Hitorijime
My Hero
CONTENTS

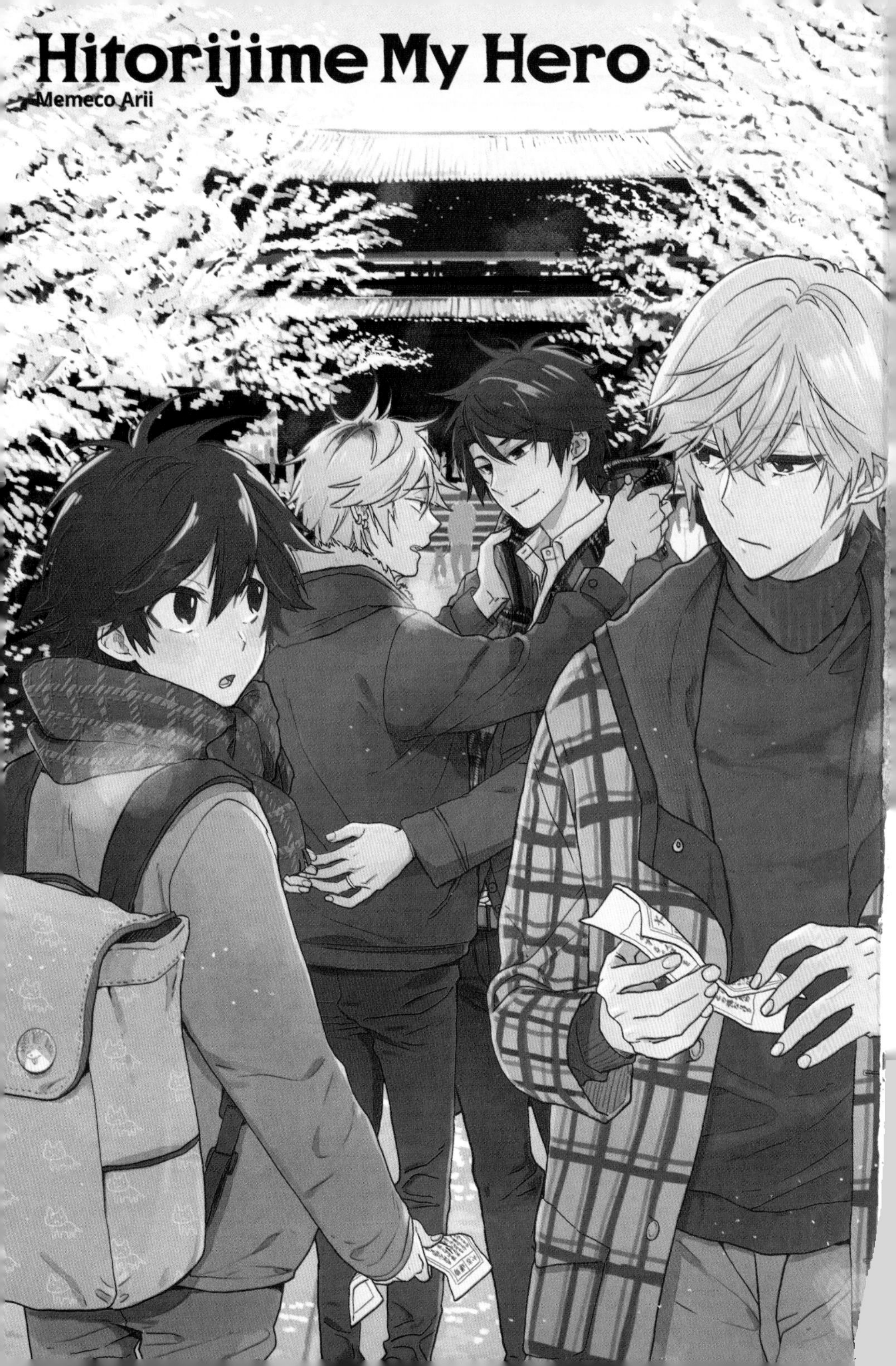
Hitorijime My Hero
Memeco Arii

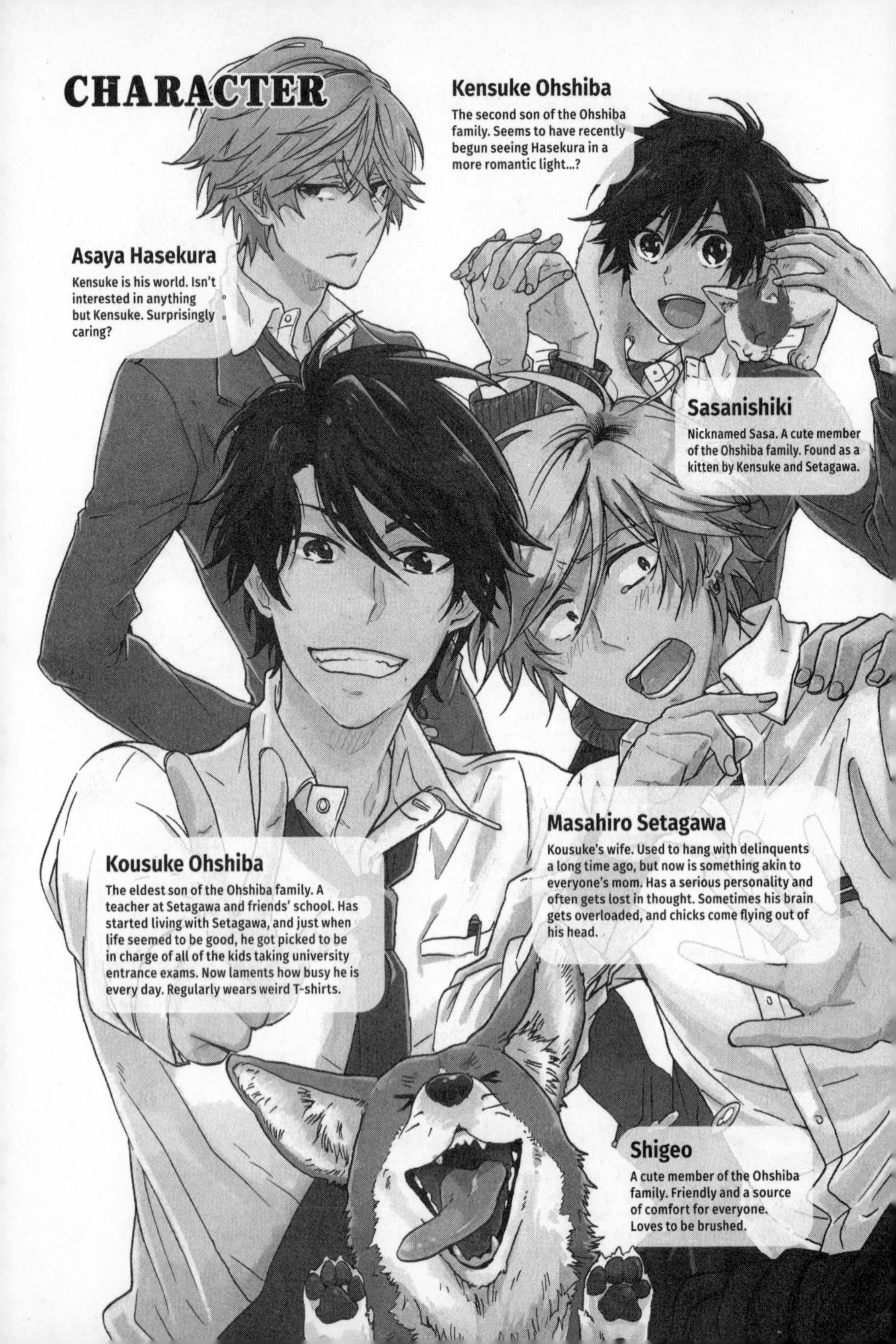

CHARACTER

Kensuke Ohshiba

The second son of the Ohshiba family. Seems to have recently begun seeing Hasekura in a more romantic light...?

Asaya Hasekura

Kensuke is his world. Isn't interested in anything but Kensuke. Surprisingly caring?

Sasanishiki

Nicknamed Sasa. A cute member of the Ohshiba family. Found as a kitten by Kensuke and Setagawa.

Masahiro Setagawa

Kousuke's wife. Used to hang with delinquents a long time ago, but now is something akin to everyone's mom. Has a serious personality and often gets lost in thought. Sometimes his brain gets overloaded, and chicks come flying out of his head.

Kousuke Ohshiba

The eldest son of the Ohshiba family. A teacher at Setagawa and friends' school. Has started living with Setagawa, and just when life seemed to be good, he got picked to be in charge of all of the kids taking university entrance exams. Now laments how busy he is every day. Regularly wears weird T-shirts.

Shigeo

A cute member of the Ohshiba family. Friendly and a source of comfort for everyone. Loves to be brushed.

Cast of Characters

Jirou Yoshida
Chairman. Tends to bear witness to things. Has some feelings for Monika.

Tsuyoshi Yamabe
Yamabe. The scarf he wears around his neck is his trademark.

Mitsuru Fukushige
Shige. Loves Setagawa as a friend and sometimes finds Kousuke irritating.

Ayaka and Tsunehito Houjou
Married couple. Ayaka is Hasekura's older sister. They're both Kousuke's friends.

Shirou Shingai
Yakuza. Kousuke's friend. Works hard at getting contracts for new homes signed.

Natsuo Nanaoka
Bar owner. Has been in love with Kousuke for a long time, but his feelings are unrequited.

Yuusei Yuge
Setagawa and friends' friend. Likes Natsuo.

Miho Ohshiba
The mom of the Ohshiba family. Loves going to karaoke.

Hasekura cult
Hasekura's obsessive fans. Secretly acting before others is taboo.

Kaide-sensei
Assistant teacher for Kousuke's class. Loves gossip.

Summary

Kensuke has started seeing Hasekura in a more romantic light and their relationship is slowly starting to change. Meanwhile, Setagawa has been watching over them in a fatherly way, but he only has another half a month of living with Kousuke. Setagawa and Kousuke are still head over heels for each other. If anything, their days of cohabitation have been brought them even closer together. But now Setagawa realizes just how lonely it is at home when Kousuke's not around...

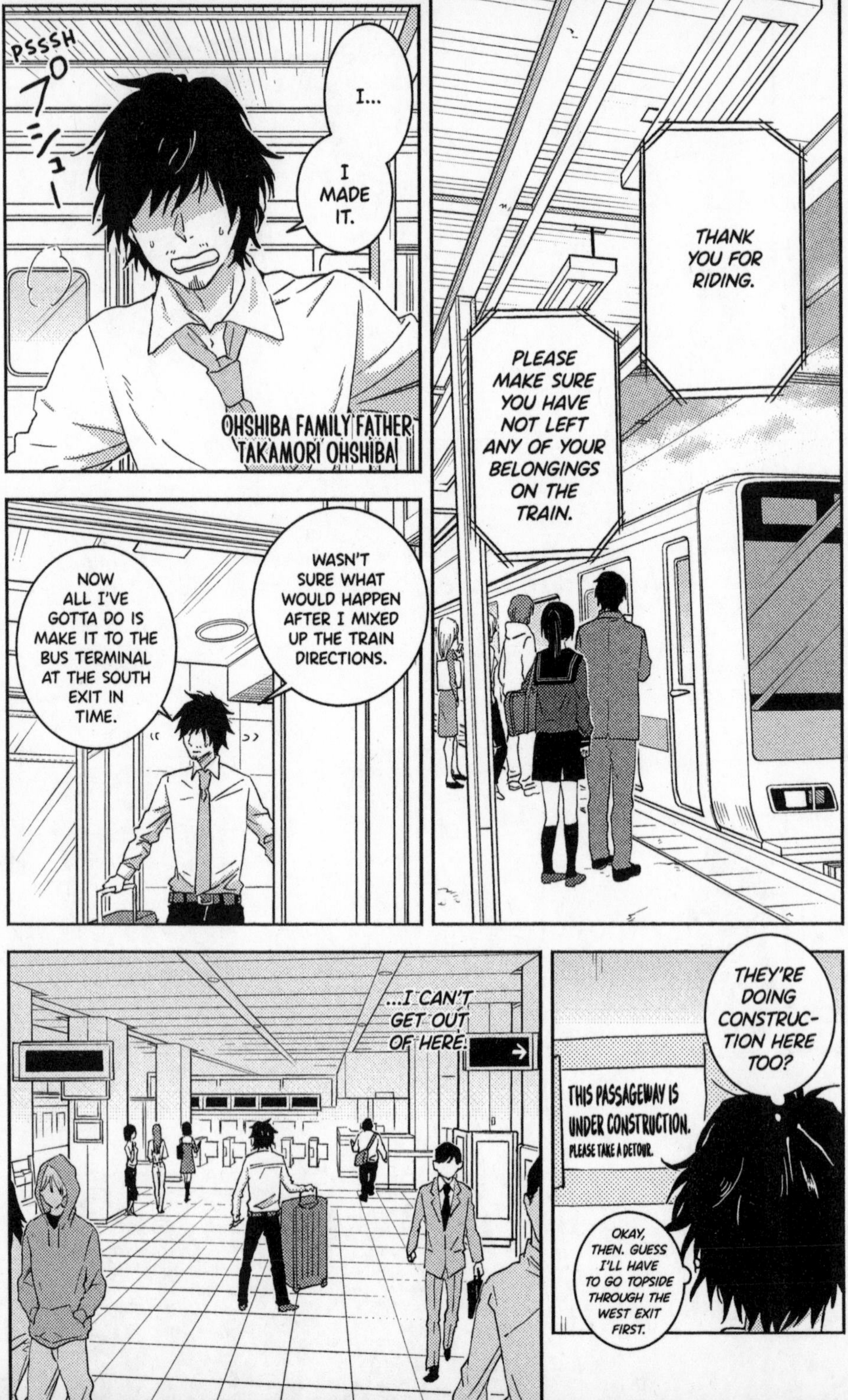
THANK YOU FOR RIDING.
PLEASE MAKE SURE YOU HAVE NOT LEFT ANY OF YOUR BELONGINGS ON THE TRAIN.
PSSSH
プシュー
I...
I MADE IT.
OHSHIBA FAMILY FATHER
TAKAMORI OHSHIBA
WASN'T SURE WHAT WOULD HAPPEN AFTER I MIXED UP THE TRAIN DIRECTIONS.
NOW ALL I'VE GOTTA DO IS MAKE IT TO THE BUS TERMINAL AT THE SOUTH EXIT IN TIME.
THEY'RE DOING CONSTRUC-TION HERE TOO?
THIS PASSAGEWAY IS UNDER CONSTRUCTION.
PLEASE TAKE A DETOUR.
OKAY, THEN. GUESS I'LL HAVE TO GO TOPSIDE THROUGH THE WEST EXIT FIRST.
...I CAN'T GET OUT OF HERE.

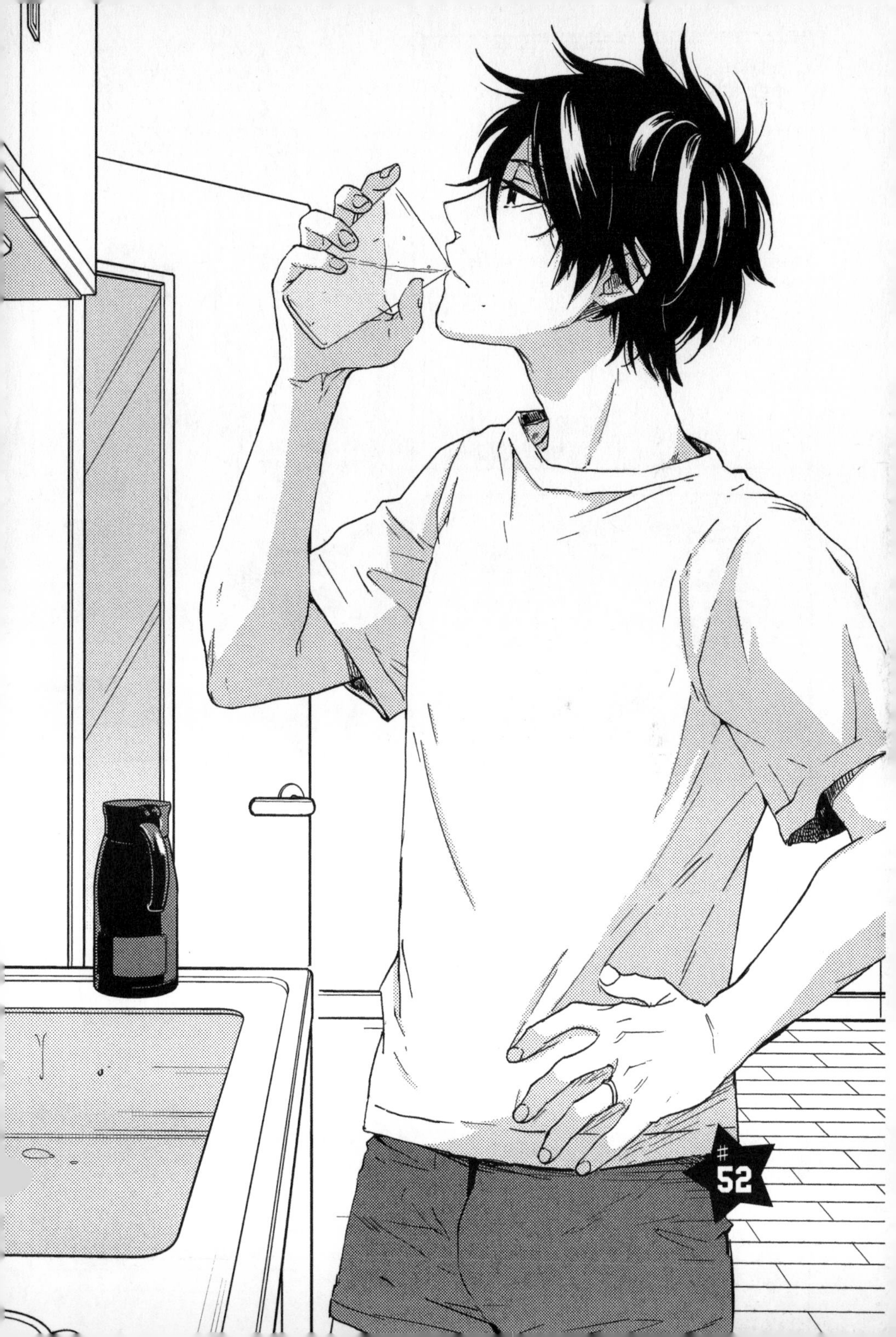

#52

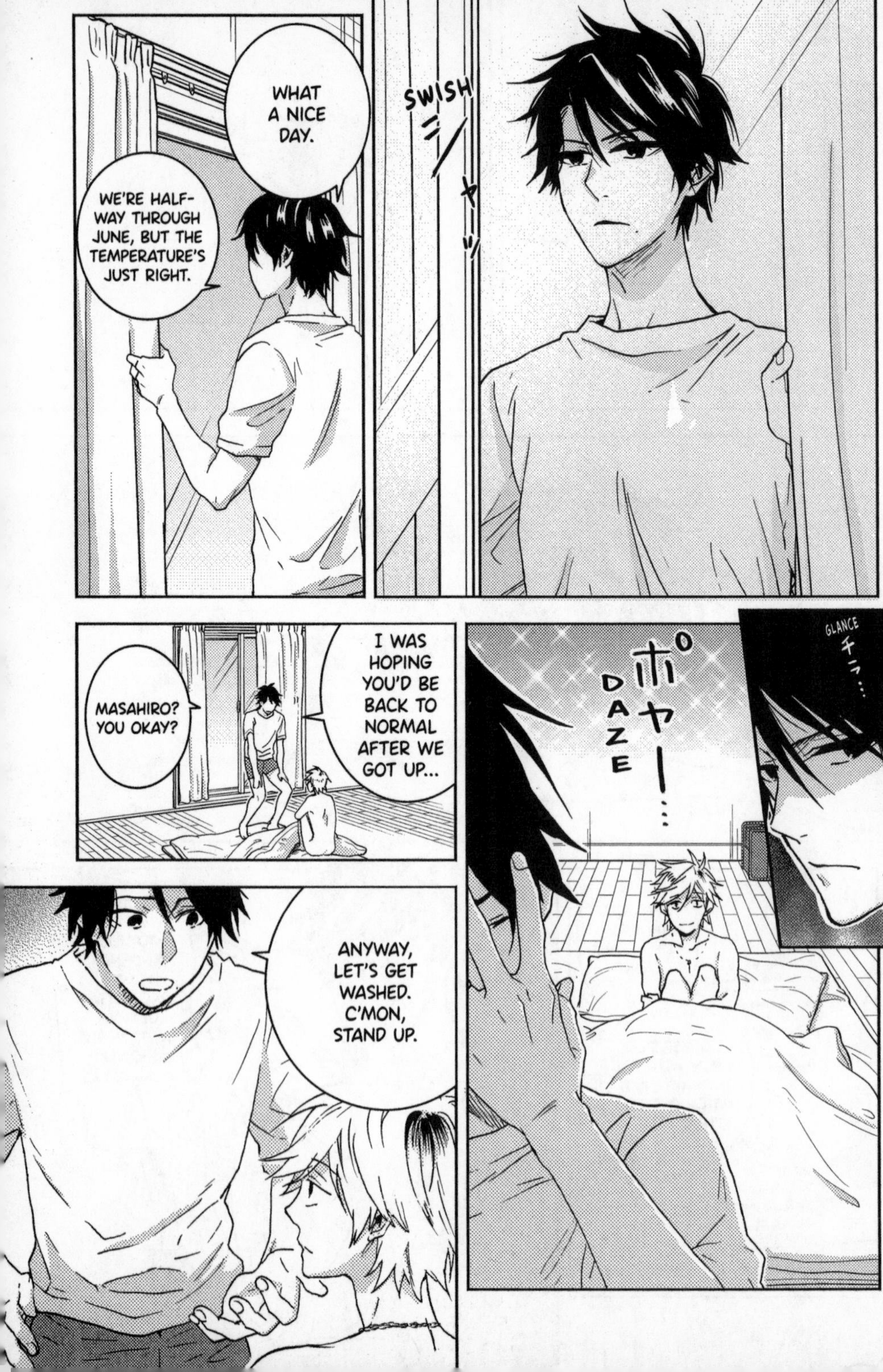
SWISH
シャッ
WHAT A NICE DAY.
WE'RE HALF-WAY THROUGH JUNE, BUT THE TEMPERATURE'S JUST RIGHT.
GLANCE
チラ…
ポヤー…
DAZE
I WAS HOPING YOU'D BE BACK TO NORMAL AFTER WE GOT UP...
MASAHIRO? YOU OKAY?
ANYWAY, LET'S GET WASHED. C'MON, STAND UP.

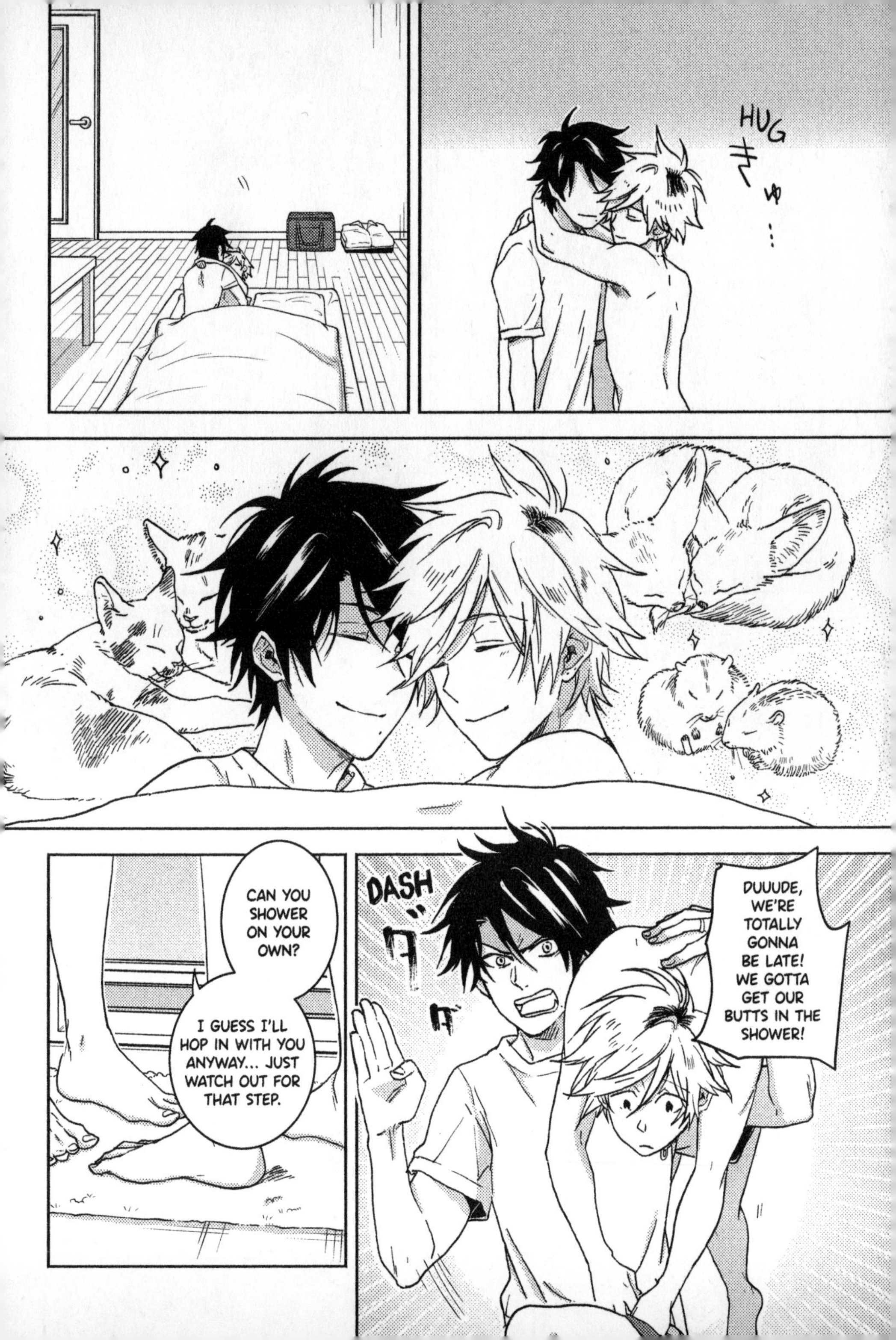
HUG
きゅ…
DASH
ダッ
DUUUDE, WE'RE TOTALLY GONNA BE LATE! WE GOTTA GET OUR BUTTS IN THE SHOWER!
CAN YOU SHOWER ON YOUR OWN?
I GUESS I'LL HOP IN WITH YOU ANYWAY... JUST WATCH OUT FOR THAT STEP.

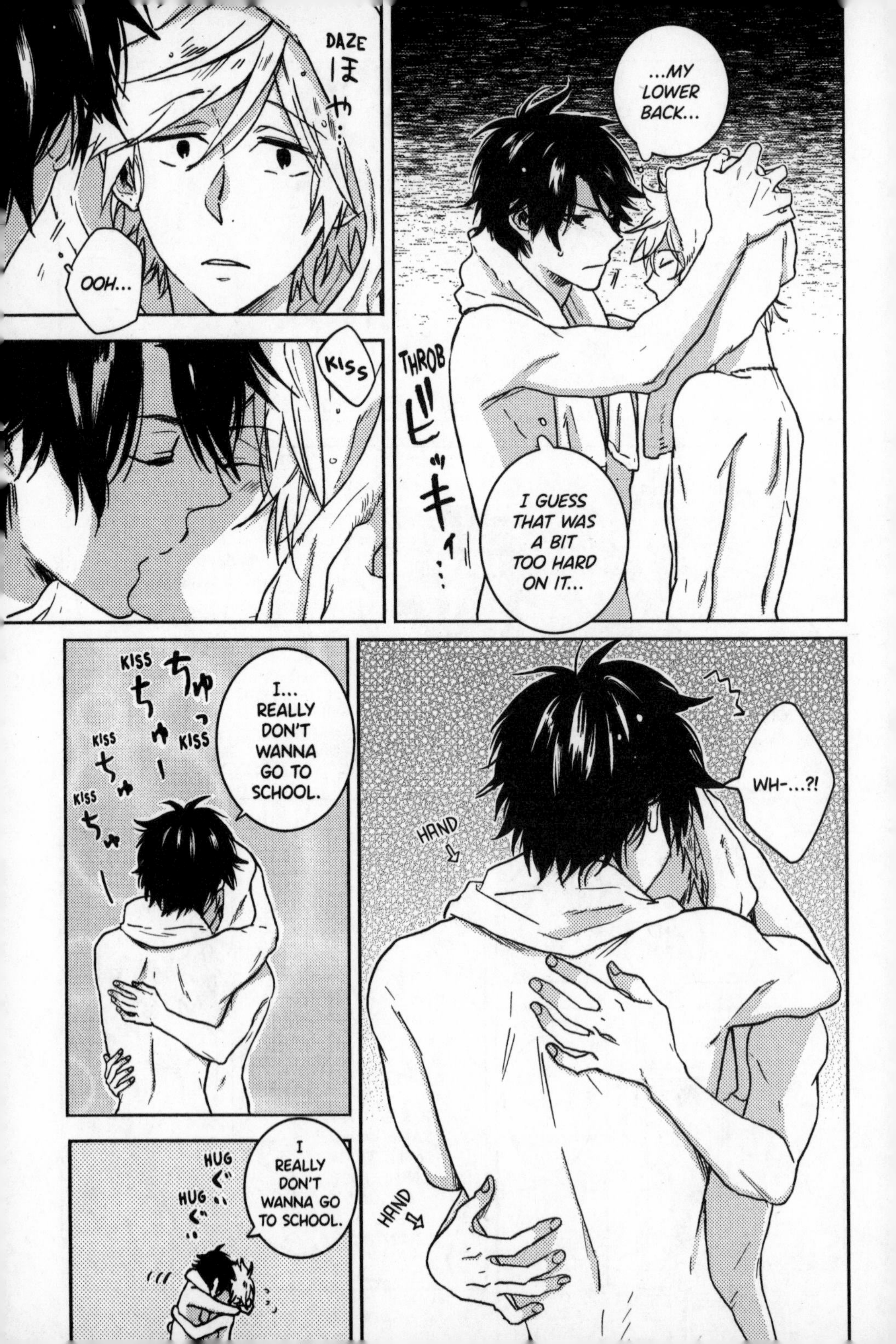
...MY LOWER BACK...
THROB
ビッキィ...
I GUESS THAT WAS A BIT TOO HARD ON IT...
DAZE
ほや...
OOH...
KISS
WH-...?!
HAND
HAND
I... REALLY DON'T WANNA GO TO SCHOOL.
KISS
KISS
KISS
KISS
I REALLY DON'T WANNA GO TO SCHOOL.
HUG
HUG

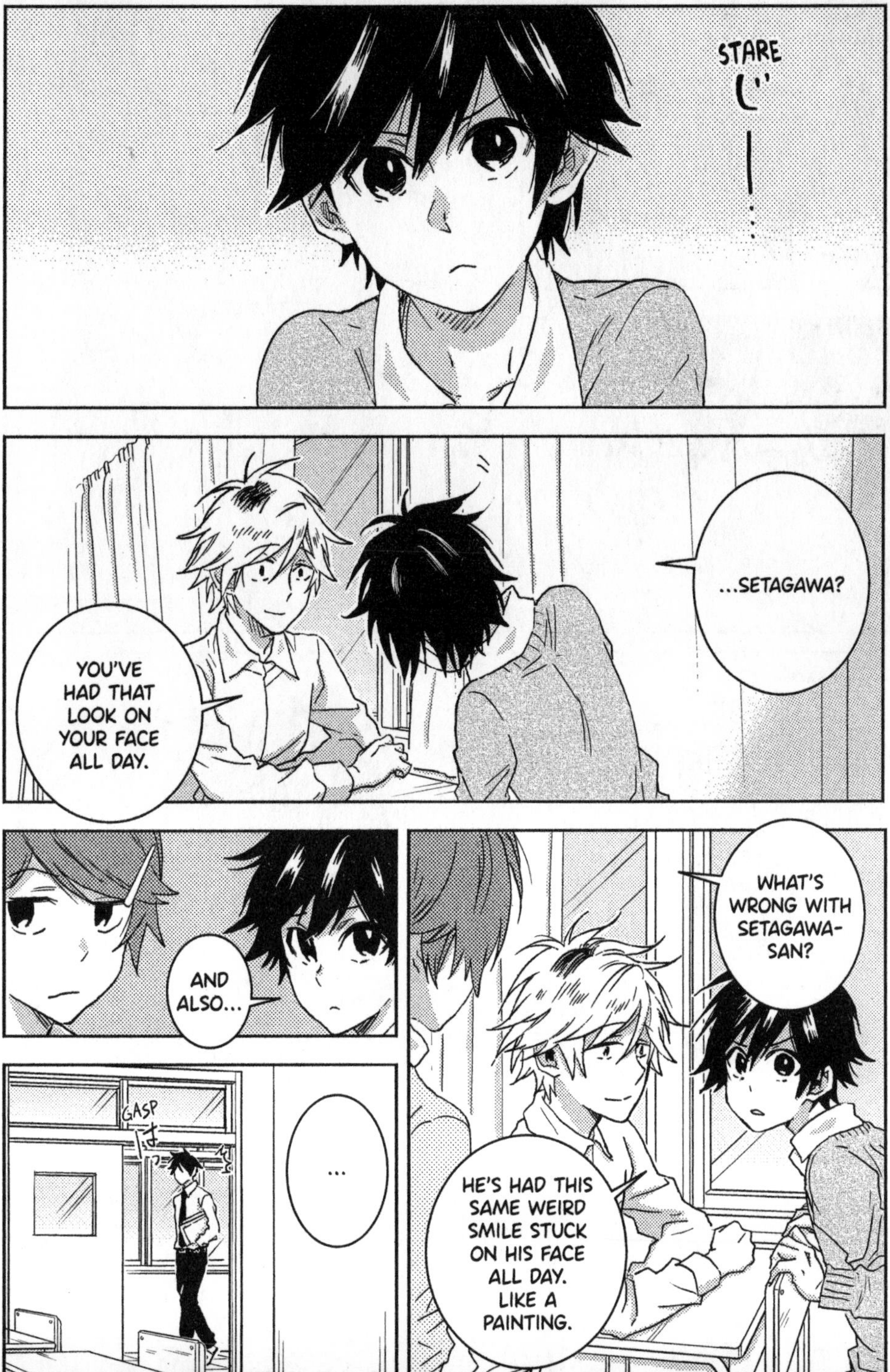
STARE
じー…
...SETAGAWA?
YOU'VE HAD THAT LOOK ON YOUR FACE ALL DAY.
WHAT'S WRONG WITH SETAGAWA-SAN?
HE'S HAD THIS SAME WEIRD SMILE STUCK ON HIS FACE ALL DAY. LIKE A PAINTING.
AND ALSO...
GASP
...

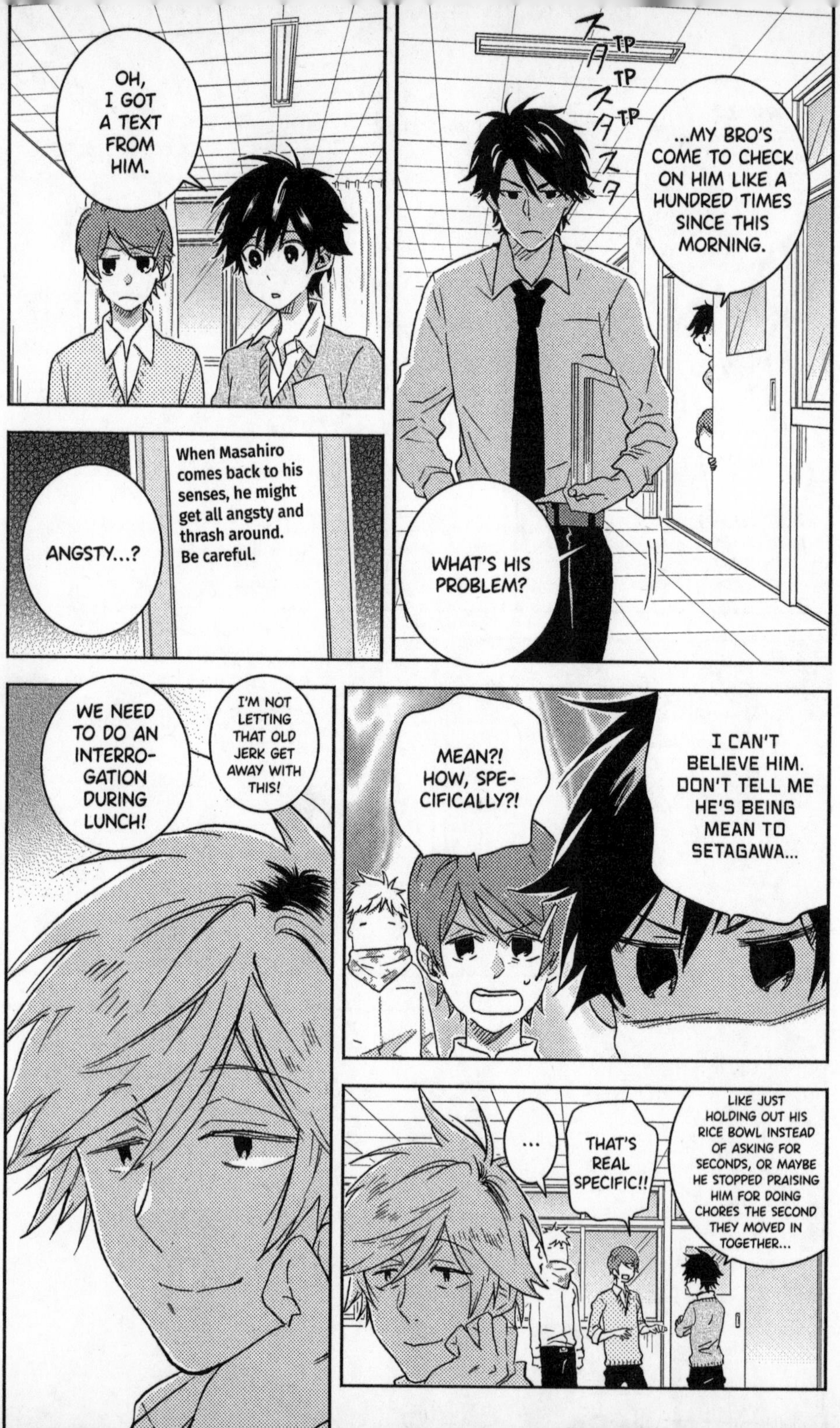
TP TP TP
...MY BRO'S COME TO CHECK ON HIM LIKE A HUNDRED TIMES SINCE THIS MORNING.
WHAT'S HIS PROBLEM?
OH, I GOT A TEXT FROM HIM.
When Masahiro comes back to his senses, he might get all angsty and thrash around. Be careful.
ANGSTY...?
I CAN'T BELIEVE HIM. DON'T TELL ME HE'S BEING MEAN TO SETAGAWA...
MEAN?! HOW, SPE-CIFICALLY?!
LIKE JUST HOLDING OUT HIS RICE BOWL INSTEAD OF ASKING FOR SECONDS, OR MAYBE HE STOPPED PRAISING HIM FOR DOING CHORES THE SECOND THEY MOVED IN TOGETHER...
THAT'S REAL SPECIFIC!!
...
I'M NOT LETTING THAT OLD JERK GET AWAY WITH THIS!
WE NEED TO DO AN INTERRO-GATION DURING LUNCH!

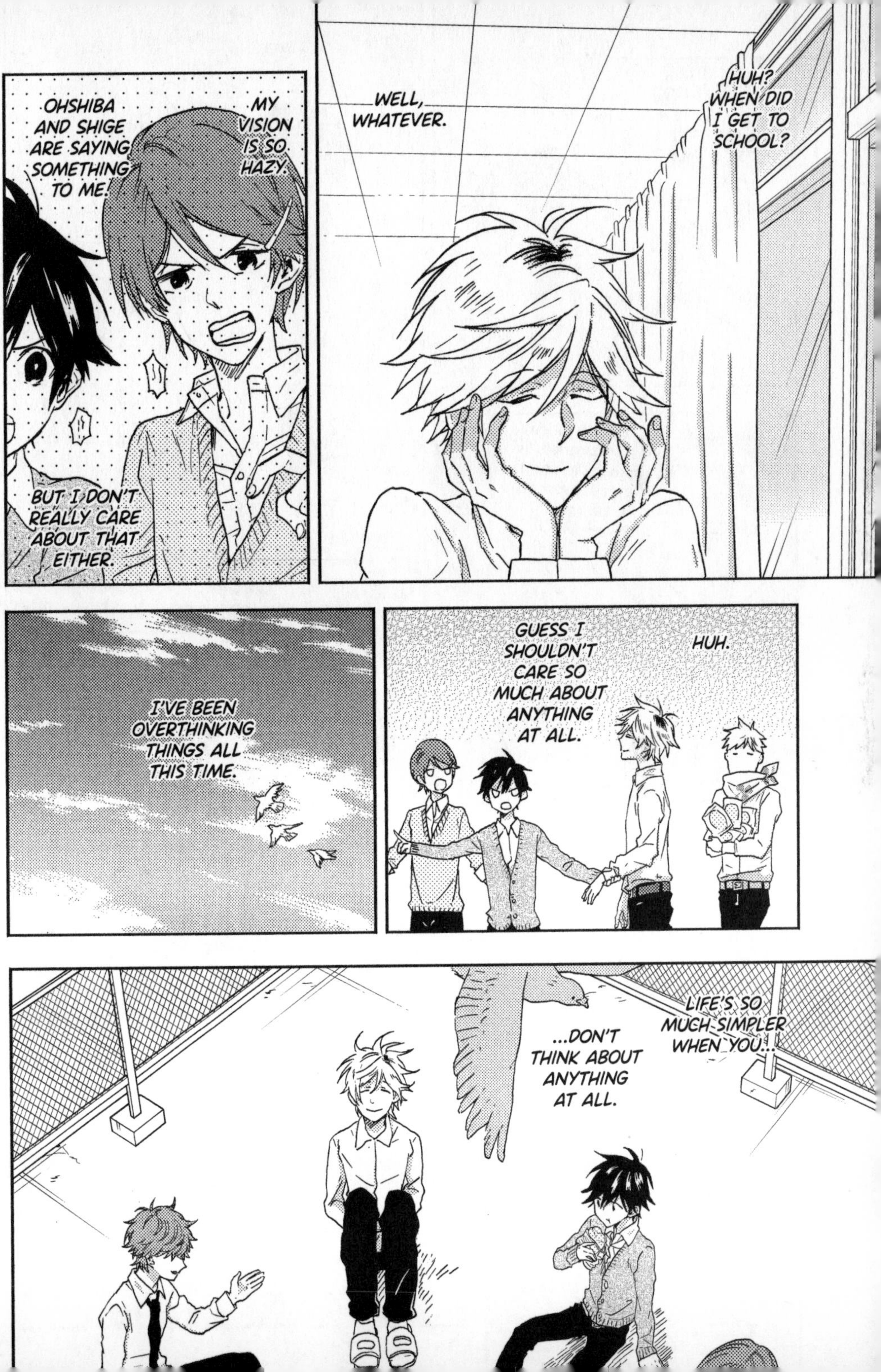
HUH? WHEN DID I GET TO SCHOOL?
WELL, WHATEVER.
MY VISION IS SO HAZY.
OHSHIBA AND SHIGE ARE SAYING SOMETHING TO ME!
BUT I DON'T REALLY CARE ABOUT THAT EITHER.
HUH.
GUESS I SHOULDN'T CARE SO MUCH ABOUT ANYTHING AT ALL.
I'VE BEEN OVERTHINKING THINGS ALL THIS TIME.
LIFE'S SO MUCH SIMPLER WHEN YOU...
...DON'T THINK ABOUT ANYTHING AT ALL.

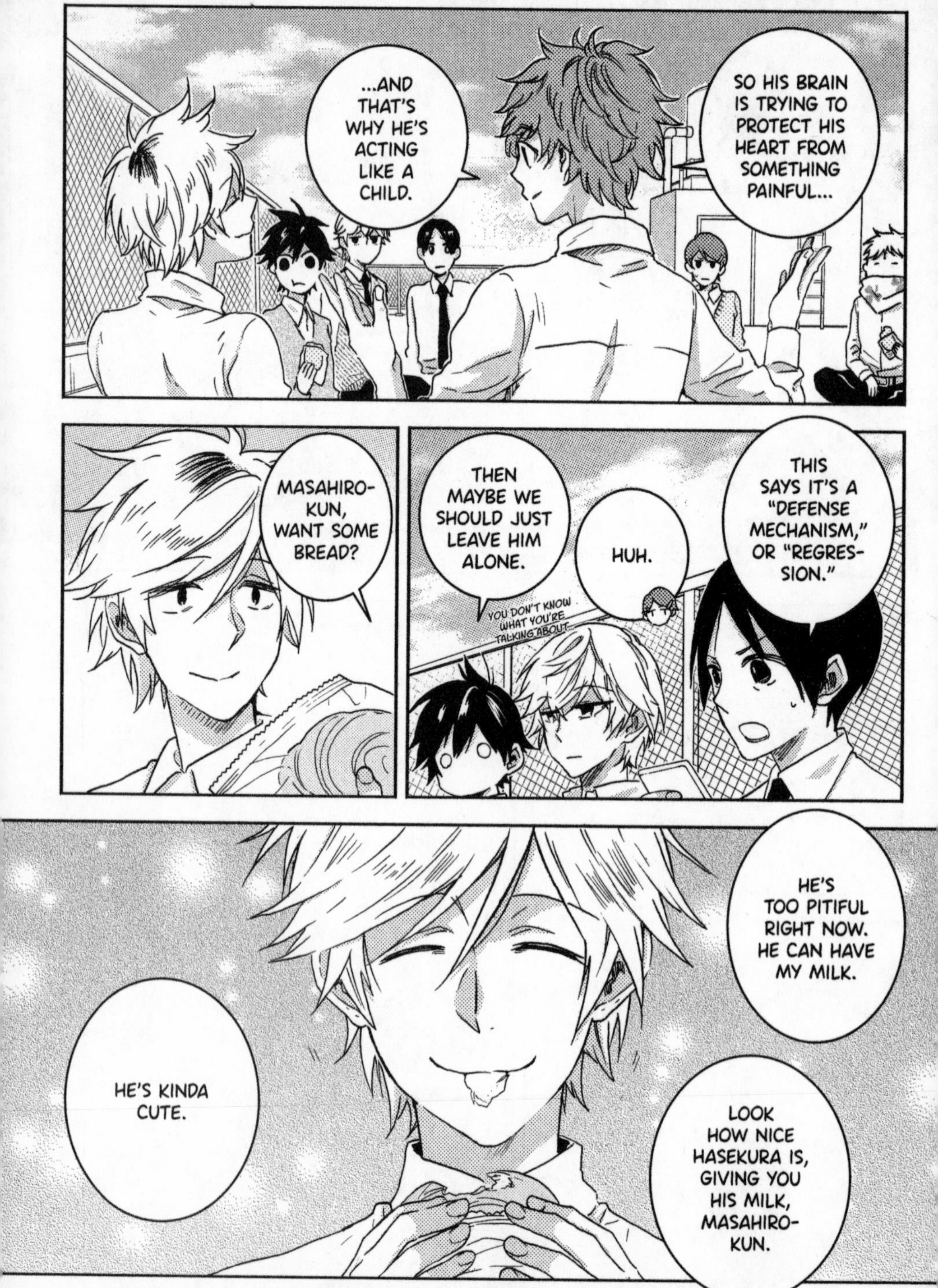
SO HIS BRAIN IS TRYING TO PROTECT HIS HEART FROM SOMETHING PAINFUL...
...AND THAT'S WHY HE'S ACTING LIKE A CHILD.
THIS SAYS IT'S A "DEFENSE MECHANISM," OR "REGRES-SION."
HUH.
THEN MAYBE WE SHOULD JUST LEAVE HIM ALONE.
YOU DON'T KNOW WHAT YOU'RE TALKING ABOUT
MASAHIRO-KUN, WANT SOME BREAD?
HE'S TOO PITIFUL RIGHT NOW. HE CAN HAVE MY MILK.
LOOK HOW NICE HASEKURA IS, GIVING YOU HIS MILK, MASAHIRO-KUN.
HE'S KINDA CUTE.

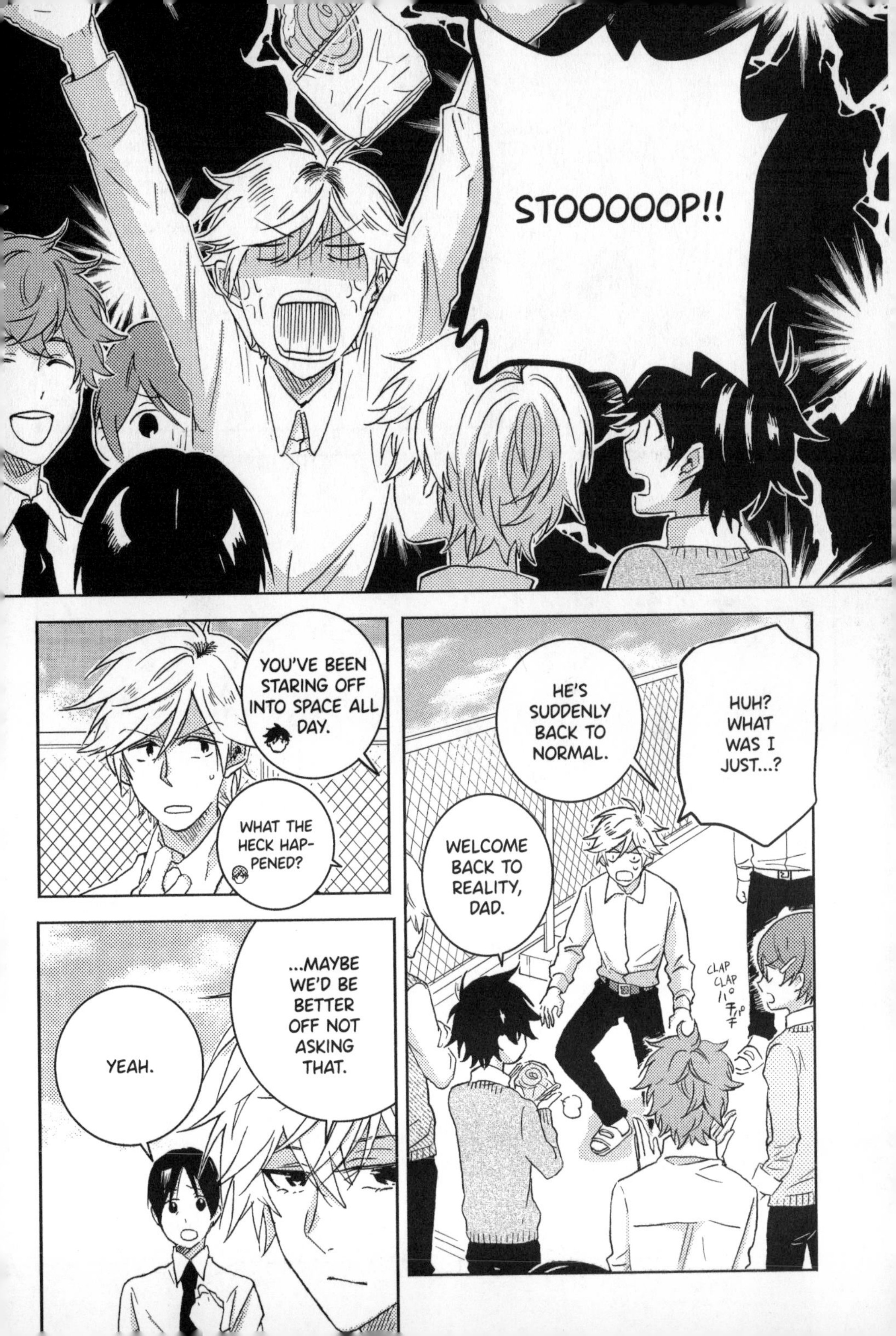
STOOOOOP!!
HUH? WHAT WAS I JUST...?
HE'S SUDDENLY BACK TO NORMAL.
WELCOME BACK TO REALITY, DAD.
CLAP CLAP
パチパチ
YOU'VE BEEN STARING OFF INTO SPACE ALL DAY.
WHAT THE HECK HAPPENED?
...MAYBE WE'D BE BETTER OFF NOT ASKING THAT.
YEAH.

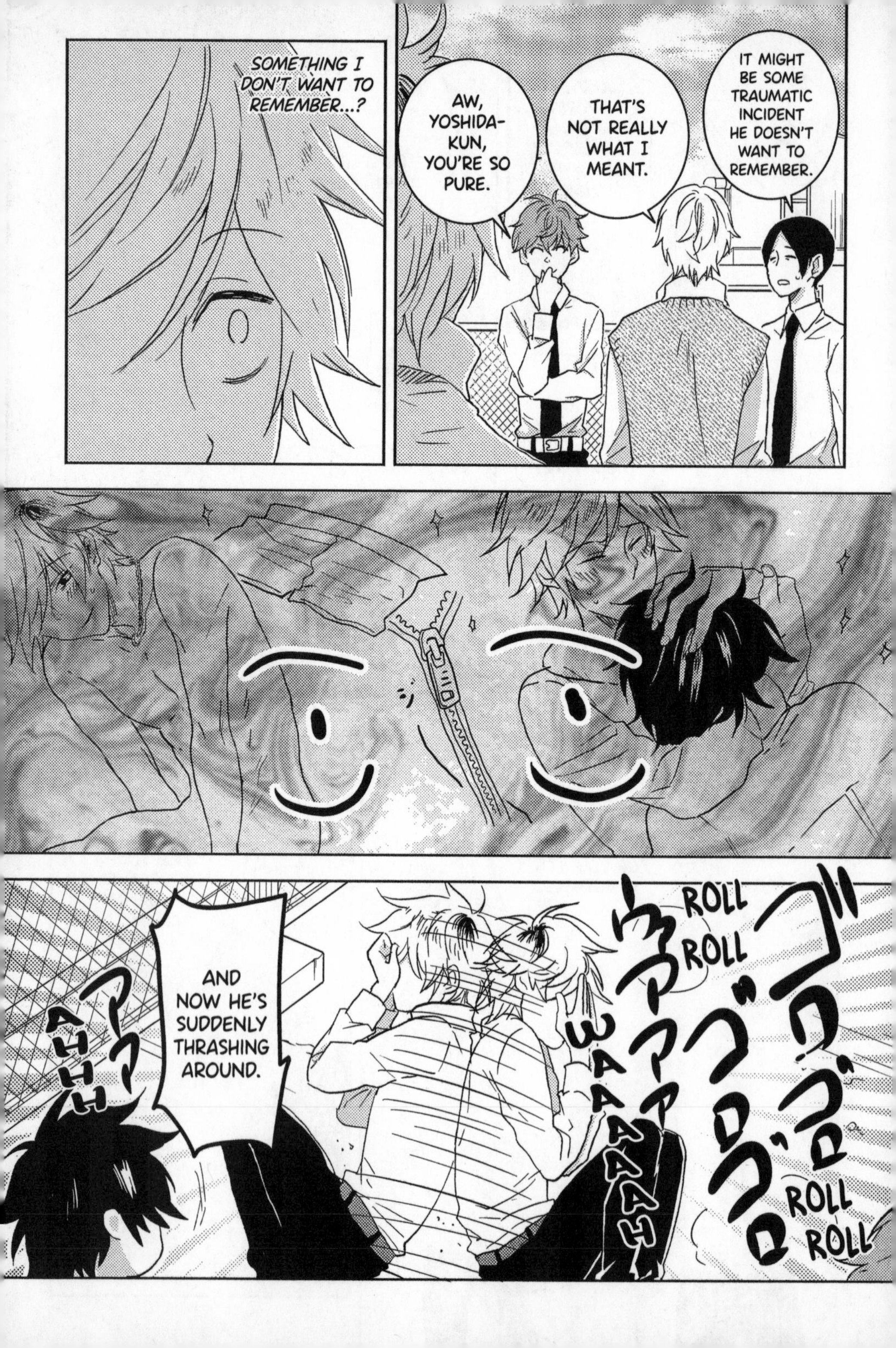
IT MIGHT BE SOME TRAUMATIC INCIDENT HE DOESN'T WANT TO REMEMBER.
THAT'S NOT REALLY WHAT I MEANT.
AW, YOSHIDA-KUN, YOU'RE SO PURE.
SOMETHING I DON'T WANT TO REMEMBER...?
ゴロゴロ
ROLL ROLL
ゴロゴロ
ROLL ROLL
ウアアアア
WAAAAAAH
AND NOW HE'S SUDDENLY THRASHING AROUND.
アアア
AHHHH

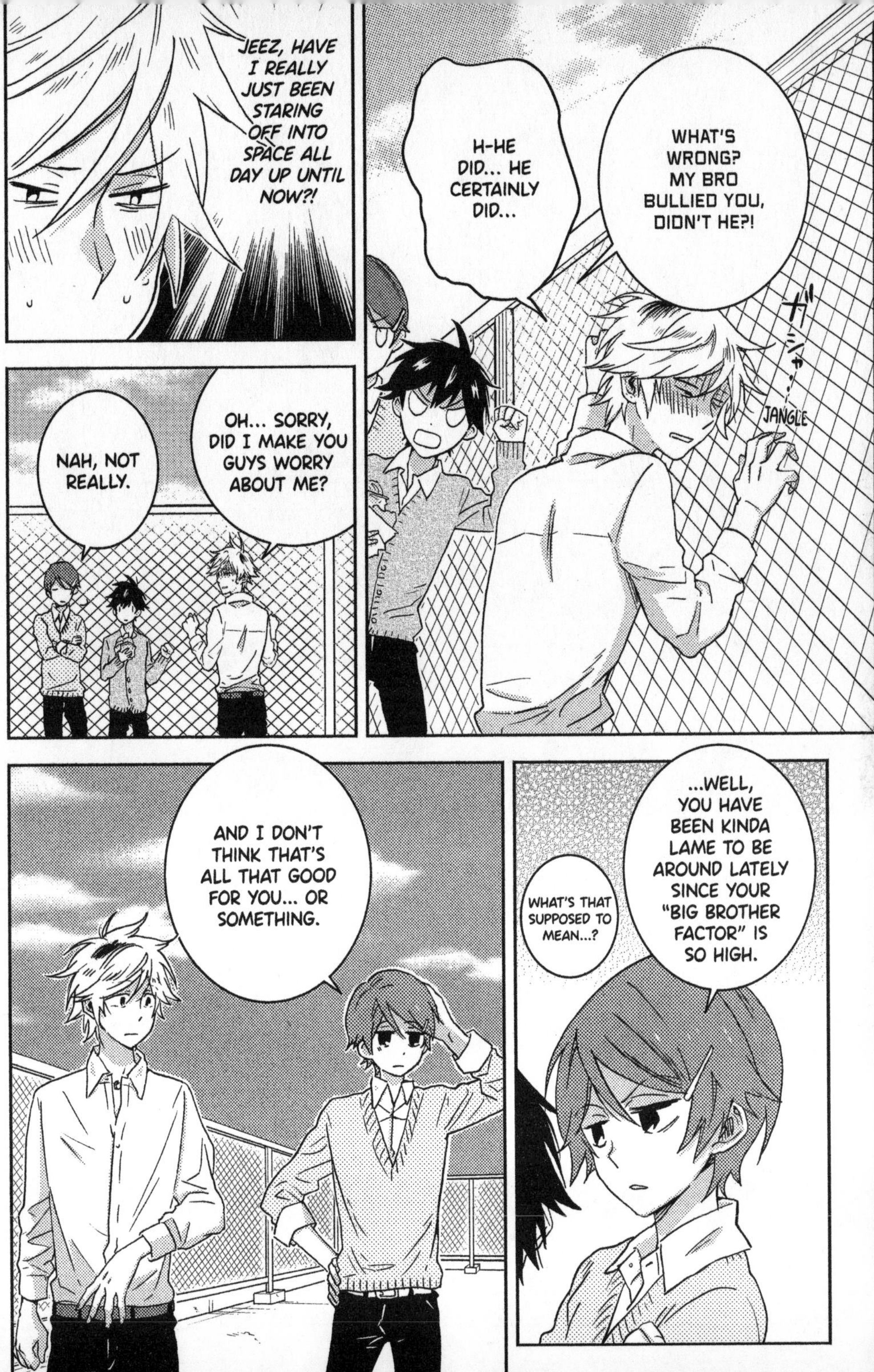
WHAT'S WRONG? MY BRO BULLIED YOU, DIDN'T HE?!
H-HE DID... HE CERTAINLY DID...
ガシャ…
JANGLE
JEEZ, HAVE I REALLY JUST BEEN STARING OFF INTO SPACE ALL DAY UP UNTIL NOW?!
OH... SORRY, DID I MAKE YOU GUYS WORRY ABOUT ME?
NAH, NOT REALLY.
...WELL, YOU HAVE BEEN KINDA LAME TO BE AROUND LATELY SINCE YOUR "BIG BROTHER FACTOR" IS SO HIGH.
WHAT'S THAT SUPPOSED TO MEAN...?
AND I DON'T THINK THAT'S ALL THAT GOOD FOR YOU... OR SOMETHING.

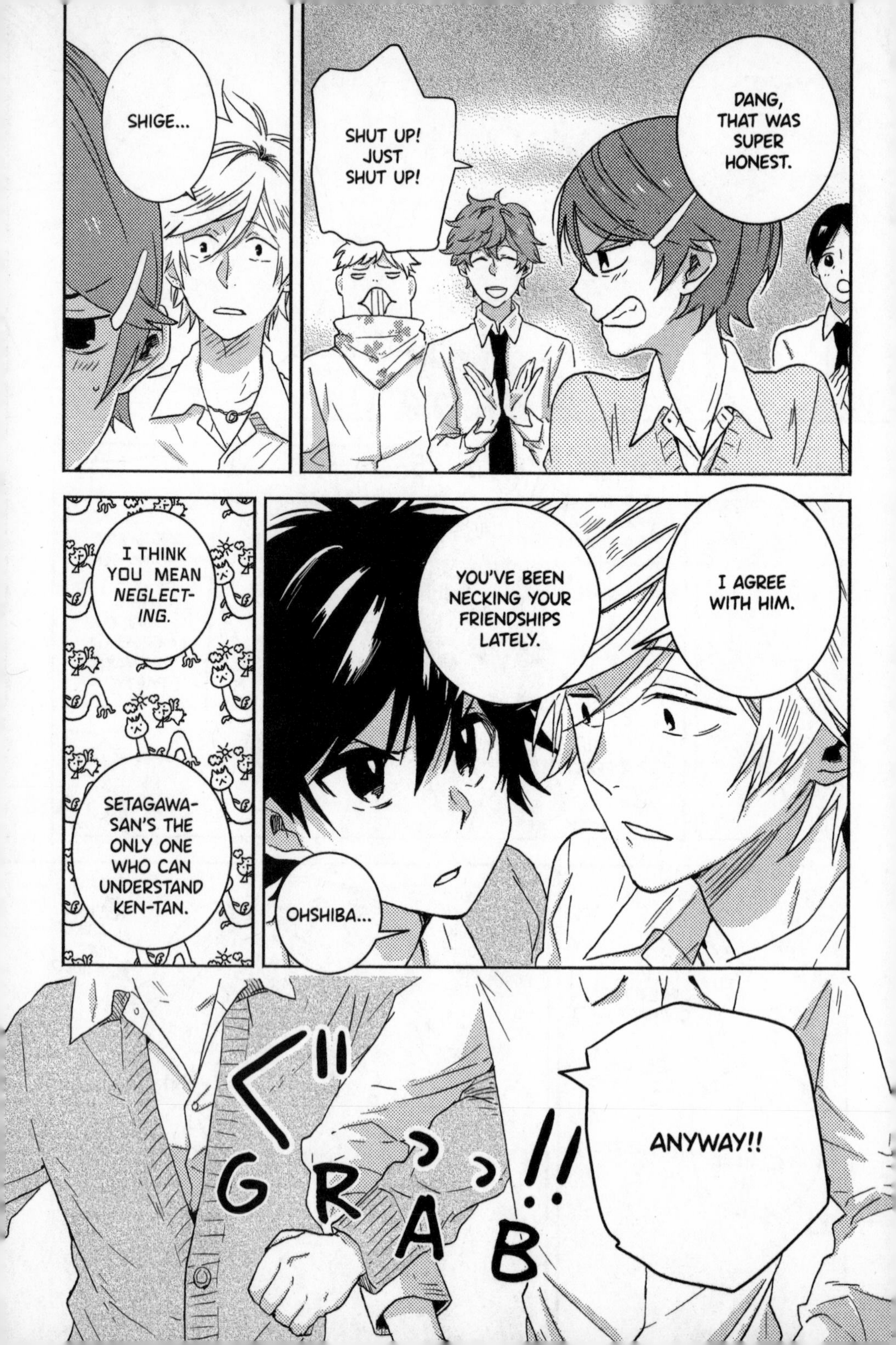

DANG, THAT WAS SUPER HONEST.
SHUT UP! JUST SHUT UP!
SHIGE...
I AGREE WITH HIM.
YOU'VE BEEN NECKING YOUR FRIENDSHIPS LATELY.
OHSHIBA...
I THINK YOU MEAN *NEGLECTING*.
SETAGAWA-SAN'S THE ONLY ONE WHO CAN UNDERSTAND KEN-TAN.
ANYWAY!!
GRAB!!

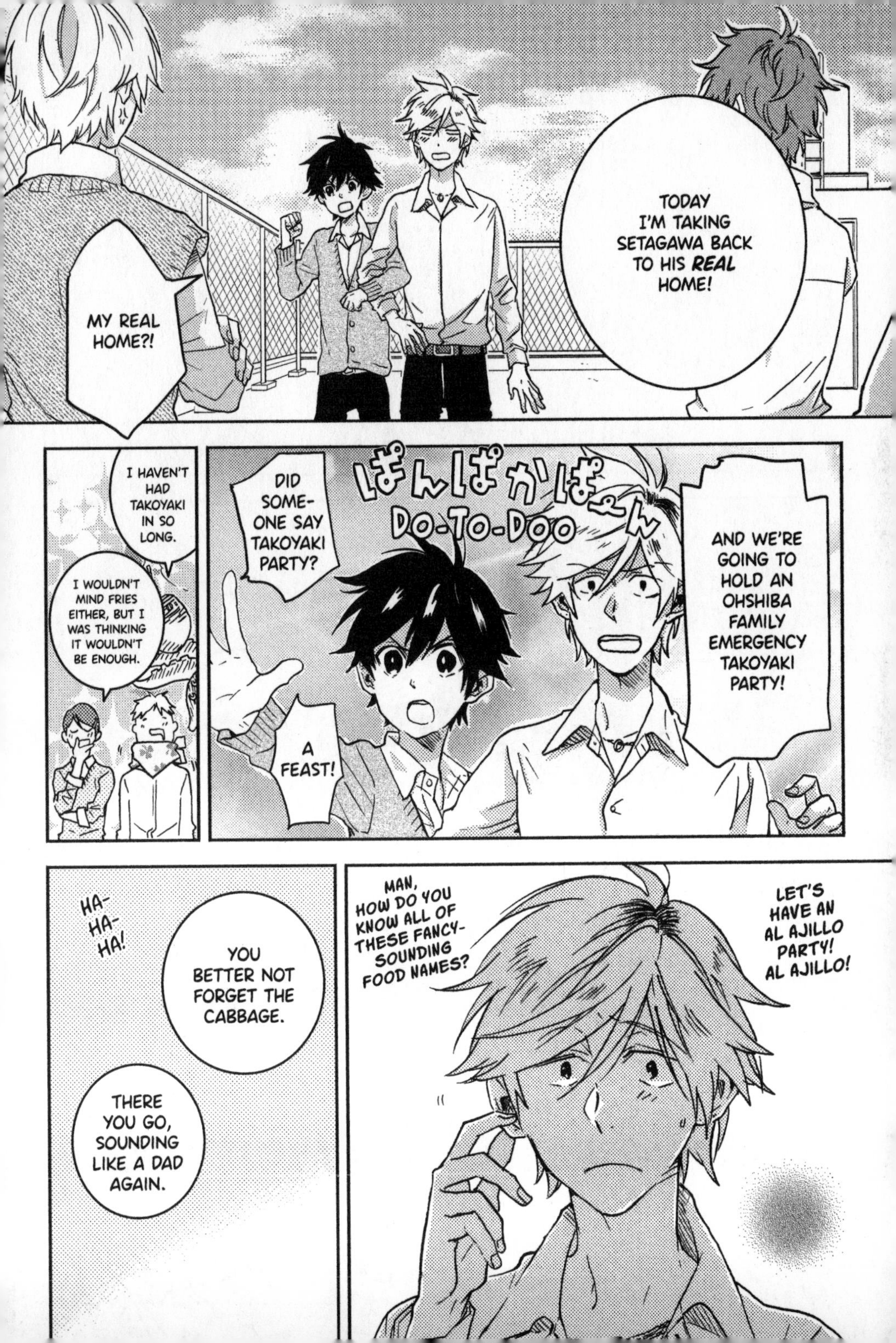
TODAY I'M TAKING SETAGAWA BACK TO HIS *REAL* HOME!
MY REAL HOME?!
AND WE'RE GOING TO HOLD AN OHSHIBA FAMILY EMERGENCY TAKOYAKI PARTY!
ぽんぱかぱーん
DO-TO-DOO
DID SOME-ONE SAY TAKOYAKI PARTY?
A FEAST!
I HAVEN'T HAD TAKOYAKI IN SO LONG.
I WOULDN'T MIND FRIES EITHER, BUT I WAS THINKING IT WOULDN'T BE ENOUGH.
LET'S HAVE AN AL AJILLO PARTY! AL AJILLO!
MAN, HOW DO YOU KNOW ALL OF THESE FANCY-SOUNDING FOOD NAMES?
HA-HA-HA!
YOU BETTER NOT FORGET THE CABBAGE.
THERE YOU GO, SOUNDING LIKE A DAD AGAIN.

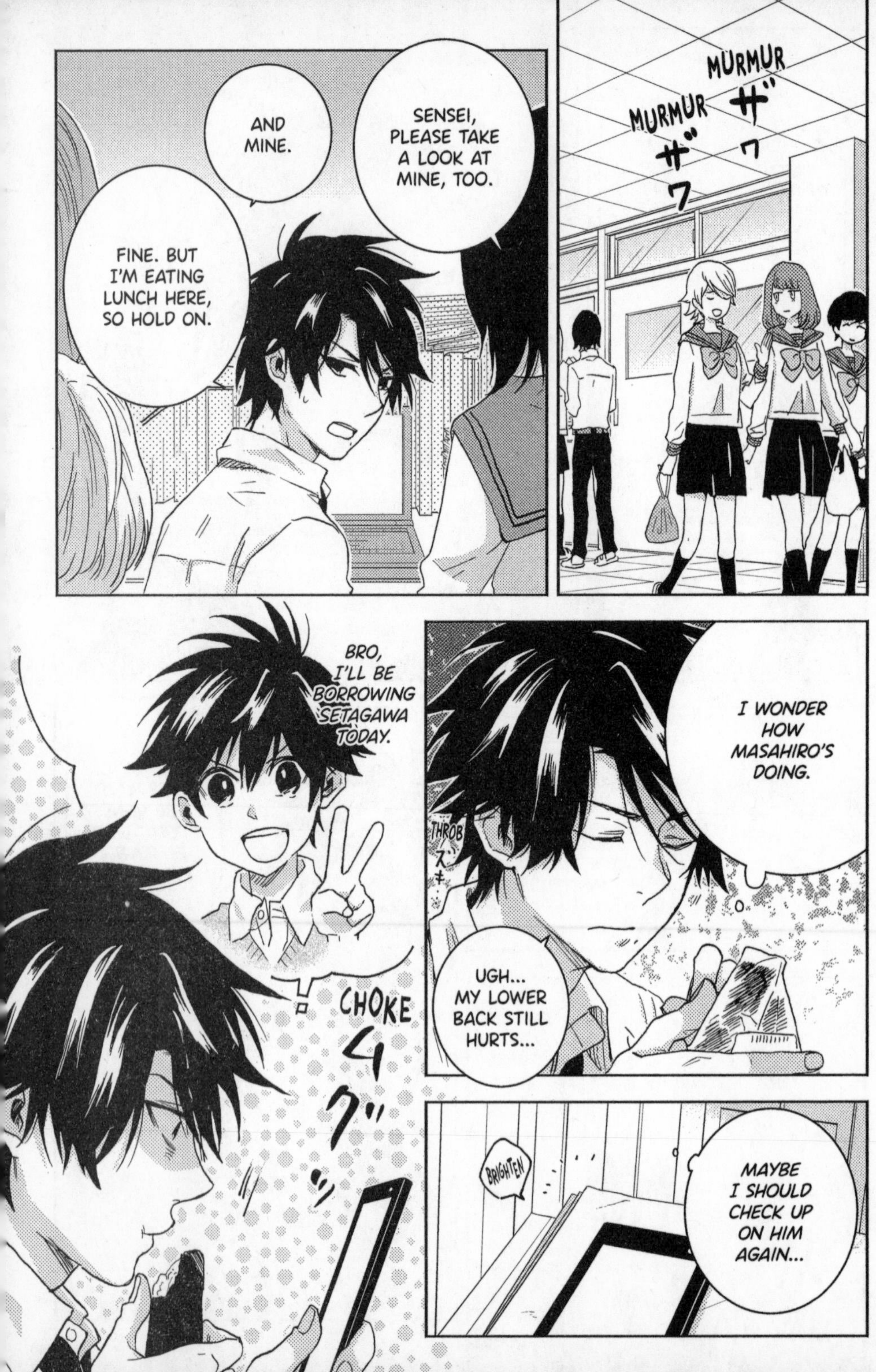
MURMUR ザワ
MURMUR ザワ
SENSEI, PLEASE TAKE A LOOK AT MINE, TOO.
AND MINE.
FINE. BUT I'M EATING LUNCH HERE, SO HOLD ON.
I WONDER HOW MASAHIRO'S DOING.
THROB ズキ…
UGH... MY LOWER BACK STILL HURTS...
BRIGHTEN
...
MAYBE I SHOULD CHECK UP ON HIM AGAIN...
BRO, I'LL BE BORROWING SETAGAWA TODAY.
!
CHOKE ムグ

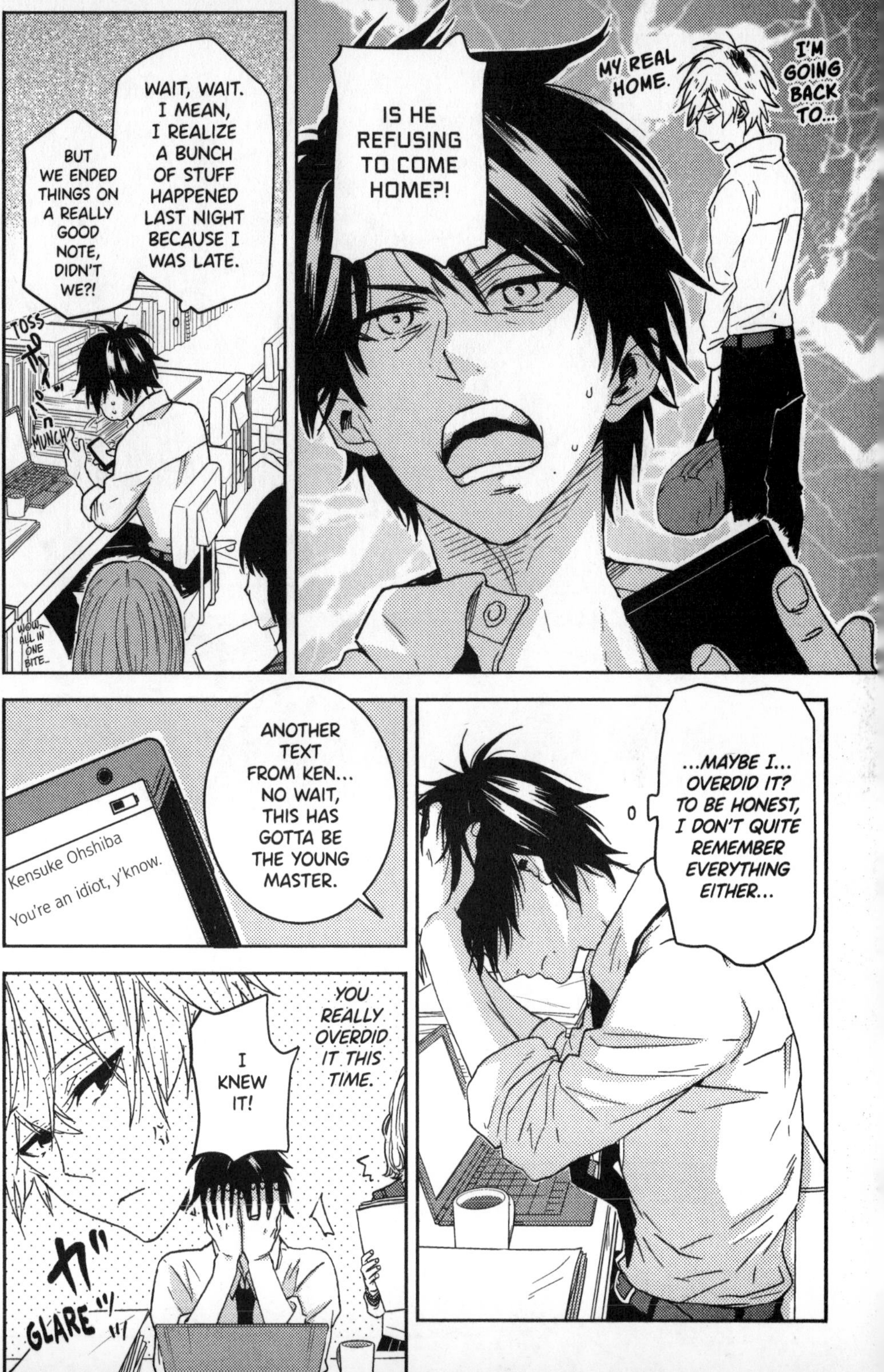
I'M GOING BACK TO...
MY REAL HOME.
IS HE REFUSING TO COME HOME?!
WAIT, WAIT. I MEAN, I REALIZE A BUNCH OF STUFF HAPPENED LAST NIGHT BECAUSE I WAS LATE.
BUT WE ENDED THINGS ON A REALLY GOOD NOTE, DIDN'T WE?!
TOSS
MUNCH
WOW, ALL IN ONE BITE...
...MAYBE I... OVERDID IT? TO BE HONEST, I DON'T QUITE REMEMBER EVERYTHING EITHER...
ANOTHER TEXT FROM KEN... NO WAIT, THIS HAS GOTTA BE THE YOUNG MASTER.
Kensuke Ohshiba
You're an idiot, y'know.
YOU REALLY OVERDID IT THIS TIME.
I KNEW IT!
GLARE

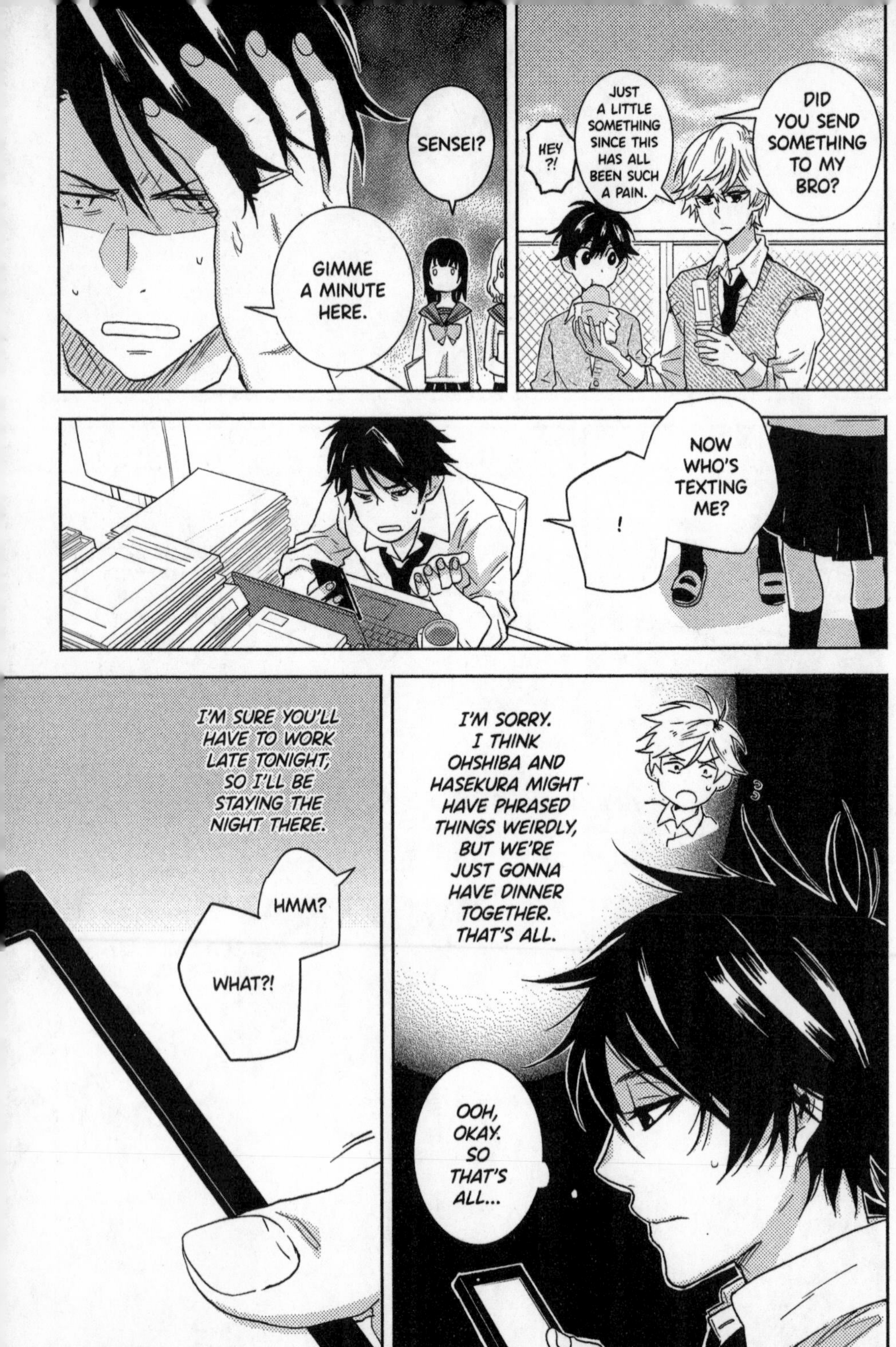
DID YOU SEND SOMETHING TO MY BRO?
JUST A LITTLE SOMETHING SINCE THIS HAS ALL BEEN SUCH A PAIN.
HEY ?!
SENSEI?
GIMME A MINUTE HERE.
NOW WHO'S TEXTING ME?
!
I'M SORRY. I THINK OHSHIBA AND HASEKURA MIGHT HAVE PHRASED THINGS WEIRDLY, BUT WE'RE JUST GONNA HAVE DINNER TOGETHER. THAT'S ALL.
OOH, OKAY. SO THAT'S ALL...
I'M SURE YOU'LL HAVE TO WORK LATE TONIGHT, SO I'LL BE STAYING THE NIGHT THERE.
HMM?
WHAT?!

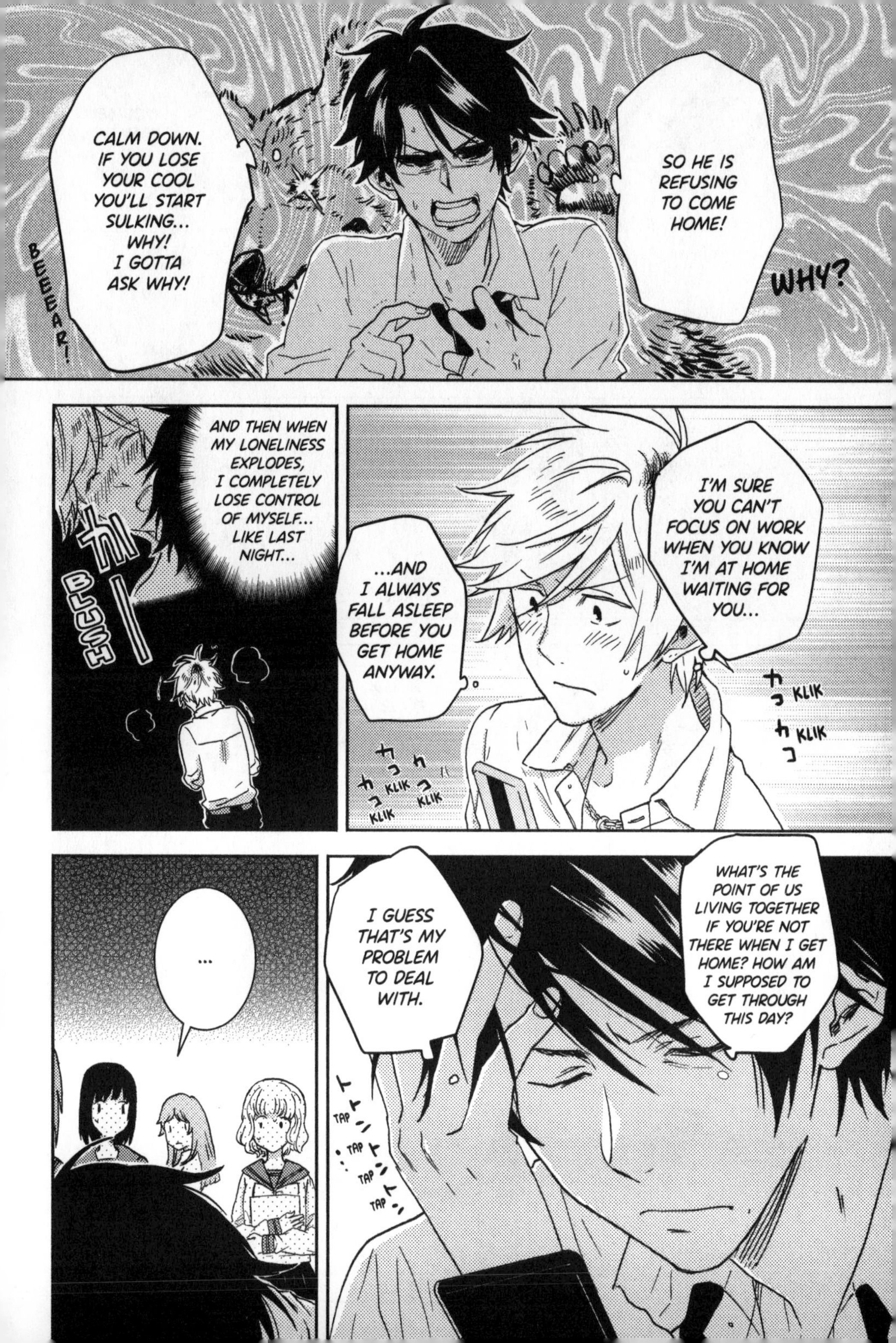
SO HE IS REFUSING TO COME HOME!
WHY?
CALM DOWN. IF YOU LOSE YOUR COOL YOU'LL START SULKING... WHY! I GOTTA ASK WHY!
BEEEAR!
I'M SURE YOU CAN'T FOCUS ON WORK WHEN YOU KNOW I'M AT HOME WAITING FOR YOU...
...AND I ALWAYS FALL ASLEEP BEFORE YOU GET HOME ANYWAY.
KLIK
KLIK
KLIK
KLIK
KLIK
AND THEN WHEN MY LONELINESS EXPLODES, I COMPLETELY LOSE CONTROL OF MYSELF... LIKE LAST NIGHT...
BLUSH
WHAT'S THE POINT OF US LIVING TOGETHER IF YOU'RE NOT THERE WHEN I GET HOME? HOW AM I SUPPOSED TO GET THROUGH THIS DAY?
I GUESS THAT'S MY PROBLEM TO DEAL WITH.
TAP
TAP
TAP
TAP
...

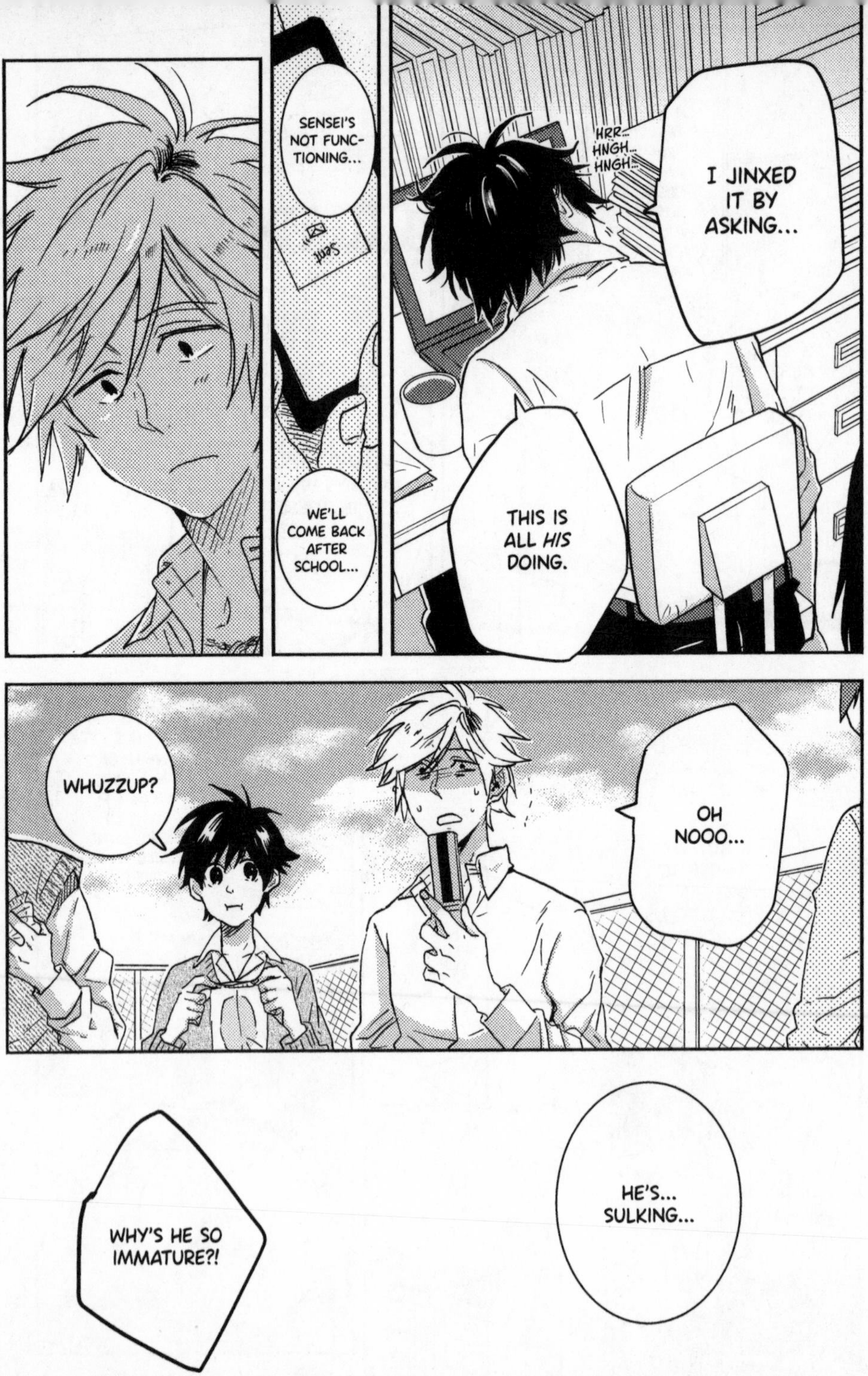
I JINXED IT BY ASKING...
HRR... HNGH... HNGH...
THIS IS ALL *HIS* DOING.
SENSEI'S NOT FUNC-TIONING...
Sent
WE'LL COME BACK AFTER SCHOOL...
OH NOOO...
WHUZZUP?
HE'S... SULKING...
WHY'S HE SO IMMATURE?!

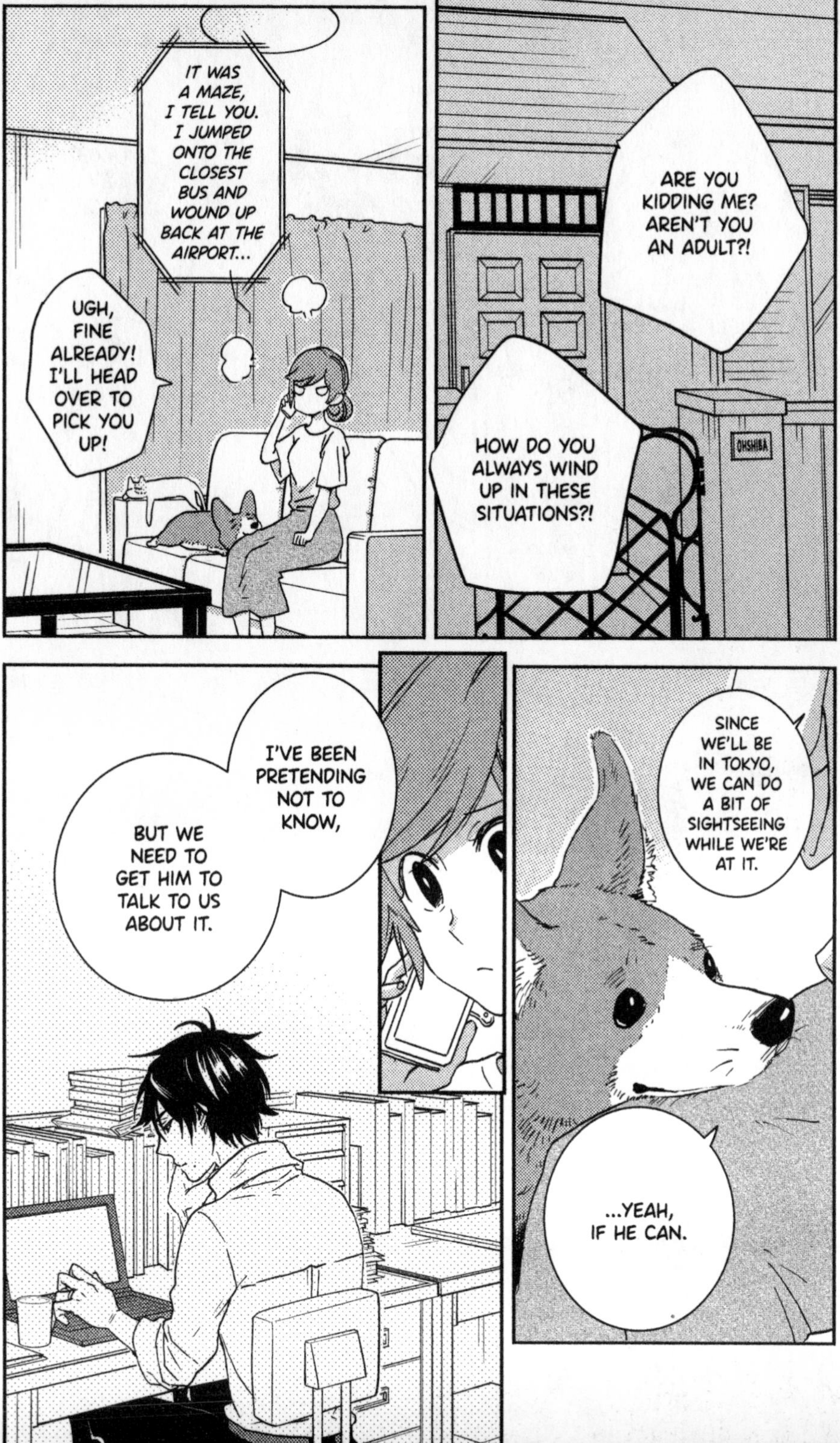
ARE YOU KIDDING ME? AREN'T YOU AN ADULT?!
OHSHIBA
HOW DO YOU ALWAYS WIND UP IN THESE SITUATIONS?!
IT WAS A MAZE, I TELL YOU. I JUMPED ONTO THE CLOSEST BUS AND WOUND UP BACK AT THE AIRPORT...
UGH, FINE ALREADY! I'LL HEAD OVER TO PICK YOU UP!
SINCE WE'LL BE IN TOKYO, WE CAN DO A BIT OF SIGHTSEEING WHILE WE'RE AT IT.
...YEAH, IF HE CAN.
I'VE BEEN PRETENDING NOT TO KNOW,
BUT WE NEED TO GET HIM TO TALK TO US ABOUT IT.

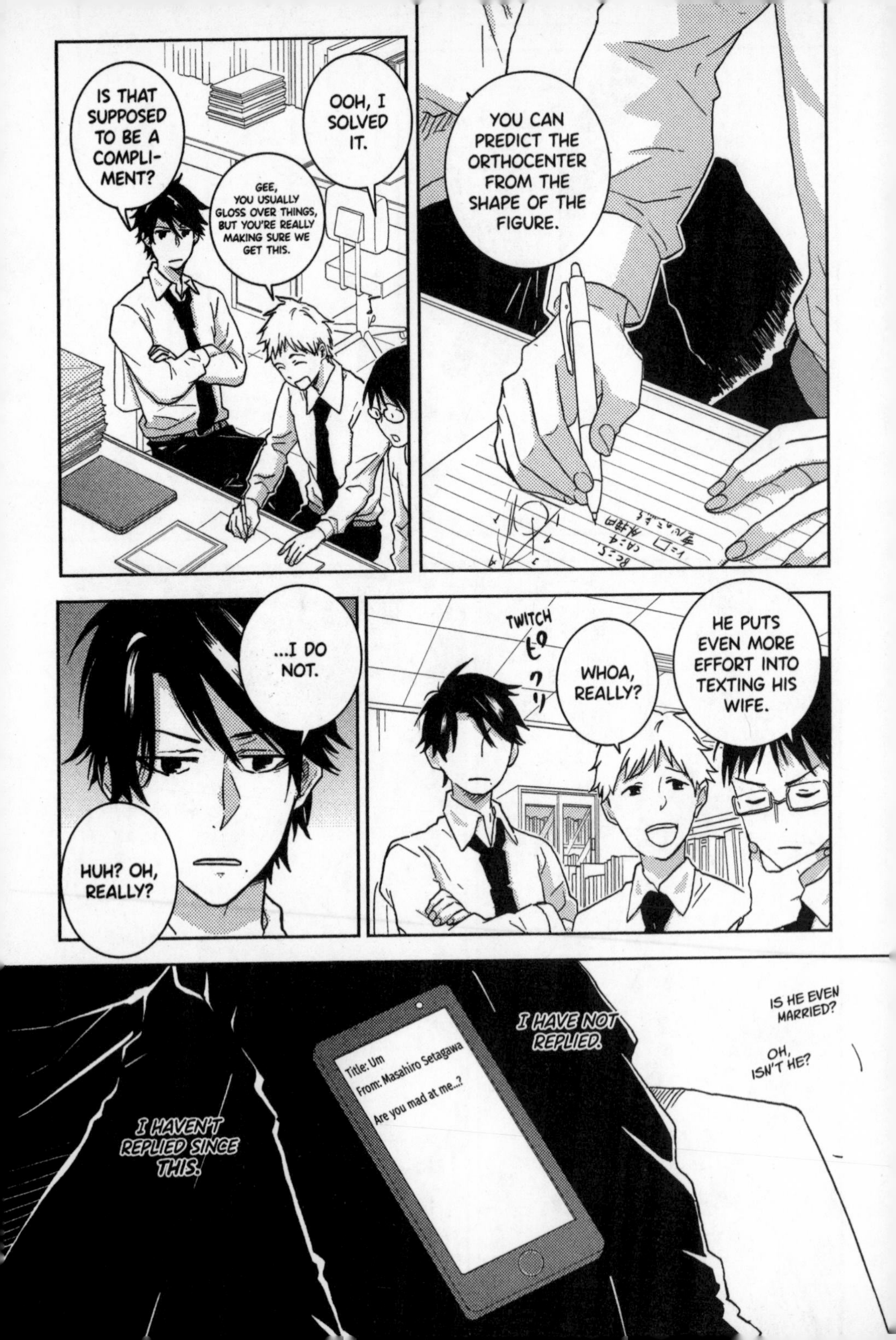

YOU CAN PREDICT THE ORTHOCENTER FROM THE SHAPE OF THE FIGURE.
OOH, I SOLVED IT.
GEE, YOU USUALLY GLOSS OVER THINGS, BUT YOU'RE REALLY MAKING SURE WE GET THIS.
IS THAT SUPPOSED TO BE A COMPLIMENT?
HE PUTS EVEN MORE EFFORT INTO TEXTING HIS WIFE.
WHOA, REALLY?
TWITCH
...I DO NOT.
HUH? OH, REALLY?
IS HE EVEN MARRIED?
OH, ISN'T HE?
I HAVE NOT REPLIED.
Title: Um
From: Masahiro Setagawa
Are you mad at me...?
I HAVEN'T REPLIED SINCE THIS.

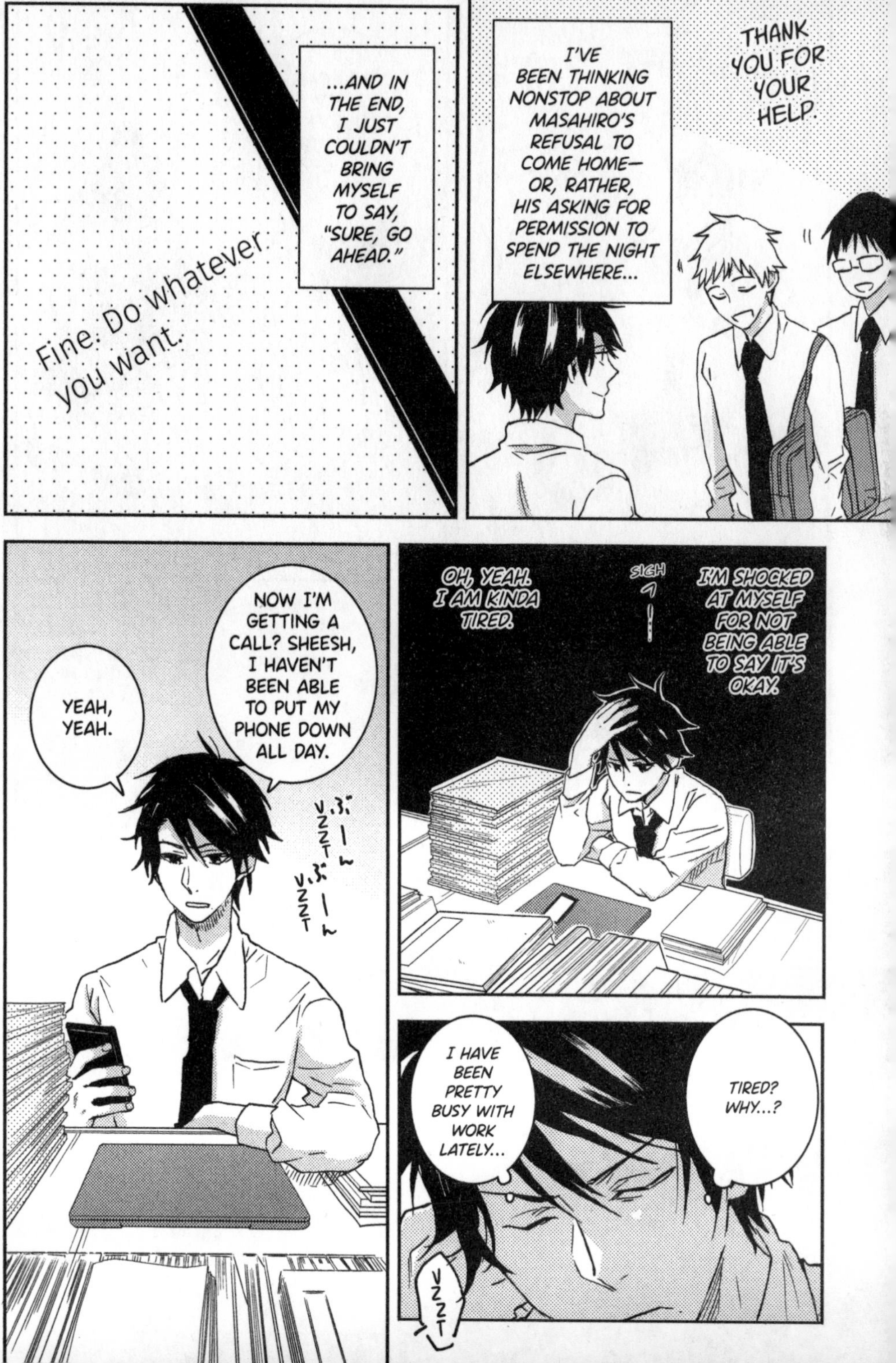
THANK YOU FOR YOUR HELP.
I'VE BEEN THINKING NONSTOP ABOUT MASAHIRO'S REFUSAL TO COME HOME—OR, RATHER, HIS ASKING FOR PERMISSION TO SPEND THE NIGHT ELSEWHERE...
...AND IN THE END, I JUST COULDN'T BRING MYSELF TO SAY, "SURE, GO AHEAD."
Fine. Do whatever you want.
I'M SHOCKED AT MYSELF FOR NOT BEING ABLE TO SAY IT'S OKAY.
SIGH
OH, YEAH. I AM KINDA TIRED.
TIRED? WHY...?
I HAVE BEEN PRETTY BUSY WITH WORK LATELY...
VZZT
NOW I'M GETTING A CALL? SHEESH, I HAVEN'T BEEN ABLE TO PUT MY PHONE DOWN ALL DAY.
YEAH, YEAH.
VZZT ぶーん
VZZT ぶーん

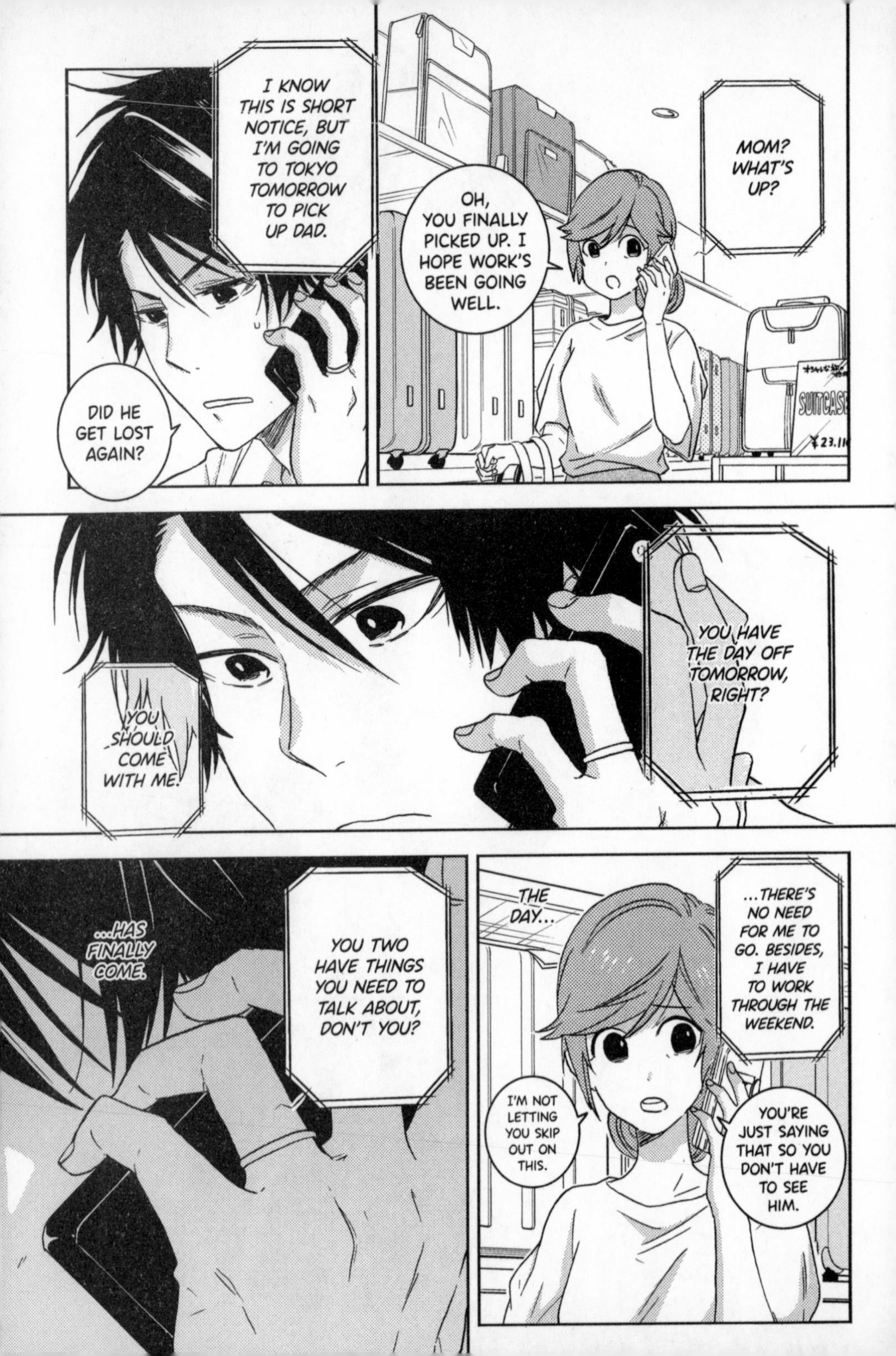
MOM? WHAT'S UP?
OH, YOU FINALLY PICKED UP. I HOPE WORK'S BEEN GOING WELL.
SUITCASE
I KNOW THIS IS SHORT NOTICE, BUT I'M GOING TO TOKYO TOMORROW TO PICK UP DAD.
DID HE GET LOST AGAIN?
YOU HAVE THE DAY OFF TOMORROW, RIGHT?
YOU SHOULD COME WITH ME.
...THERE'S NO NEED FOR ME TO GO. BESIDES, I HAVE TO WORK THROUGH THE WEEKEND.
THE DAY...
YOU'RE JUST SAYING THAT SO YOU DON'T HAVE TO SEE HIM.
I'M NOT LETTING YOU SKIP OUT ON THIS.
YOU TWO HAVE THINGS YOU NEED TO TALK ABOUT, DON'T YOU?
...HAS FINALLY COME.

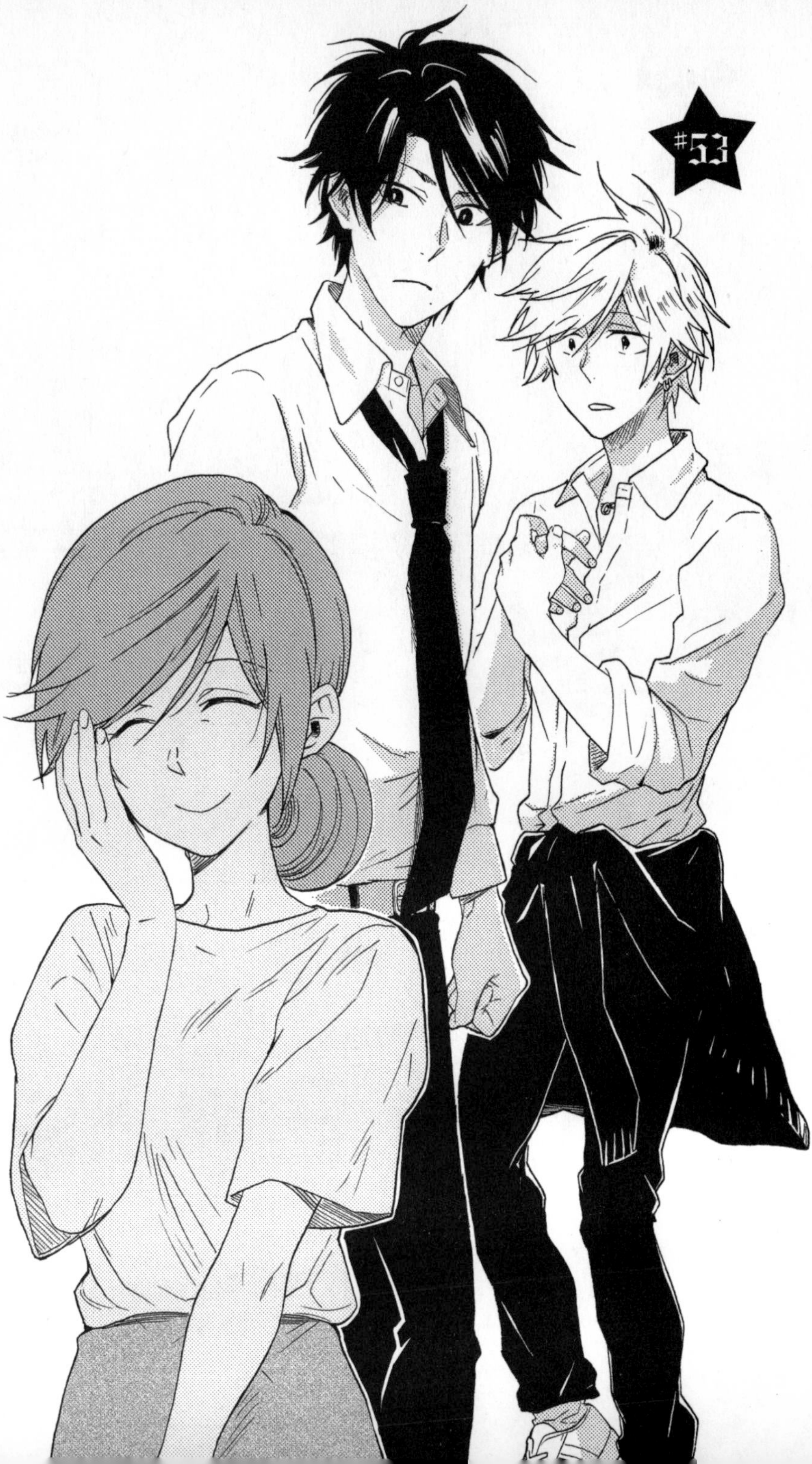
#53

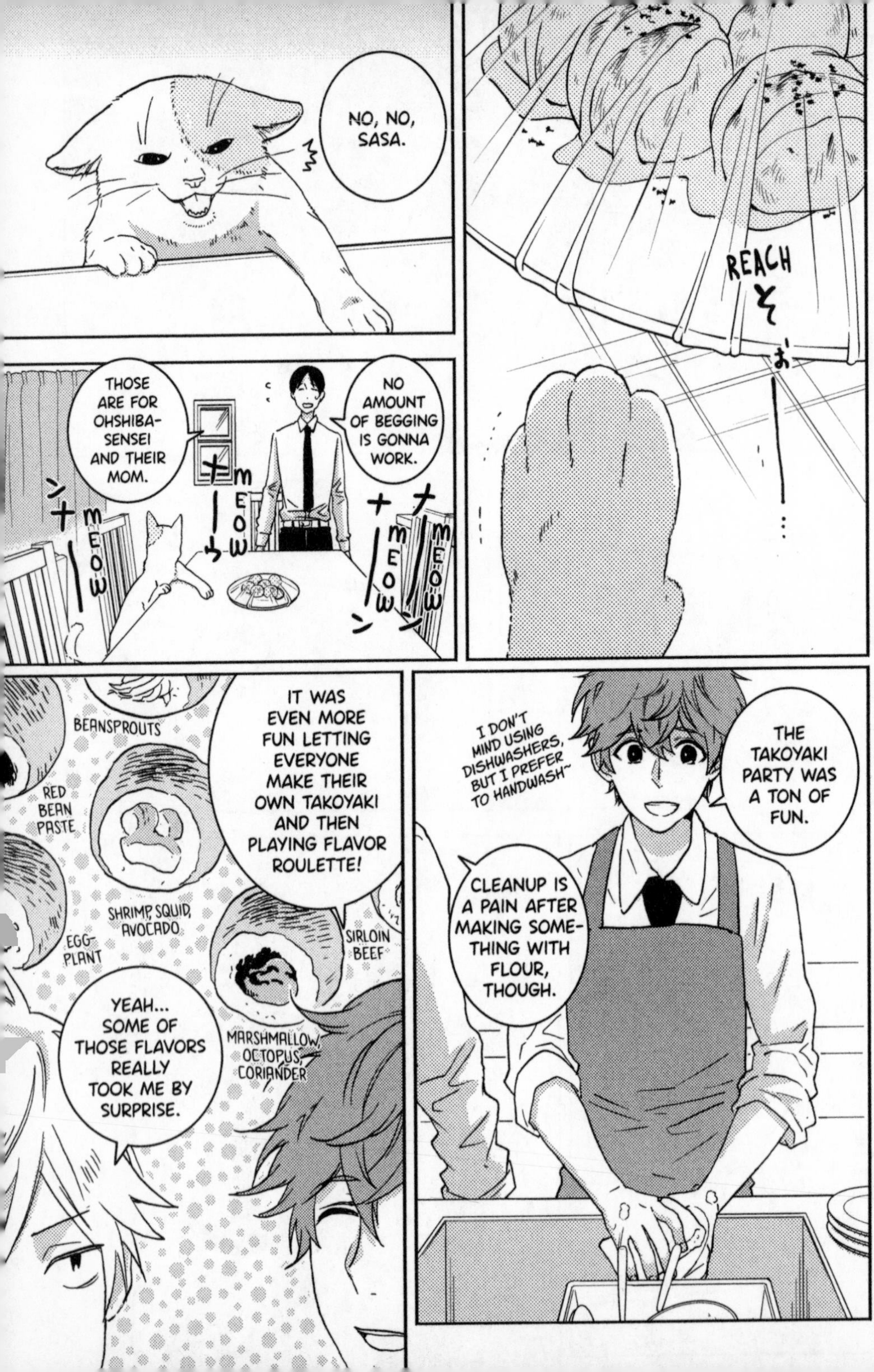
REACH
そ
ぉ
NO, NO, SASA.
NO AMOUNT OF BEGGING IS GONNA WORK.
MEOW
MEOW
THOSE ARE FOR OHSHIBA-SENSEI AND THEIR MOM.
MEOW
MEOW
THE TAKOYAKI PARTY WAS A TON OF FUN.
I DON'T MIND USING DISHWASHERS, BUT I PREFER TO HANDWASH~
CLEANUP IS A PAIN AFTER MAKING SOME-THING WITH FLOUR, THOUGH.
IT WAS EVEN MORE FUN LETTING EVERYONE MAKE THEIR OWN TAKOYAKI AND THEN PLAYING FLAVOR ROULETTE!
BEANSPROUTS
RED BEAN PASTE
SHRIMP, SQUID, AVOCADO
SIRLOIN BEEF
EGG-PLANT
MARSHMALLOW, OCTOPUS, CORIANDER
YEAH... SOME OF THOSE FLAVORS REALLY TOOK ME BY SURPRISE.

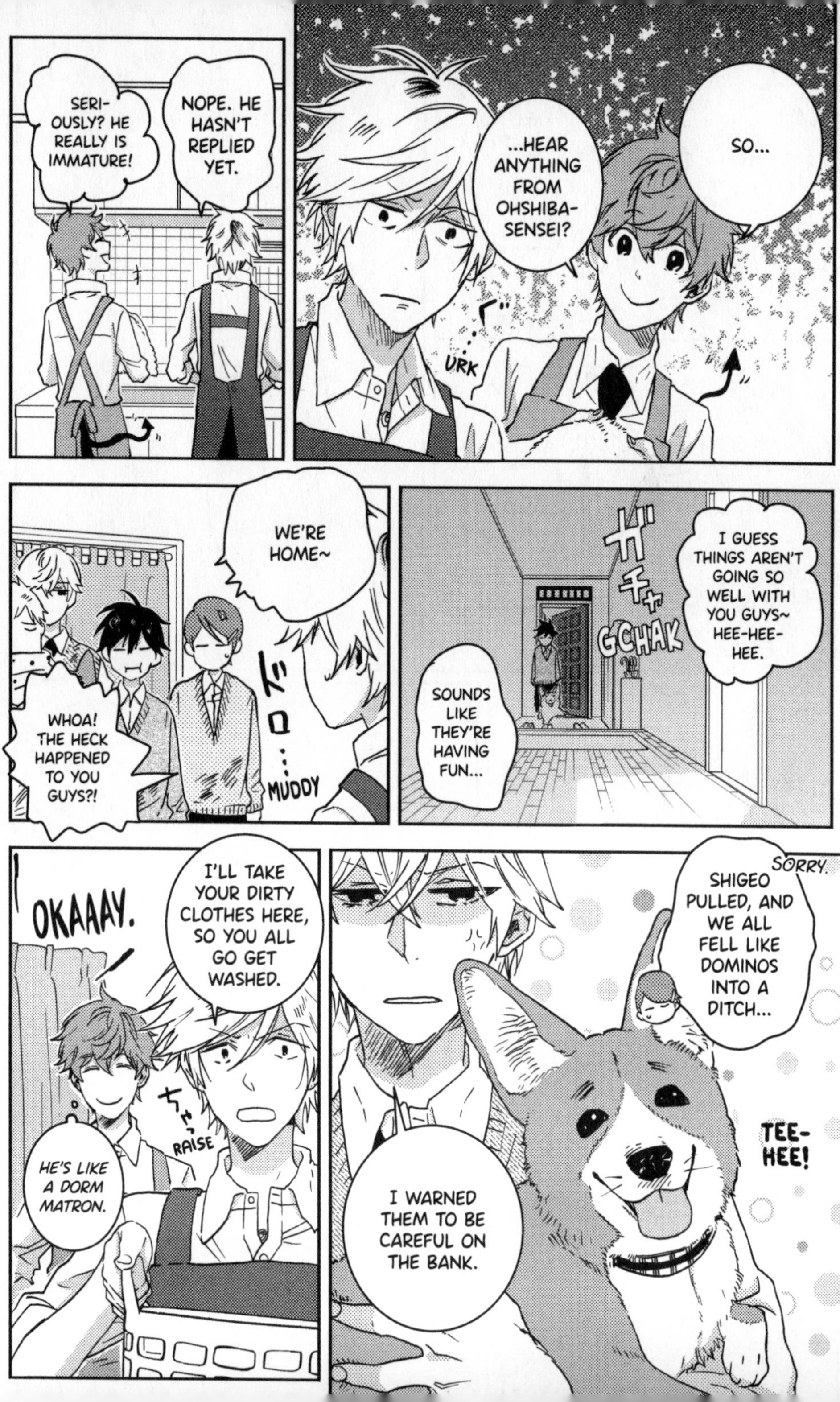
SO...
...HEAR ANYTHING FROM OHSHIBA-SENSEI?
URK
NOPE. HE HASN'T REPLIED YET.
SERIOUSLY? HE REALLY IS IMMATURE!
I GUESS THINGS AREN'T GOING SO WELL WITH YOU GUYS~ HEE-HEE-HEE.
GCHAK
SOUNDS LIKE THEY'RE HAVING FUN...
WE'RE HOME~
MUDDY
WHOA! THE HECK HAPPENED TO YOU GUYS?!
SORRY.
SHIGEO PULLED, AND WE ALL FELL LIKE DOMINOS INTO A DITCH...
TEE-HEE!
I WARNED THEM TO BE CAREFUL ON THE BANK.
OKAAAY.
I'LL TAKE YOUR DIRTY CLOTHES HERE, SO YOU ALL GO GET WASHED.
RAISE
HE'S LIKE A DORM MATRON.

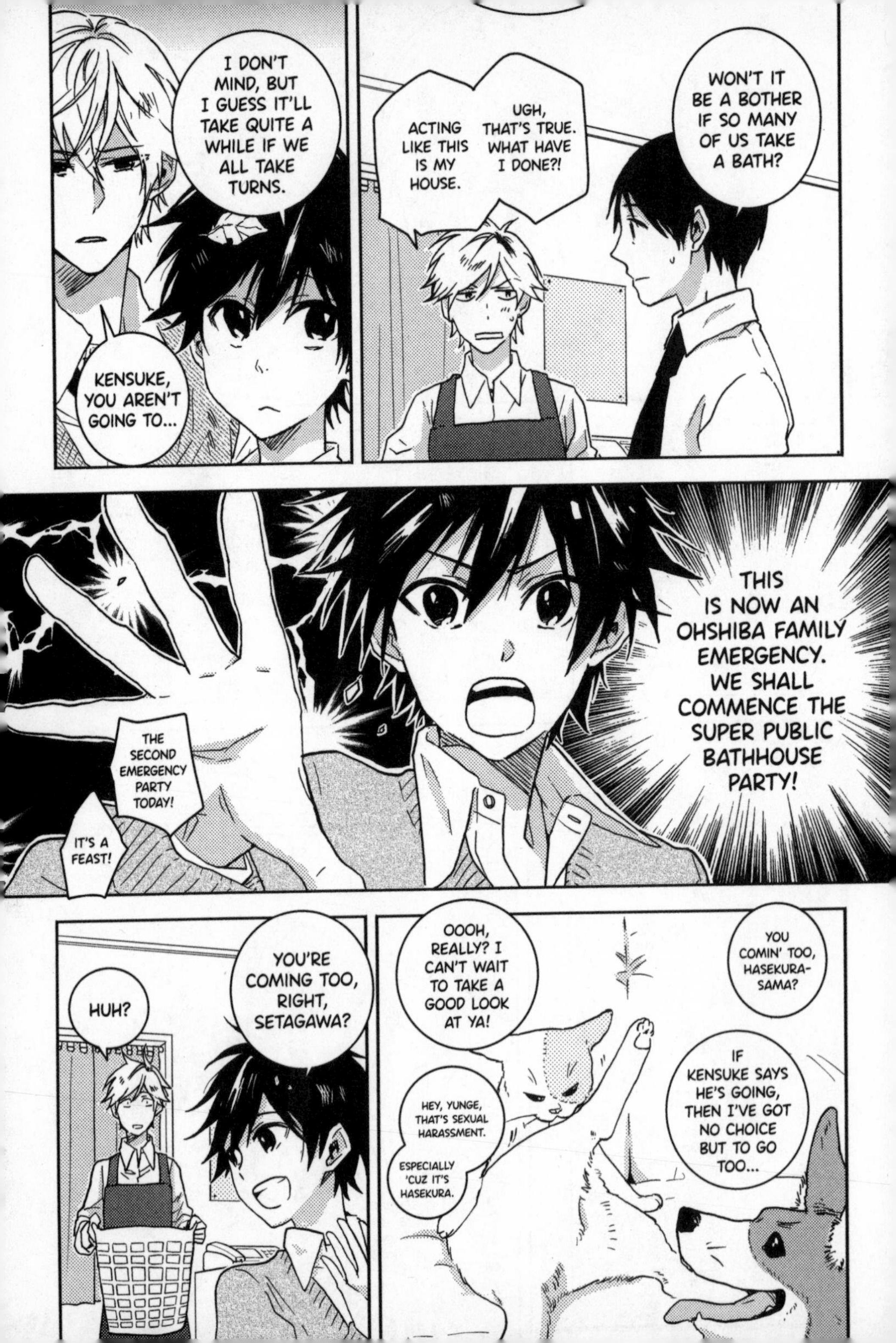
WON'T IT BE A BOTHER IF SO MANY OF US TAKE A BATH?
UGH, THAT'S TRUE. WHAT HAVE I DONE?!
ACTING LIKE THIS IS MY HOUSE.
I DON'T MIND, BUT I GUESS IT'LL TAKE QUITE A WHILE IF WE ALL TAKE TURNS.
KENSUKE, YOU AREN'T GOING TO...
THIS IS NOW AN OHSHIBA FAMILY EMERGENCY. WE SHALL COMMENCE THE SUPER PUBLIC BATHHOUSE PARTY!
THE SECOND EMERGENCY PARTY TODAY!
IT'S A FEAST!
YOU COMIN' TOO, HASEKURA-SAMA?
OOOH, REALLY? I CAN'T WAIT TO TAKE A GOOD LOOK AT YA!
IF KENSUKE SAYS HE'S GOING, THEN I'VE GOT NO CHOICE BUT TO GO TOO...
HEY, YUNGE, THAT'S SEXUAL HARASSMENT.
ESPECIALLY 'CUZ IT'S HASEKURA.
YOU'RE COMING TOO, RIGHT, SETAGAWA?
HUH?

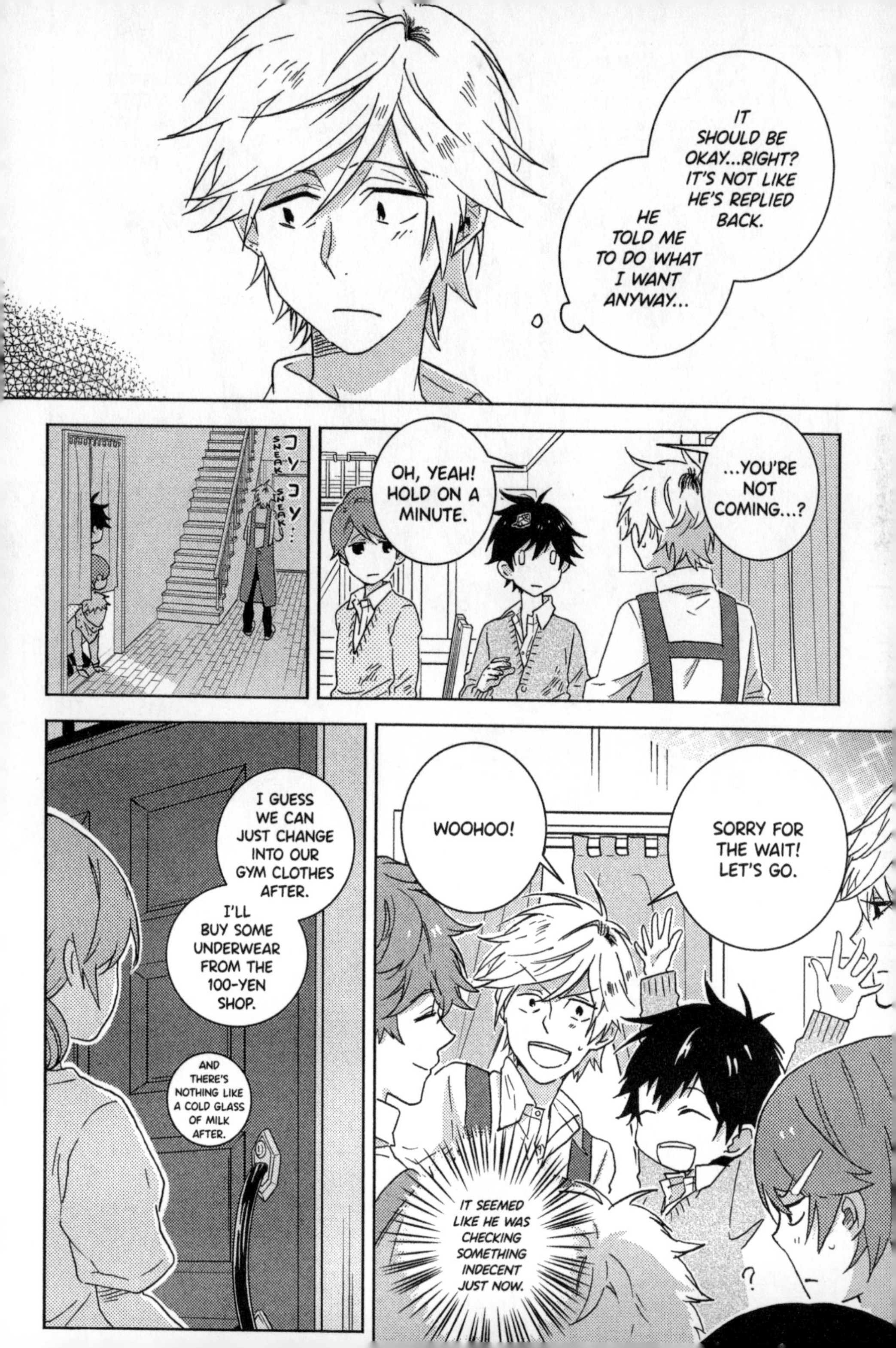
IT SHOULD BE OKAY...RIGHT? IT'S NOT LIKE HE'S REPLIED BACK.
HE TOLD ME TO DO WHAT I WANT ANYWAY...
...YOU'RE NOT COMING...?
OH, YEAH! HOLD ON A MINUTE.
コソコソ
SNEAK SNEAK...
SORRY FOR THE WAIT! LET'S GO.
WOOHOO!
IT SEEMED LIKE HE WAS CHECKING SOMETHING INDECENT JUST NOW.
?
I GUESS WE CAN JUST CHANGE INTO OUR GYM CLOTHES AFTER.
I'LL BUY SOME UNDERWEAR FROM THE 100-YEN SHOP.
AND THERE'S NOTHING LIKE A COLD GLASS OF MILK AFTER.

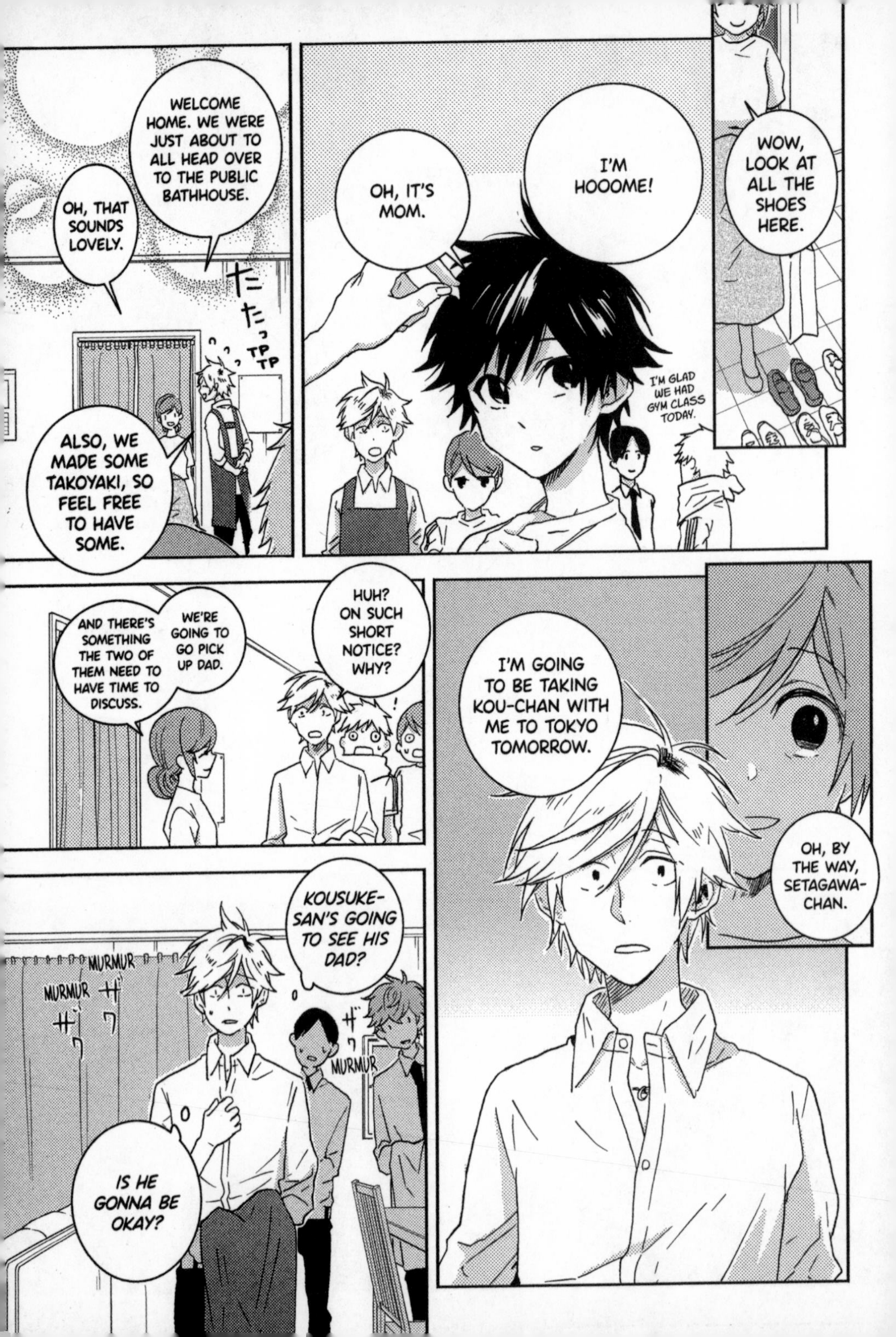
WOW, LOOK AT ALL THE SHOES HERE.
I'M HOOOME!
OH, IT'S MOM.
I'M GLAD WE HAD GYM CLASS TODAY.
WELCOME HOME. WE WERE JUST ABOUT TO ALL HEAD OVER TO THE PUBLIC BATHHOUSE.
OH, THAT SOUNDS LOVELY.
たたっ TP TP
ALSO, WE MADE SOME TAKOYAKI, SO FEEL FREE TO HAVE SOME.
OH, BY THE WAY, SETAGAWA-CHAN.
I'M GOING TO BE TAKING KOU-CHAN WITH ME TO TOKYO TOMORROW.
HUH? ON SUCH SHORT NOTICE? WHY?
WE'RE GOING TO GO PICK UP DAD.
AND THERE'S SOMETHING THE TWO OF THEM NEED TO HAVE TIME TO DISCUSS.
KOUSUKE-SAN'S GOING TO SEE HIS DAD?
ザワ MURMUR
ザワ MURMUR
ザワ MURMUR
IS HE GONNA BE OKAY?

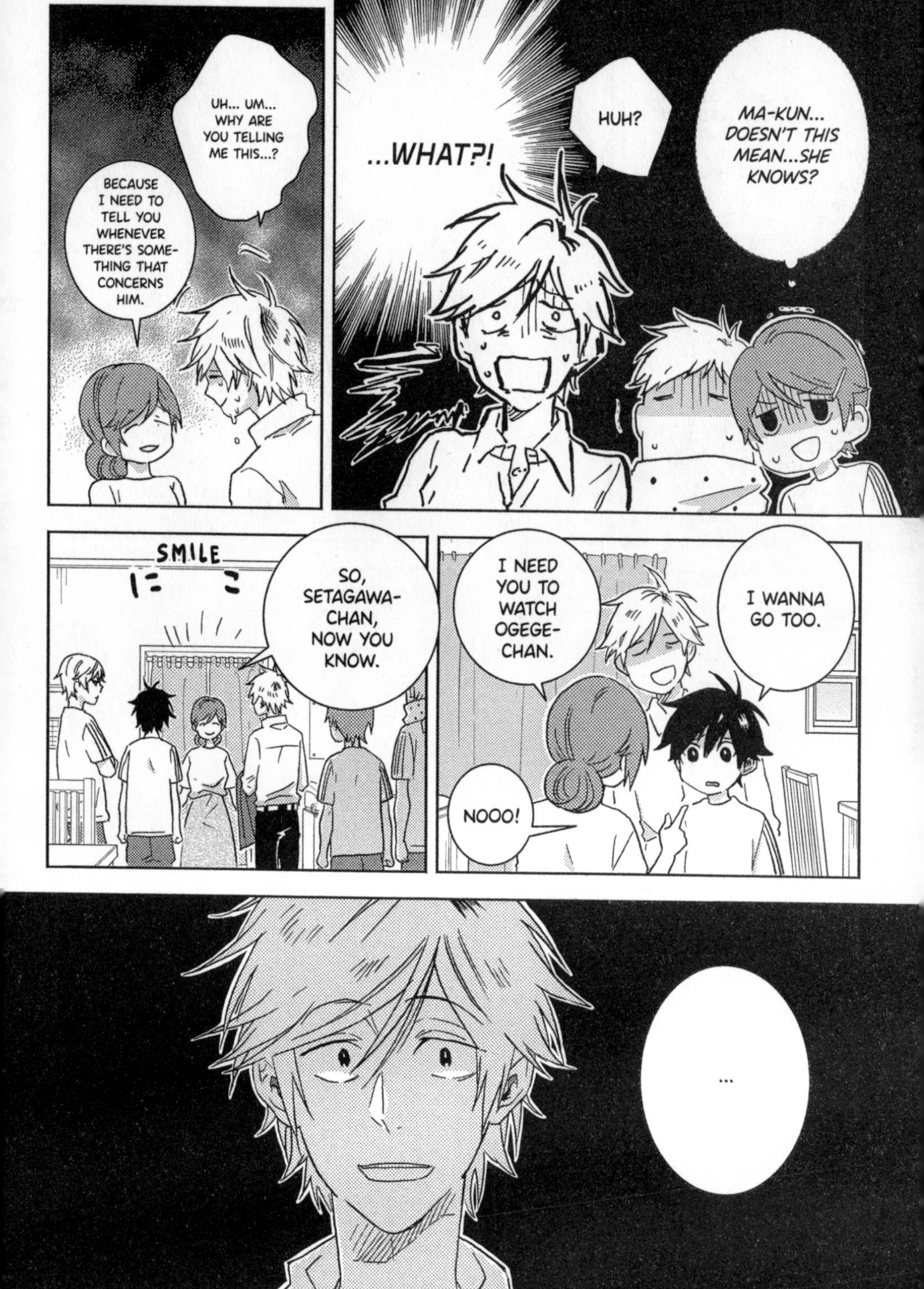
MA-KUN... DOESN'T THIS MEAN...SHE KNOWS?
HUH?
...WHAT?!
UH... UM... WHY ARE YOU TELLING ME THIS...?
BECAUSE I NEED TO TELL YOU WHENEVER THERE'S SOME-THING THAT CONCERNS HIM.
I WANNA GO TOO.
I NEED YOU TO WATCH OGEGE-CHAN.
NOOO!
SO, SETAGAWA-CHAN, NOW YOU KNOW.
SMILE
にこ
...

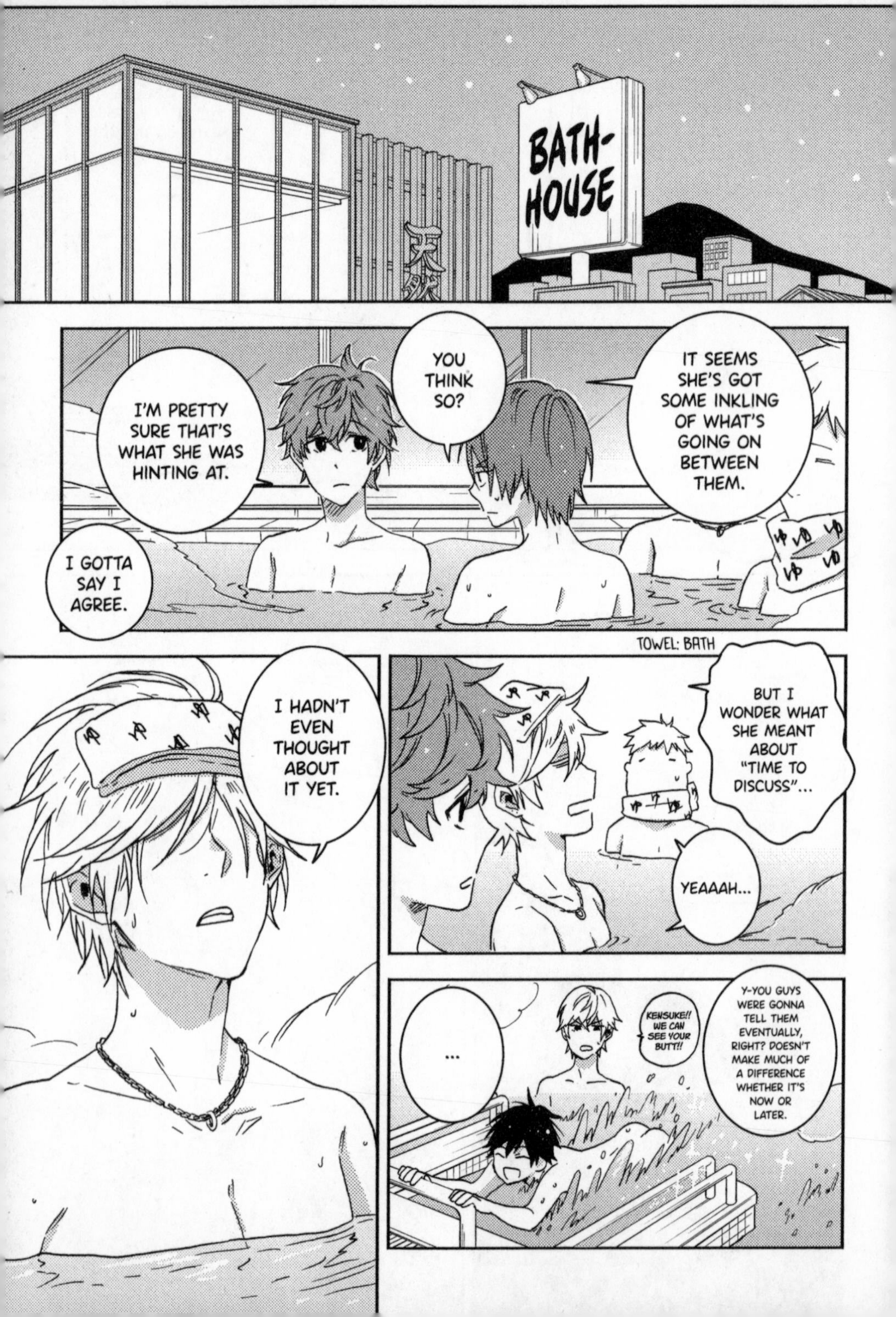
BATH-HOUSE
IT SEEMS SHE'S GOT SOME INKLING OF WHAT'S GOING ON BETWEEN THEM.
YOU THINK SO?
I'M PRETTY SURE THAT'S WHAT SHE WAS HINTING AT.
I GOTTA SAY I AGREE.
TOWEL: BATH
BUT I WONDER WHAT SHE MEANT ABOUT "TIME TO DISCUSS"...
YEAAAH...
Y-YOU GUYS WERE GONNA TELL THEM EVENTUALLY, RIGHT? DOESN'T MAKE MUCH OF A DIFFERENCE WHETHER IT'S NOW OR LATER.
KENSUKE!! WE CAN SEE YOUR BUTT!!
...
I HADN'T EVEN THOUGHT ABOUT IT YET.

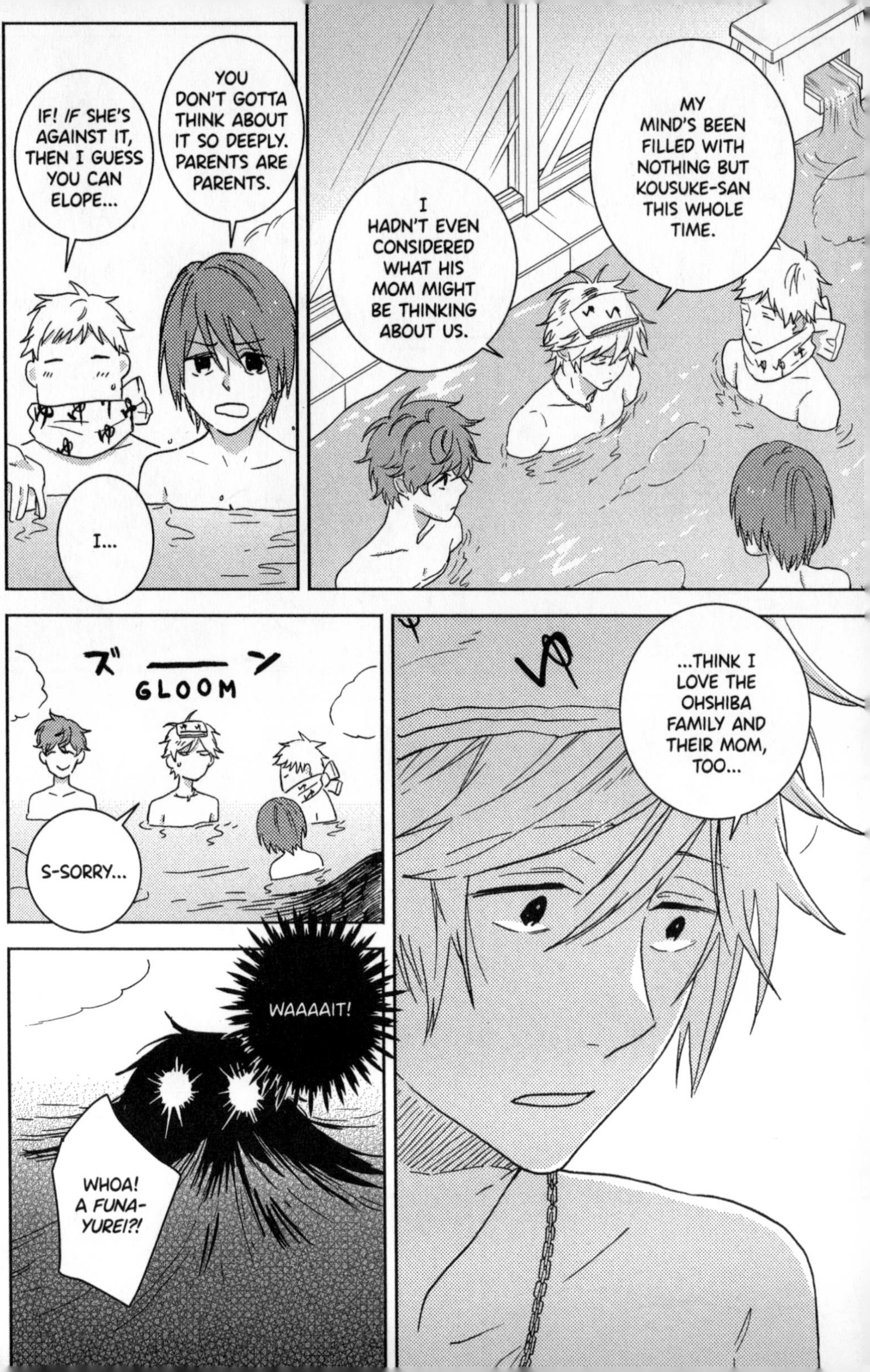
MY MIND'S BEEN FILLED WITH NOTHING BUT KOUSUKE-SAN THIS WHOLE TIME.
I HADN'T EVEN CONSIDERED WHAT HIS MOM MIGHT BE THINKING ABOUT US.
YOU DON'T GOTTA THINK ABOUT IT SO DEEPLY. PARENTS ARE PARENTS.
IF! *IF* SHE'S AGAINST IT, THEN I GUESS YOU CAN ELOPE...
I...
...THINK I LOVE THE OHSHIBA FAMILY AND THEIR MOM, TOO...
ズーーン
GLOOM
S-SORRY...
WAAAAIT!
WHOA! A FUNA-YUREI!?!

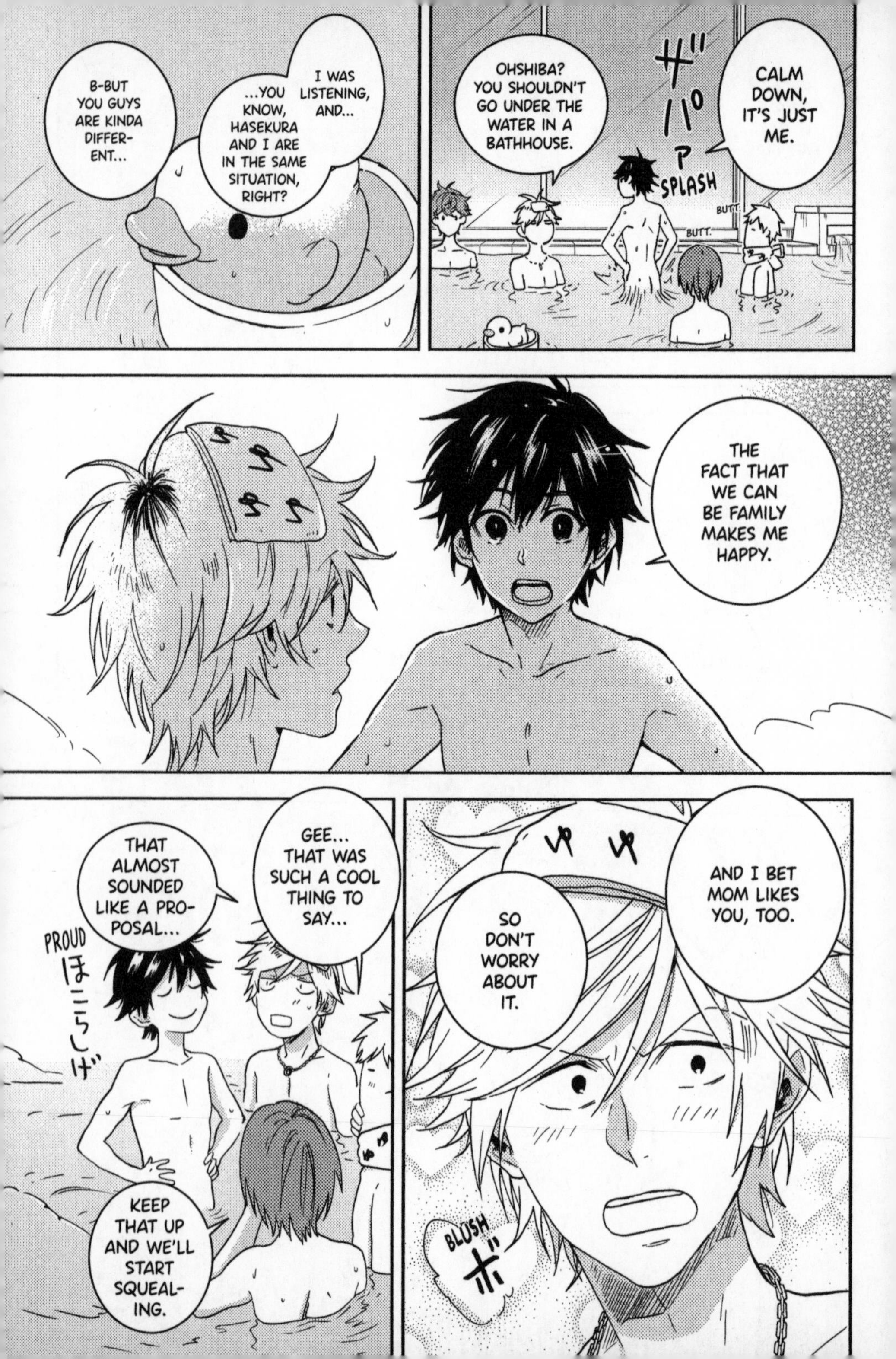
CALM DOWN, IT'S JUST ME.
ザバァ
SPLASH
OHSHIBA? YOU SHOULDN'T GO UNDER THE WATER IN A BATHHOUSE.
BUTT.
BUTT.
I WAS LISTENING, AND...
...YOU KNOW, HASEKURA AND I ARE IN THE SAME SITUATION, RIGHT?
B-BUT YOU GUYS ARE KINDA DIFFERENT...
THE FACT THAT WE CAN BE FAMILY MAKES ME HAPPY.
AND I BET MOM LIKES YOU, TOO.
SO DON'T WORRY ABOUT IT.
BLUSH
ボッ
GEE... THAT WAS SUCH A COOL THING TO SAY...
THAT ALMOST SOUNDED LIKE A PROPOSAL...
PROUD
ほこらしげ
KEEP THAT UP AND WE'LL START SQUEALING.

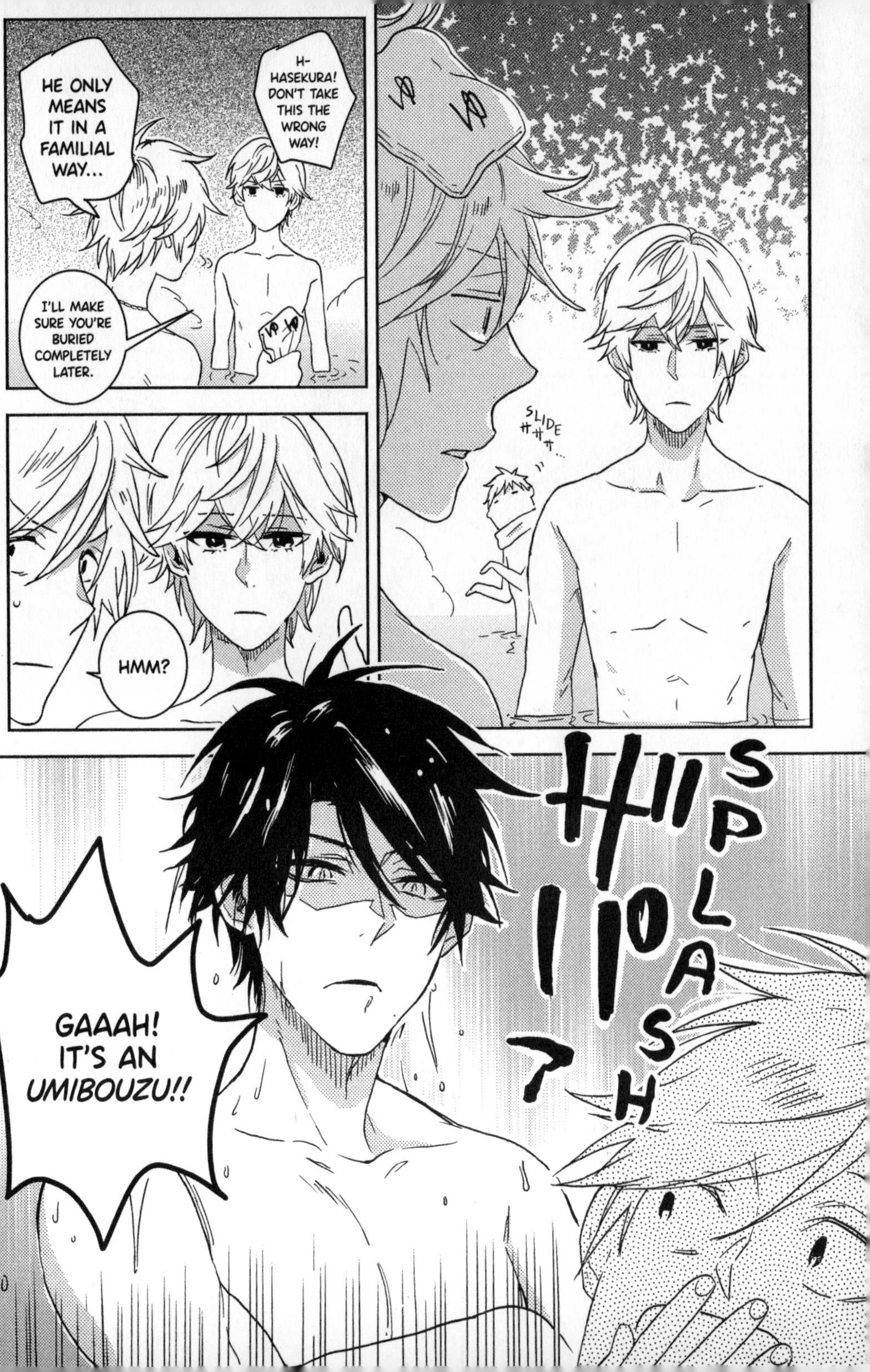
SLIDE
H-HASEKURA! DON'T TAKE THIS THE WRONG WAY!
HE ONLY MEANS IT IN A FAMILIAL WAY...
I'LL MAKE SURE YOU'RE BURIED COMPLETELY LATER.
HMM?
SPLASH
GAAAH! IT'S AN UMIBOUZU!!

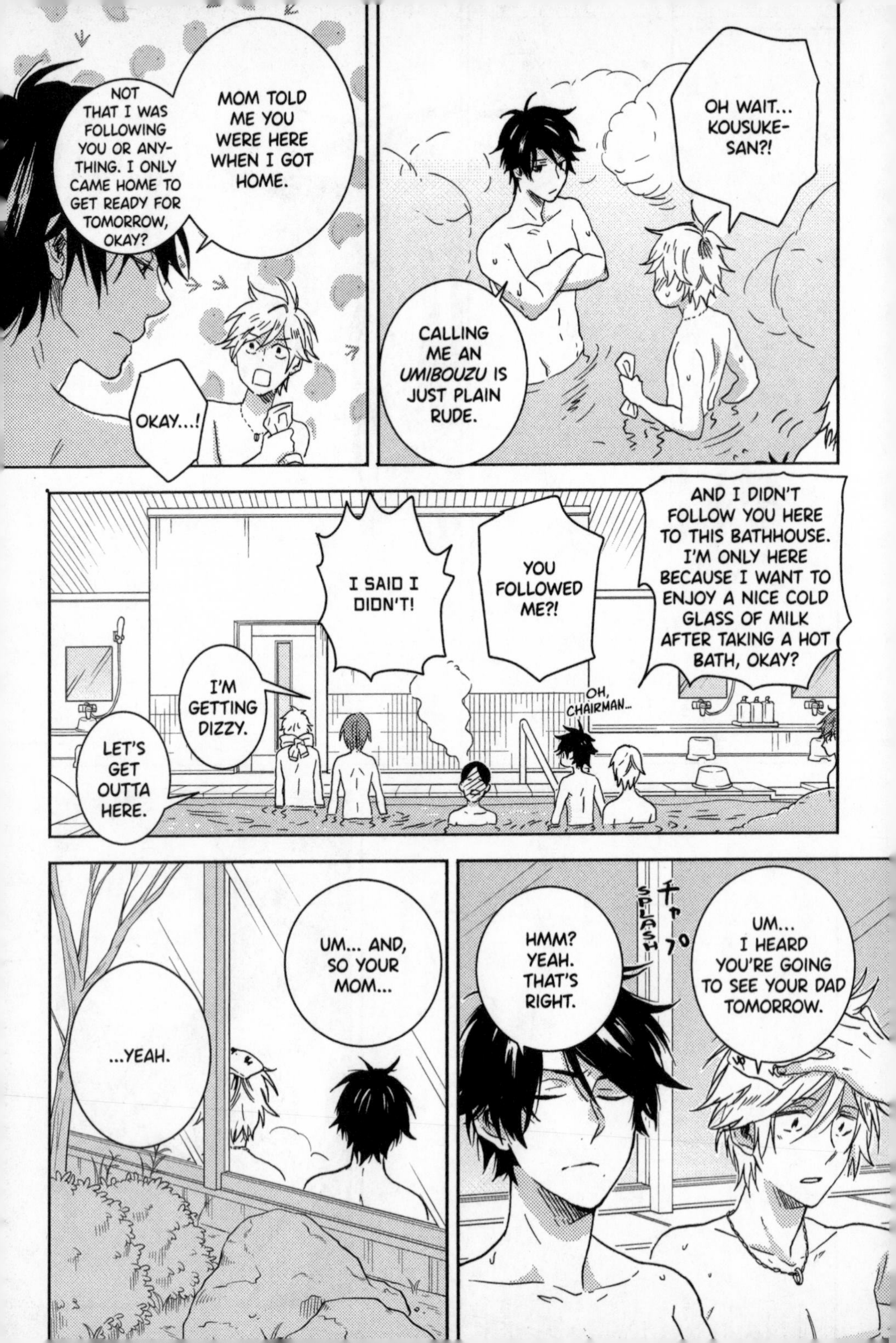
OH WAIT... KOUSUKE-SAN?!
CALLING ME AN UMIBOUZU IS JUST PLAIN RUDE.
MOM TOLD ME YOU WERE HERE WHEN I GOT HOME.
NOT THAT I WAS FOLLOWING YOU OR ANYTHING. I ONLY CAME HOME TO GET READY FOR TOMORROW, OKAY?
OKAY...!
AND I DIDN'T FOLLOW YOU HERE TO THIS BATHHOUSE. I'M ONLY HERE BECAUSE I WANT TO ENJOY A NICE COLD GLASS OF MILK AFTER TAKING A HOT BATH, OKAY?
YOU FOLLOWED ME?!
I SAID I DIDN'T!
OH, CHAIRMAN...
I'M GETTING DIZZY.
LET'S GET OUTTA HERE.
UM... I HEARD YOU'RE GOING TO SEE YOUR DAD TOMORROW.
チャプ
SPLASH
HMM? YEAH. THAT'S RIGHT.
UM... AND, SO YOUR MOM...
...YEAH.

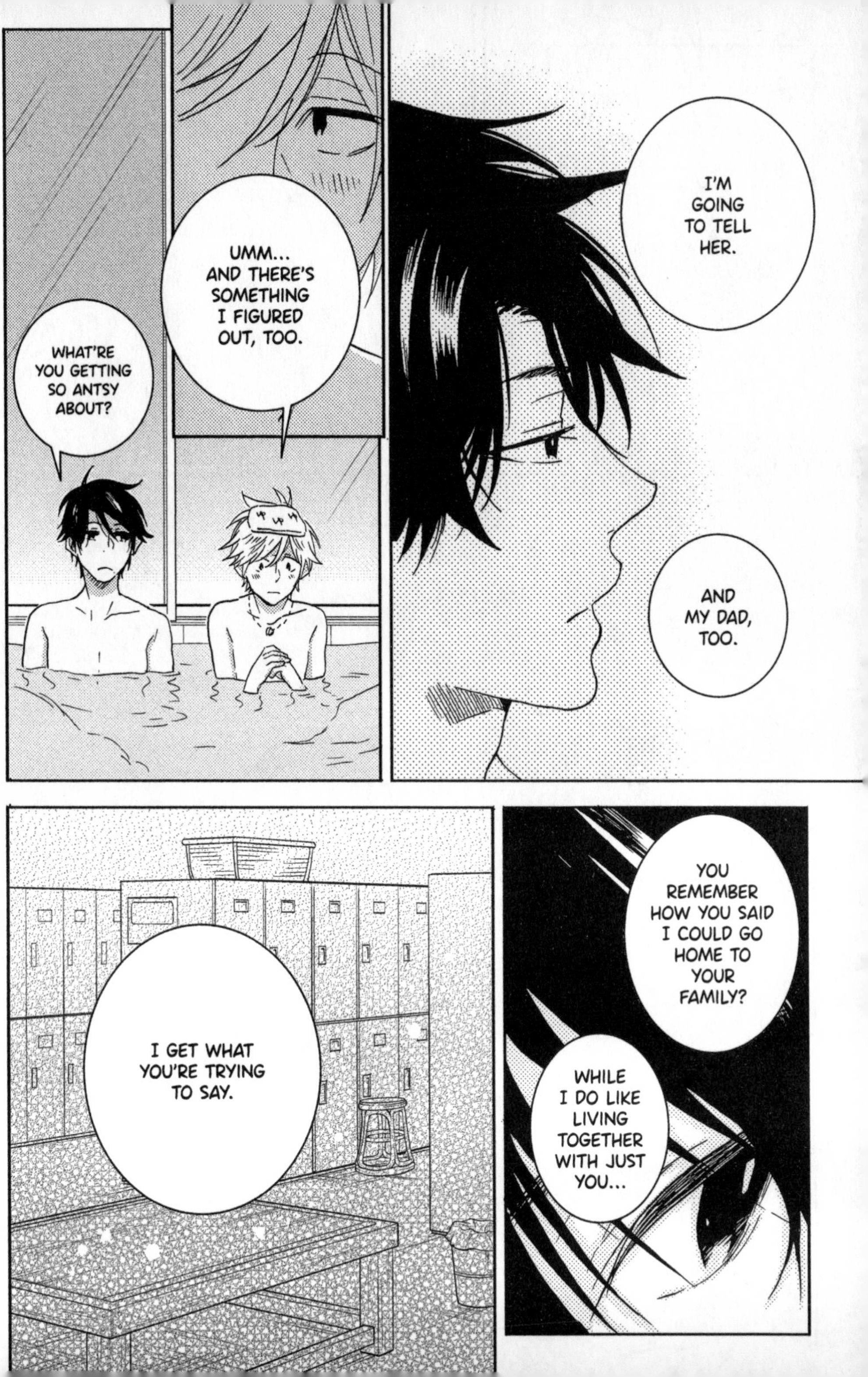
I'M GOING TO TELL HER.
AND MY DAD, TOO.
UMM... AND THERE'S SOMETHING I FIGURED OUT, TOO.
WHAT'RE YOU GETTING SO ANTSY ABOUT?
YOU REMEMBER HOW YOU SAID I COULD GO HOME TO YOUR FAMILY?
WHILE I DO LIKE LIVING TOGETHER WITH JUST YOU...
I GET WHAT YOU'RE TRYING TO SAY.

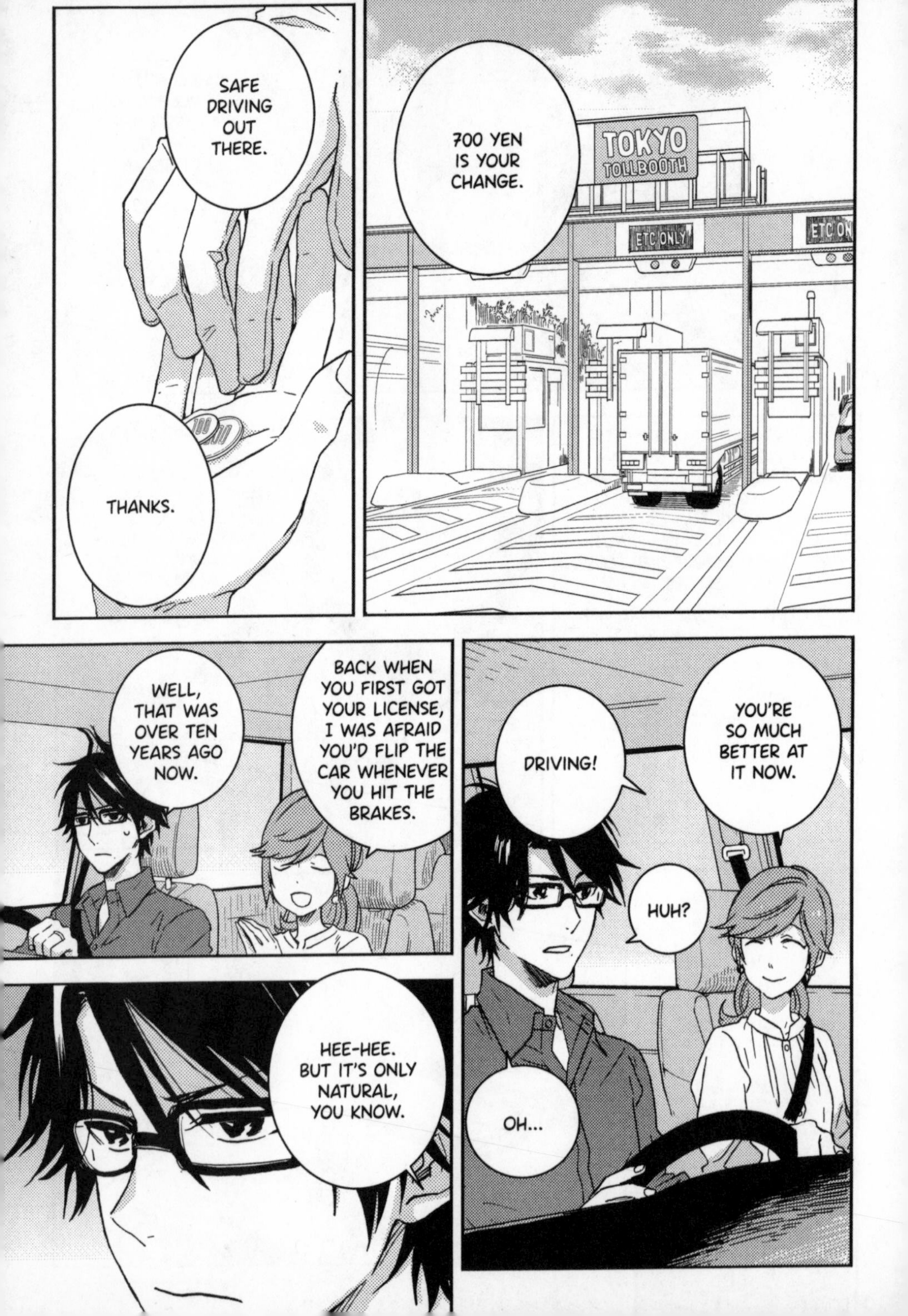
700 YEN IS YOUR CHANGE.
TOKYO TOLLBOOTH
ETC ONLY
SAFE DRIVING OUT THERE.
THANKS.
YOU'RE SO MUCH BETTER AT IT NOW.
DRIVING!
HUH?
OH...
BACK WHEN YOU FIRST GOT YOUR LICENSE, I WAS AFRAID YOU'D FLIP THE CAR WHENEVER YOU HIT THE BRAKES.
WELL, THAT WAS OVER TEN YEARS AGO NOW.
HEE-HEE. BUT IT'S ONLY NATURAL, YOU KNOW.

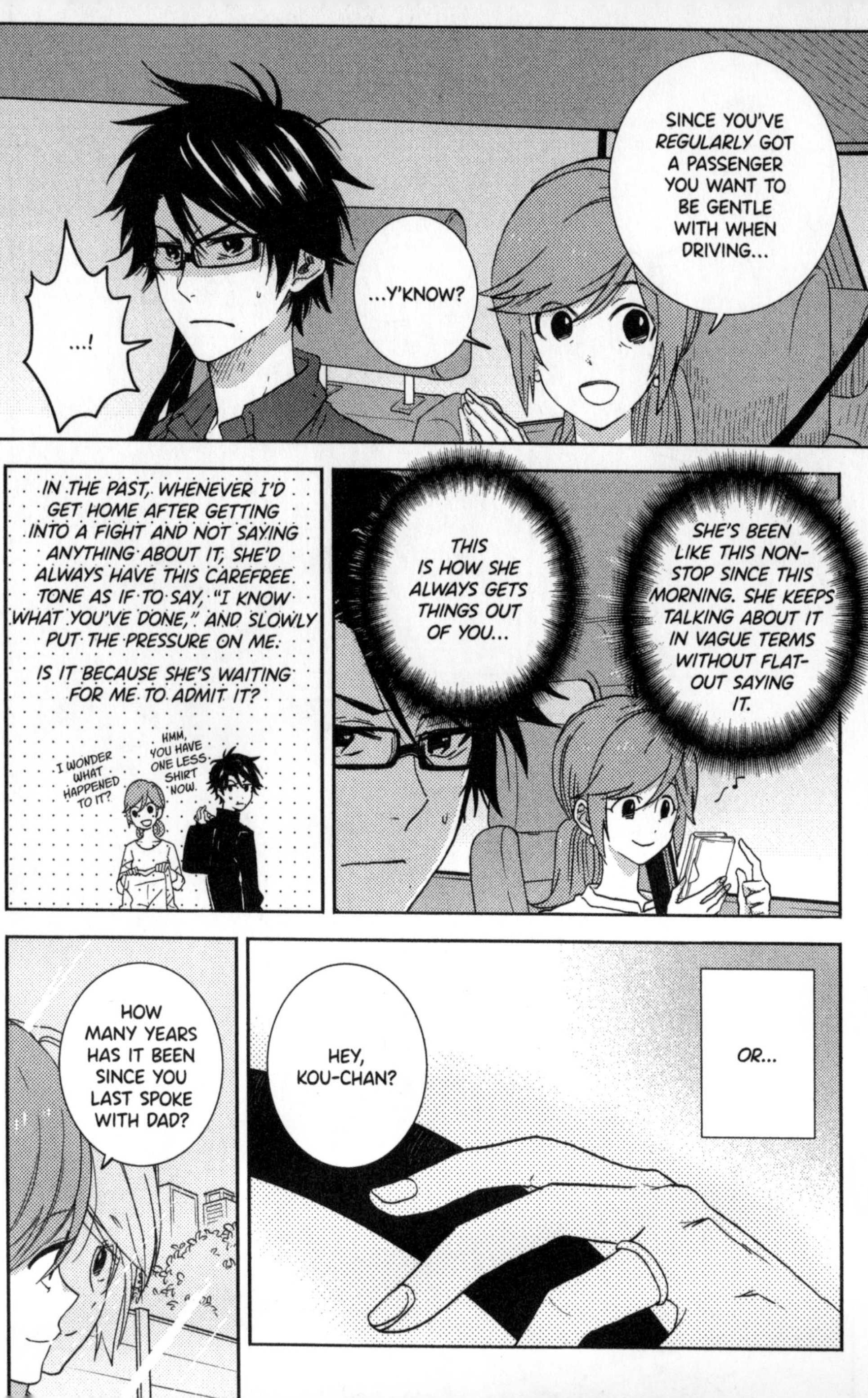
SINCE YOU'VE REGULARLY GOT A PASSENGER YOU WANT TO BE GENTLE WITH WHEN DRIVING...
...Y'KNOW?
...!
SHE'S BEEN LIKE THIS NON-STOP SINCE THIS MORNING. SHE KEEPS TALKING ABOUT IT IN VAGUE TERMS WITHOUT FLAT-OUT SAYING IT.
THIS IS HOW SHE ALWAYS GETS THINGS OUT OF YOU...
IN THE PAST, WHENEVER I'D GET HOME AFTER GETTING INTO A FIGHT AND NOT SAYING ANYTHING ABOUT IT, SHE'D ALWAYS HAVE THIS CAREFREE TONE AS IF TO SAY, "I KNOW WHAT YOU'VE DONE," AND SLOWLY PUT THE PRESSURE ON ME.
IS IT BECAUSE SHE'S WAITING FOR ME TO ADMIT IT?
HMM, YOU HAVE ONE LESS SHIRT NOW.
I WONDER WHAT HAPPENED TO IT?
OR...
HEY, KOU-CHAN?
HOW MANY YEARS HAS IT BEEN SINCE YOU LAST SPOKE WITH DAD?

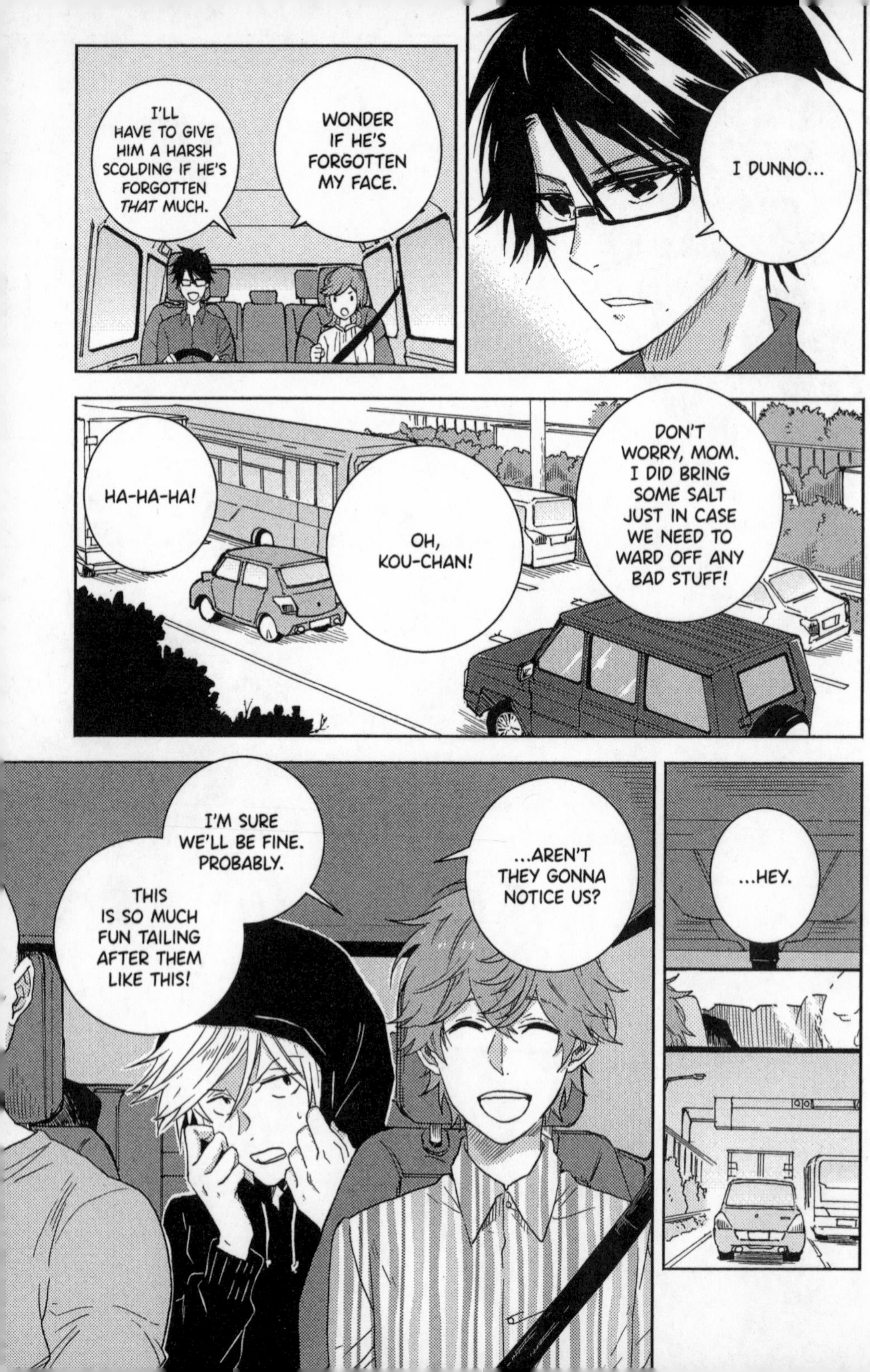
I DUNNO...
WONDER IF HE'S FORGOTTEN MY FACE.
I'LL HAVE TO GIVE HIM A HARSH SCOLDING IF HE'S FORGOTTEN *THAT* MUCH.
DON'T WORRY, MOM. I DID BRING SOME SALT JUST IN CASE WE NEED TO WARD OFF ANY BAD STUFF!
OH, KOU-CHAN!
HA-HA-HA!
...HEY.
...AREN'T THEY GONNA NOTICE US?
I'M SURE WE'LL BE FINE. PROBABLY.
THIS IS SO MUCH FUN TAILING AFTER THEM LIKE THIS!

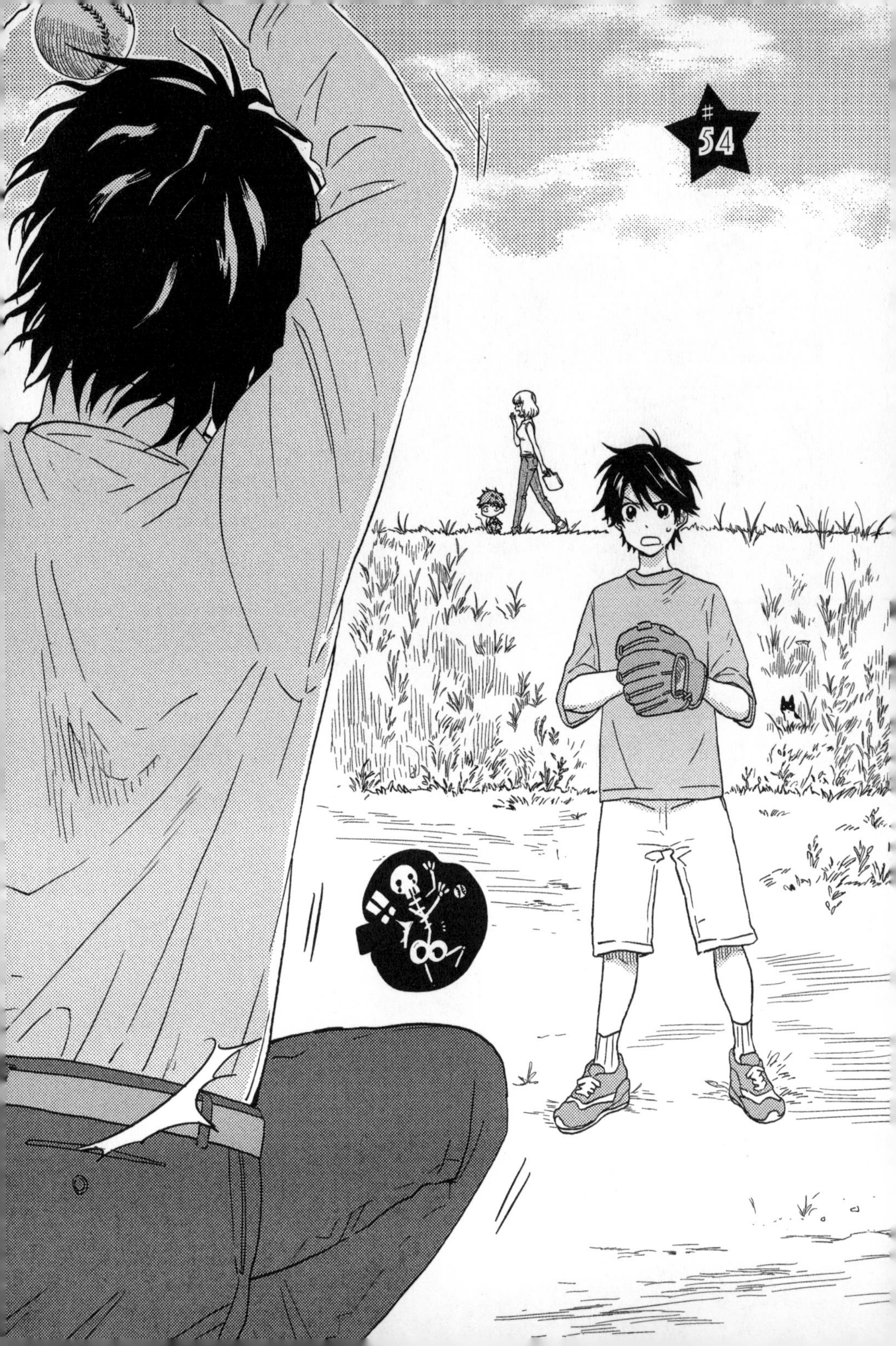
#54

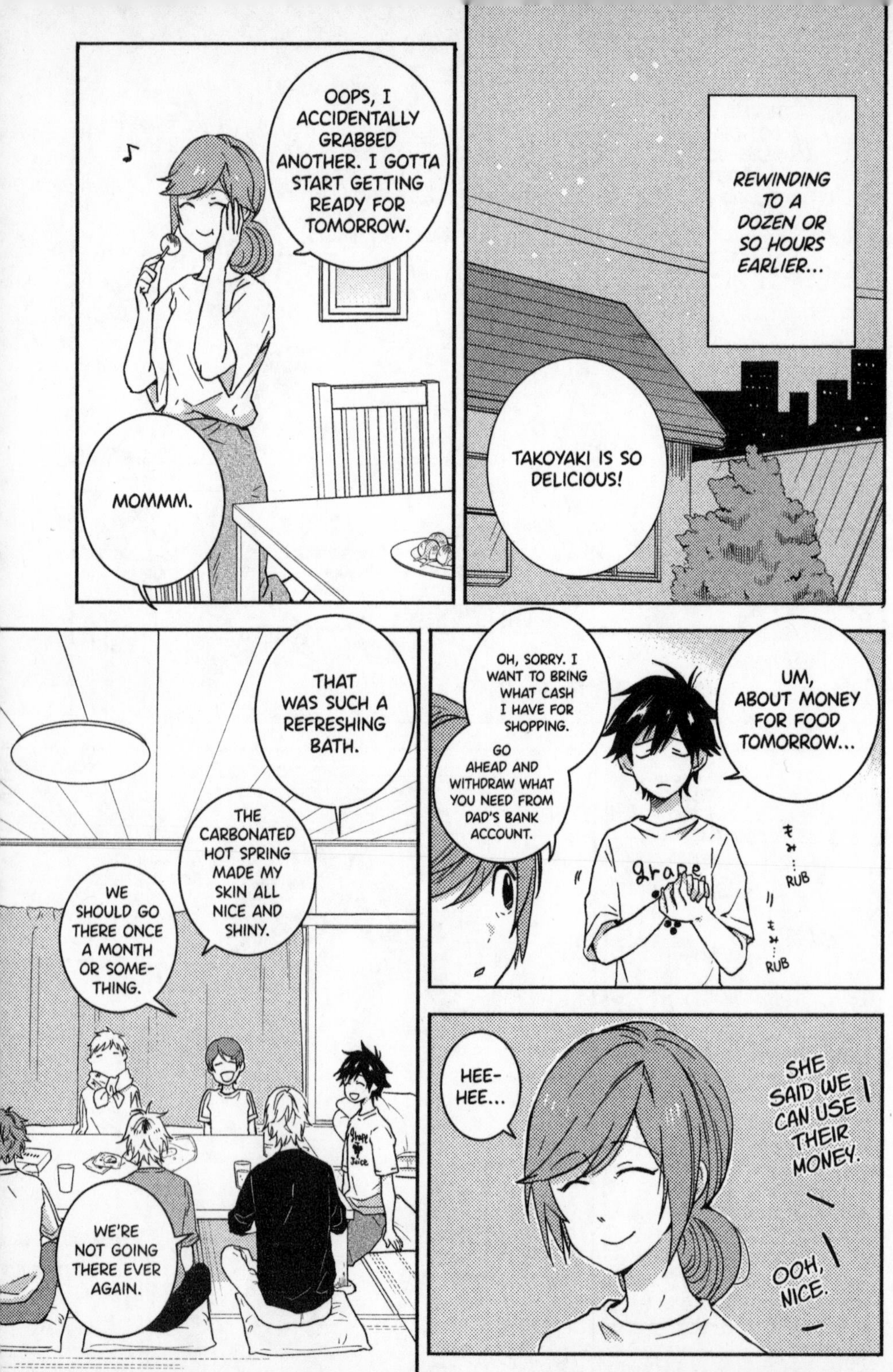
REWINDING TO A DOZEN OR SO HOURS EARLIER...
TAKOYAKI IS SO DELICIOUS!
OOPS, I ACCIDENTALLY GRABBED ANOTHER. I GOTTA START GETTING READY FOR TOMORROW.
MOMMM.
UM, ABOUT MONEY FOR FOOD TOMORROW...
OH, SORRY. I WANT TO BRING WHAT CASH I HAVE FOR SHOPPING.
GO AHEAD AND WITHDRAW WHAT YOU NEED FROM DAD'S BANK ACCOUNT.
RUB
RUB
SHE SAID WE CAN USE THEIR MONEY.
HEE-HEE...
OOH, NICE.
THAT WAS SUCH A REFRESHING BATH.
THE CARBONATED HOT SPRING MADE MY SKIN ALL NICE AND SHINY.
WE SHOULD GO THERE ONCE A MONTH OR SOME-THING.
WE'RE NOT GOING THERE EVER AGAIN.

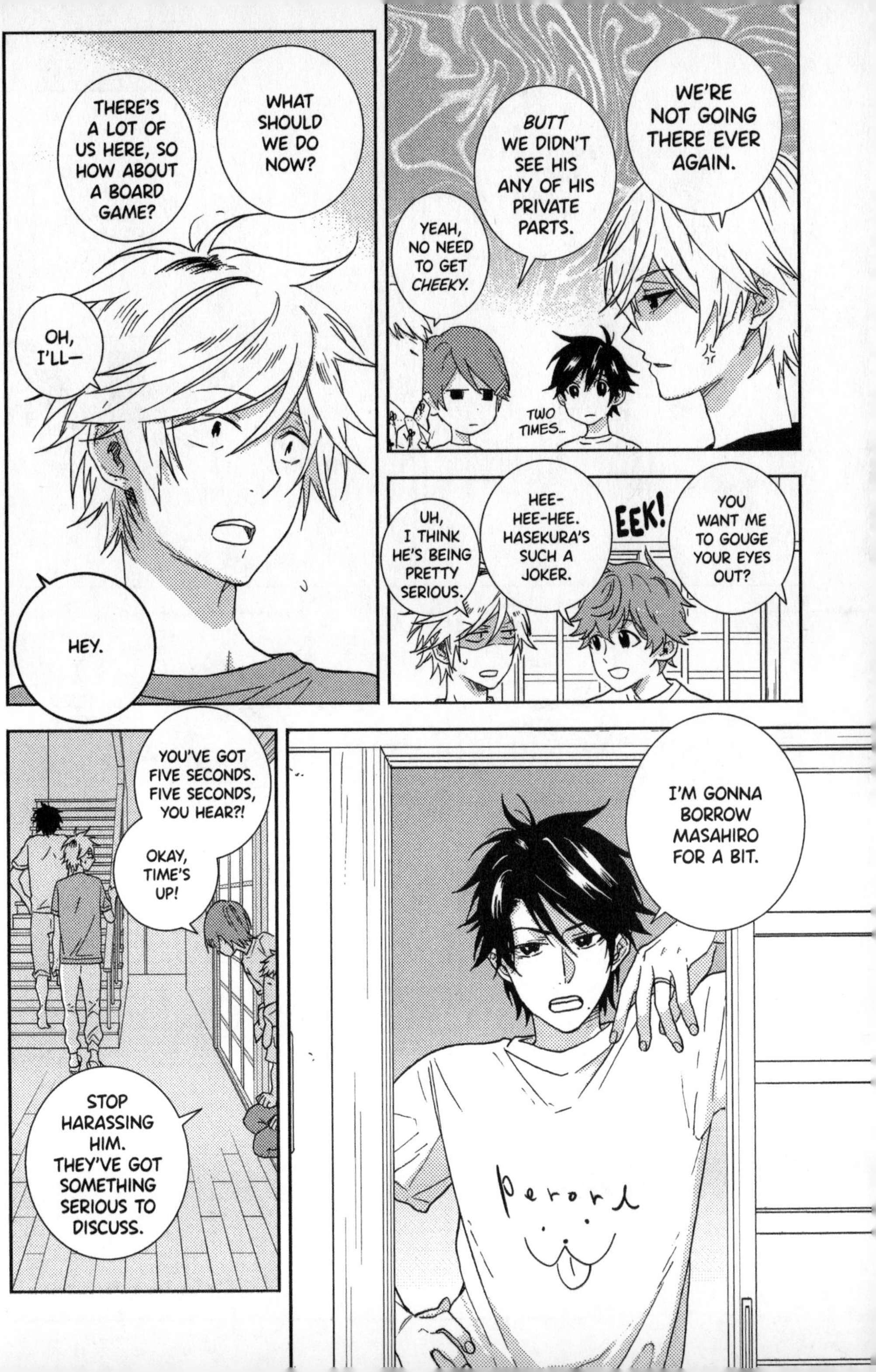
WE'RE NOT GOING THERE EVER AGAIN.
BUTT WE DIDN'T SEE HIS ANY OF HIS PRIVATE PARTS.
YEAH, NO NEED TO GET CHEEKY.
TWO TIMES...
YOU WANT ME TO GOUGE YOUR EYES OUT?
EEK!
HEE-HEE-HEE. HASEKURA'S SUCH A JOKER.
UH, I THINK HE'S BEING PRETTY SERIOUS.
WHAT SHOULD WE DO NOW?
THERE'S A LOT OF US HERE, SO HOW ABOUT A BOARD GAME?
OH, I'LL—
HEY.
I'M GONNA BORROW MASAHIRO FOR A BIT.
YOU'VE GOT FIVE SECONDS. FIVE SECONDS, YOU HEAR?!
OKAY, TIME'S UP!
STOP HARASSING HIM. THEY'VE GOT SOMETHING SERIOUS TO DISCUSS.

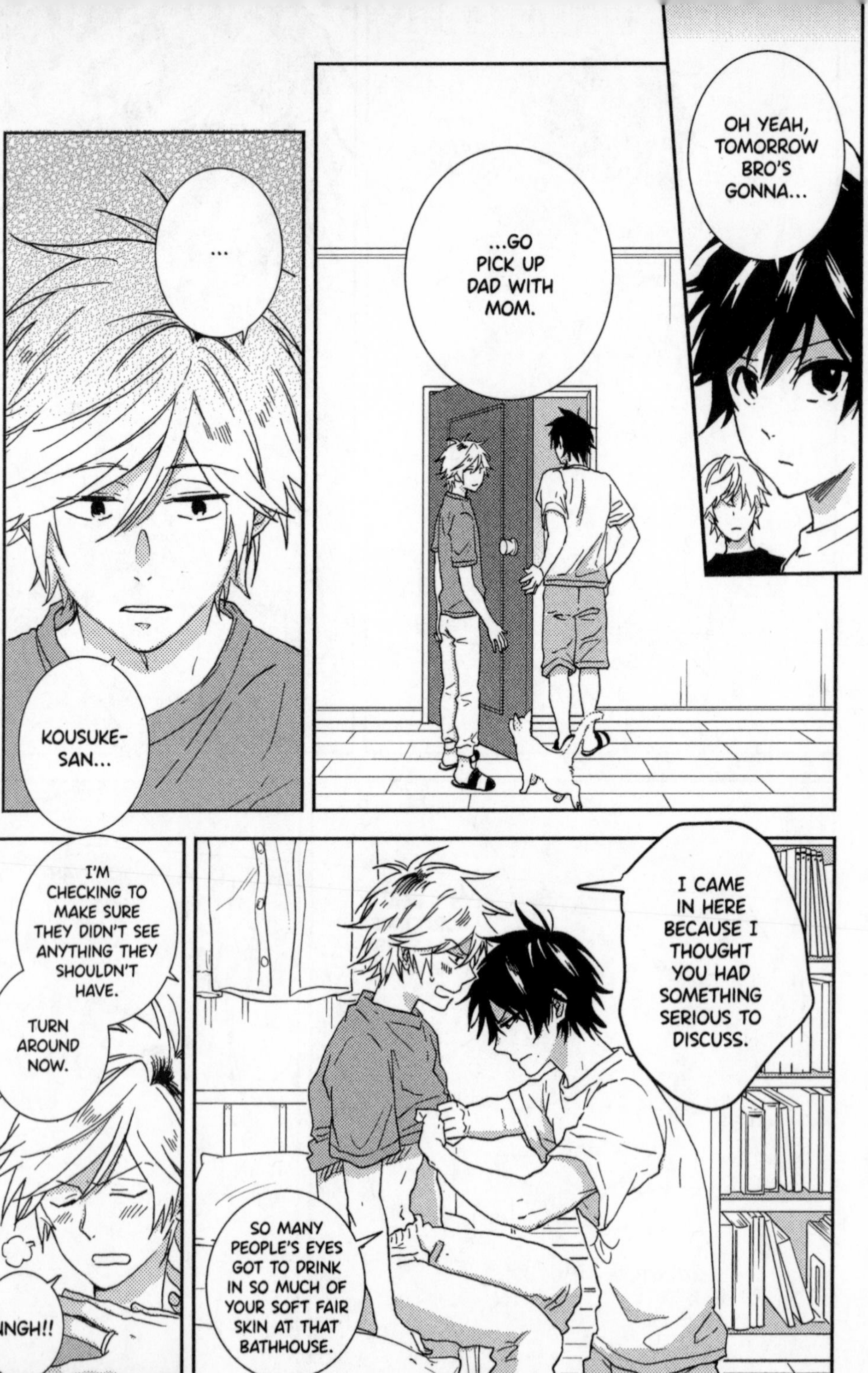
OH YEAH, TOMORROW BRO'S GONNA...
...GO PICK UP DAD WITH MOM.
...
KOUSUKE-SAN...
I CAME IN HERE BECAUSE I THOUGHT YOU HAD SOMETHING SERIOUS TO DISCUSS.
SO MANY PEOPLE'S EYES GOT TO DRINK IN SO MUCH OF YOUR SOFT FAIR SKIN AT THAT BATHHOUSE.
I'M CHECKING TO MAKE SURE THEY DIDN'T SEE ANYTHING THEY SHOULDN'T HAVE.
TURN AROUND NOW.
NNGH!!

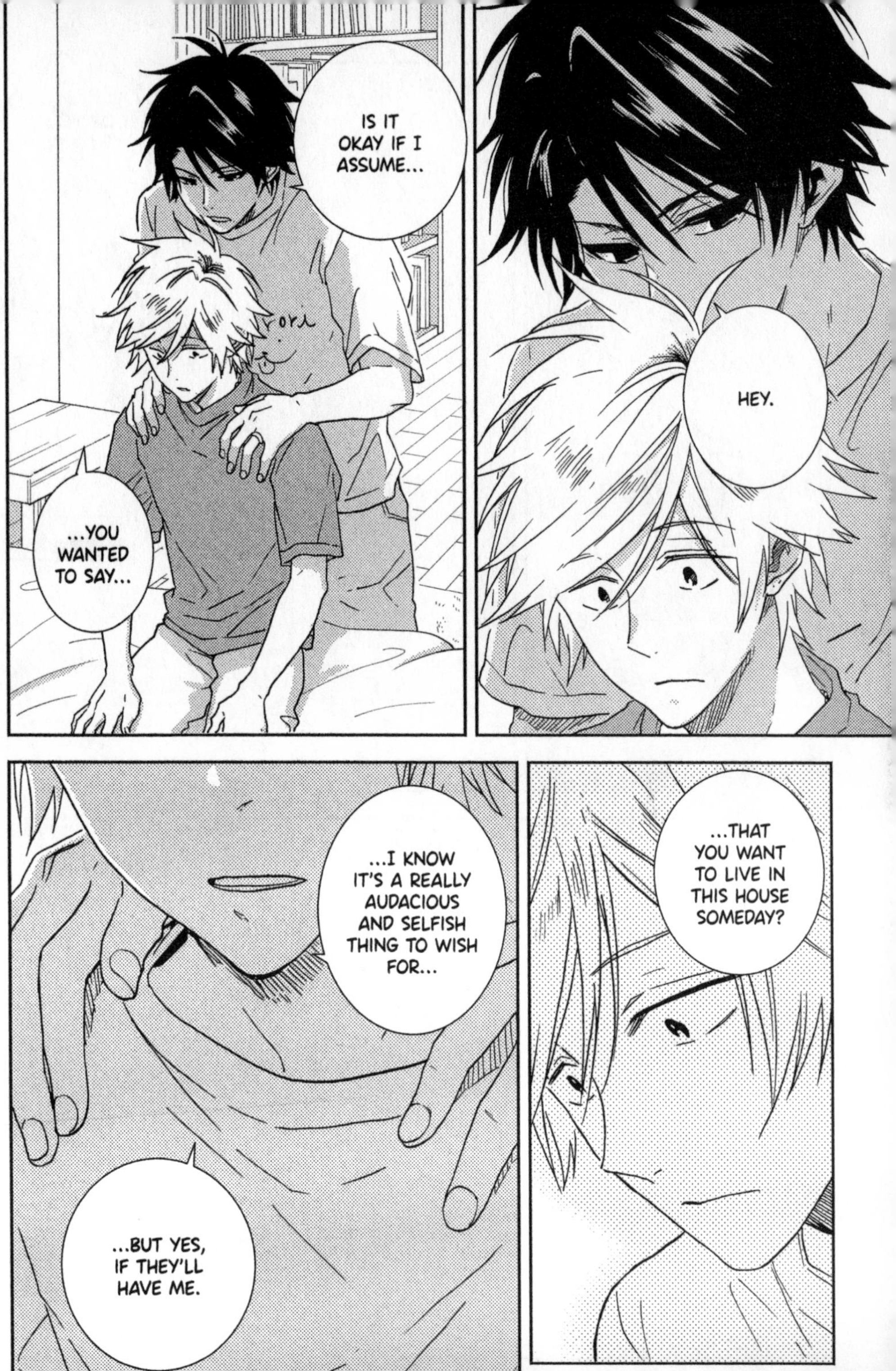
HEY.
IS IT OKAY IF I ASSUME...
...YOU WANTED TO SAY...
...THAT YOU WANT TO LIVE IN THIS HOUSE SOMEDAY?
...I KNOW IT'S A REALLY AUDACIOUS AND SELFISH THING TO WISH FOR...
...BUT YES, IF THEY'LL HAVE ME.

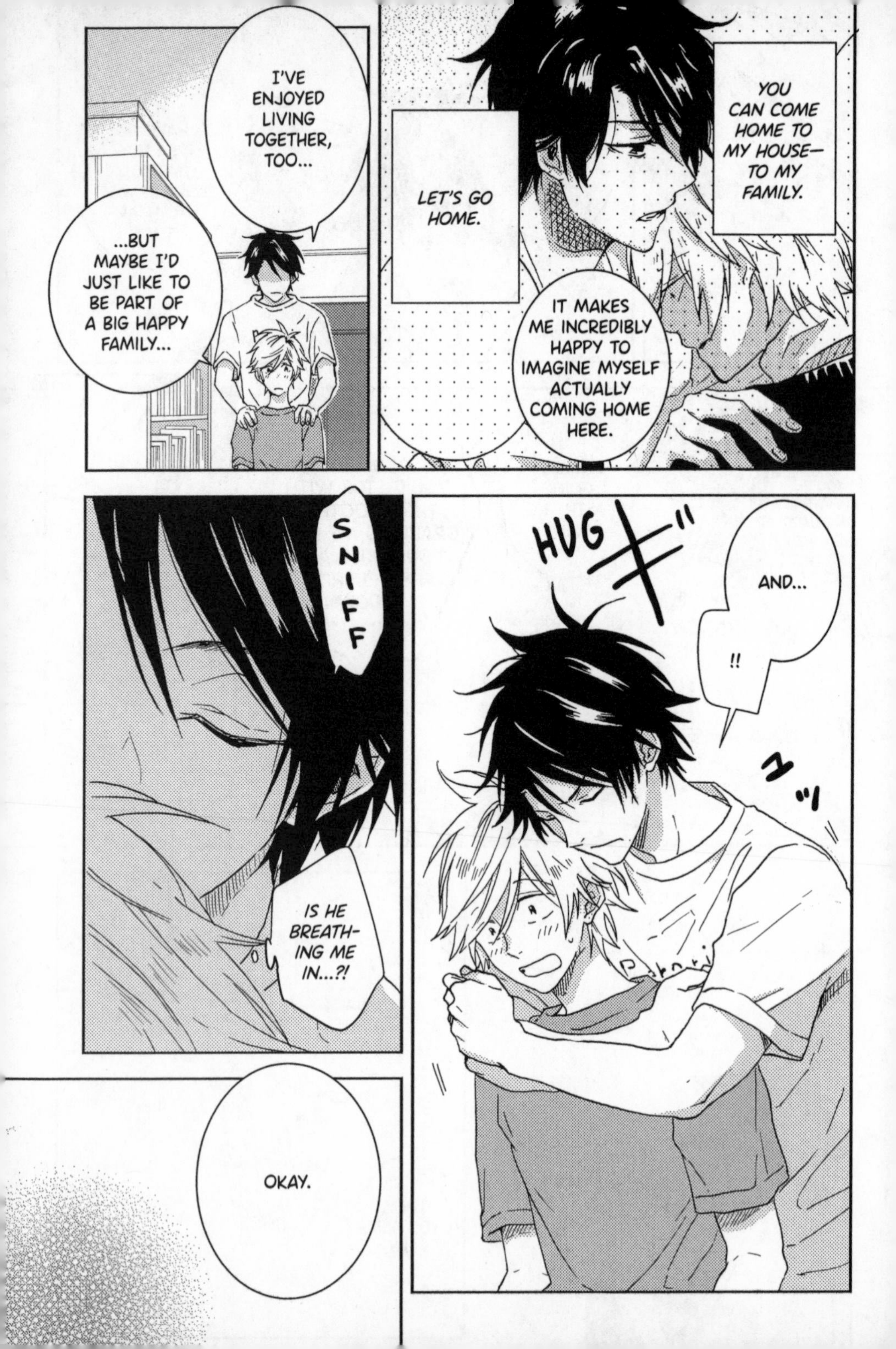
YOU CAN COME HOME TO MY HOUSE— TO MY FAMILY.
LET'S GO HOME.
IT MAKES ME INCREDIBLY HAPPY TO IMAGINE MYSELF ACTUALLY COMING HOME HERE.
I'VE ENJOYED LIVING TOGETHER, TOO...
...BUT MAYBE I'D JUST LIKE TO BE PART OF A BIG HAPPY FAMILY...
AND...
!!
HUG
SNIFF
IS HE BREATHING ME IN...?!
OKAY.

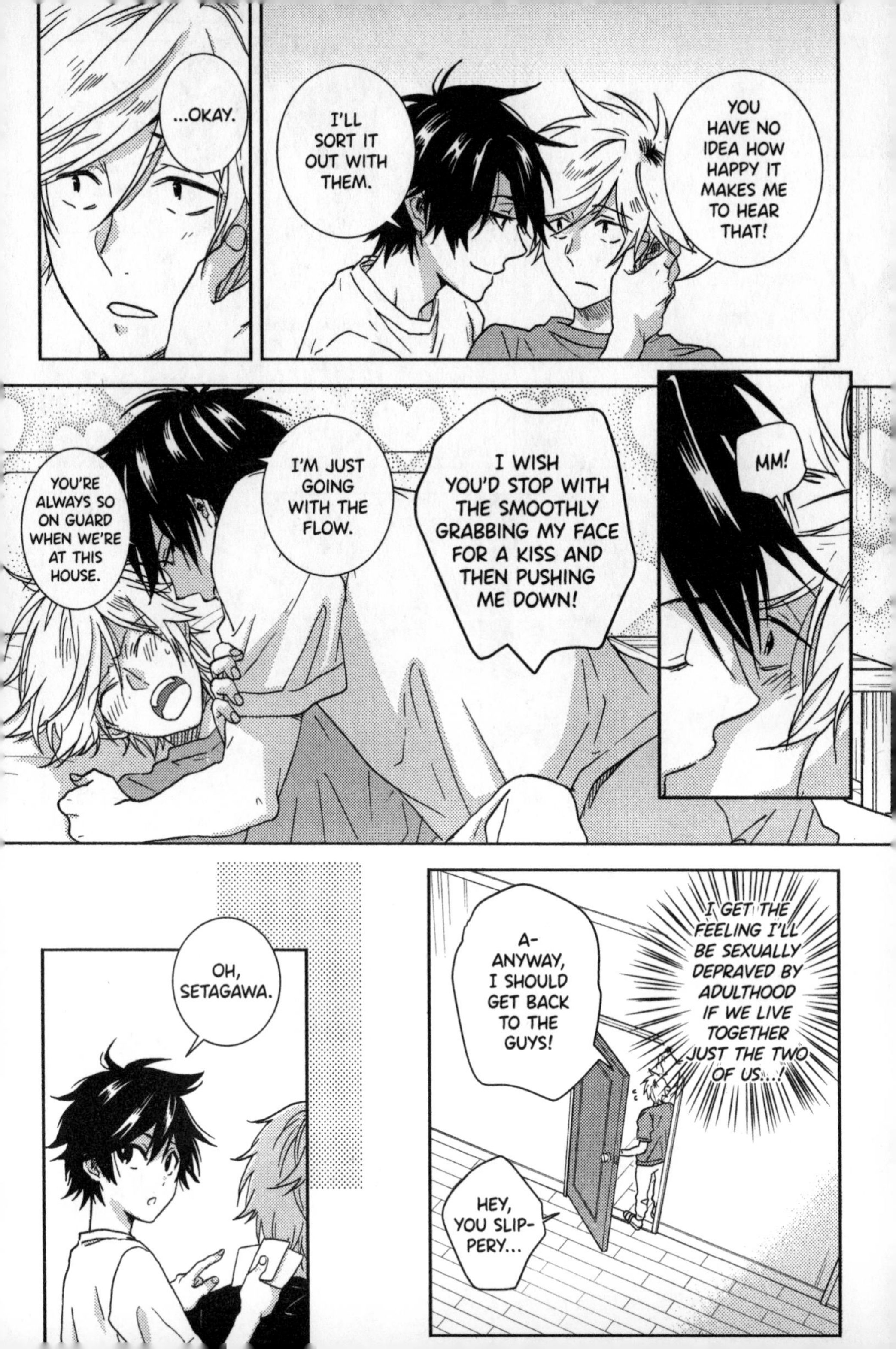
YOU HAVE NO IDEA HOW HAPPY IT MAKES ME TO HEAR THAT!
I'LL SORT IT OUT WITH THEM.
...OKAY.
MM!
I WISH YOU'D STOP WITH THE SMOOTHLY GRABBING MY FACE FOR A KISS AND THEN PUSHING ME DOWN!
I'M JUST GOING WITH THE FLOW.
YOU'RE ALWAYS SO ON GUARD WHEN WE'RE AT THIS HOUSE.
I GET THE FEELING I'LL BE SEXUALLY DEPRAVED BY ADULTHOOD IF WE LIVE TOGETHER JUST THE TWO OF US...!
A-ANYWAY, I SHOULD GET BACK TO THE GUYS!
HEY, YOU SLIP-PERY...
OH, SETAGAWA.

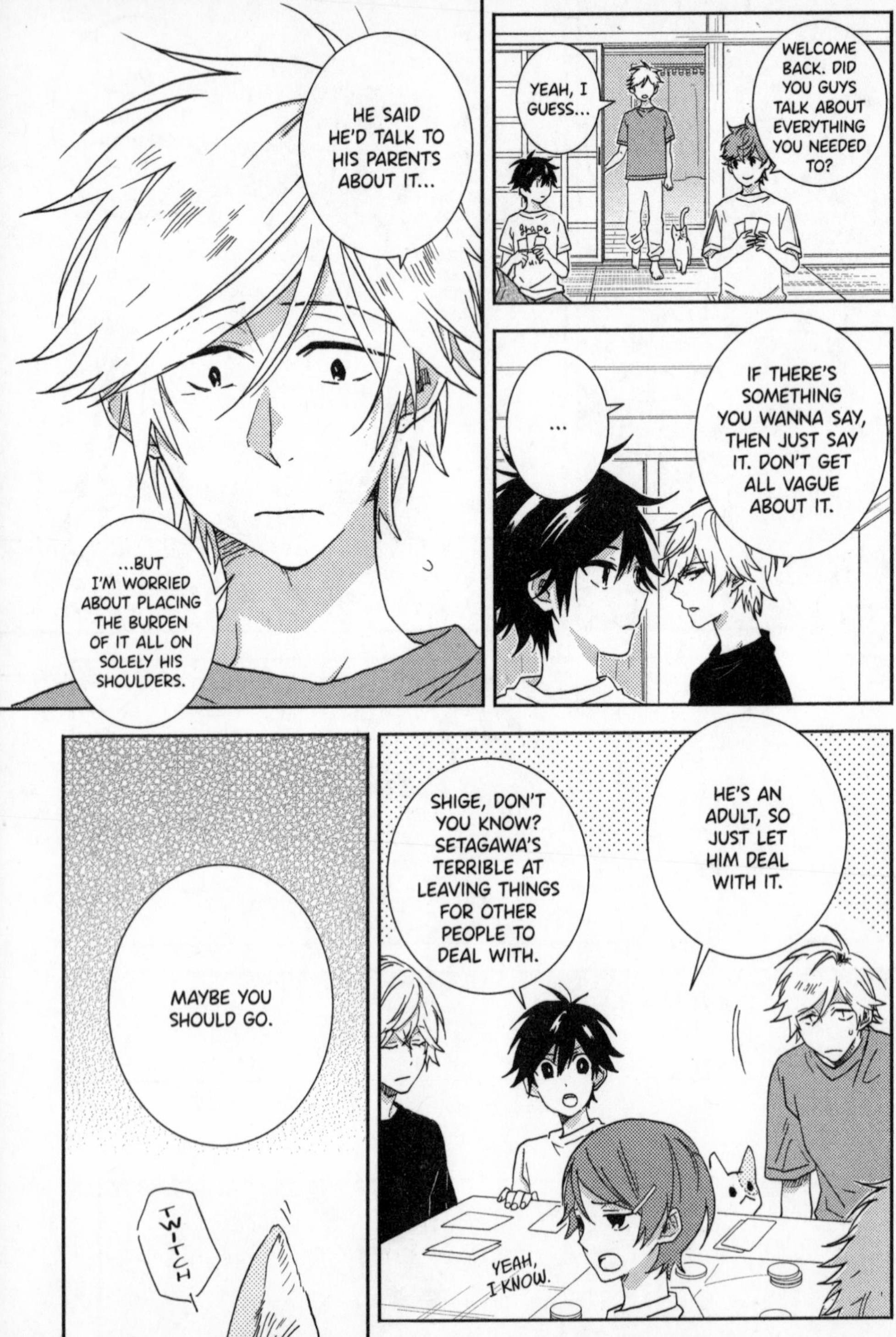
WELCOME BACK. DID YOU GUYS TALK ABOUT EVERYTHING YOU NEEDED TO?
YEAH, I GUESS...
IF THERE'S SOMETHING YOU WANNA SAY, THEN JUST SAY IT. DON'T GET ALL VAGUE ABOUT IT.
...
HE SAID HE'D TALK TO HIS PARENTS ABOUT IT...
...BUT I'M WORRIED ABOUT PLACING THE BURDEN OF IT ALL ON SOLELY HIS SHOULDERS.
HE'S AN ADULT, SO JUST LET HIM DEAL WITH IT.
SHIGE, DON'T YOU KNOW? SETAGAWA'S TERRIBLE AT LEAVING THINGS FOR OTHER PEOPLE TO DEAL WITH.
YEAH, I KNOW.
MAYBE YOU SHOULD GO.
TWITCH

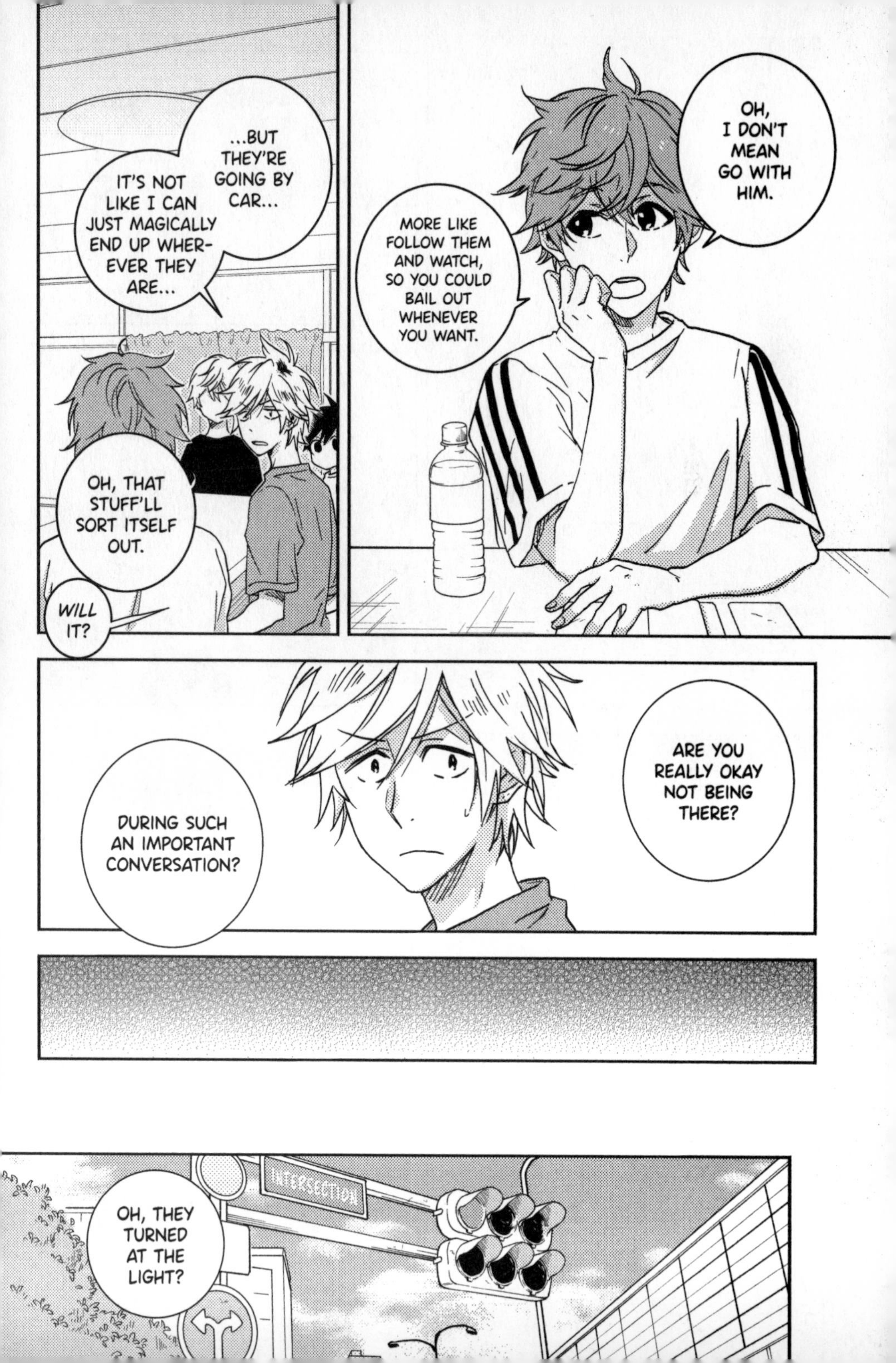
OH, I DON'T MEAN GO WITH HIM.
MORE LIKE FOLLOW THEM AND WATCH, SO YOU COULD BAIL OUT WHENEVER YOU WANT.
...BUT THEY'RE GOING BY CAR...
IT'S NOT LIKE I CAN JUST MAGICALLY END UP WHER-EVER THEY ARE...
OH, THAT STUFF'LL SORT ITSELF OUT.
WILL IT?
ARE YOU REALLY OKAY NOT BEING THERE?
DURING SUCH AN IMPORTANT CONVERSATION?
INTERSECTION
OH, THEY TURNED AT THE LIGHT?

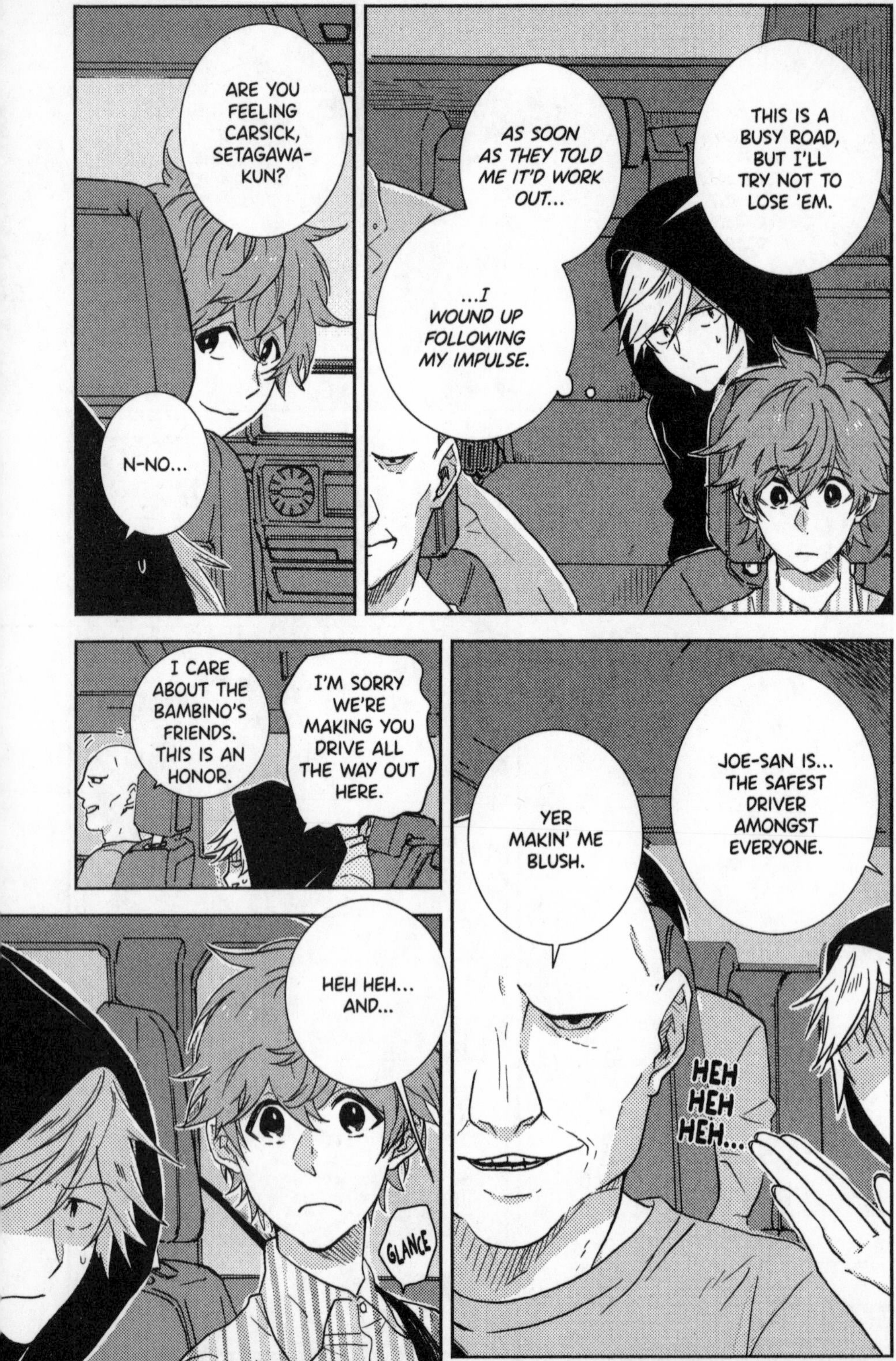
THIS IS A BUSY ROAD, BUT I'LL TRY NOT TO LOSE 'EM.
AS SOON AS THEY TOLD ME IT'D WORK OUT...
...I WOUND UP FOLLOWING MY IMPULSE.
ARE YOU FEELING CARSICK, SETAGAWA-KUN?
N-NO...
JOE-SAN IS... THE SAFEST DRIVER AMONGST EVERYONE.
YER MAKIN' ME BLUSH.
HEH HEH HEH...
I'M SORRY WE'RE MAKING YOU DRIVE ALL THE WAY OUT HERE.
I CARE ABOUT THE BAMBINO'S FRIENDS. THIS IS AN HONOR.
HEH HEH... AND...
GLANCE

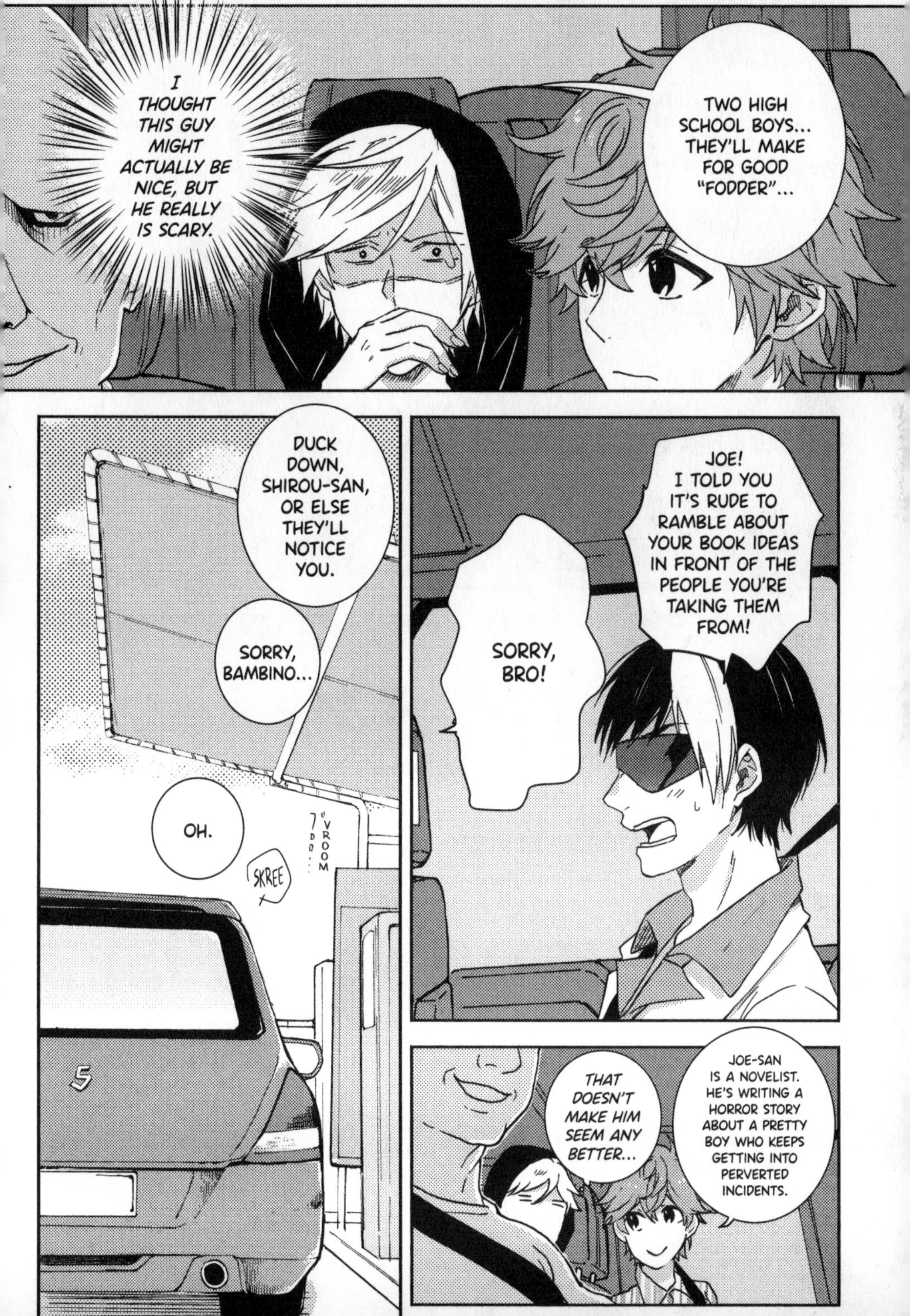
TWO HIGH SCHOOL BOYS... THEY'LL MAKE FOR GOOD "FODDER"...
I THOUGHT THIS GUY MIGHT ACTUALLY BE NICE, BUT HE REALLY IS SCARY.
JOE! I TOLD YOU IT'S RUDE TO RAMBLE ABOUT YOUR BOOK IDEAS IN FRONT OF THE PEOPLE YOU'RE TAKING THEM FROM!
SORRY, BRO!
JOE-SAN IS A NOVELIST. HE'S WRITING A HORROR STORY ABOUT A PRETTY BOY WHO KEEPS GETTING INTO PERVERTED INCIDENTS.
THAT DOESN'T MAKE HIM SEEM ANY BETTER...
DUCK DOWN, SHIROU-SAN, OR ELSE THEY'LL NOTICE YOU.
SORRY, BAMBINO...
OH.
VROOM
SKREE

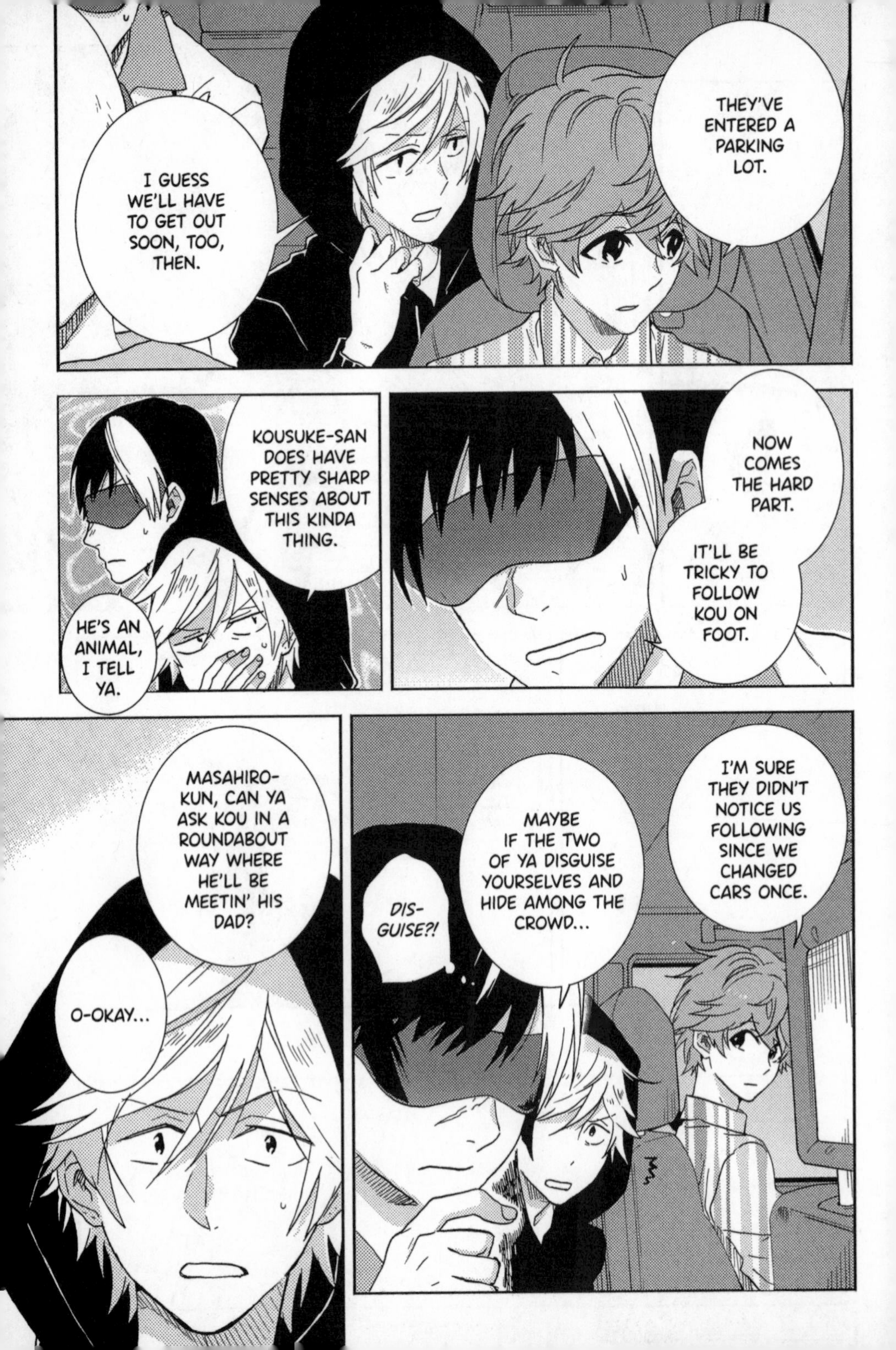
THEY'VE ENTERED A PARKING LOT.
I GUESS WE'LL HAVE TO GET OUT SOON, TOO, THEN.
NOW COMES THE HARD PART.
IT'LL BE TRICKY TO FOLLOW KOU ON FOOT.
KOUSUKE-SAN DOES HAVE PRETTY SHARP SENSES ABOUT THIS KINDA THING.
HE'S AN ANIMAL, I TELL YA.
I'M SURE THEY DIDN'T NOTICE US FOLLOWING SINCE WE CHANGED CARS ONCE.
MAYBE IF THE TWO OF YA DISGUISE YOURSELVES AND HIDE AMONG THE CROWD...
DIS-GUISE?!
MASAHIRO-KUN, CAN YA ASK KOU IN A ROUNDABOUT WAY WHERE HE'LL BE MEETIN' HIS DAD?
O-OKAY...

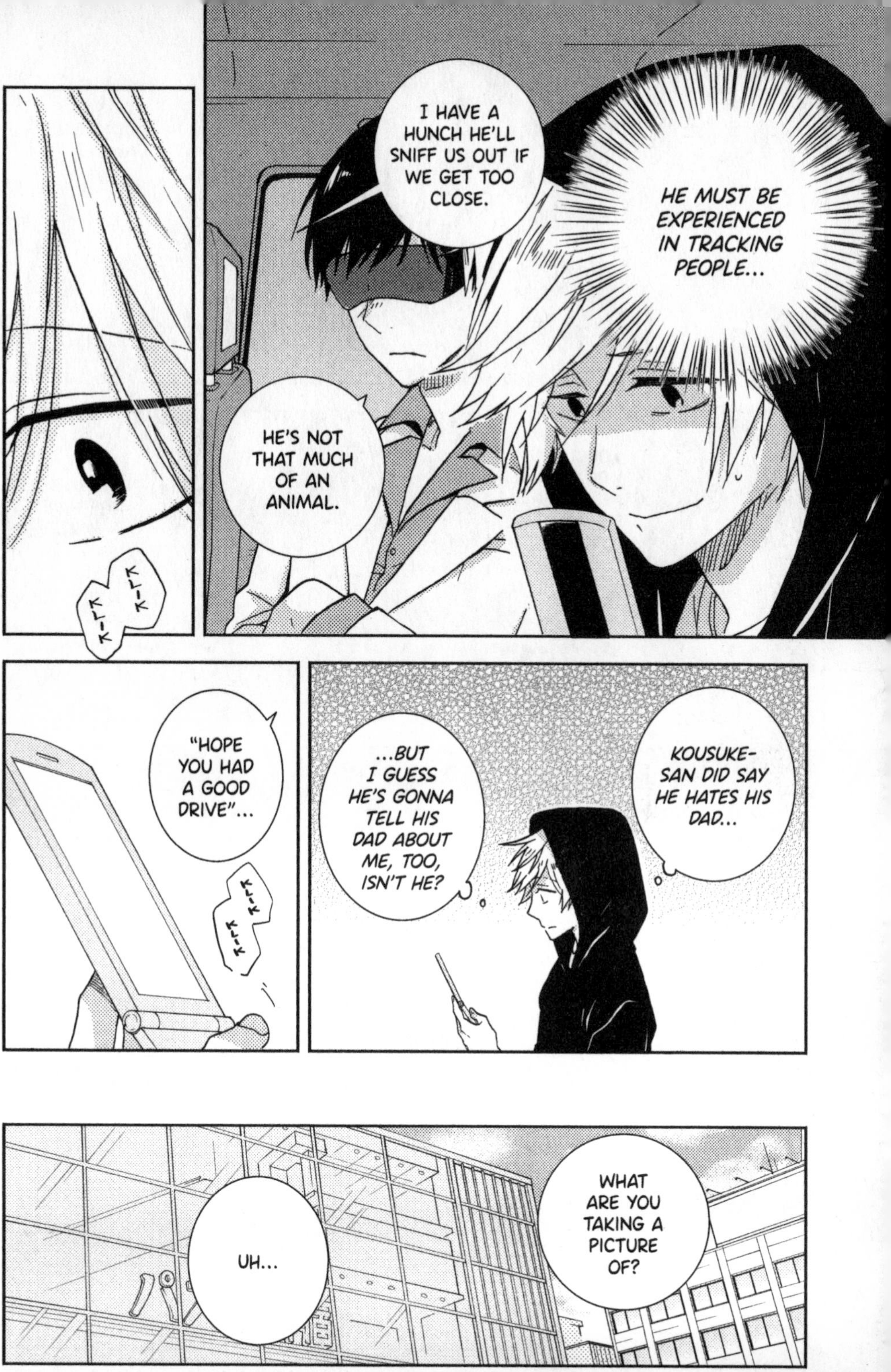
I HAVE A HUNCH HE'LL SNIFF US OUT IF WE GET TOO CLOSE.
HE MUST BE EXPERIENCED IN TRACKING PEOPLE...
HE'S NOT THAT MUCH OF AN ANIMAL.
KL-K
KL-K
KOUSUKE-SAN DID SAY HE HATES HIS DAD...
...BUT I GUESS HE'S GONNA TELL HIS DAD ABOUT ME, TOO, ISN'T HE?
"HOPE YOU HAD A GOOD DRIVE"...
KL-K
KL-K
WHAT ARE YOU TAKING A PICTURE OF?
UH...

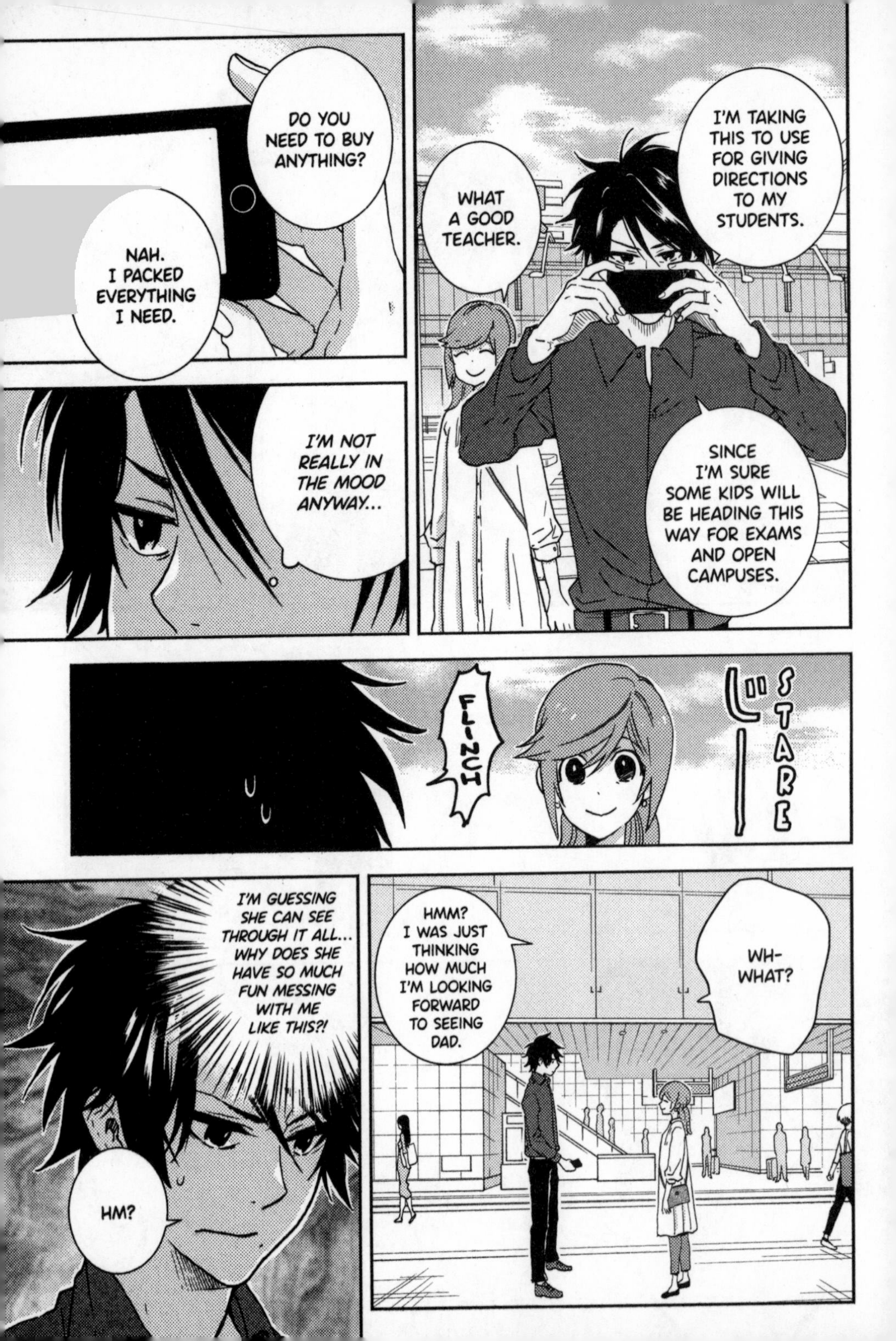
I'M TAKING THIS TO USE FOR GIVING DIRECTIONS TO MY STUDENTS.
WHAT A GOOD TEACHER.
SINCE I'M SURE SOME KIDS WILL BE HEADING THIS WAY FOR EXAMS AND OPEN CAMPUSES.
DO YOU NEED TO BUY ANYTHING?
NAH. I PACKED EVERYTHING I NEED.
I'M NOT REALLY IN THE MOOD ANYWAY...
じー STARE
FLINCH
WH- WHAT?
HMM? I WAS JUST THINKING HOW MUCH I'M LOOKING FORWARD TO SEEING DAD.
I'M GUESSING SHE CAN SEE THROUGH IT ALL... WHY DOES SHE HAVE SO MUCH FUN MESSING WITH ME LIKE THIS?!
HM?

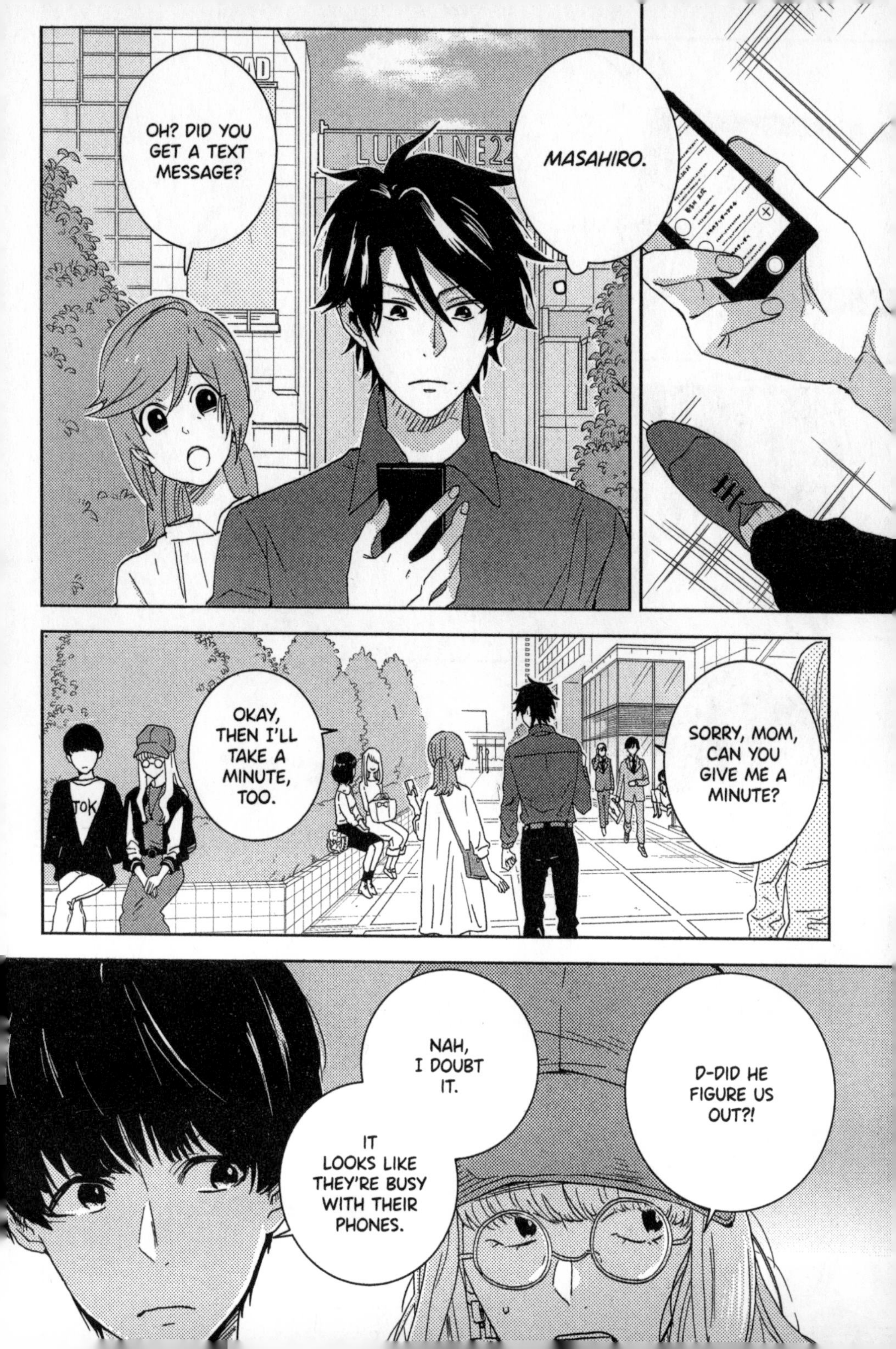
MASAHIRO.
OH? DID YOU GET A TEXT MESSAGE?
SORRY, MOM, CAN YOU GIVE ME A MINUTE?
OKAY, THEN I'LL TAKE A MINUTE, TOO.
D-DID HE FIGURE US OUT?!
NAH, I DOUBT IT.
IT LOOKS LIKE THEY'RE BUSY WITH THEIR PHONES.

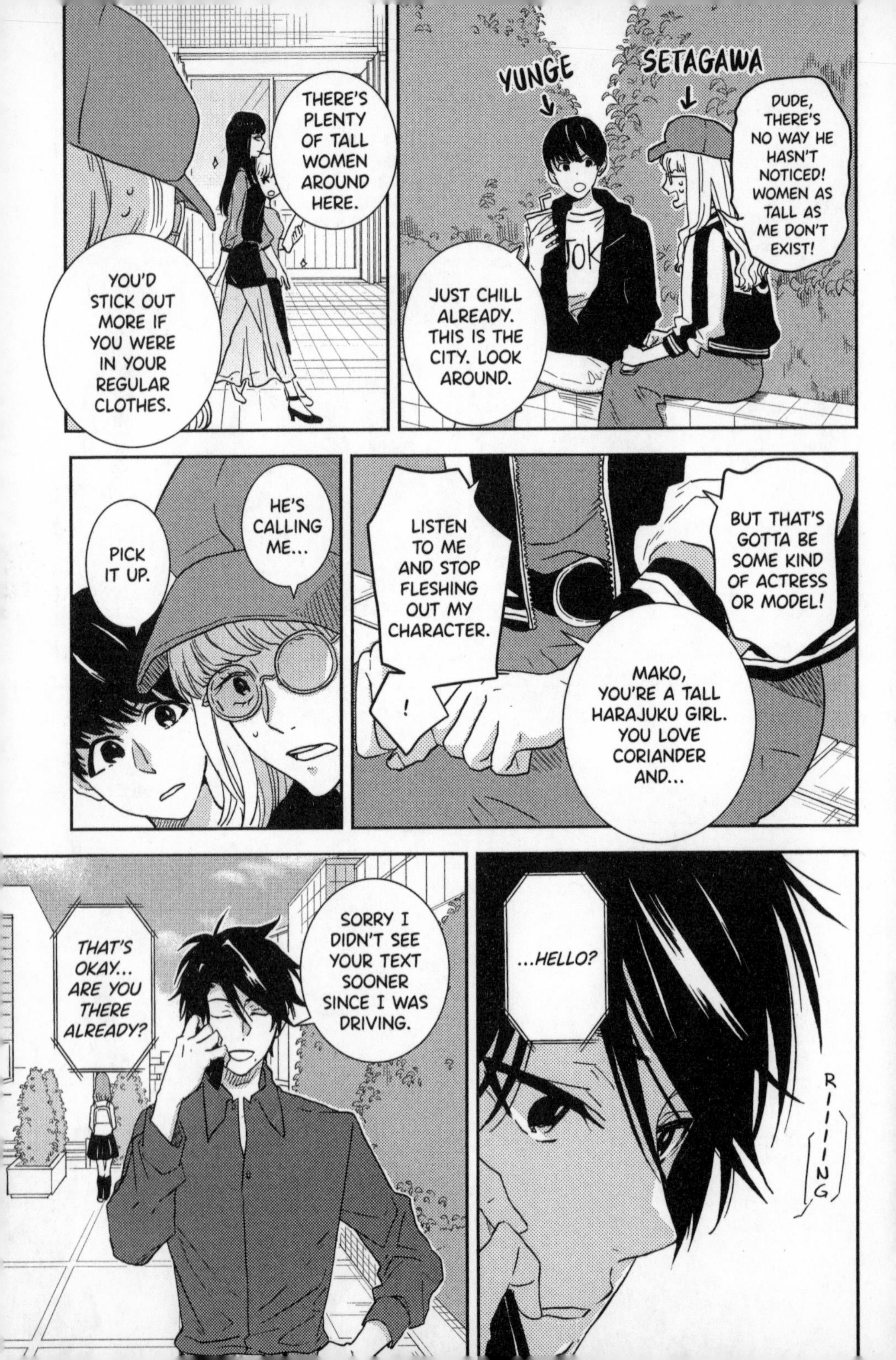

YUNGE
SETAGAWA
DUDE, THERE'S NO WAY HE HASN'T NOTICED! WOMEN AS TALL AS ME DON'T EXIST!
JUST CHILL ALREADY. THIS IS THE CITY. LOOK AROUND.
THERE'S PLENTY OF TALL WOMEN AROUND HERE.
YOU'D STICK OUT MORE IF YOU WERE IN YOUR REGULAR CLOTHES.
BUT THAT'S GOTTA BE SOME KIND OF ACTRESS OR MODEL!
LISTEN TO ME AND STOP FLESHING OUT MY CHARACTER.
!
MAKO, YOU'RE A TALL HARAJUKU GIRL. YOU LOVE CORIANDER AND...
HE'S CALLING ME...
PICK IT UP.
RIIIING
...HELLO?
SORRY I DIDN'T SEE YOUR TEXT SOONER SINCE I WAS DRIVING.
THAT'S OKAY... ARE YOU THERE ALREADY?

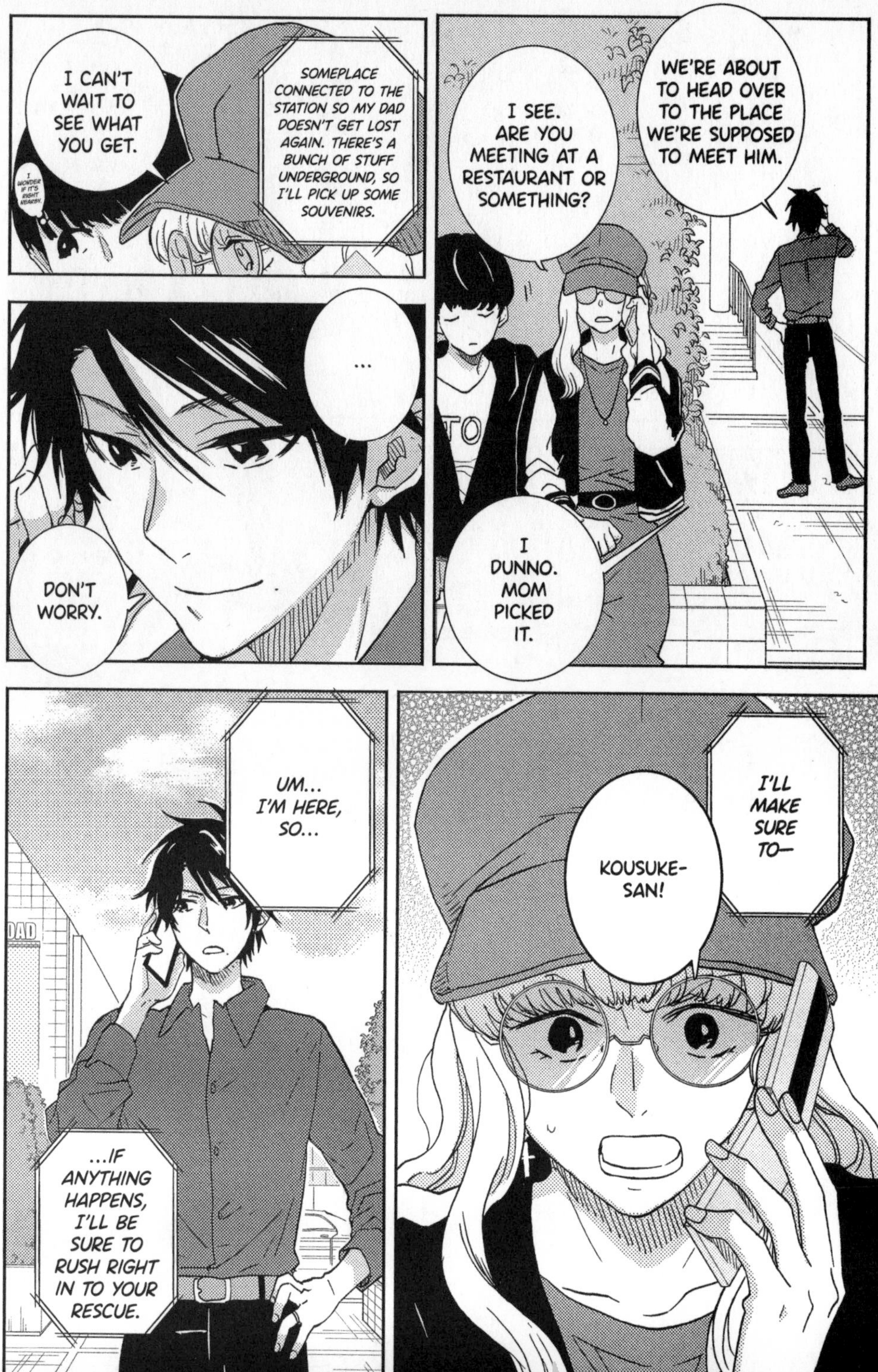
WE'RE ABOUT TO HEAD OVER TO THE PLACE WE'RE SUPPOSED TO MEET HIM.
I SEE. ARE YOU MEETING AT A RESTAURANT OR SOMETHING?
I DUNNO. MOM PICKED IT.
SOMEPLACE CONNECTED TO THE STATION SO MY DAD DOESN'T GET LOST AGAIN. THERE'S A BUNCH OF STUFF UNDERGROUND, SO I'LL PICK UP SOME SOUVENIRS.
I CAN'T WAIT TO SEE WHAT YOU GET.
I WONDER IF IT'S RIGHT NEARBY.
...
DON'T WORRY.
I'LL MAKE SURE TO—
KOUSUKE-SAN!
UM... I'M HERE, SO...
...IF ANYTHING HAPPENS, I'LL BE SURE TO RUSH RIGHT IN TO YOUR RESCUE.

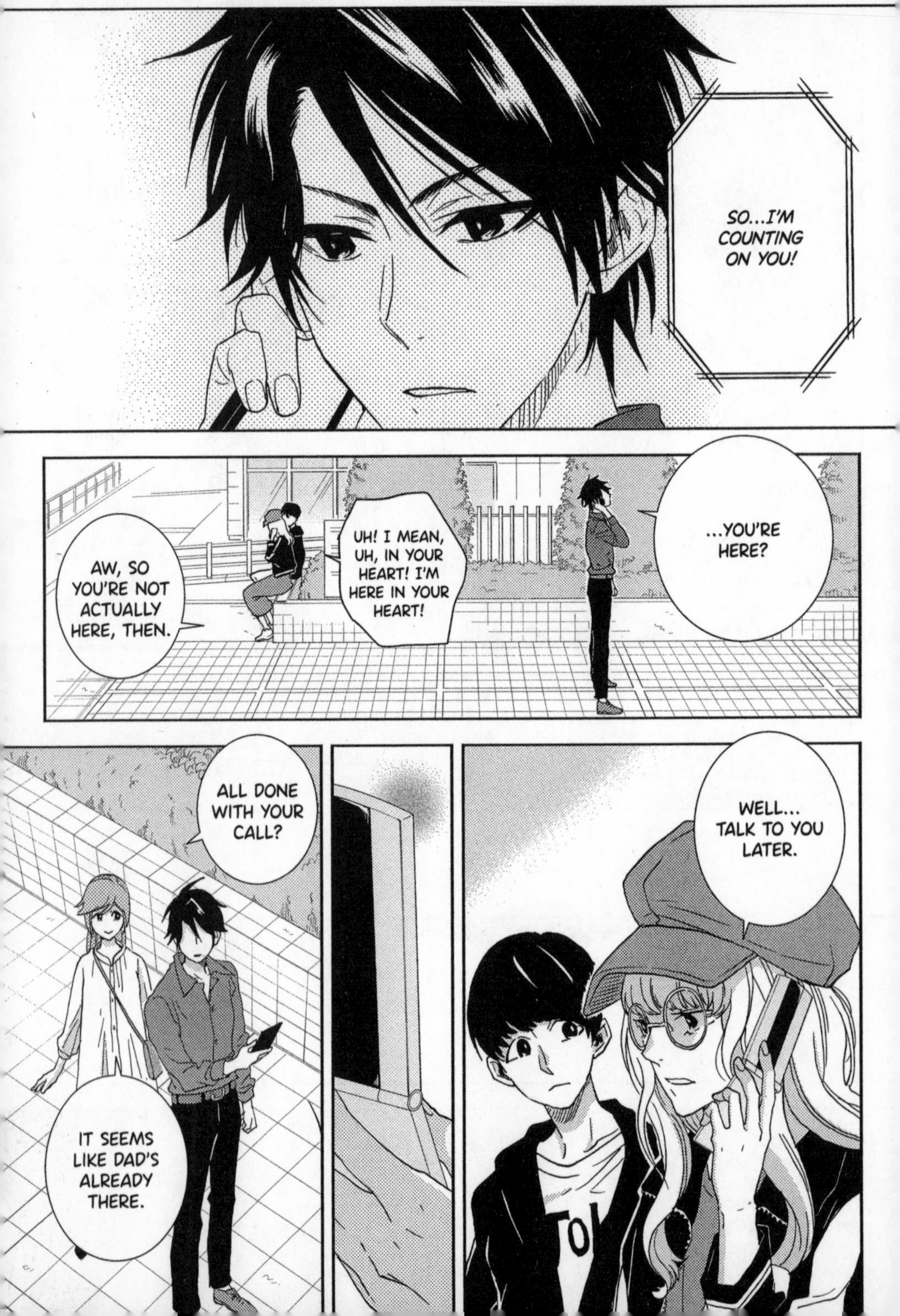

SO...I'M COUNTING ON YOU!
...YOU'RE HERE?
UH! I MEAN, UH, IN YOUR HEART! I'M HERE IN YOUR HEART!
AW, SO YOU'RE NOT ACTUALLY HERE, THEN.
WELL... TALK TO YOU LATER.
ALL DONE WITH YOUR CALL?
IT SEEMS LIKE DAD'S ALREADY THERE.

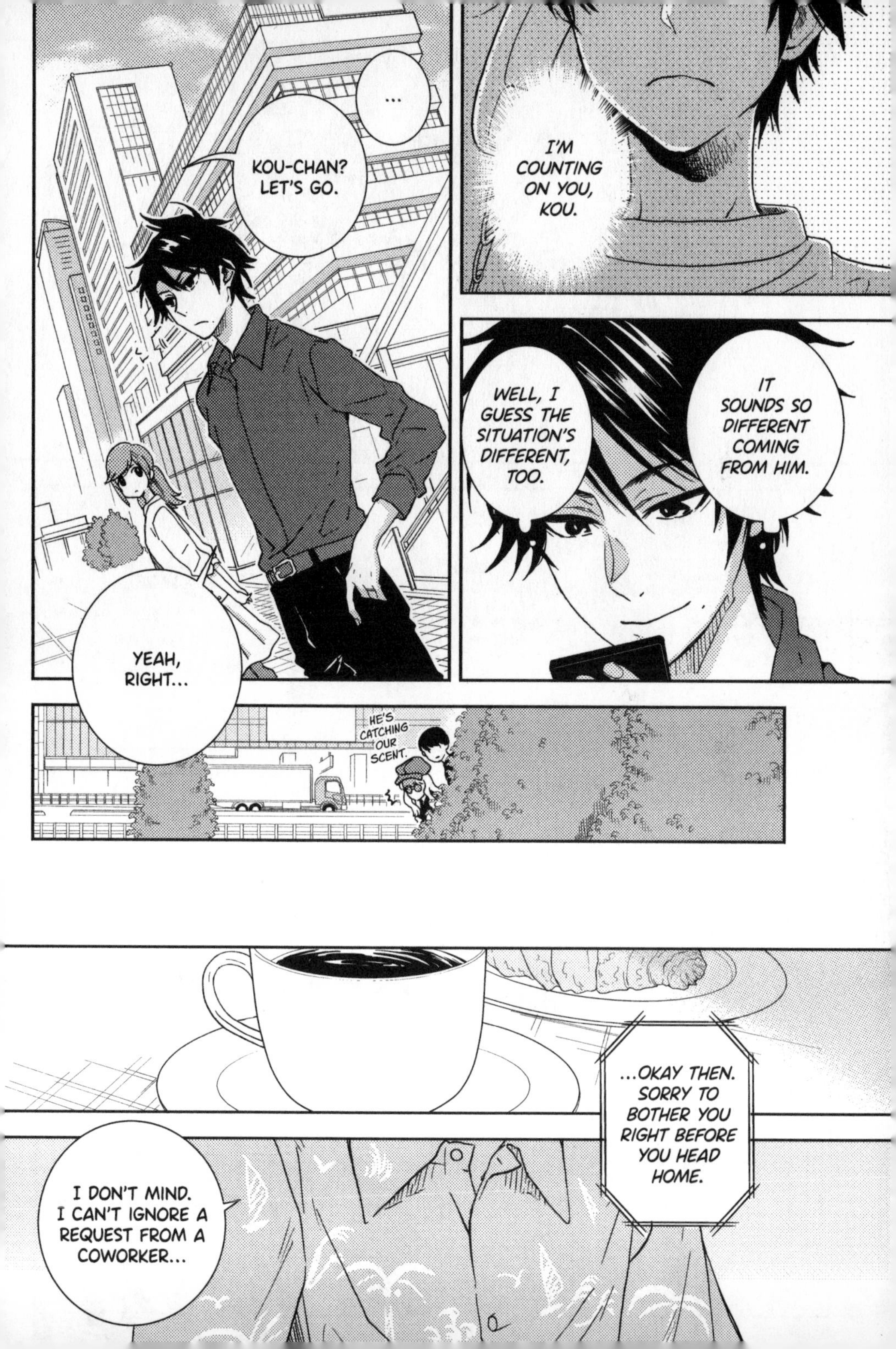
I'M COUNTING ON YOU, KOU.
IT SOUNDS SO DIFFERENT COMING FROM HIM.
WELL, I GUESS THE SITUATION'S DIFFERENT, TOO.
...
KOU-CHAN? LET'S GO.
YEAH, RIGHT...
HE'S CATCHING OUR SCENT.
...OKAY THEN. SORRY TO BOTHER YOU RIGHT BEFORE YOU HEAD HOME.
I DON'T MIND. I CAN'T IGNORE A REQUEST FROM A COWORKER...

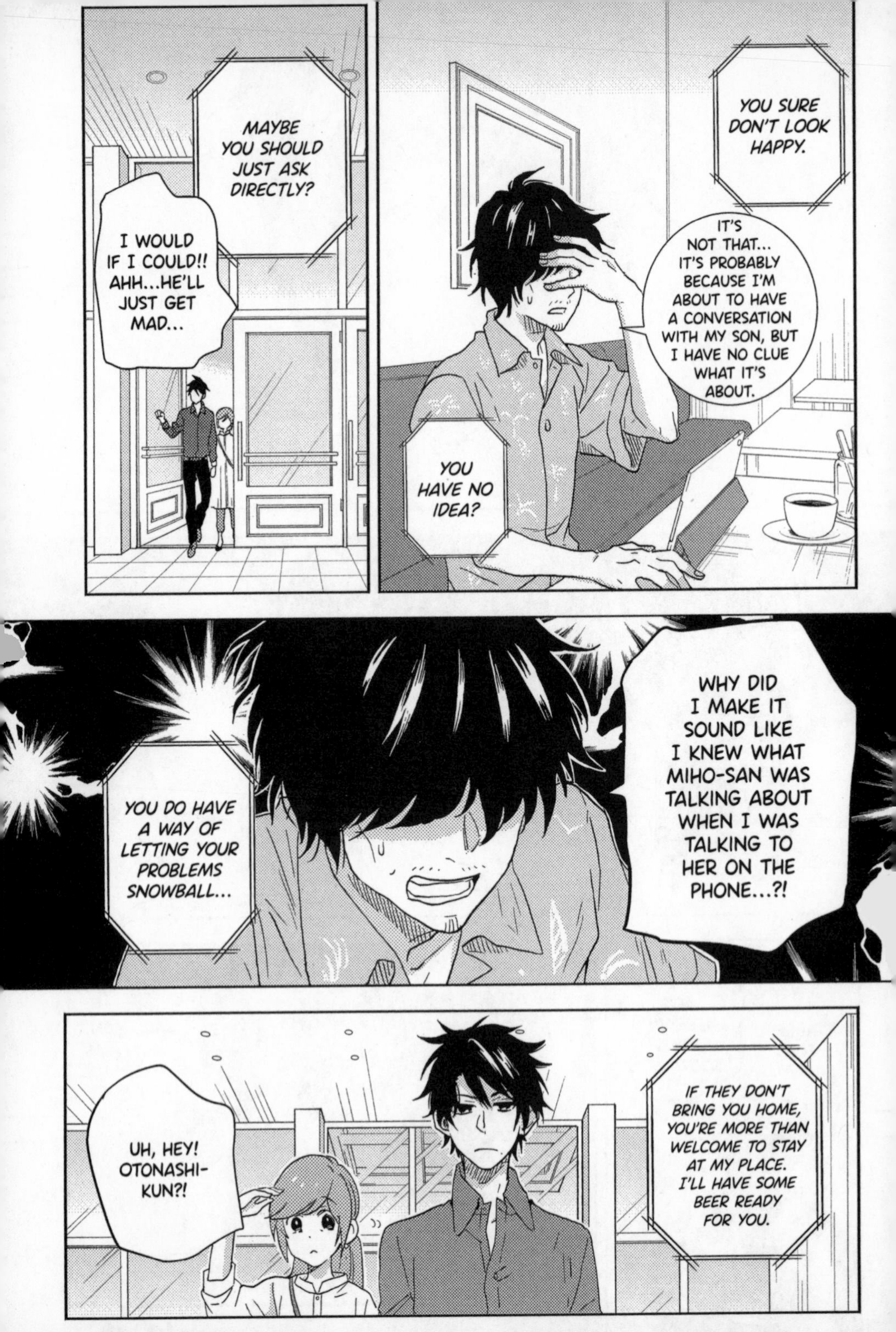
YOU SURE DON'T LOOK HAPPY.
IT'S NOT THAT... IT'S PROBABLY BECAUSE I'M ABOUT TO HAVE A CONVERSATION WITH MY SON, BUT I HAVE NO CLUE WHAT IT'S ABOUT.
YOU HAVE NO IDEA?
MAYBE YOU SHOULD JUST ASK DIRECTLY?
I WOULD IF I COULD!! AHH...HE'LL JUST GET MAD...
WHY DID I MAKE IT SOUND LIKE I KNEW WHAT MIHO-SAN WAS TALKING ABOUT WHEN I WAS TALKING TO HER ON THE PHONE...?!
YOU DO HAVE A WAY OF LETTING YOUR PROBLEMS SNOWBALL...
IF THEY DON'T BRING YOU HOME, YOU'RE MORE THAN WELCOME TO STAY AT MY PLACE. I'LL HAVE SOME BEER READY FOR YOU.
UH, HEY! OTONASHI-KUN?!

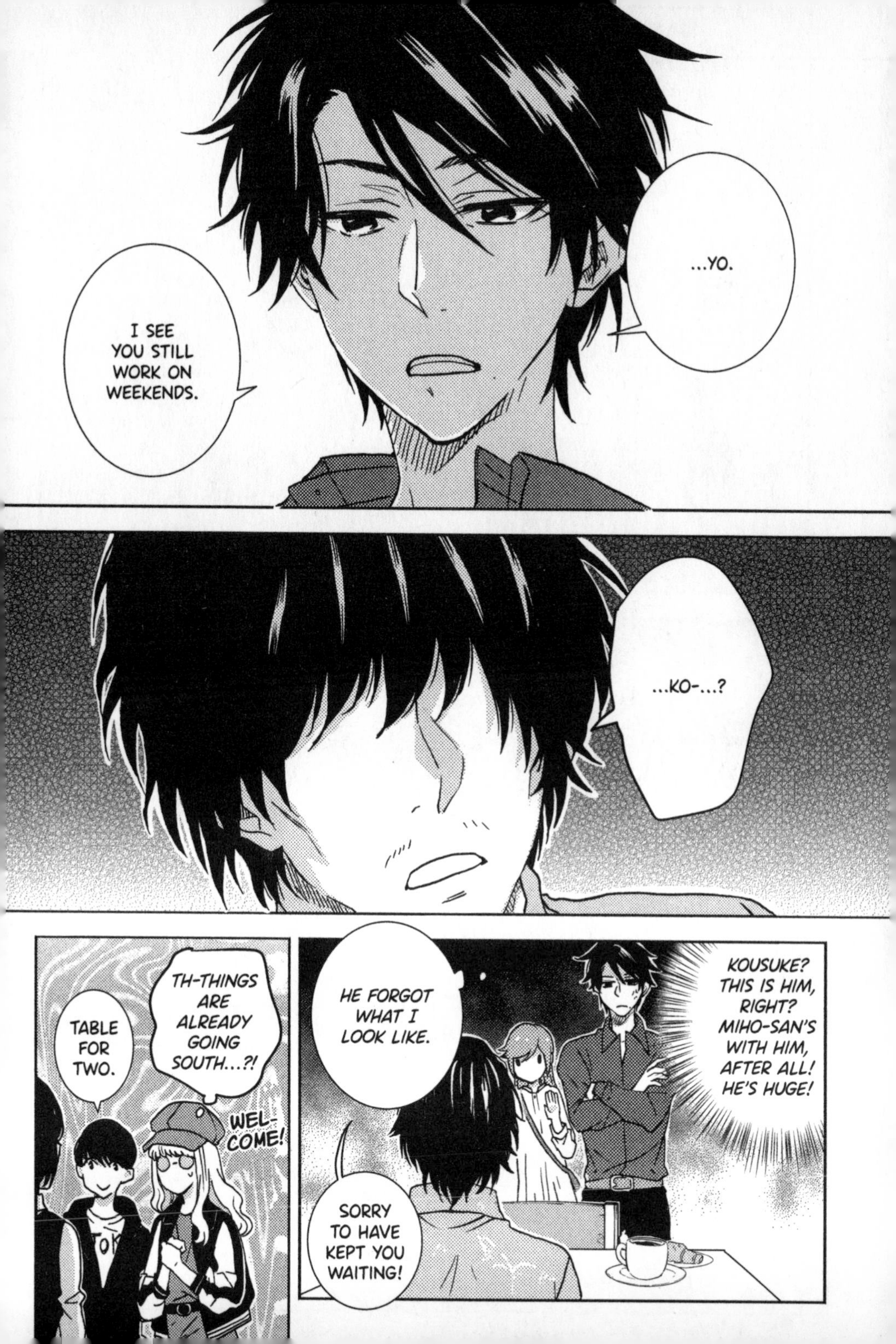
...YO.
I SEE YOU STILL WORK ON WEEKENDS.
...KO-...?
KOUSUKE? THIS IS HIM, RIGHT? MIHO-SAN'S WITH HIM, AFTER ALL! HE'S HUGE!
HE FORGOT WHAT I LOOK LIKE.
SORRY TO HAVE KEPT YOU WAITING!
TH-THINGS ARE ALREADY GOING SOUTH...?!
TABLE FOR TWO.
WEL-COME!

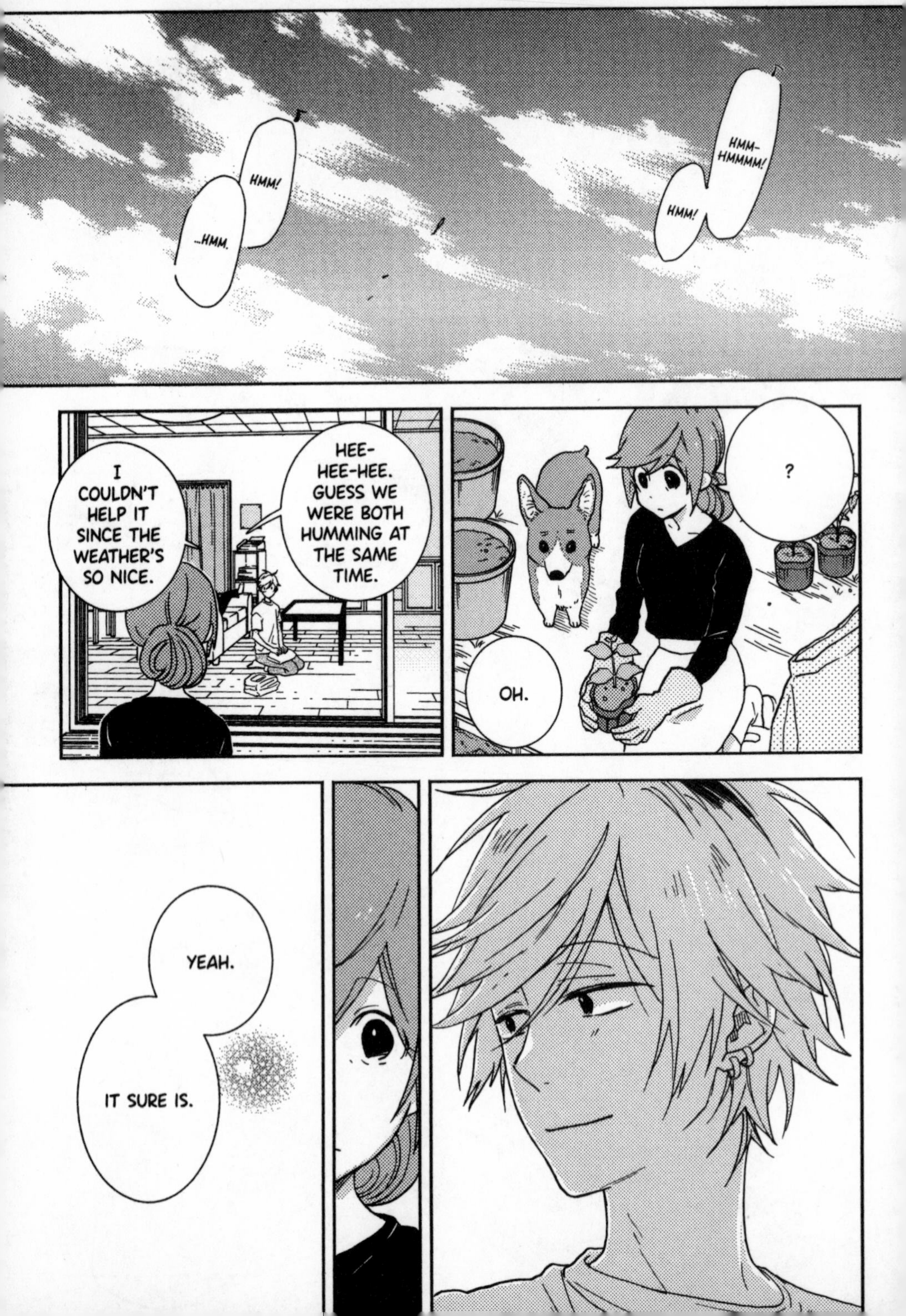
HMM-HMMMM!
HMM!
HMM!
...HMM.
?
OH.
HEE-HEE-HEE. GUESS WE WERE BOTH HUMMING AT THE SAME TIME.
I COULDN'T HELP IT SINCE THE WEATHER'S SO NICE.
YEAH.
IT SURE IS.

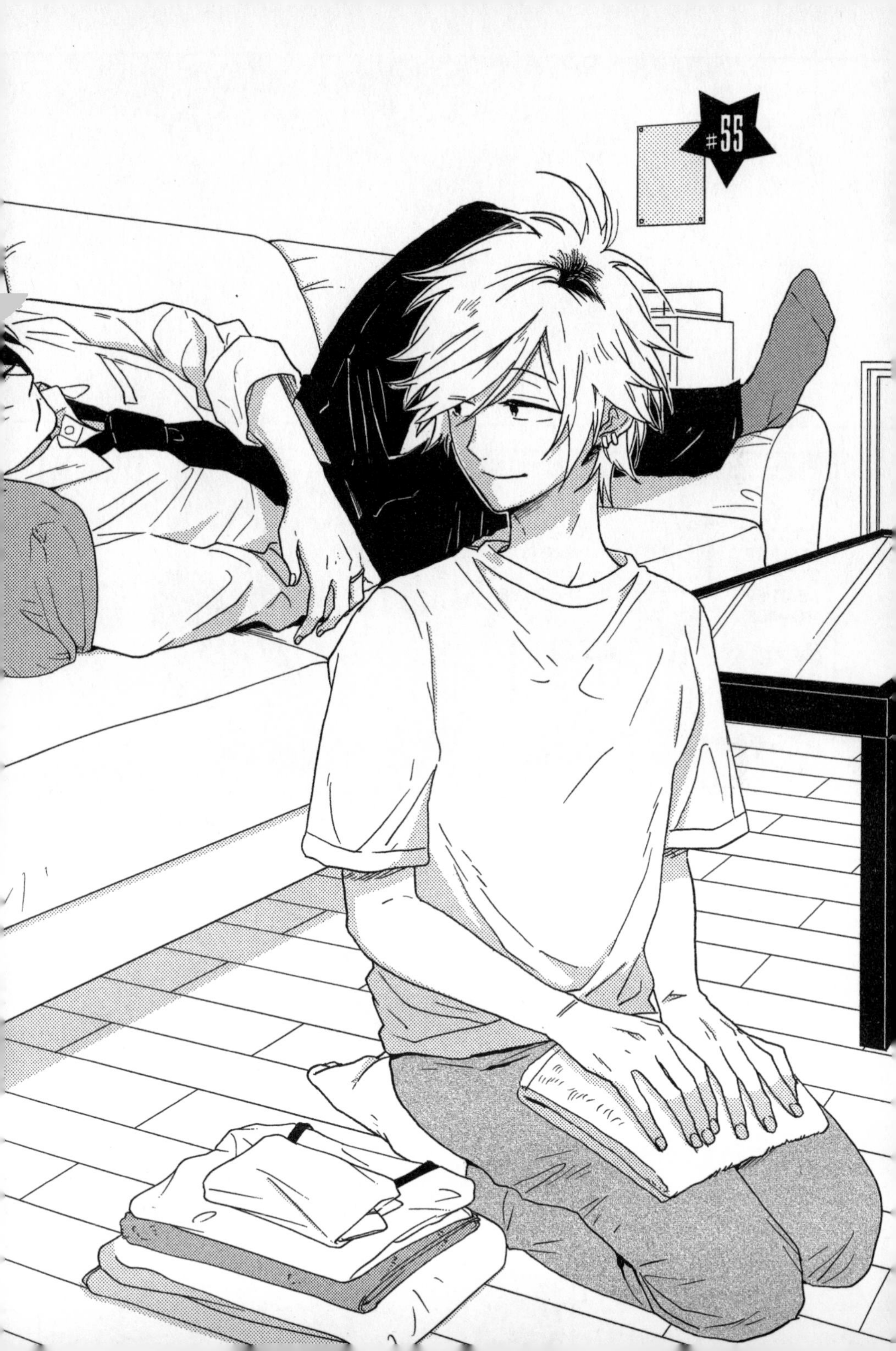
#55

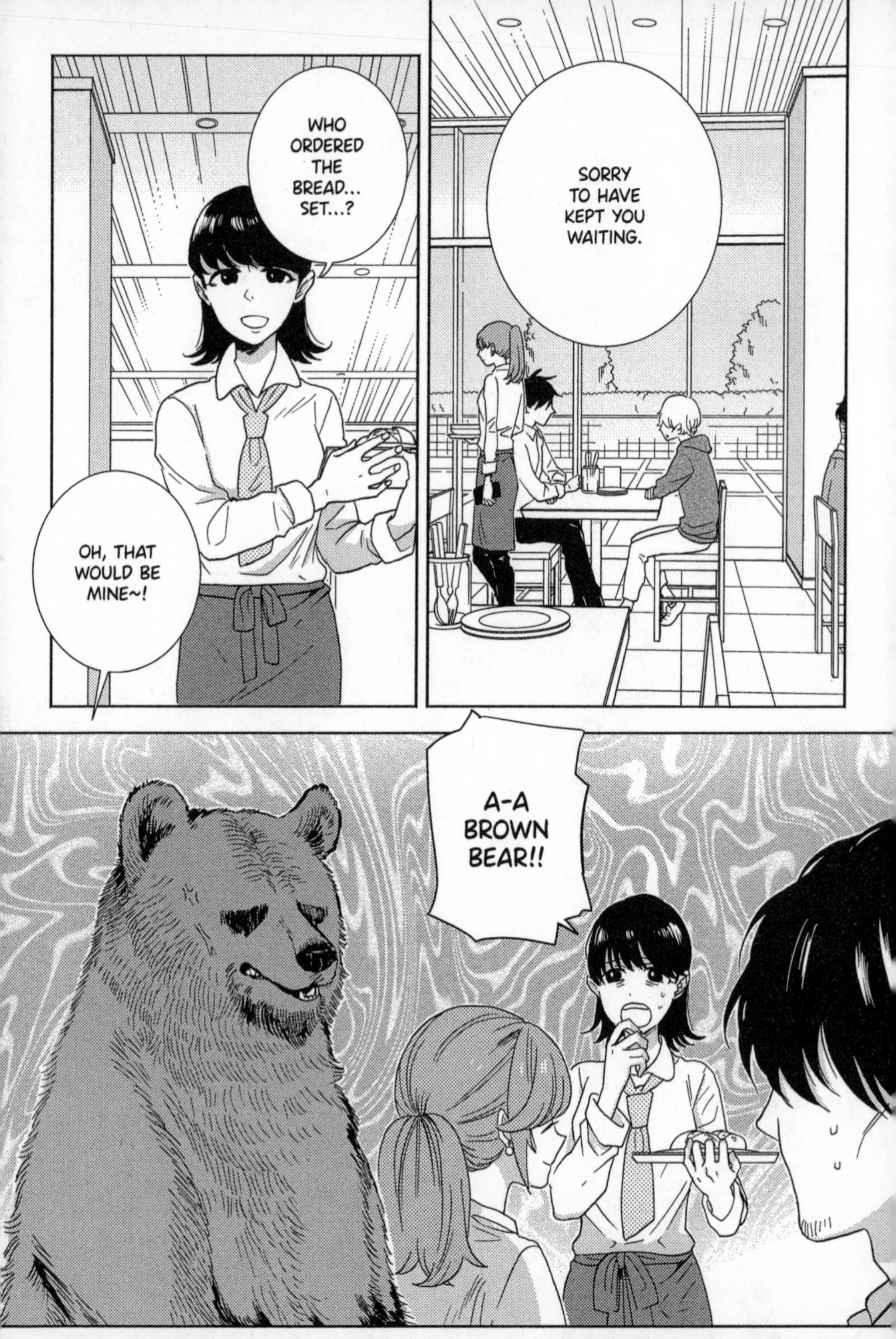
SORRY TO HAVE KEPT YOU WAITING.
WHO ORDERED THE BREAD... SET...?
OH, THAT WOULD BE MINE~!
A-A BROWN BEAR!!

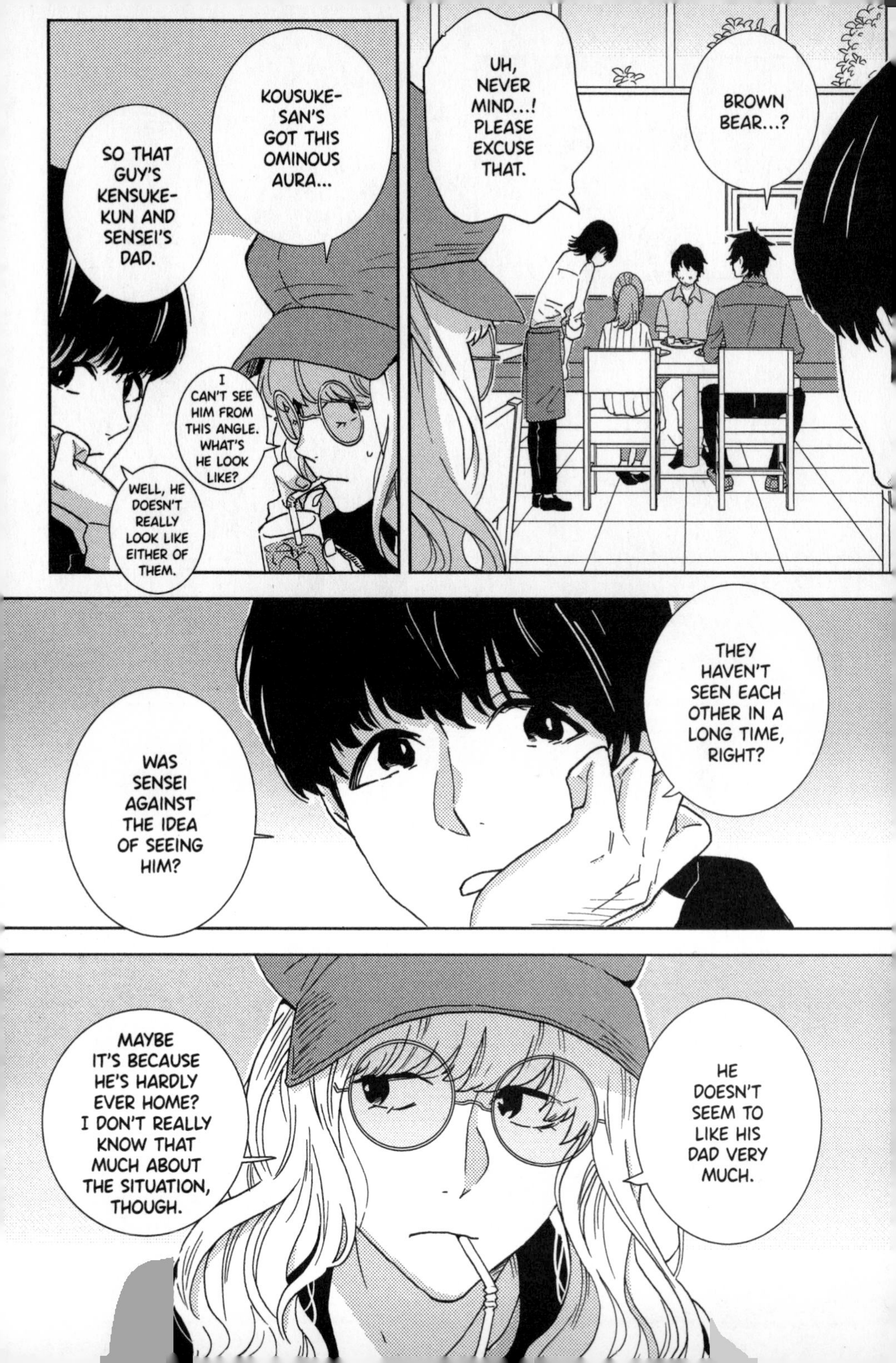
BROWN BEAR...?
UH, NEVER MIND...! PLEASE EXCUSE THAT.
KOUSUKE-SAN'S GOT THIS OMINOUS AURA...
SO THAT GUY'S KENSUKE-KUN AND SENSEI'S DAD.
I CAN'T SEE HIM FROM THIS ANGLE. WHAT'S HE LOOK LIKE?
WELL, HE DOESN'T REALLY LOOK LIKE EITHER OF THEM.
THEY HAVEN'T SEEN EACH OTHER IN A LONG TIME, RIGHT?
WAS SENSEI AGAINST THE IDEA OF SEEING HIM?
HE DOESN'T SEEM TO LIKE HIS DAD VERY MUCH.
MAYBE IT'S BECAUSE HE'S HARDLY EVER HOME? I DON'T REALLY KNOW THAT MUCH ABOUT THE SITUATION, THOUGH.

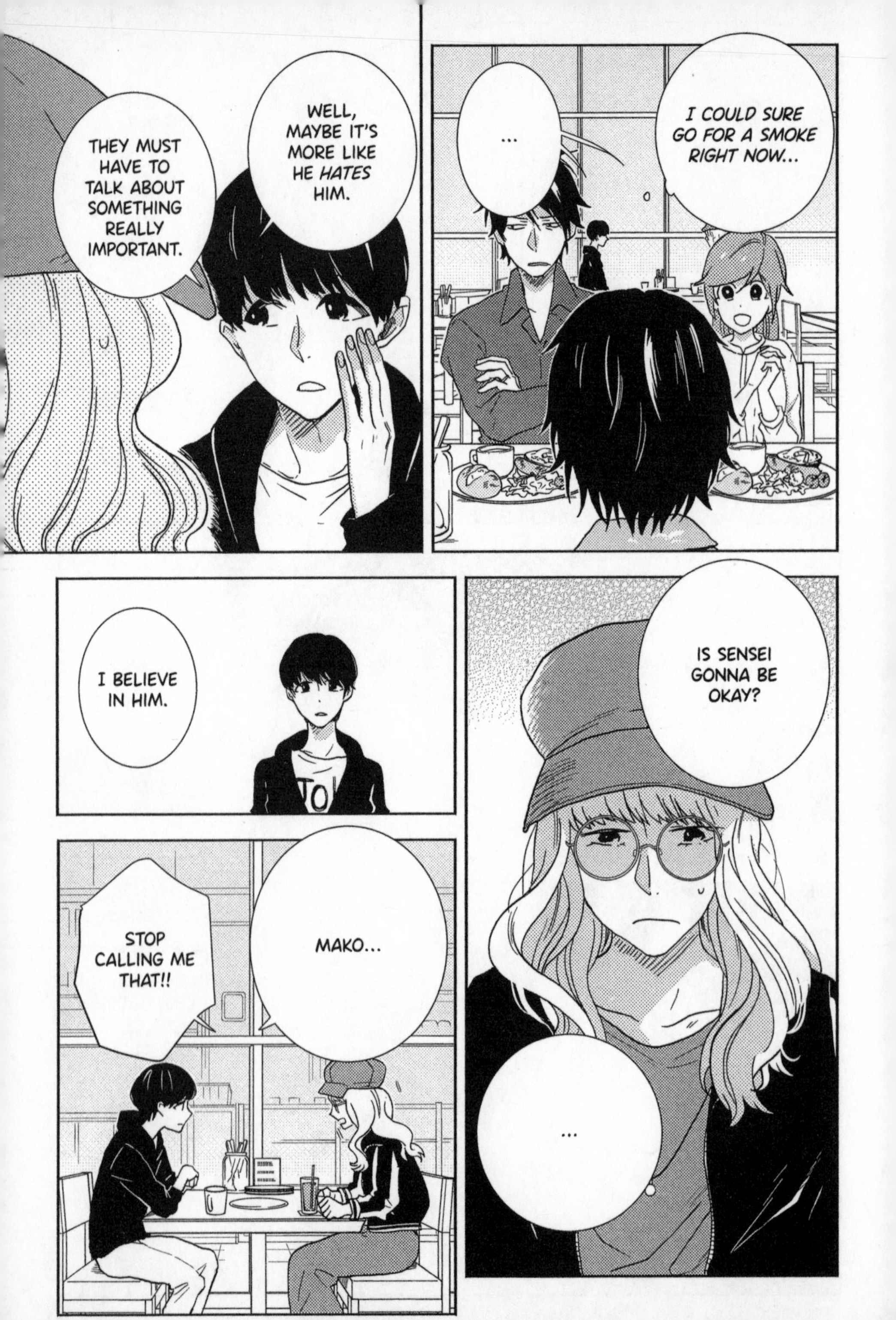
I COULD SURE GO FOR A SMOKE RIGHT NOW...
...
WELL, MAYBE IT'S MORE LIKE HE *HATES* HIM.
THEY MUST HAVE TO TALK ABOUT SOMETHING REALLY IMPORTANT.
IS SENSEI GONNA BE OKAY?
...
I BELIEVE IN HIM.
MAKO...
STOP CALLING ME THAT!!

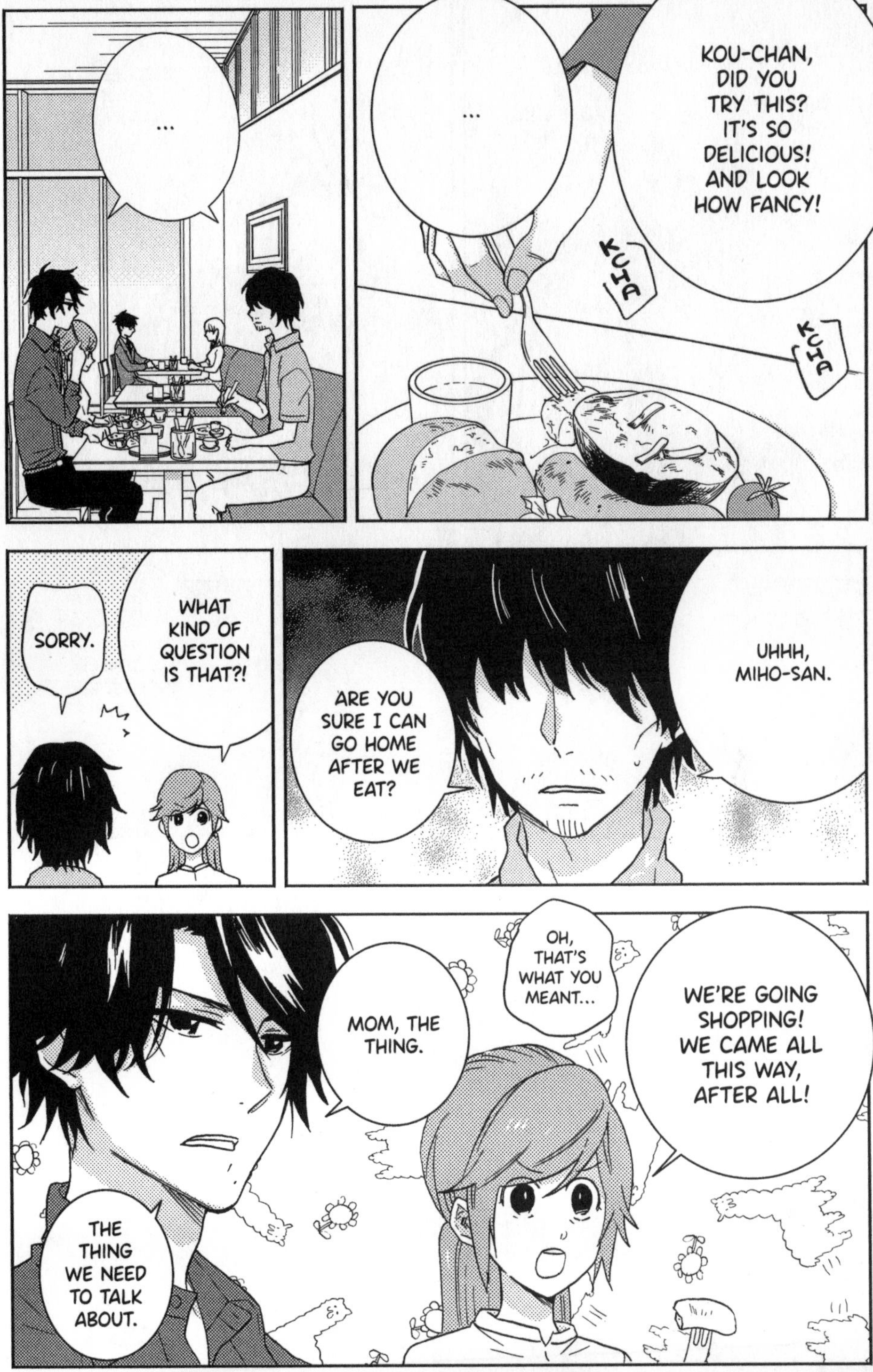
KOU-CHAN, DID YOU TRY THIS? IT'S SO DELICIOUS! AND LOOK HOW FANCY!
KUHA
KUHA
...
...
UHHH, MIHO-SAN.
ARE YOU SURE I CAN GO HOME AFTER WE EAT?
WHAT KIND OF QUESTION IS THAT?!
SORRY.
WE'RE GOING SHOPPING! WE CAME ALL THIS WAY, AFTER ALL!
OH, THAT'S WHAT YOU MEANT...
MOM, THE THING.
THE THING WE NEED TO TALK ABOUT.

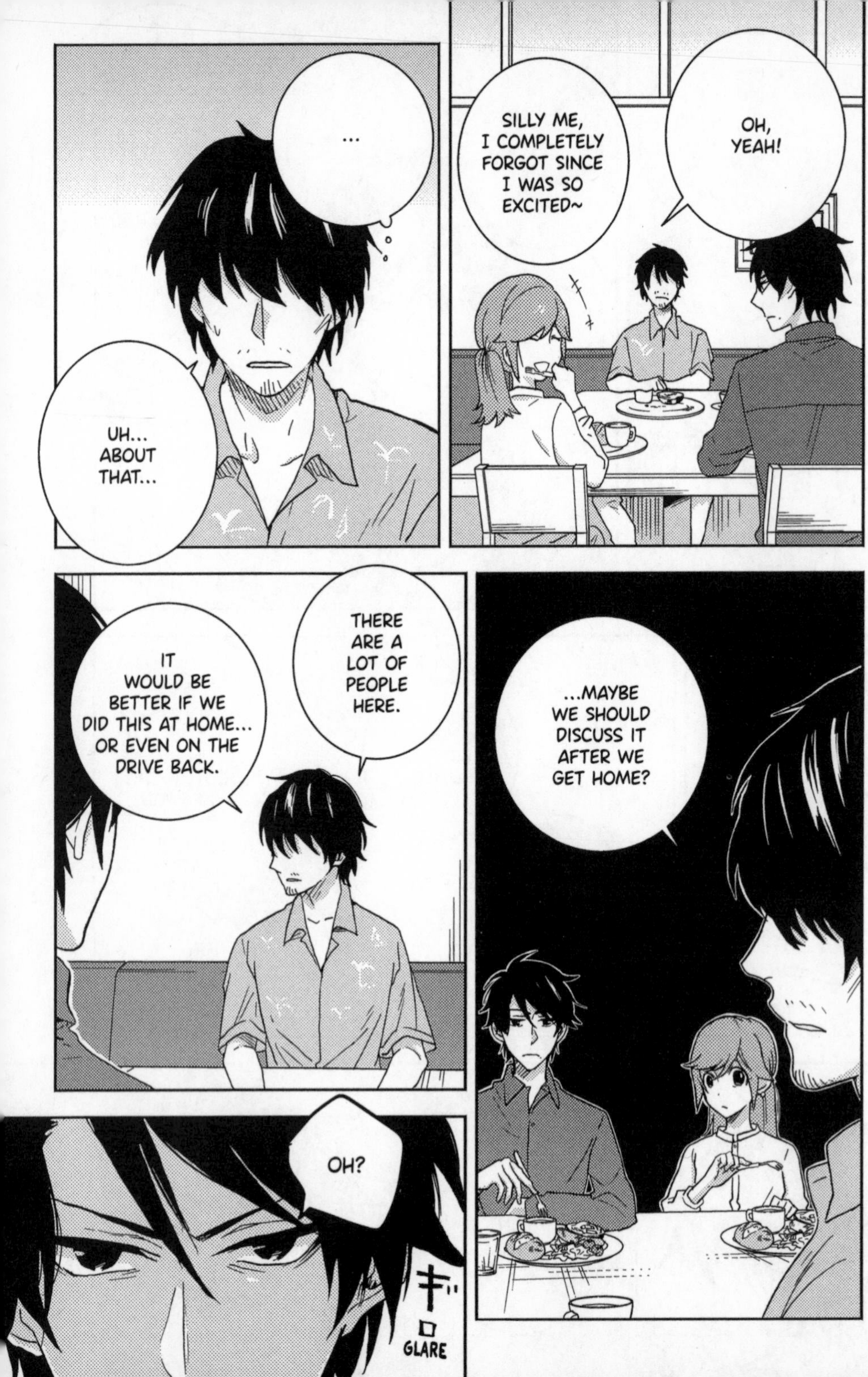
OH, YEAH!
SILLY ME, I COMPLETELY FORGOT SINCE I WAS SO EXCITED~
...
UH... ABOUT THAT...
...MAYBE WE SHOULD DISCUSS IT AFTER WE GET HOME?
THERE ARE A LOT OF PEOPLE HERE.
IT WOULD BE BETTER IF WE DID THIS AT HOME... OR EVEN ON THE DRIVE BACK.
OH?
GLARE

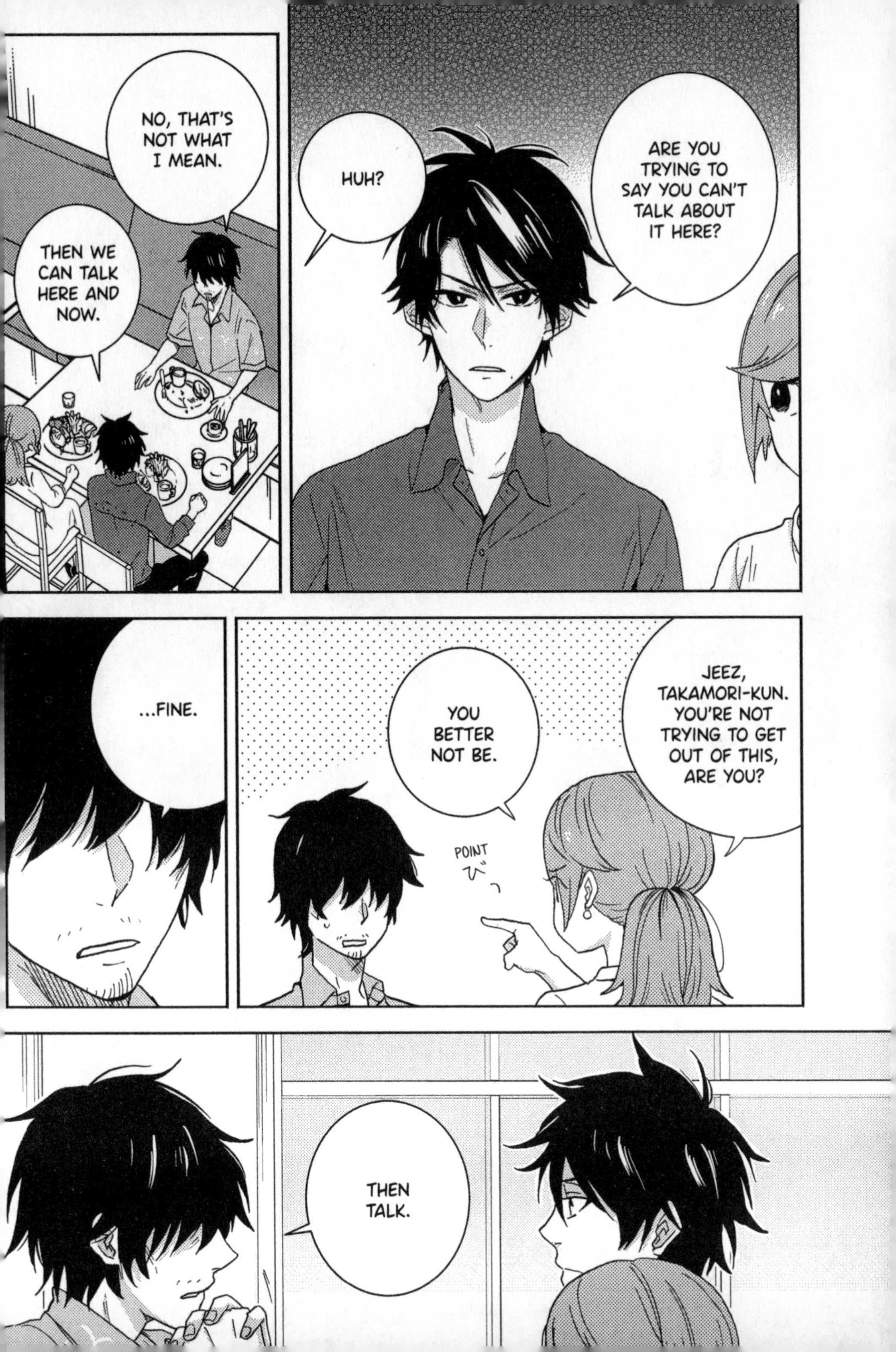
ARE YOU TRYING TO SAY YOU CAN'T TALK ABOUT IT HERE?
HUH?
NO, THAT'S NOT WHAT I MEAN.
THEN WE CAN TALK HERE AND NOW.
JEEZ, TAKAMORI-KUN. YOU'RE NOT TRYING TO GET OUT OF THIS, ARE YOU?
YOU BETTER NOT BE.
POINT
びっ
...FINE.
THEN TALK.

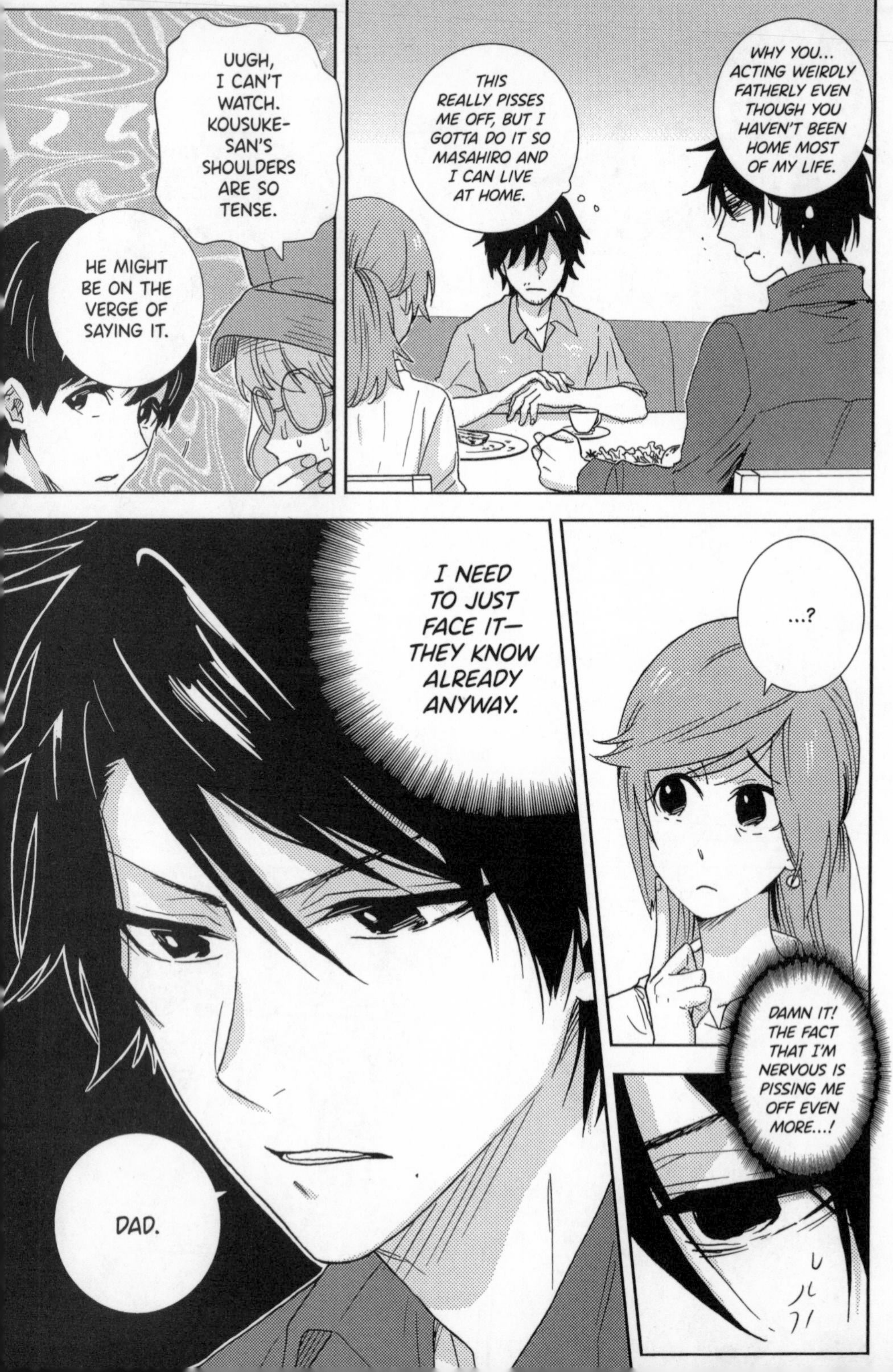

WHY YOU... ACTING WEIRDLY FATHERLY EVEN THOUGH YOU HAVEN'T BEEN HOME MOST OF MY LIFE.
THIS REALLY PISSES ME OFF, BUT I GOTTA DO IT SO MASAHIRO AND I CAN LIVE AT HOME.
UUGH, I CAN'T WATCH. KOUSUKE-SAN'S SHOULDERS ARE SO TENSE.
HE MIGHT BE ON THE VERGE OF SAYING IT.
...?
DAMN IT! THE FACT THAT I'M NERVOUS IS PISSING ME OFF EVEN MORE...!
I NEED TO JUST FACE IT—THEY KNOW ALREADY ANYWAY.
DAD.

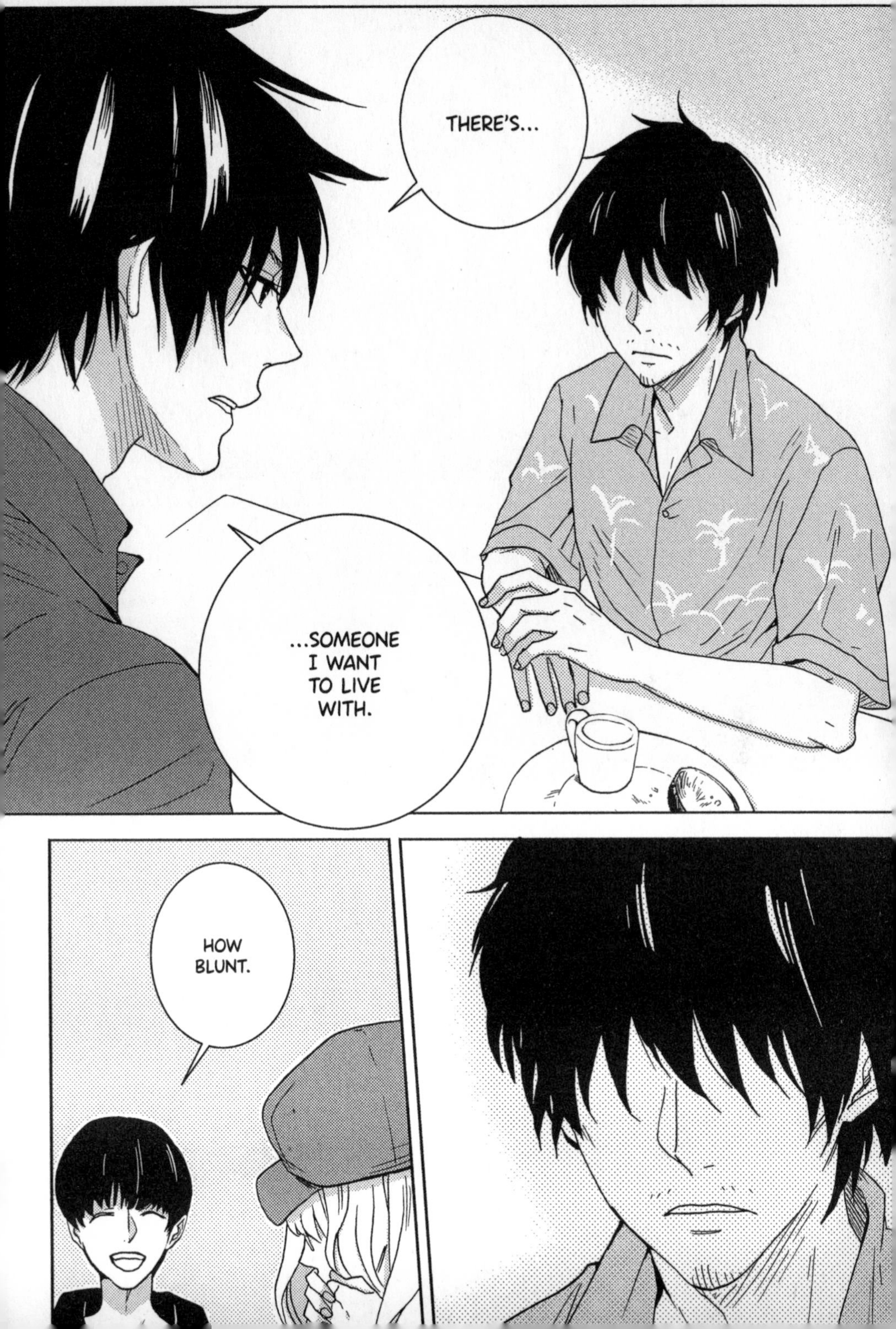
THERE'S...
...SOMEONE I WANT TO LIVE WITH.
HOW BLUNT.

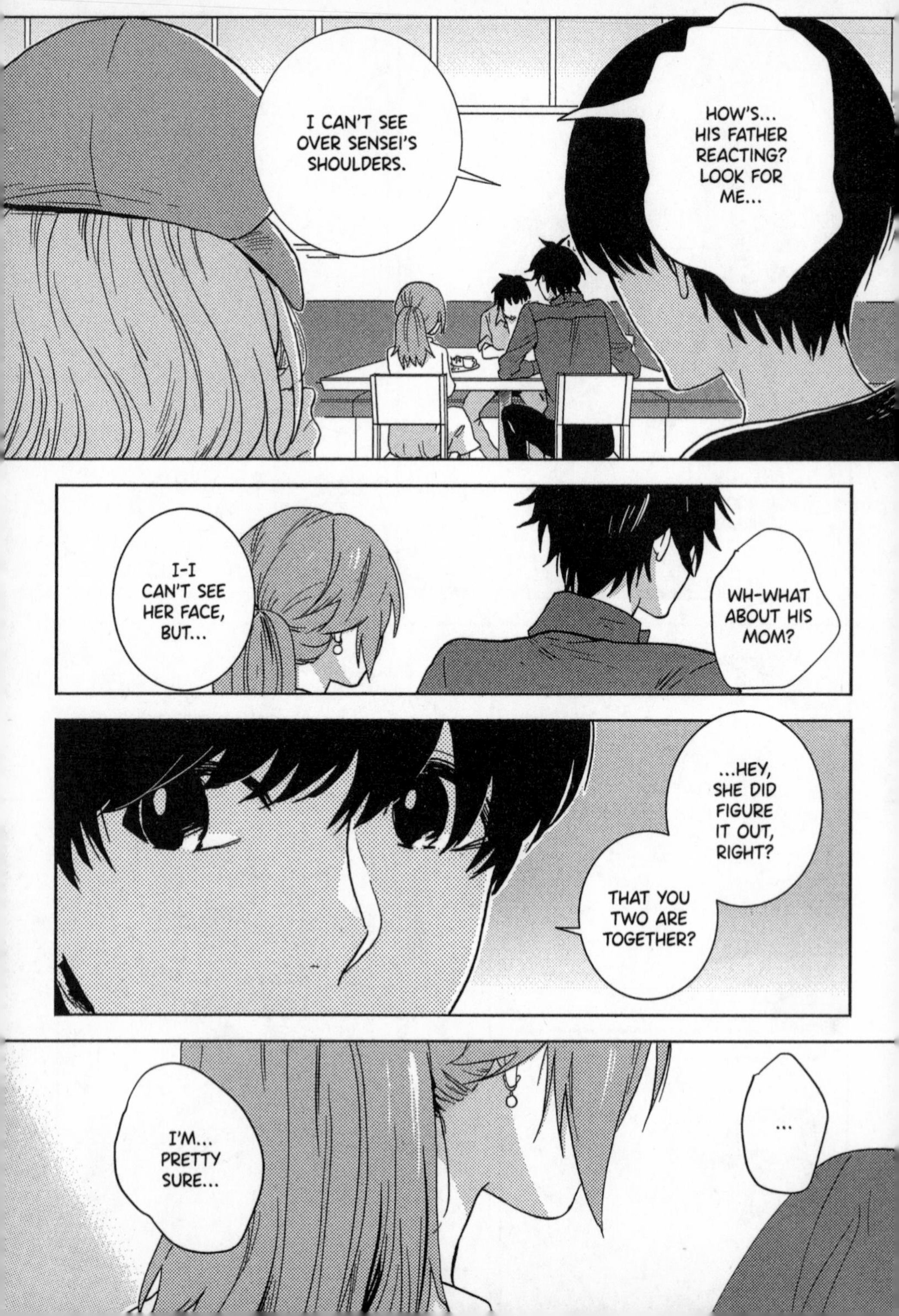
HOW'S... HIS FATHER REACTING? LOOK FOR ME...
I CAN'T SEE OVER SENSEI'S SHOULDERS.
WH-WHAT ABOUT HIS MOM?
I-I CAN'T SEE HER FACE, BUT...
...HEY, SHE DID FIGURE IT OUT, RIGHT?
THAT YOU TWO ARE TOGETHER?
...
I'M... PRETTY SURE...

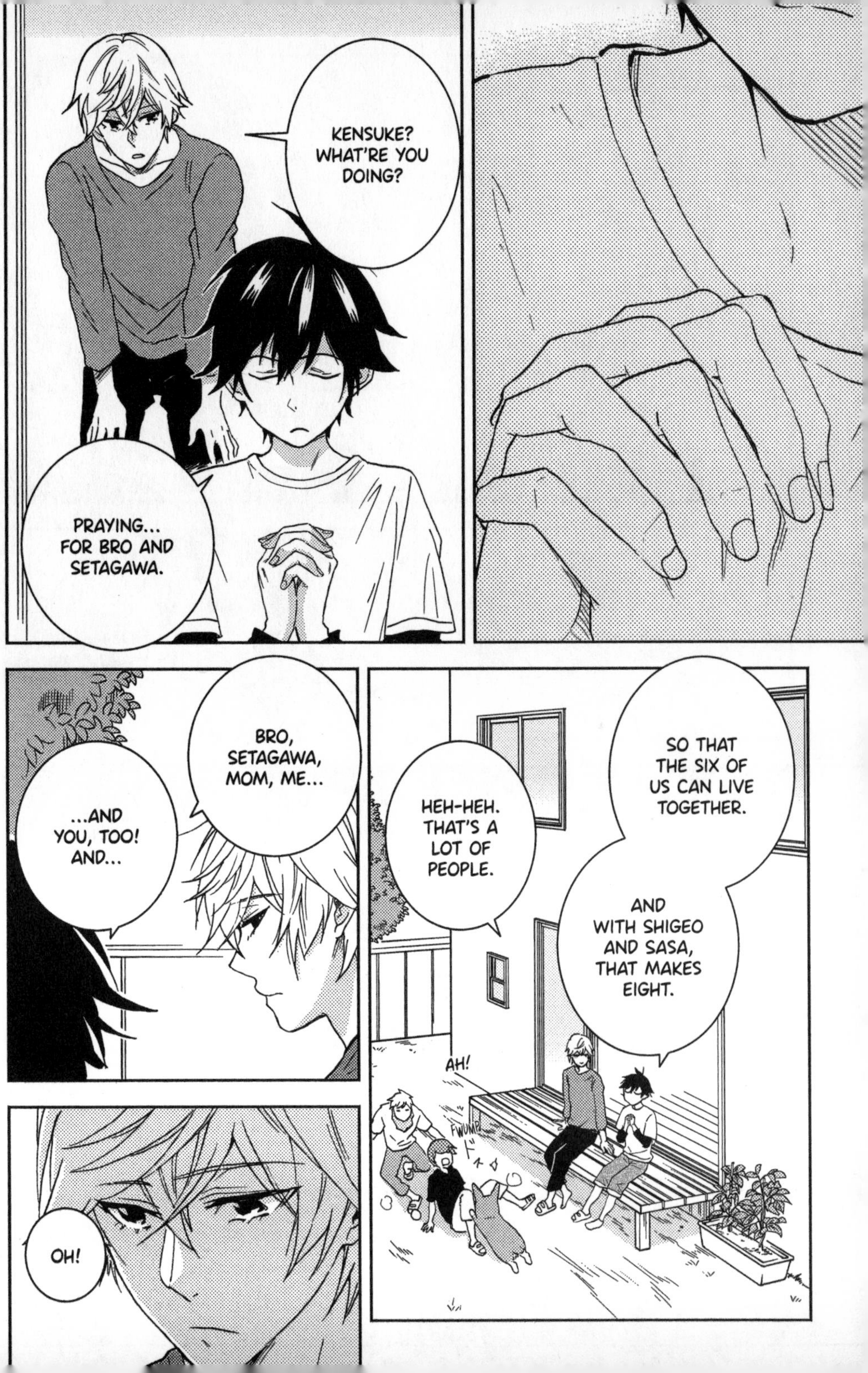
KENSUKE? WHAT'RE YOU DOING?
PRAYING... FOR BRO AND SETAGAWA.
SO THAT THE SIX OF US CAN LIVE TOGETHER.
HEH-HEH. THAT'S A LOT OF PEOPLE.
AND WITH SHIGEO AND SASA, THAT MAKES EIGHT.
AH!
FWUMP
BRO, SETAGAWA, MOM, ME...
...AND YOU, TOO! AND...
OH!

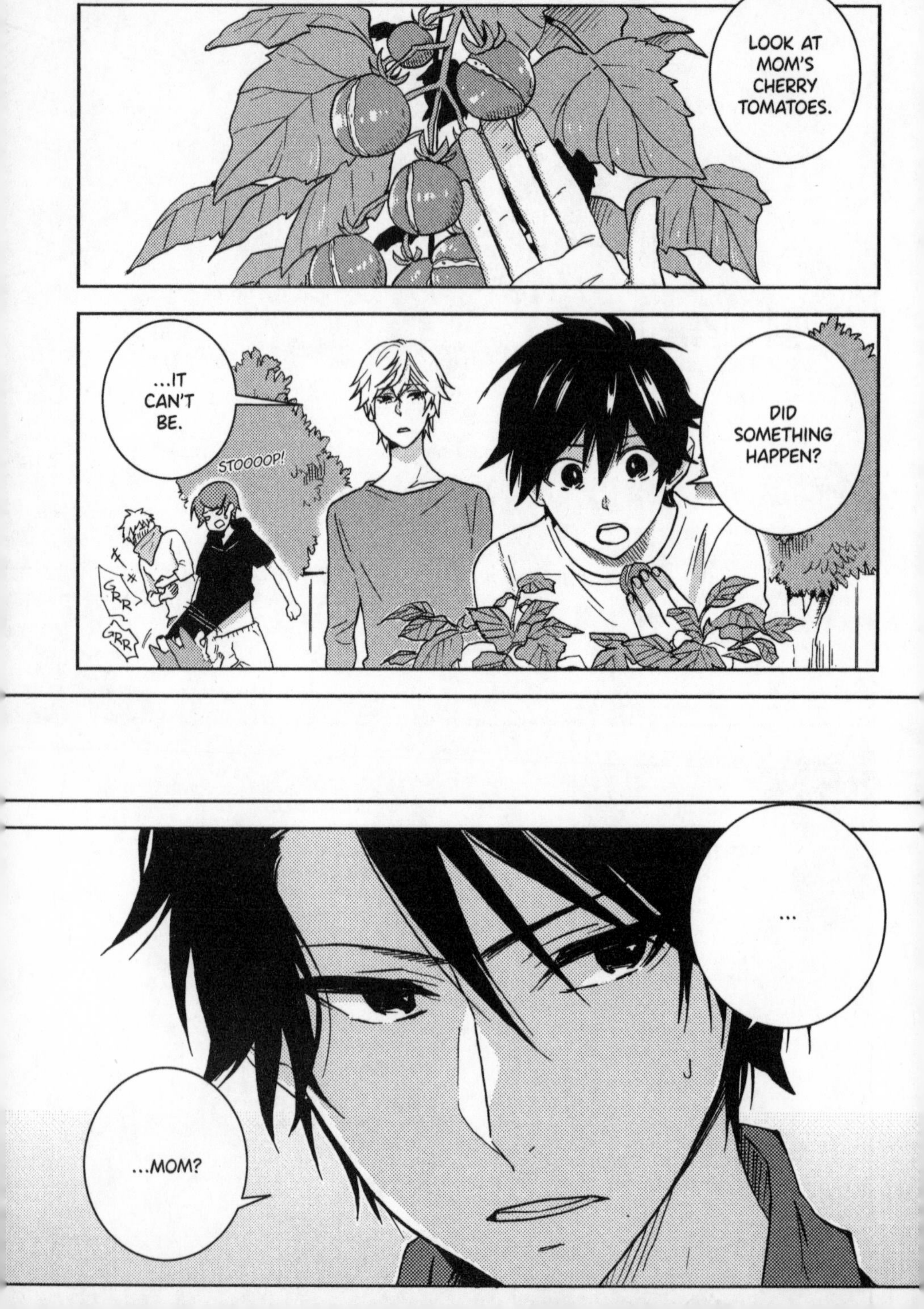
LOOK AT MOM'S CHERRY TOMATOES.
DID SOMETHING HAPPEN?
...IT CAN'T BE.
STOOOOP!
GRR
GRR
...
...MOM?

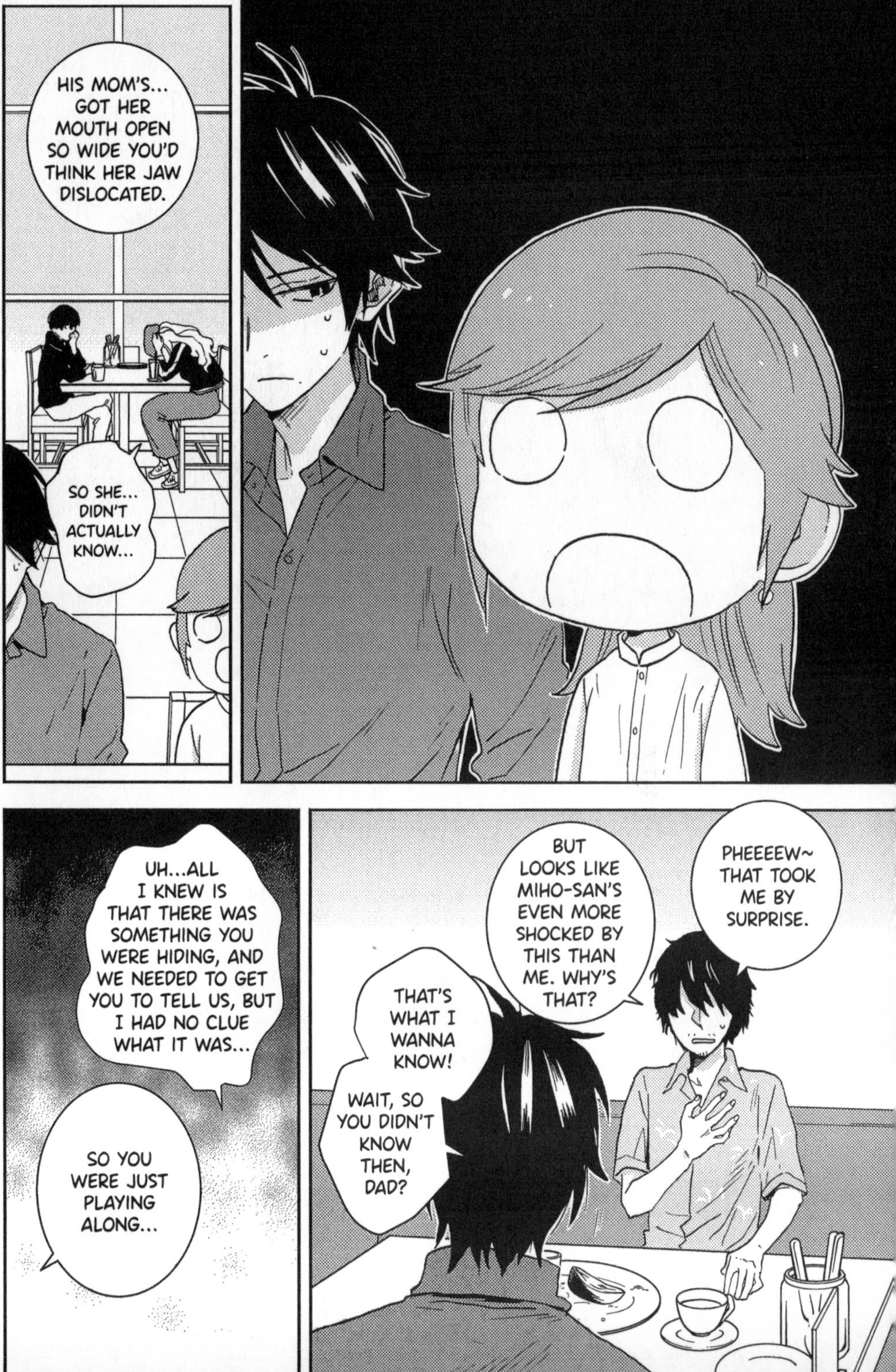
HIS MOM'S... GOT HER MOUTH OPEN SO WIDE YOU'D THINK HER JAW DISLOCATED.
SO SHE... DIDN'T ACTUALLY KNOW...
PHEEEEW~ THAT TOOK ME BY SURPRISE.
BUT LOOKS LIKE MIHO-SAN'S EVEN MORE SHOCKED BY THIS THAN ME. WHY'S THAT?
THAT'S WHAT I WANNA KNOW!
WAIT, SO YOU DIDN'T KNOW THEN, DAD?
UH...ALL I KNEW IS THAT THERE WAS SOMETHING YOU WERE HIDING, AND WE NEEDED TO GET YOU TO TELL US, BUT I HAD NO CLUE WHAT IT WAS...
SO YOU WERE JUST PLAYING ALONG...

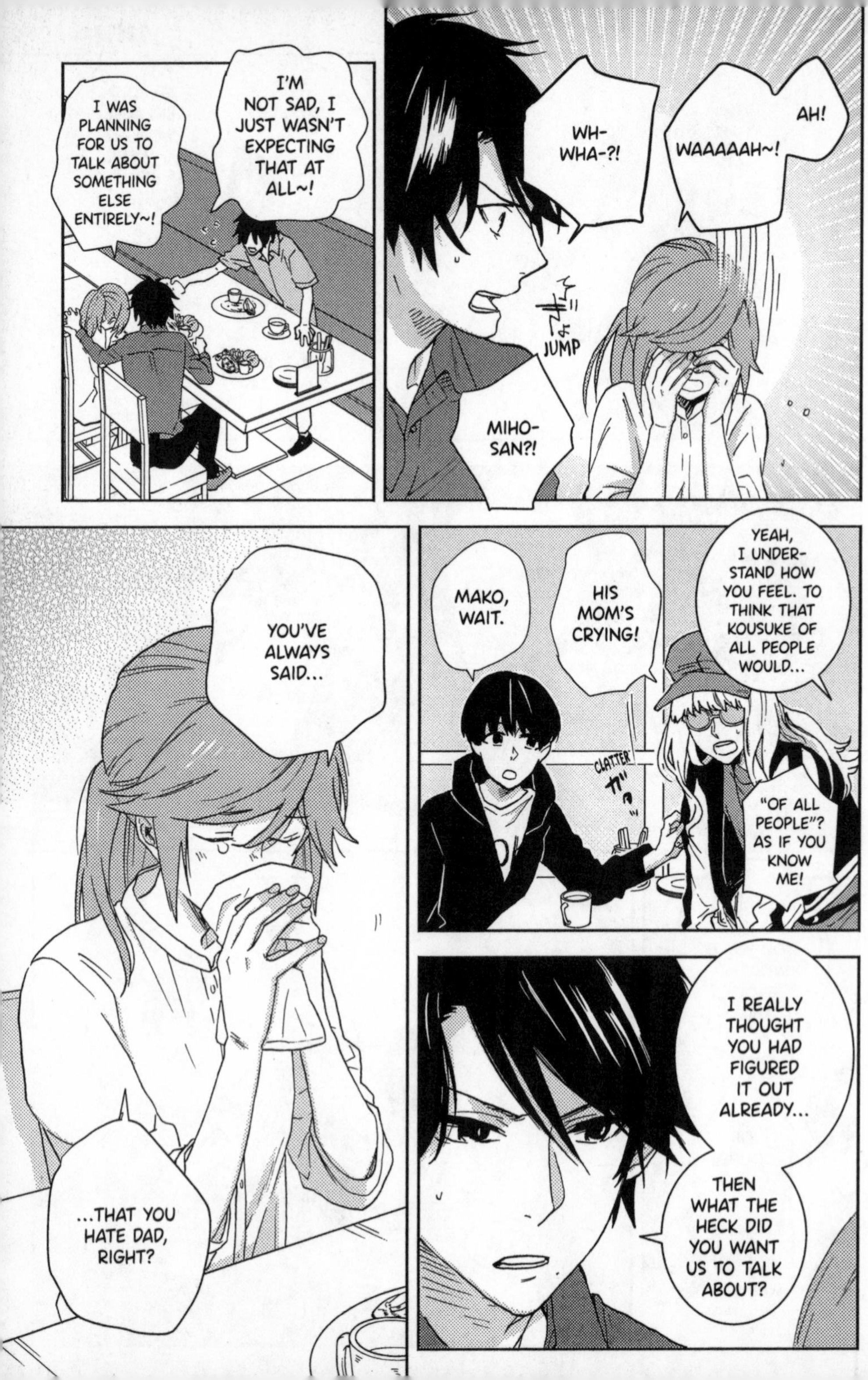

AH!
WAAAAAH~!
WH- WHA-?!
JUMP
MIHO-SAN?!
I'M NOT SAD, I JUST WASN'T EXPECTING THAT AT ALL~!
I WAS PLANNING FOR US TO TALK ABOUT SOMETHING ELSE ENTIRELY~!
YEAH, I UNDER-STAND HOW YOU FEEL. TO THINK THAT KOUSUKE OF ALL PEOPLE WOULD...
HIS MOM'S CRYING!
MAKO, WAIT.
CLATTER
"OF ALL PEOPLE"? AS IF YOU KNOW ME!
I REALLY THOUGHT YOU HAD FIGURED IT OUT ALREADY...
THEN WHAT THE HECK DID YOU WANT US TO TALK ABOUT?
YOU'VE ALWAYS SAID...
...THAT YOU HATE DAD, RIGHT?

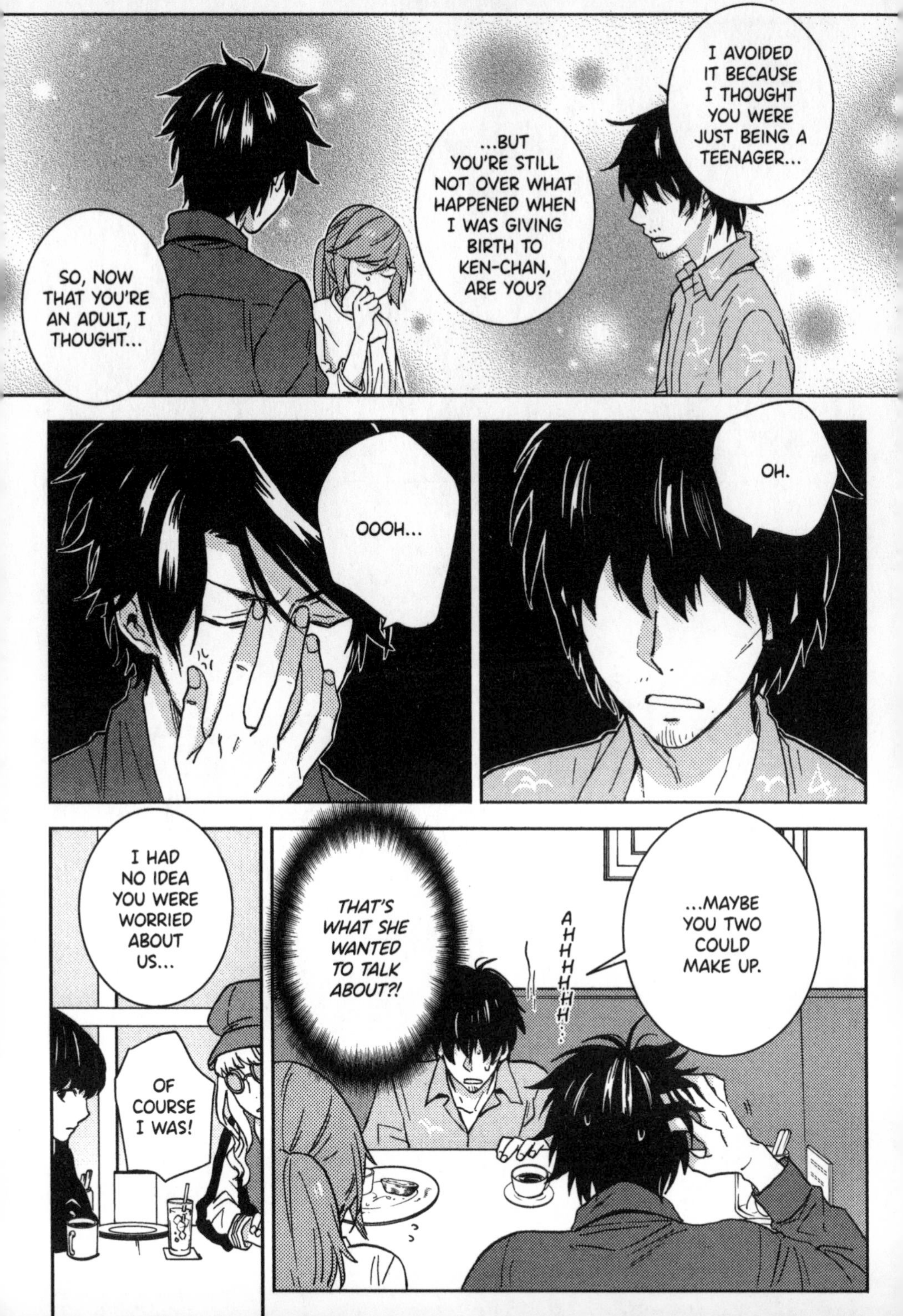
I AVOIDED IT BECAUSE I THOUGHT YOU WERE JUST BEING A TEENAGER...
...BUT YOU'RE STILL NOT OVER WHAT HAPPENED WHEN I WAS GIVING BIRTH TO KEN-CHAN, ARE YOU?
SO, NOW THAT YOU'RE AN ADULT, I THOUGHT...
OH.
OOOH...
...MAYBE YOU TWO COULD MAKE UP.
AHHHHHH...
THAT'S WHAT SHE WANTED TO TALK ABOUT?!
I HAD NO IDEA YOU WERE WORRIED ABOUT US...
OF COURSE I WAS!

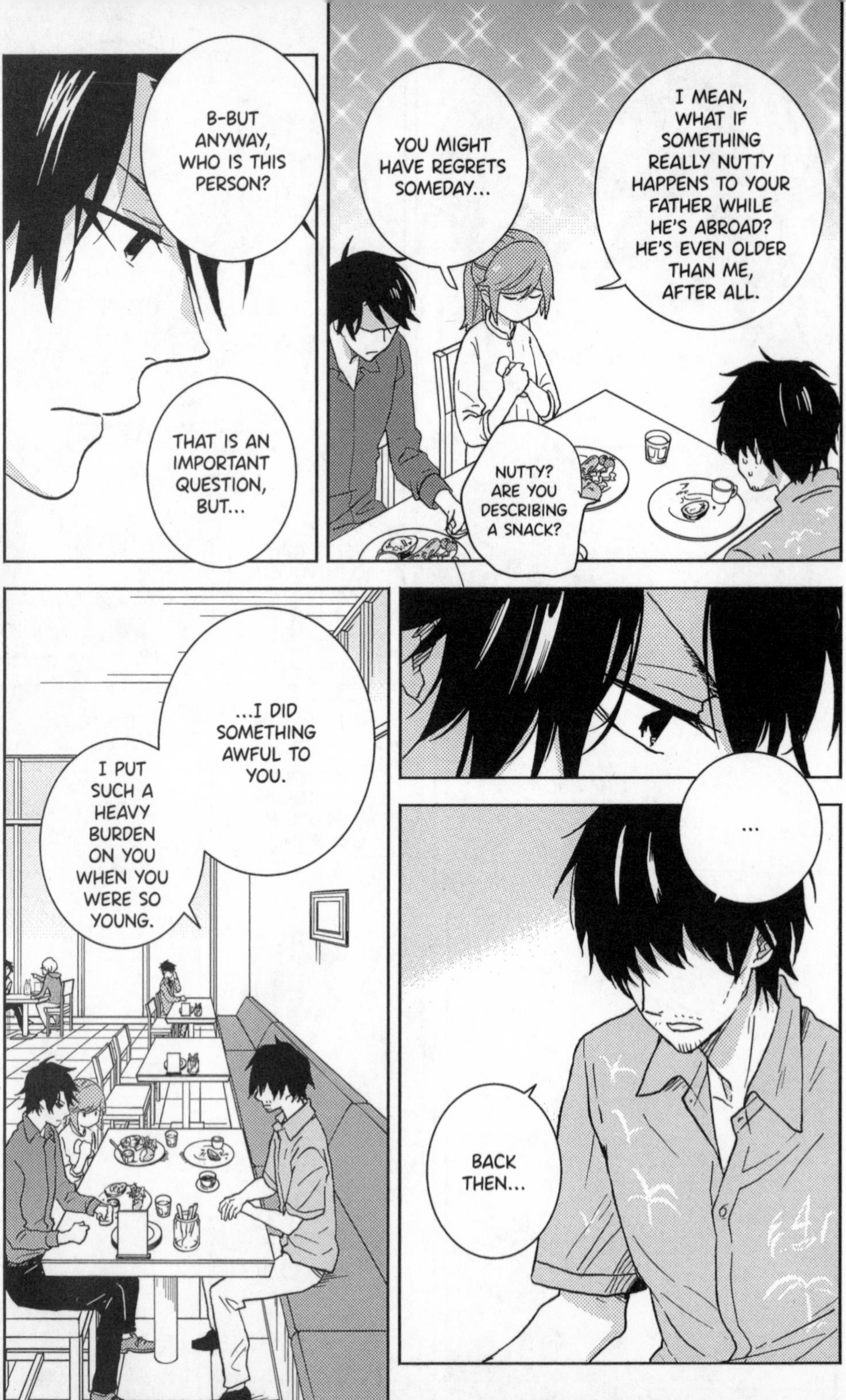
I MEAN, WHAT IF SOMETHING REALLY NUTTY HAPPENS TO YOUR FATHER WHILE HE'S ABROAD? HE'S EVEN OLDER THAN ME, AFTER ALL.
YOU MIGHT HAVE REGRETS SOMEDAY...
NUTTY? ARE YOU DESCRIBING A SNACK?
B-BUT ANYWAY, WHO IS THIS PERSON?
THAT IS AN IMPORTANT QUESTION, BUT...
...
BACK THEN...
...I DID SOMETHING AWFUL TO YOU.
I PUT SUCH A HEAVY BURDEN ON YOU WHEN YOU WERE SO YOUNG.

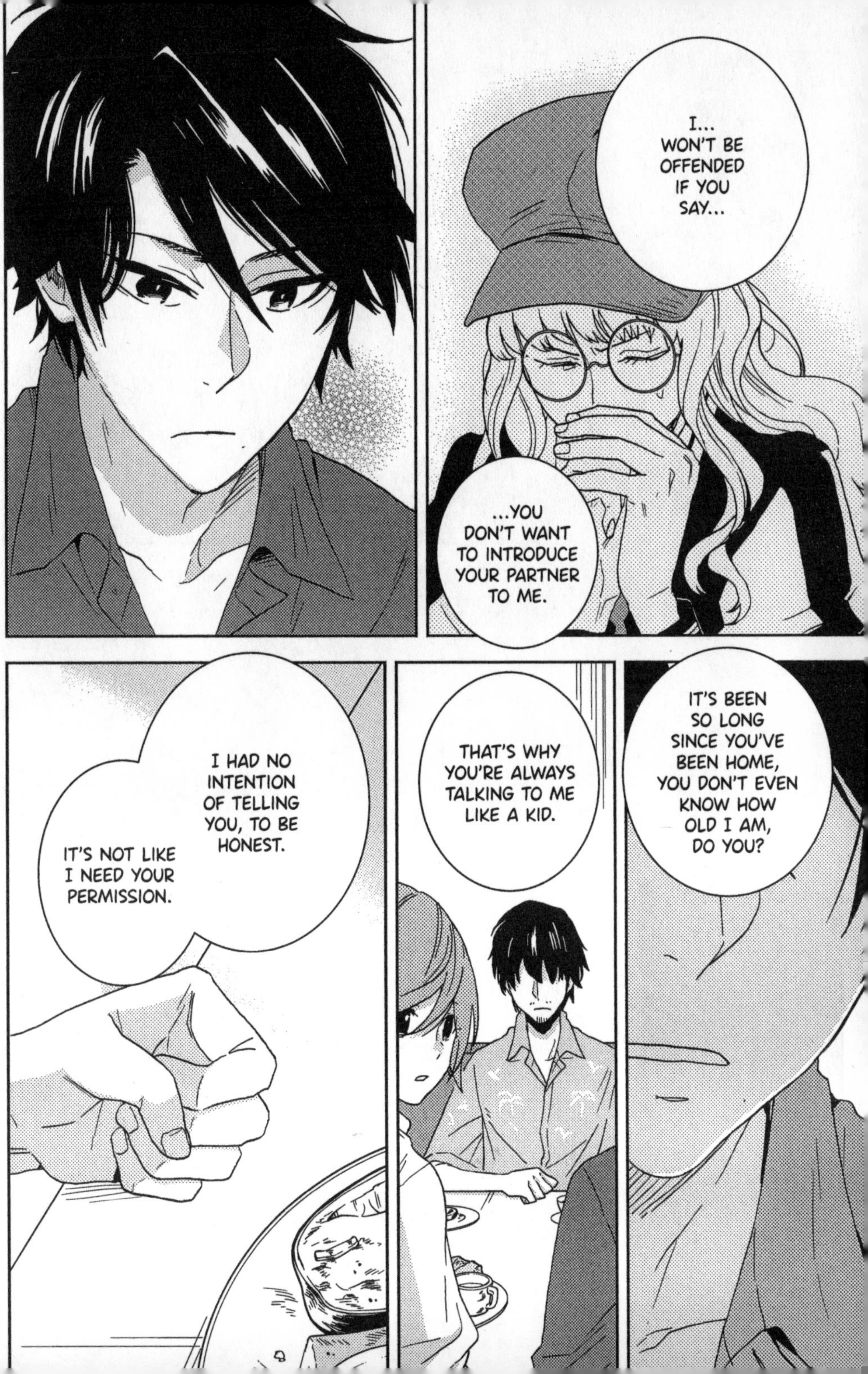
I... WON'T BE OFFENDED IF YOU SAY...
...YOU DON'T WANT TO INTRODUCE YOUR PARTNER TO ME.
IT'S BEEN SO LONG SINCE YOU'VE BEEN HOME, YOU DON'T EVEN KNOW HOW OLD I AM, DO YOU?
THAT'S WHY YOU'RE ALWAYS TALKING TO ME LIKE A KID.
I HAD NO INTENTION OF TELLING YOU, TO BE HONEST.
IT'S NOT LIKE I NEED YOUR PERMISSION.

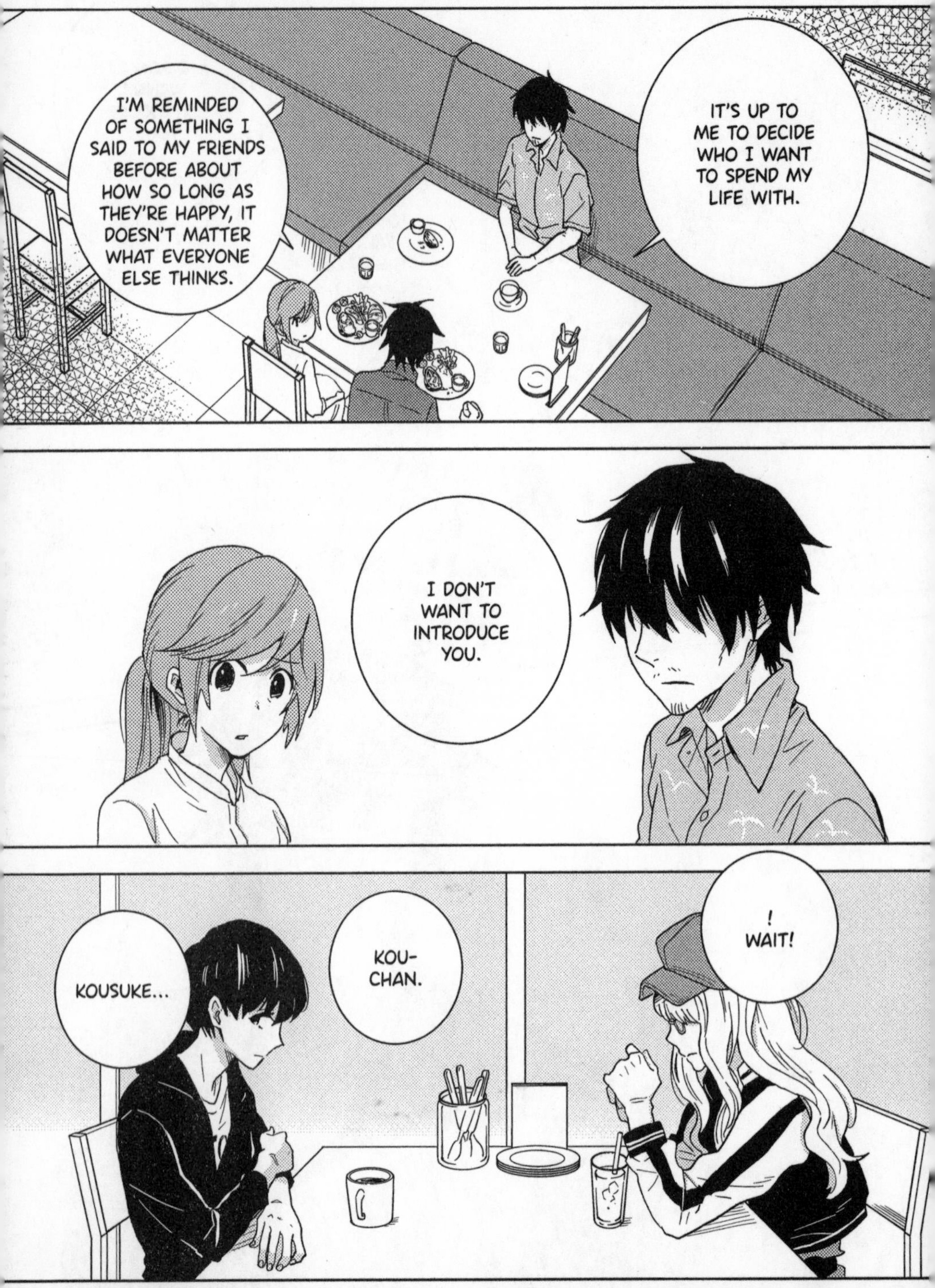
IT'S UP TO ME TO DECIDE WHO I WANT TO SPEND MY LIFE WITH.
I'M REMINDED OF SOMETHING I SAID TO MY FRIENDS BEFORE ABOUT HOW SO LONG AS THEY'RE HAPPY, IT DOESN'T MATTER WHAT EVERYONE ELSE THINKS.
I DON'T WANT TO INTRODUCE YOU.
! WAIT!
KOU-CHAN.
KOUSUKE...

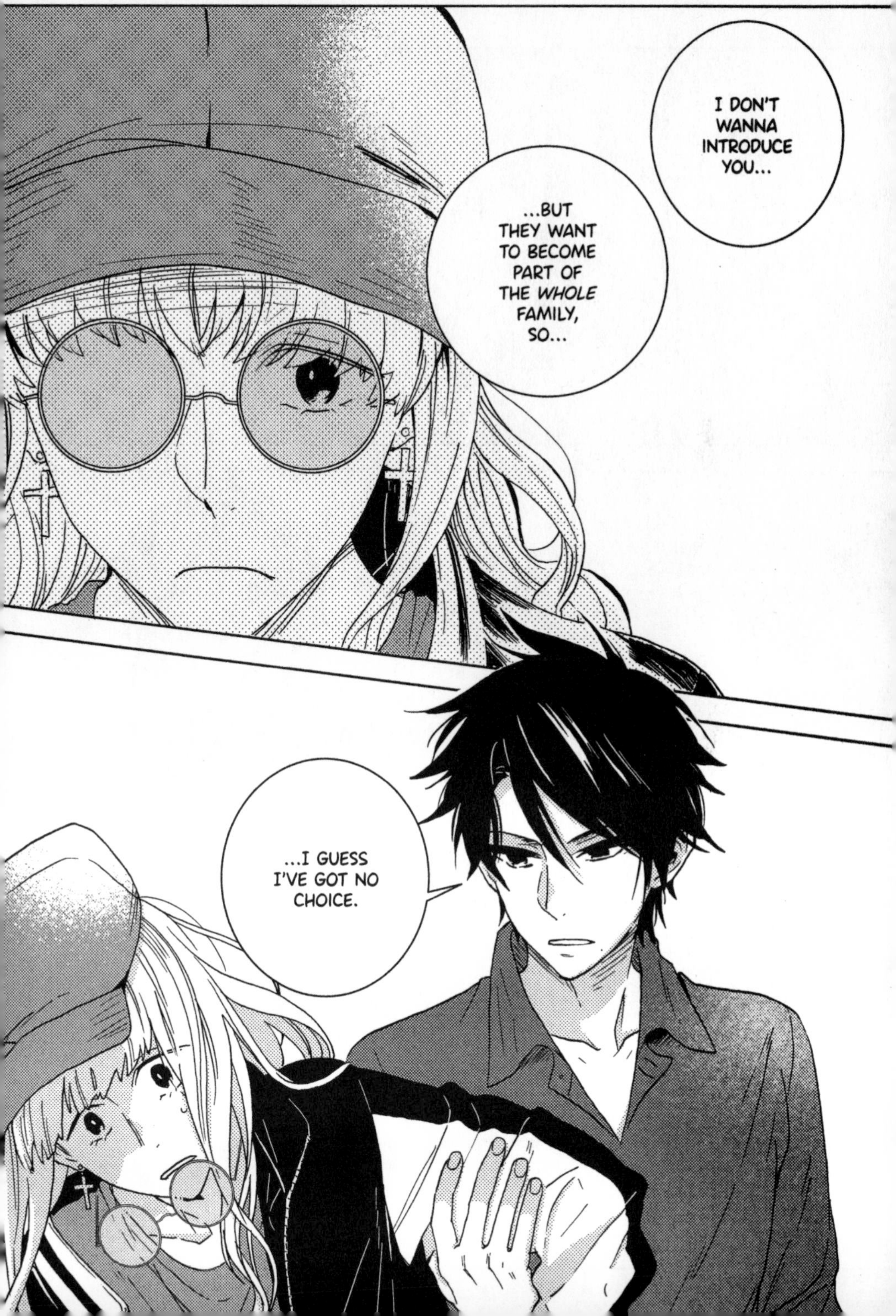
I DON'T WANNA INTRODUCE YOU...
...BUT THEY WANT TO BECOME PART OF THE *WHOLE* FAMILY, SO...
...I GUESS I'VE GOT NO CHOICE.

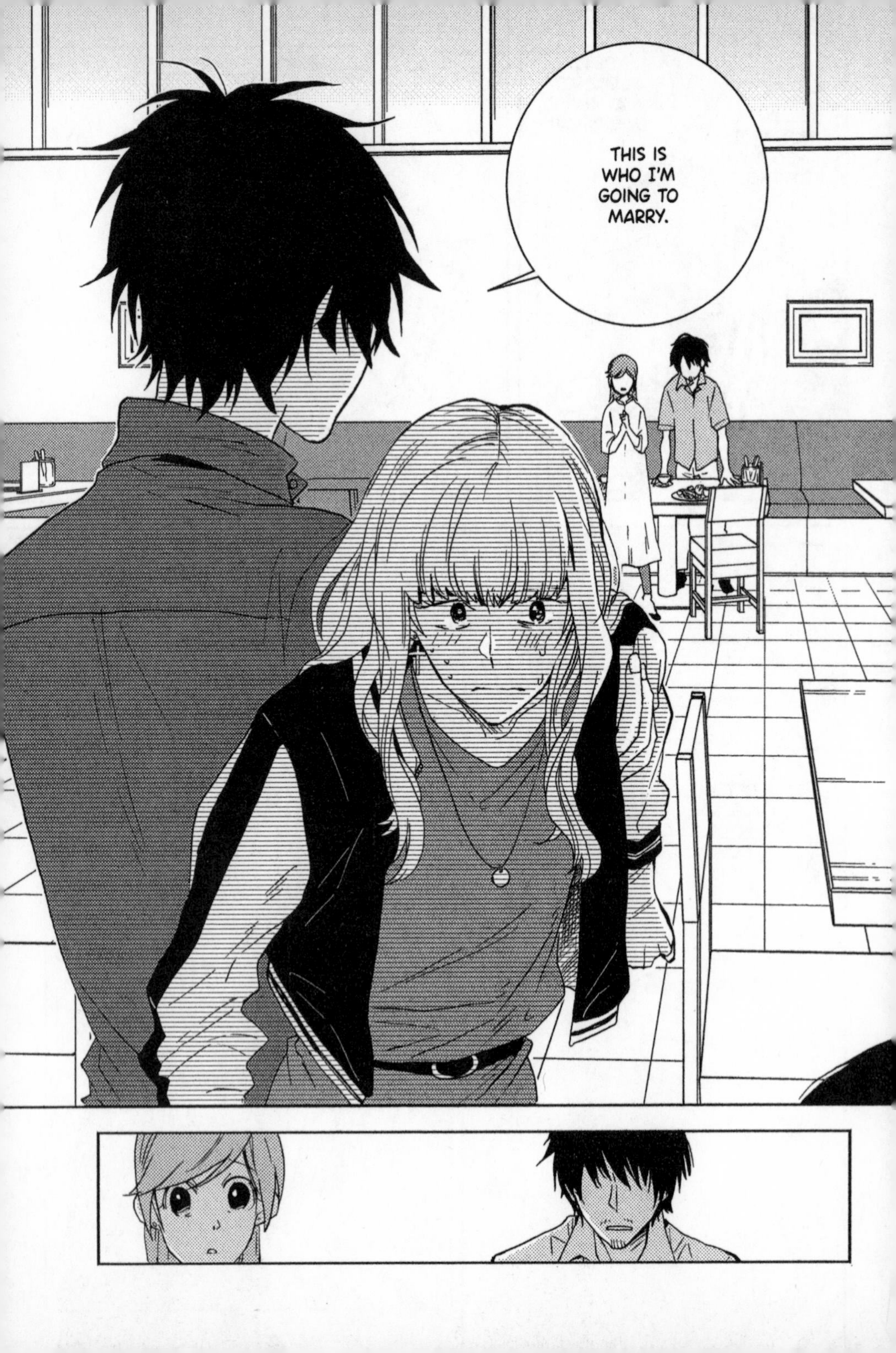
THIS IS WHO I'M GOING TO MARRY.

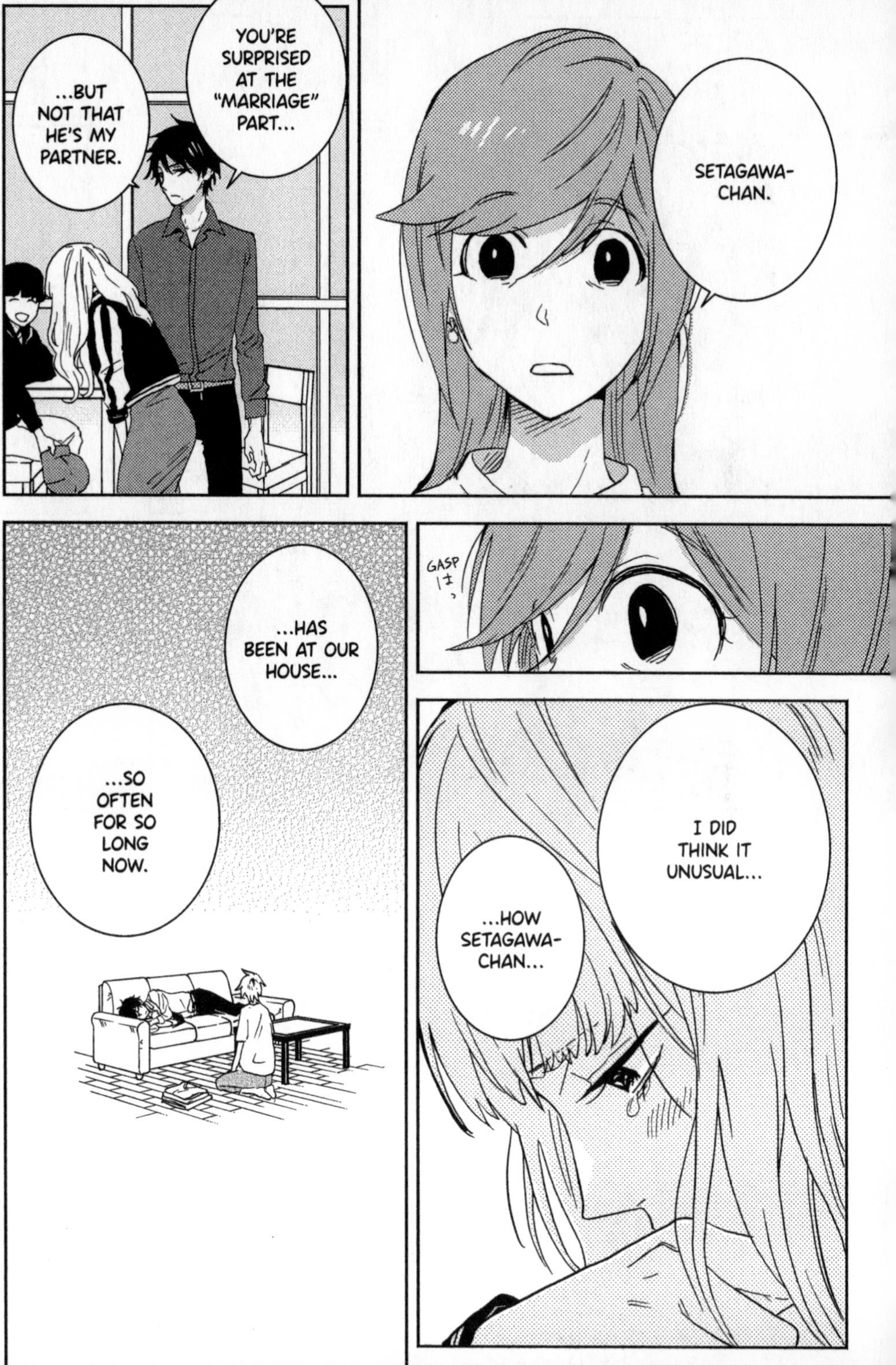
SETAGAWA-CHAN.
YOU'RE SURPRISED AT THE "MARRIAGE" PART...
...BUT NOT THAT HE'S MY PARTNER.
GASP
はっ
I DID THINK IT UNUSUAL...
...HOW SETAGAWA-CHAN...
...HAS BEEN AT OUR HOUSE...
...SO OFTEN FOR SO LONG NOW.

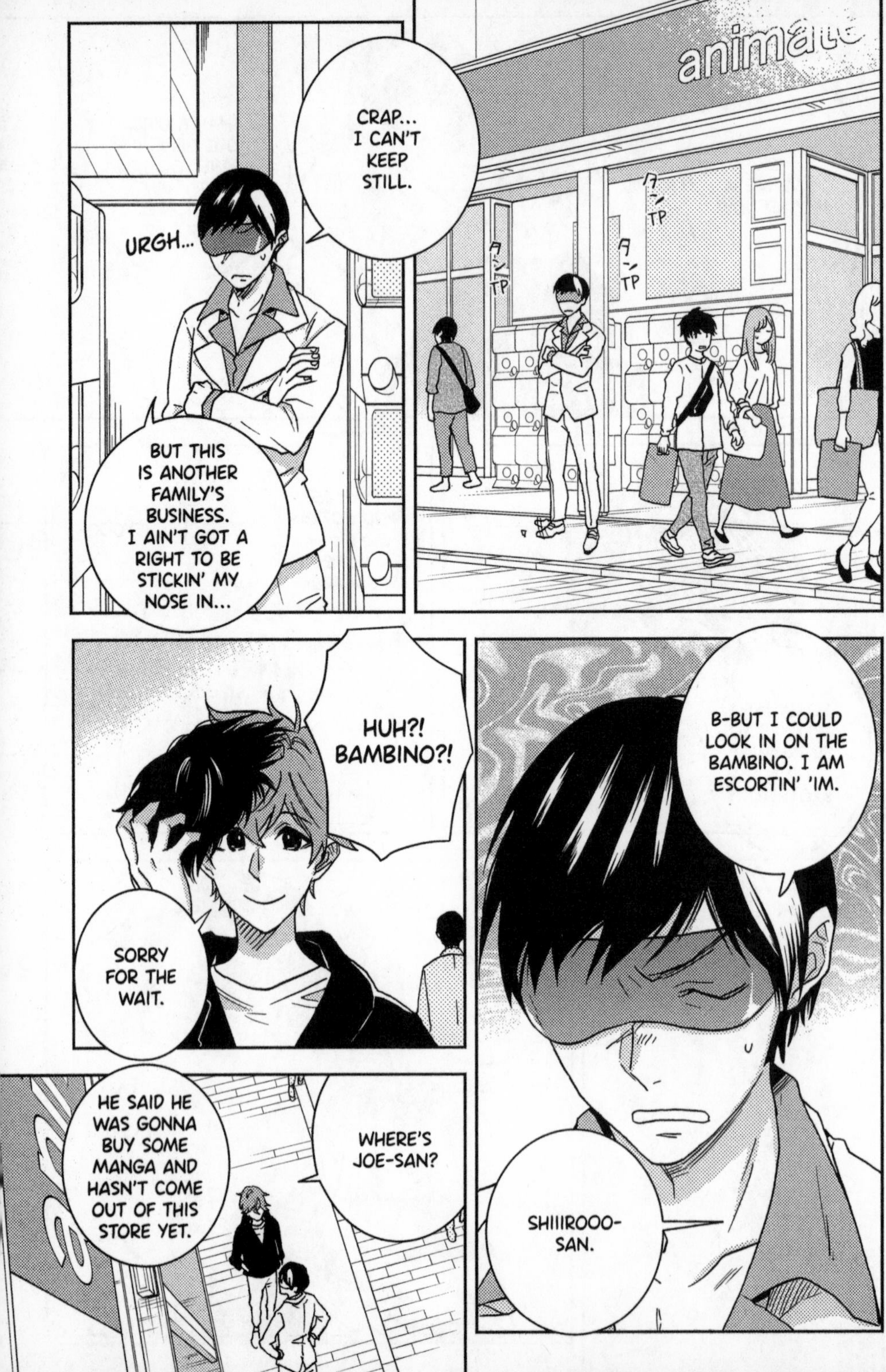
animate
TP
TP
TP
CRAP... I CAN'T KEEP STILL.
URGH...
BUT THIS IS ANOTHER FAMILY'S BUSINESS. I AIN'T GOT A RIGHT TO BE STICKIN' MY NOSE IN...
B-BUT I COULD LOOK IN ON THE BAMBINO. I AM ESCORTIN' 'IM.
SHIIIROOO-SAN.
HUH?! BAMBINO?!
SORRY FOR THE WAIT.
WHERE'S JOE-SAN?
HE SAID HE WAS GONNA BUY SOME MANGA AND HASN'T COME OUT OF THIS STORE YET.

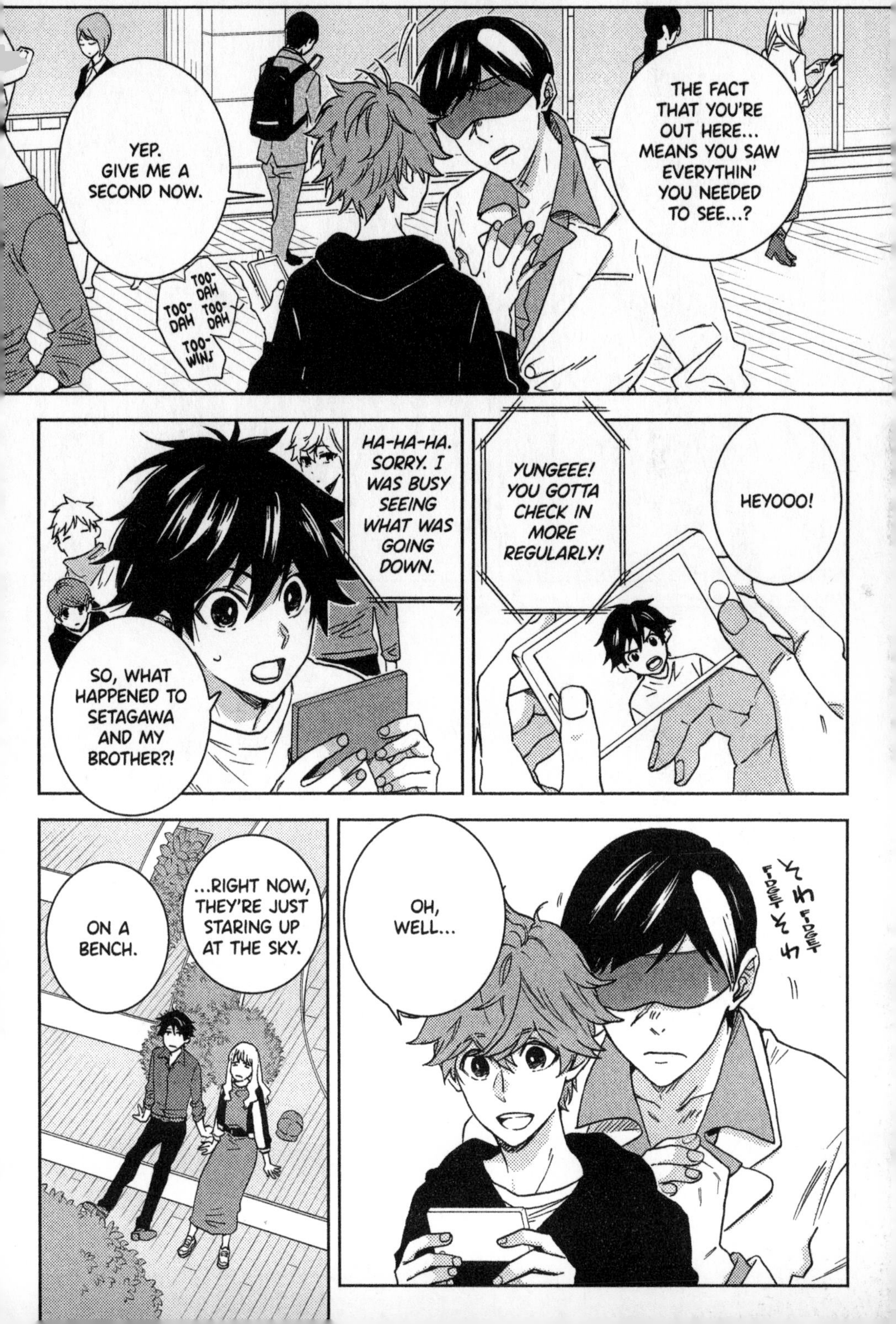
THE FACT THAT YOU'RE OUT HERE... MEANS YOU SAW EVERYTHIN' YOU NEEDED TO SEE...?
YEP. GIVE ME A SECOND NOW.
TOO-DAH TOO-DAH TOO-DAH TOO-DAH TOO-WIN♪
HEYOOO!
YUNGEEE! YOU GOTTA CHECK IN MORE REGULARLY!
HA-HA-HA. SORRY. I WAS BUSY SEEING WHAT WAS GOING DOWN.
SO, WHAT HAPPENED TO SETAGAWA AND MY BROTHER?!
そわ そわ FIDGET FIDGET
OH, WELL...
...RIGHT NOW, THEY'RE JUST STARING UP AT THE SKY.
ON A BENCH.

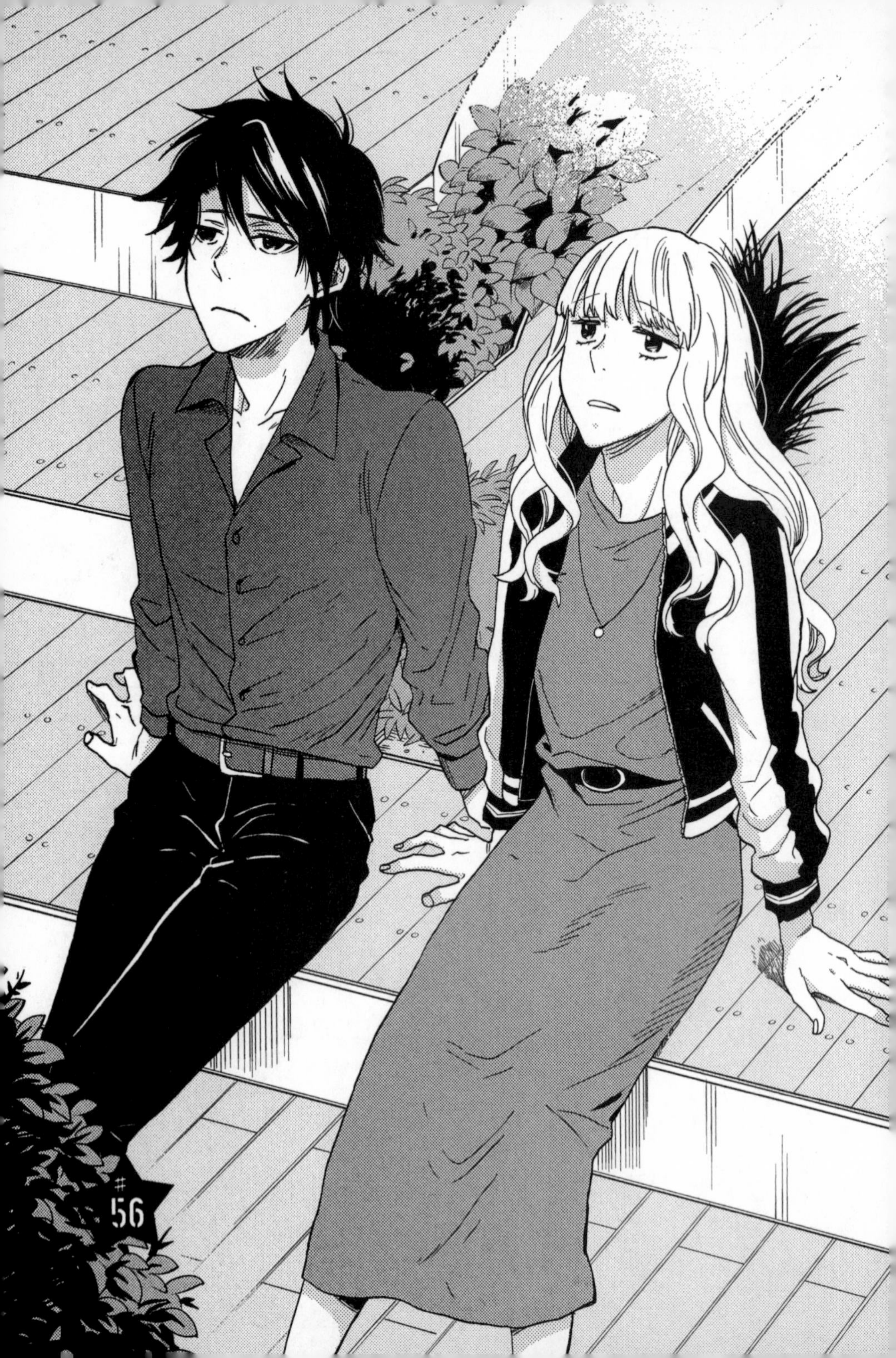
#56

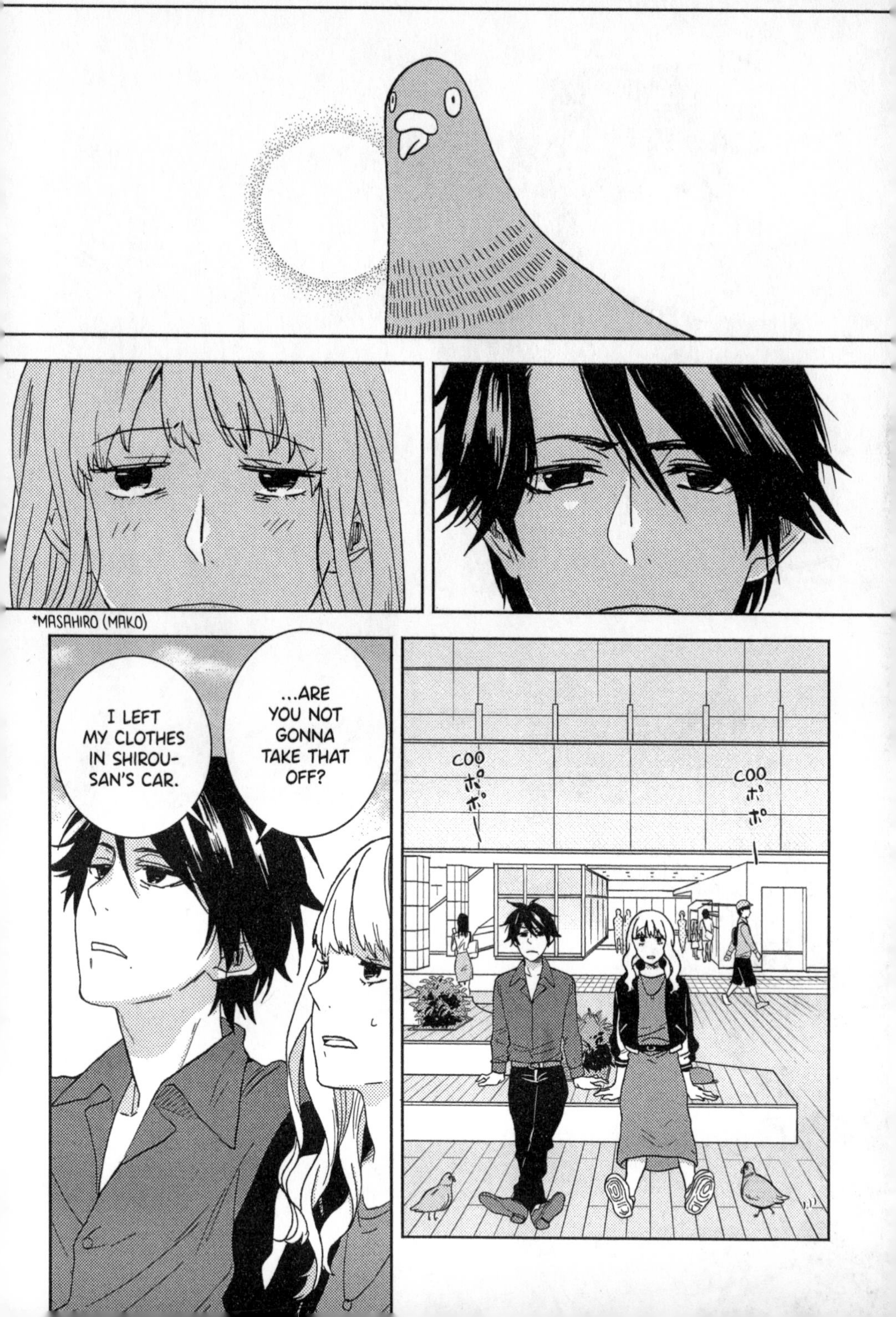
*MASAHIRO (MAKO)
COO ポポー
COO ポポー
...ARE YOU NOT GONNA TAKE THAT OFF?
I LEFT MY CLOTHES IN SHIROU-SAN'S CAR.

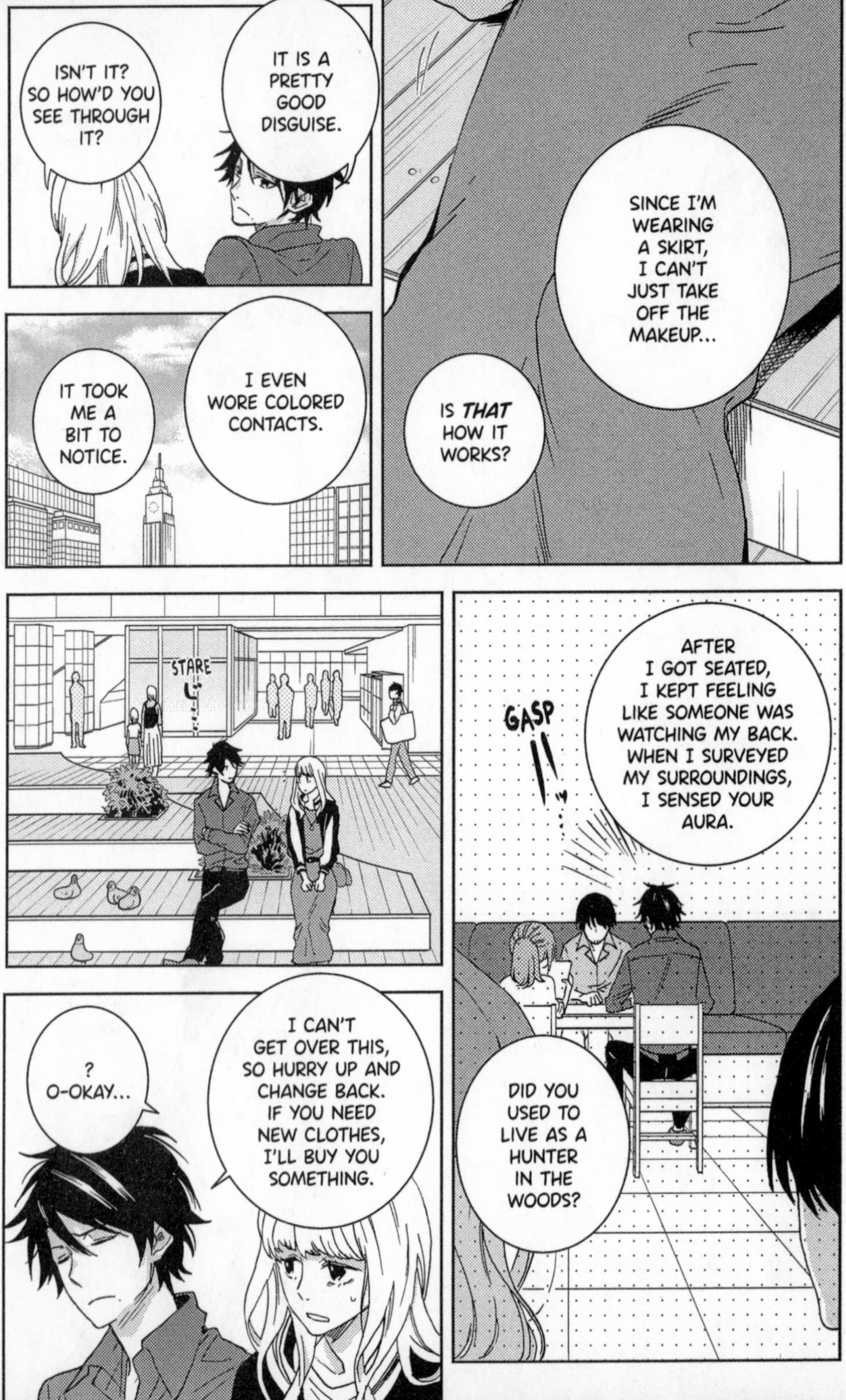
SINCE I'M WEARING A SKIRT, I CAN'T JUST TAKE OFF THE MAKEUP...
IS *THAT* HOW IT WORKS?
IT IS A PRETTY GOOD DISGUISE.
ISN'T IT? SO HOW'D YOU SEE THROUGH IT?
I EVEN WORE COLORED CONTACTS.
IT TOOK ME A BIT TO NOTICE.
AFTER I GOT SEATED, I KEPT FEELING LIKE SOMEONE WAS WATCHING MY BACK. WHEN I SURVEYED MY SURROUNDINGS, I SENSED YOUR AURA.
GASP
DID YOU USED TO LIVE AS A HUNTER IN THE WOODS?
STARE
I CAN'T GET OVER THIS, SO HURRY UP AND CHANGE BACK. IF YOU NEED NEW CLOTHES, I'LL BUY YOU SOMETHING.
? O-OKAY...

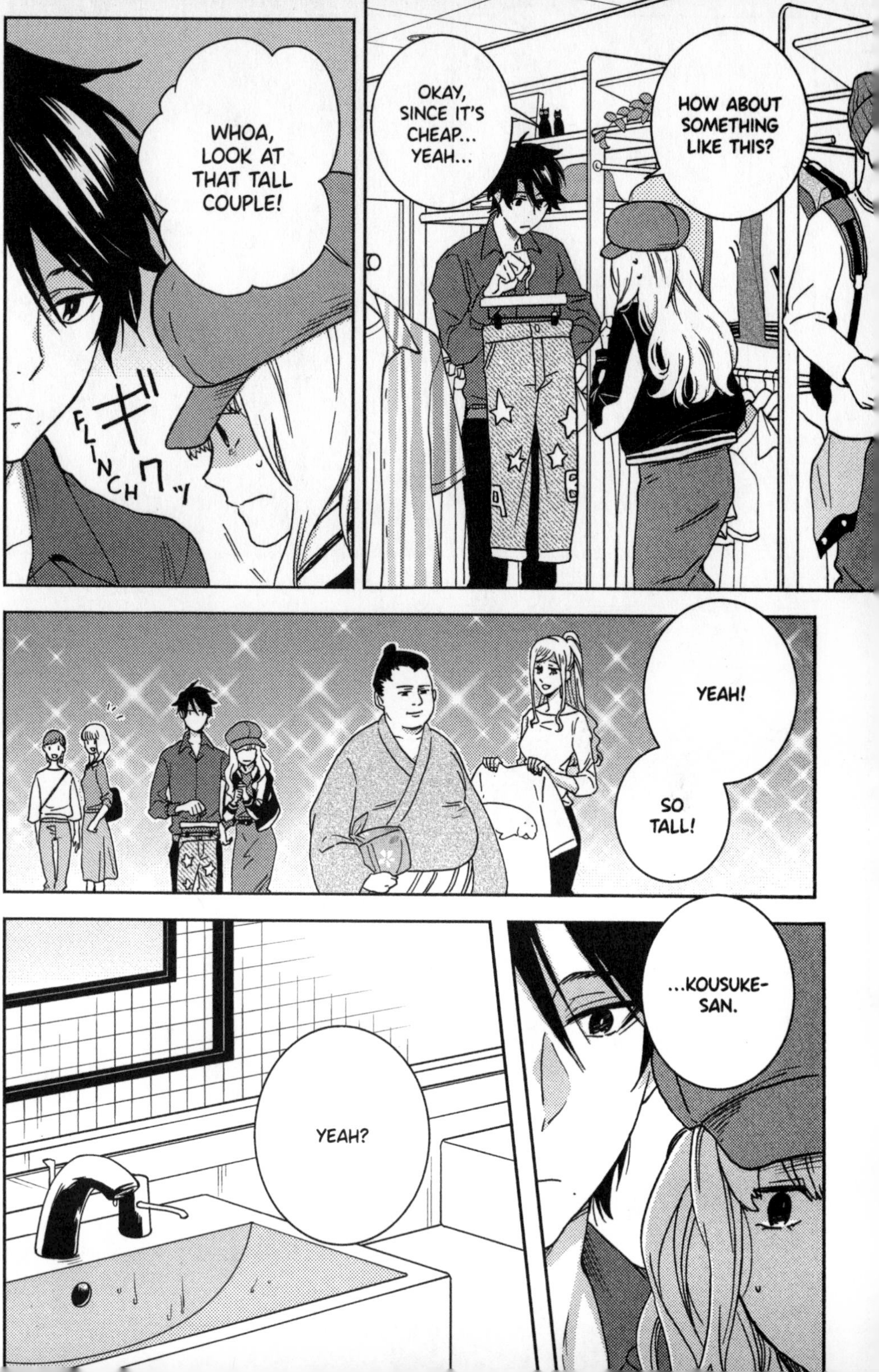
HOW ABOUT SOMETHING LIKE THIS?
OKAY, SINCE IT'S CHEAP... YEAH...
WHOA, LOOK AT THAT TALL COUPLE!
FLINCH
YEAH!
SO TALL!
...KOUSUKE-SAN.
YEAH?

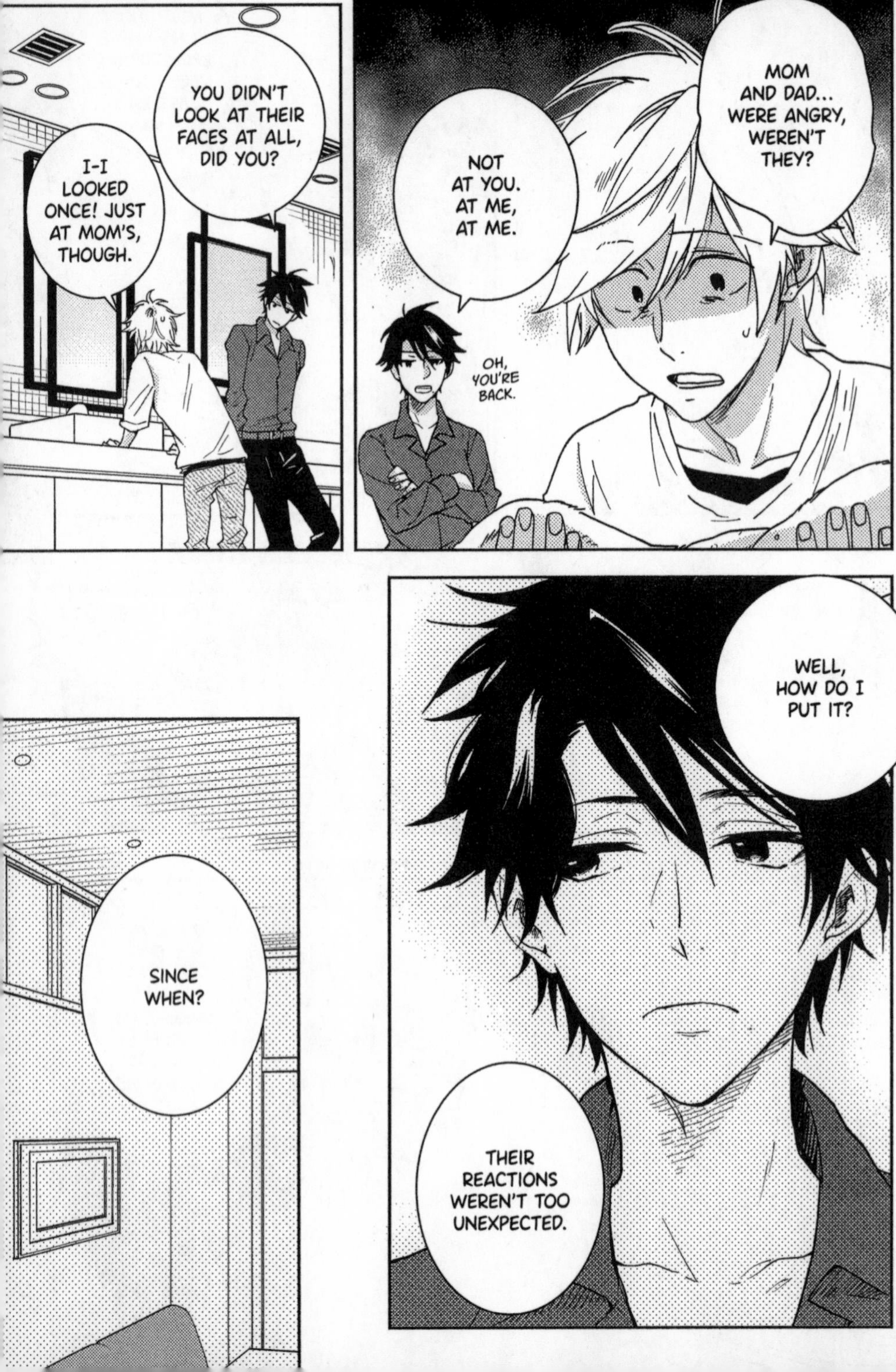
MOM AND DAD... WERE ANGRY, WEREN'T THEY?
NOT AT YOU. AT ME, AT ME.
OH, YOU'RE BACK.
YOU DIDN'T LOOK AT THEIR FACES AT ALL, DID YOU?
I-I LOOKED ONCE! JUST AT MOM'S, THOUGH.
WELL, HOW DO I PUT IT?
THEIR REACTIONS WEREN'T TOO UNEXPECTED.
SINCE WHEN?

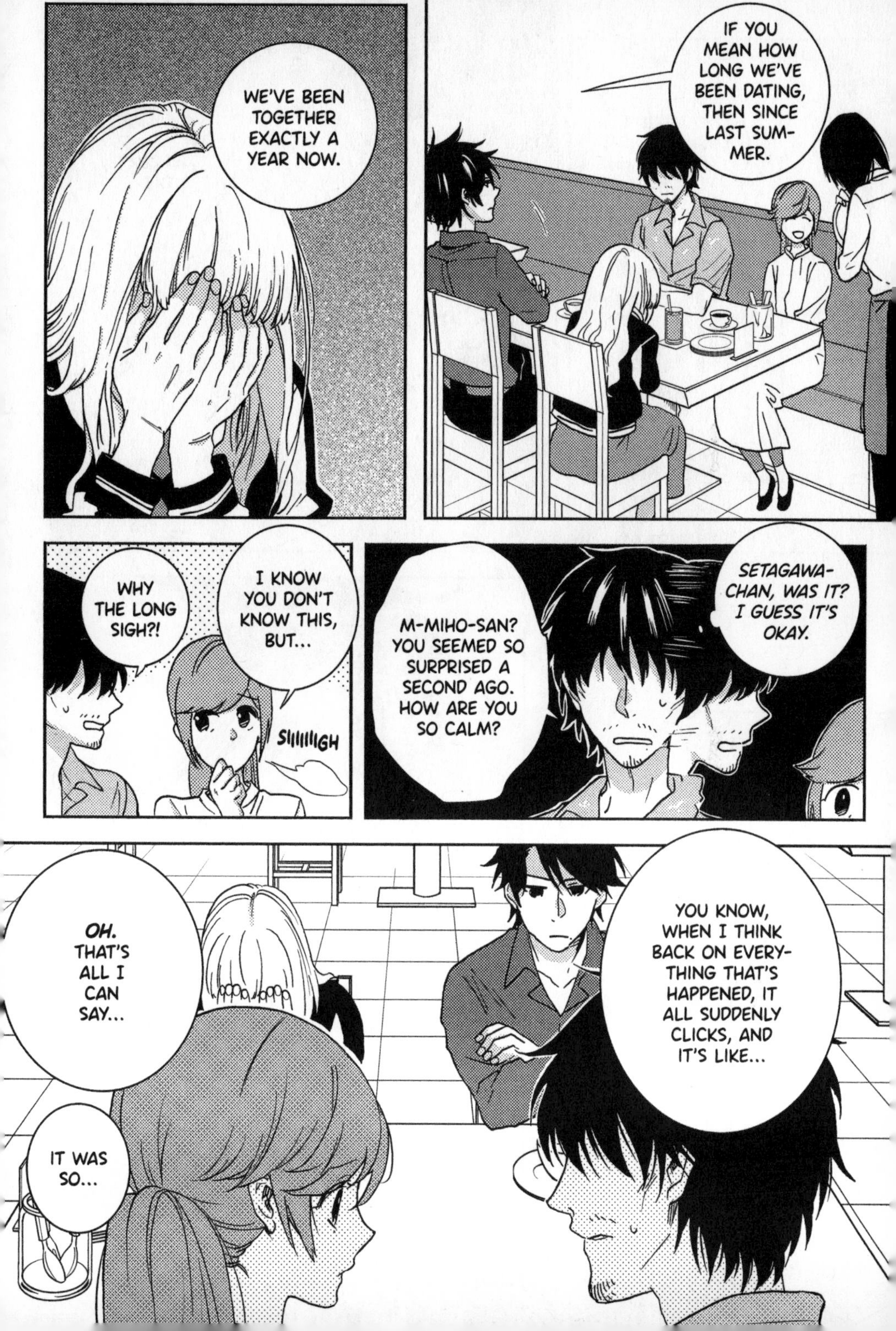
IF YOU MEAN HOW LONG WE'VE BEEN DATING, THEN SINCE LAST SUM-MER.
WE'VE BEEN TOGETHER EXACTLY A YEAR NOW.
SETAGAWA-CHAN, WAS IT? I GUESS IT'S OKAY.
M-MIHO-SAN? YOU SEEMED SO SURPRISED A SECOND AGO. HOW ARE YOU SO CALM?
I KNOW YOU DON'T KNOW THIS, BUT...
SIIIIIGH
WHY THE LONG SIGH?!
YOU KNOW, WHEN I THINK BACK ON EVERY-THING THAT'S HAPPENED, IT ALL SUDDENLY CLICKS, AND IT'S LIKE...
OH. THAT'S ALL I CAN SAY...
IT WAS SO...

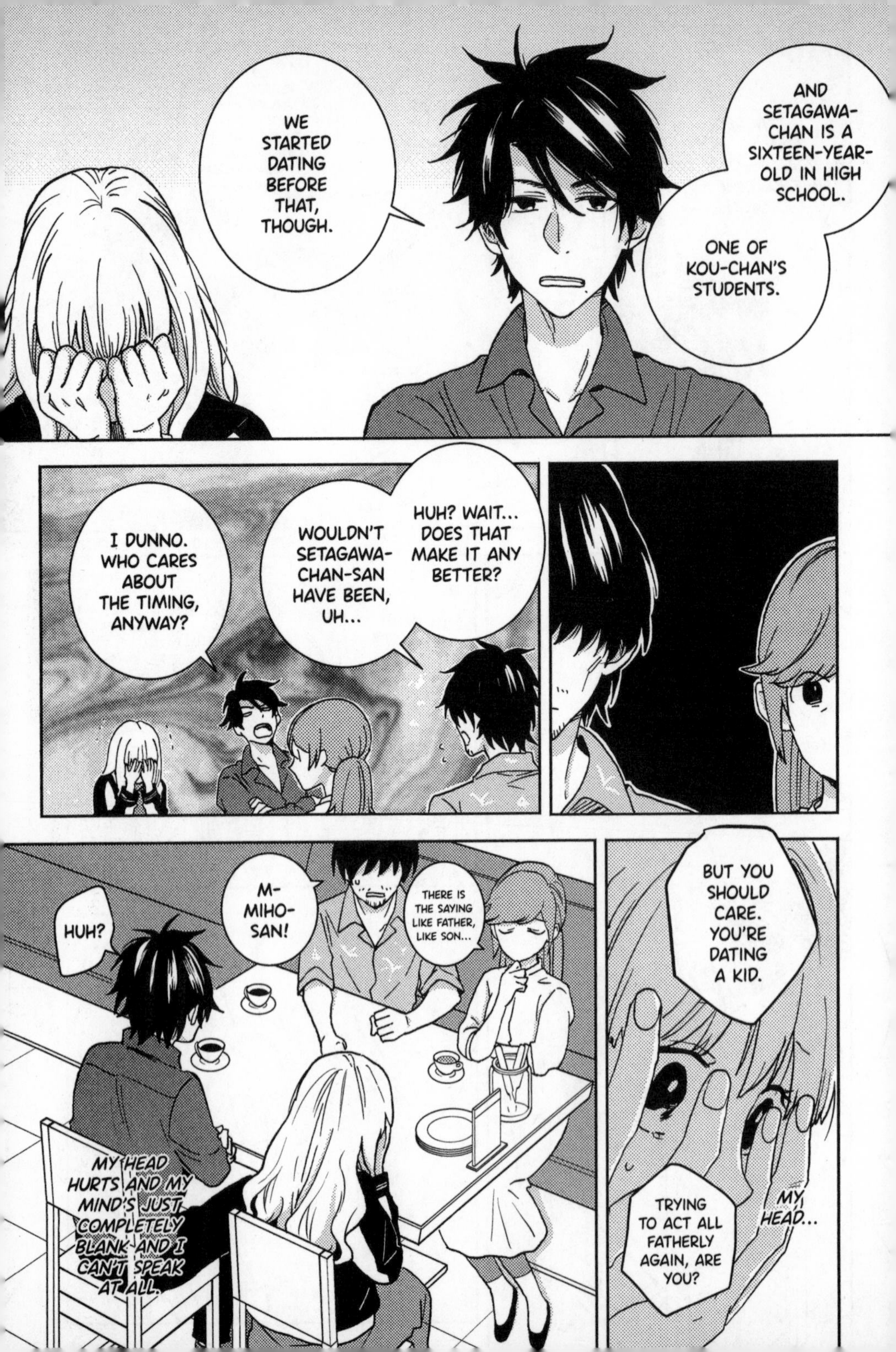
AND SETAGAWA-CHAN IS A SIXTEEN-YEAR-OLD IN HIGH SCHOOL.
ONE OF KOU-CHAN'S STUDENTS.
WE STARTED DATING BEFORE THAT, THOUGH.
HUH? WAIT... DOES THAT MAKE IT ANY BETTER?
WOULDN'T SETAGAWA-CHAN-SAN HAVE BEEN, UH...
I DUNNO. WHO CARES ABOUT THE TIMING, ANYWAY?
BUT YOU SHOULD CARE. YOU'RE DATING A KID.
MY HEAD...
TRYING TO ACT ALL FATHERLY AGAIN, ARE YOU?
THERE IS THE SAYING LIKE FATHER, LIKE SON...
M-MIHO-SAN!
HUH?
MY HEAD HURTS AND MY MIND'S JUST COMPLETELY BLANK AND I CAN'T SPEAK AT ALL.

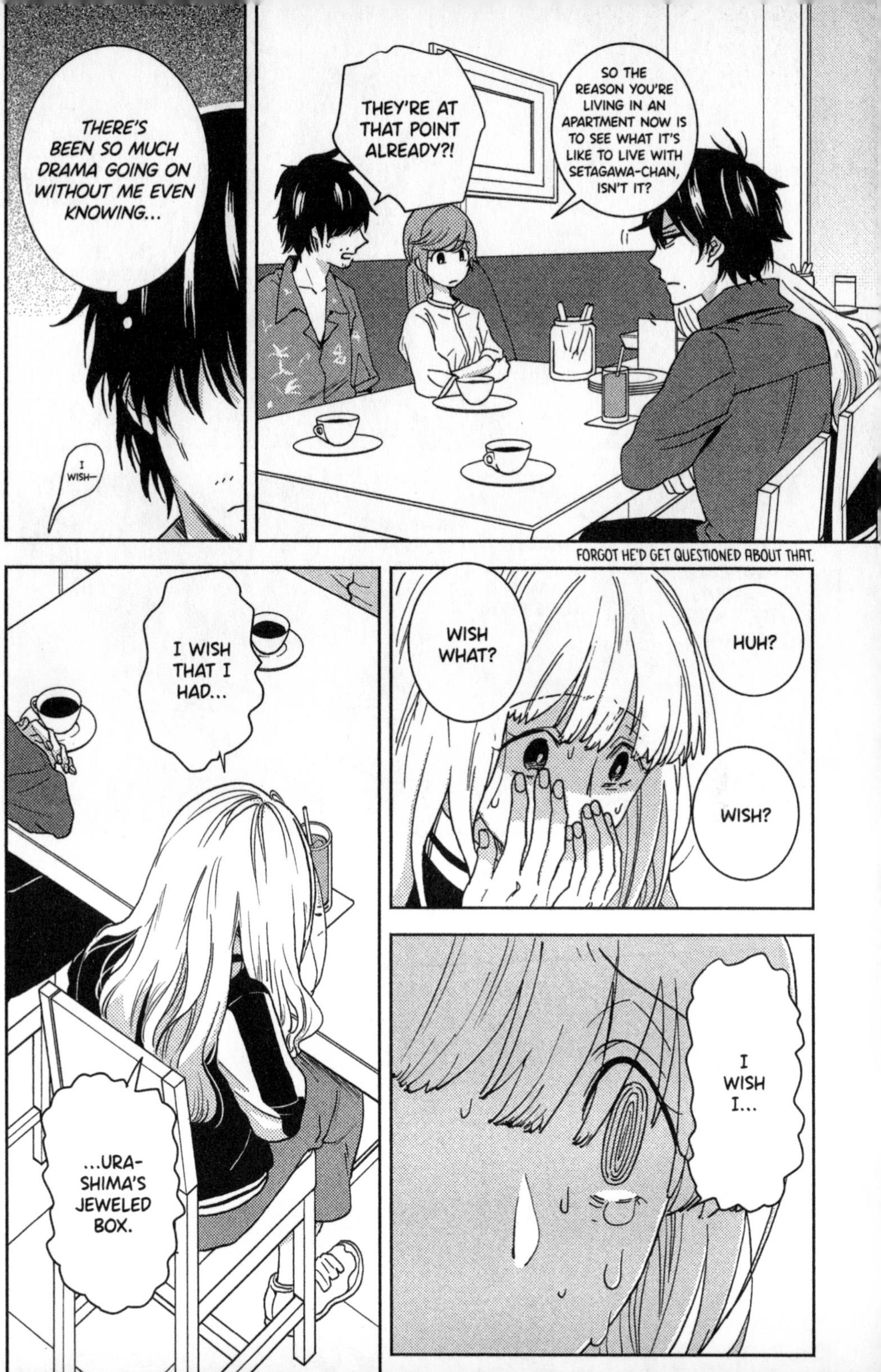
SO THE REASON YOU'RE LIVING IN AN APARTMENT NOW IS TO SEE WHAT IT'S LIKE TO LIVE WITH SETAGAWA-CHAN, ISN'T IT?
THEY'RE AT THAT POINT ALREADY?!
THERE'S BEEN SO MUCH DRAMA GOING ON WITHOUT ME EVEN KNOWING...
I WISH—
FORGOT HE'D GET QUESTIONED ABOUT THAT.
HUH?
WISH?
WISH WHAT?
I WISH I...
I WISH THAT I HAD...
...URA-SHIMA'S JEWELED BOX.

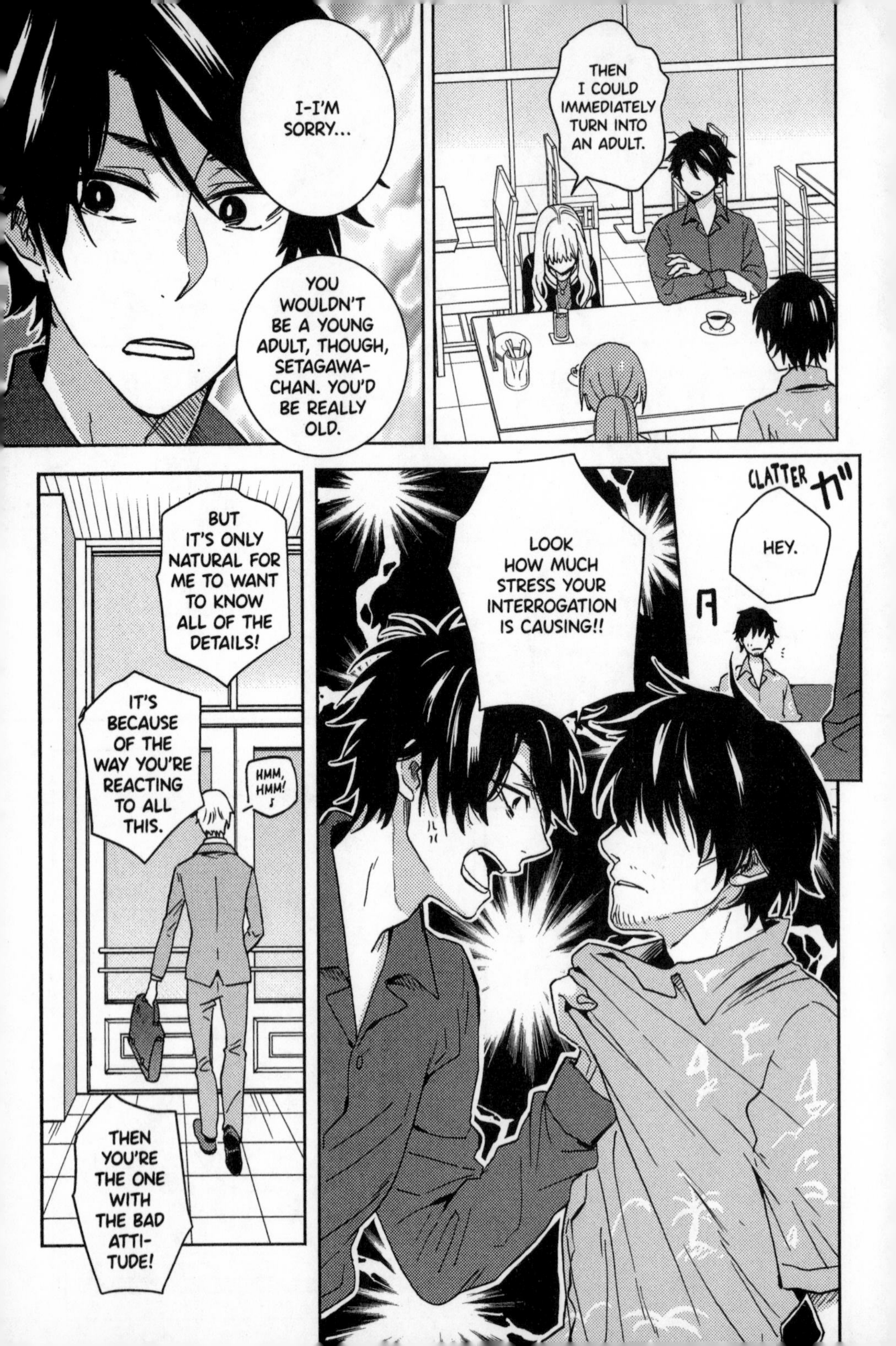
THEN I COULD IMMEDIATELY TURN INTO AN ADULT.
I-I'M SORRY...
YOU WOULDN'T BE A YOUNG ADULT, THOUGH, SETAGAWA-CHAN. YOU'D BE REALLY OLD.
CLATTER
ガ
HEY.
LOOK HOW MUCH STRESS YOUR INTERROGATION IS CAUSING!!
BUT IT'S ONLY NATURAL FOR ME TO WANT TO KNOW ALL OF THE DETAILS!
IT'S BECAUSE OF THE WAY YOU'RE REACTING TO ALL THIS.
HMM, HMM! ♪
THEN YOU'RE THE ONE WITH THE BAD ATTI-TUDE!

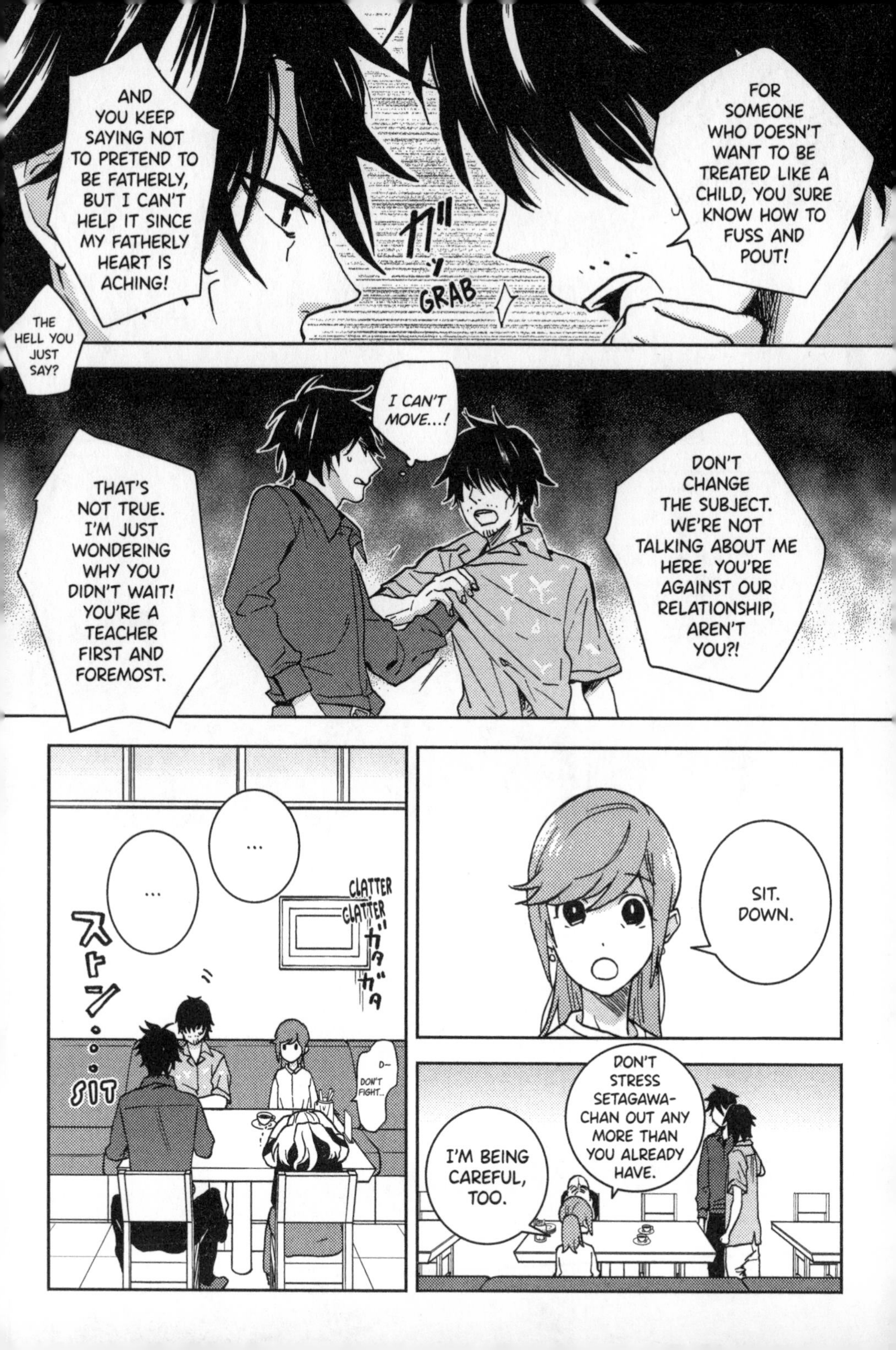
FOR SOMEONE WHO DOESN'T WANT TO BE TREATED LIKE A CHILD, YOU SURE KNOW HOW TO FUSS AND POUT!
ガッ
GRAB
AND YOU KEEP SAYING NOT TO PRETEND TO BE FATHERLY, BUT I CAN'T HELP IT SINCE MY FATHERLY HEART IS ACHING!
THE HELL YOU JUST SAY?
DON'T CHANGE THE SUBJECT. WE'RE NOT TALKING ABOUT ME HERE. YOU'RE AGAINST OUR RELATIONSHIP, AREN'T YOU?!
I CAN'T MOVE...!
THAT'S NOT TRUE. I'M JUST WONDERING WHY YOU DIDN'T WAIT! YOU'RE A TEACHER FIRST AND FOREMOST.
SIT. DOWN.
DON'T STRESS SETAGAWA-CHAN OUT ANY MORE THAN YOU ALREADY HAVE.
I'M BEING CAREFUL, TOO.
...
...
CLATTER CLATTER
ガタガタ
ストン。。。
SIT
D– DON'T FIGHT...

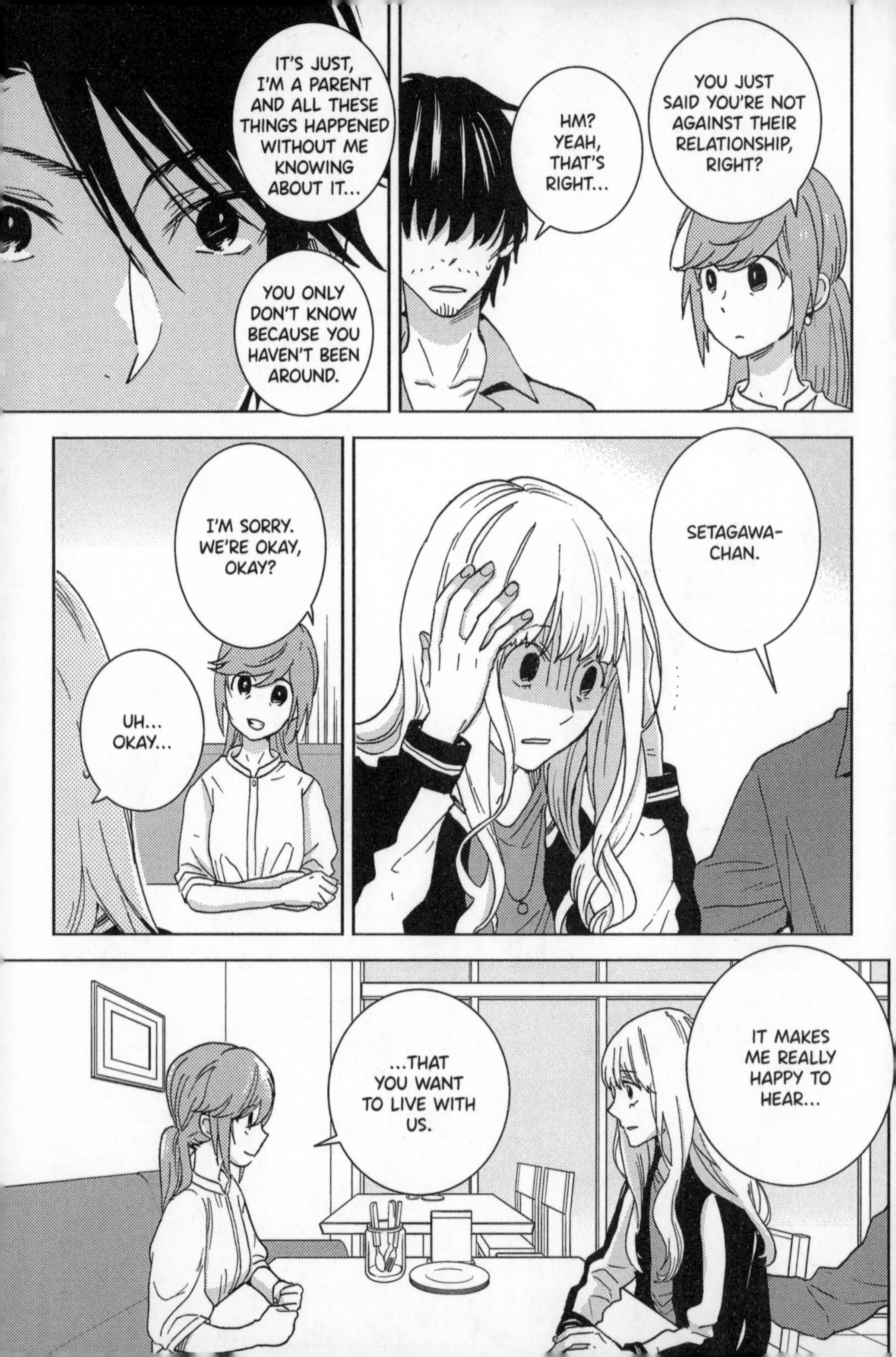
YOU JUST SAID YOU'RE NOT AGAINST THEIR RELATIONSHIP, RIGHT?
HM? YEAH, THAT'S RIGHT...
IT'S JUST, I'M A PARENT AND ALL THESE THINGS HAPPENED WITHOUT ME KNOWING ABOUT IT...
YOU ONLY DON'T KNOW BECAUSE YOU HAVEN'T BEEN AROUND.
SETAGAWA-CHAN.
I'M SORRY. WE'RE OKAY, OKAY?
UH... OKAY...
IT MAKES ME REALLY HAPPY TO HEAR...
...THAT YOU WANT TO LIVE WITH US.

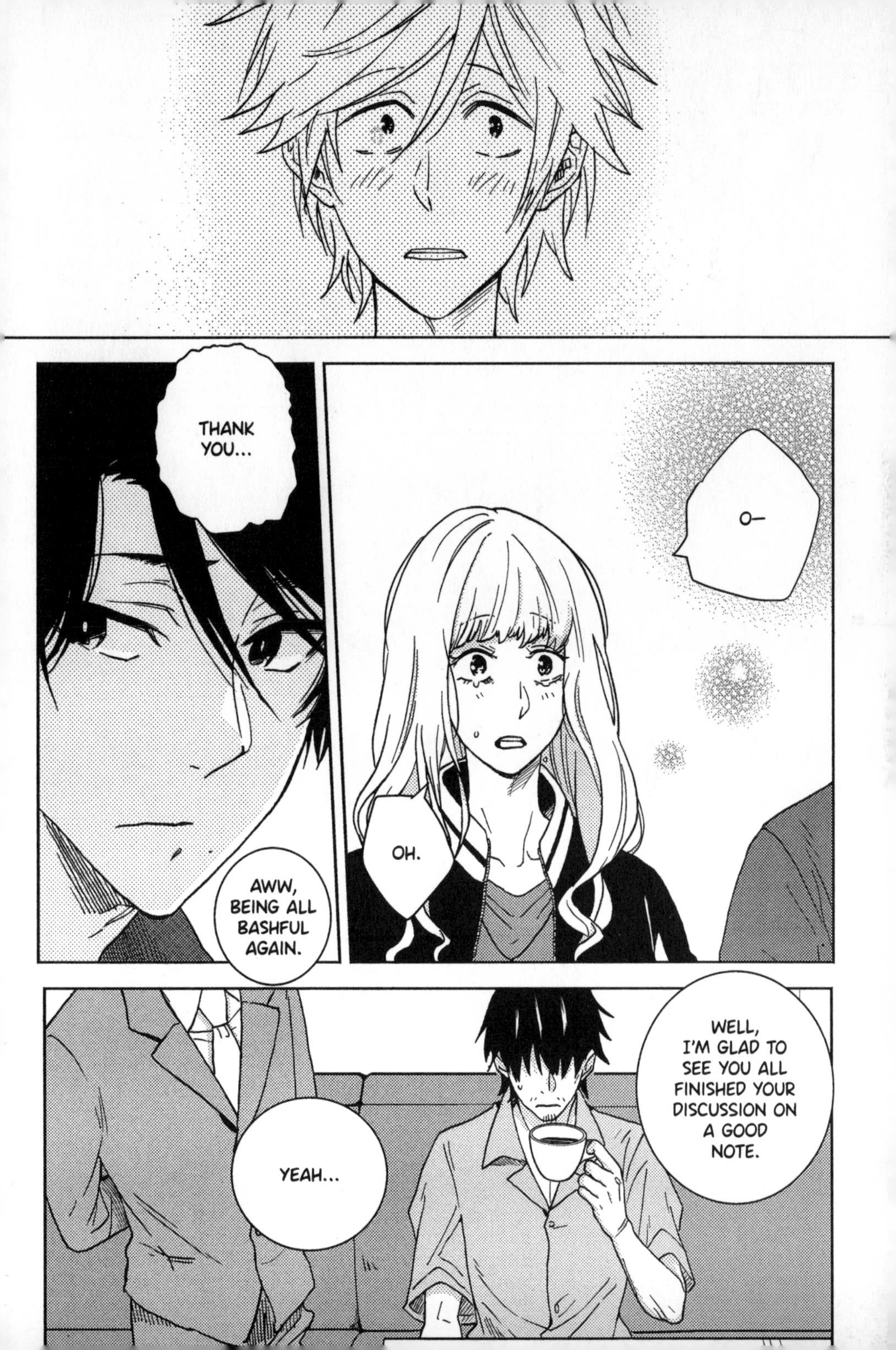
O—
OH.
THANK YOU...
AWW, BEING ALL BASHFUL AGAIN.
WELL, I'M GLAD TO SEE YOU ALL FINISHED YOUR DISCUSSION ON A GOOD NOTE.
YEAH...

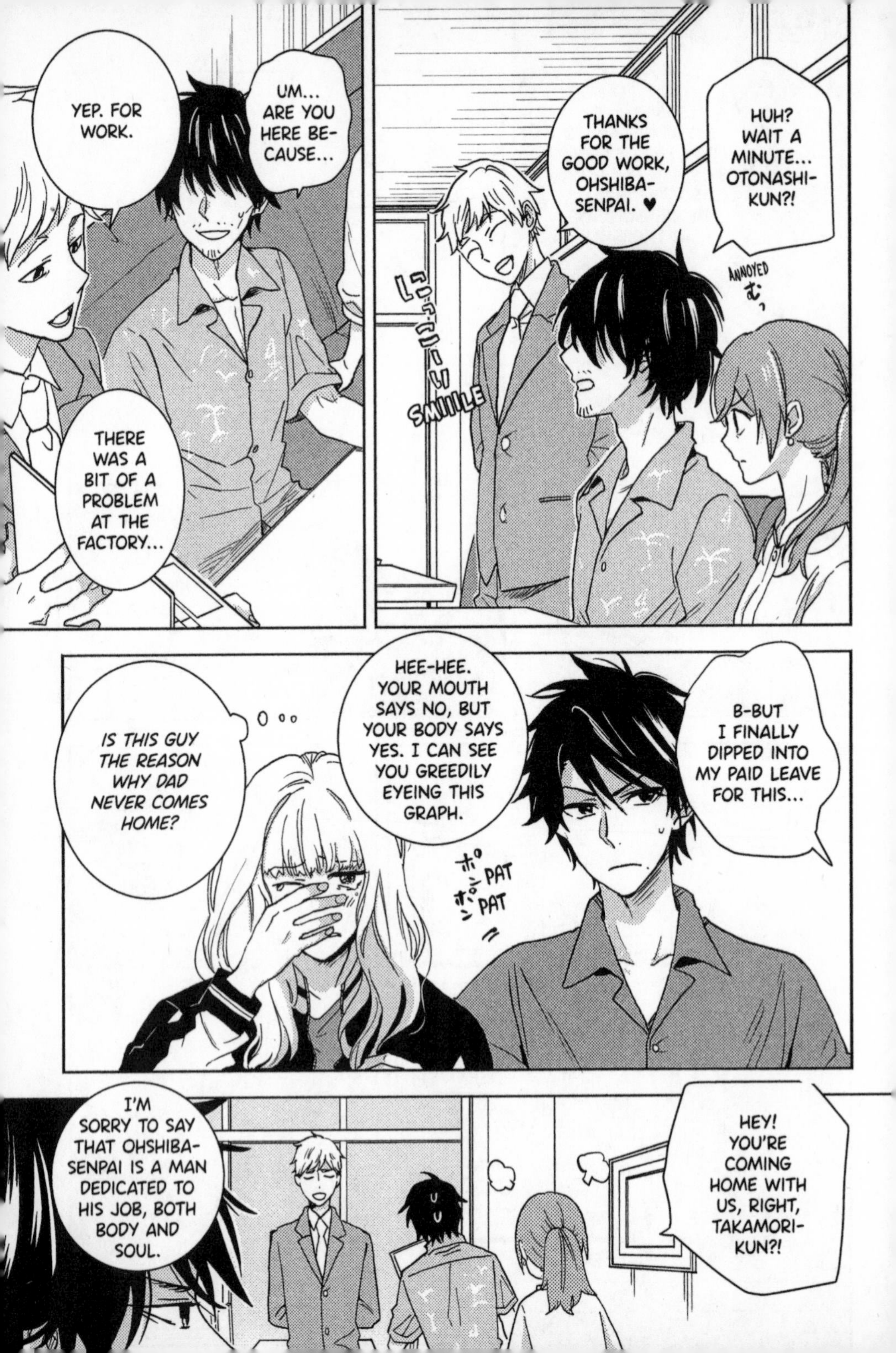
HUH? WAIT A MINUTE... OTONASHI-KUN?!
ANNOYED
THANKS FOR THE GOOD WORK, OHSHIBA-SENPAI. ♥
SMIIIILE
UM... ARE YOU HERE BE-CAUSE...
YEP. FOR WORK.
THERE WAS A BIT OF A PROBLEM AT THE FACTORY...
B-BUT I FINALLY DIPPED INTO MY PAID LEAVE FOR THIS...
HEE-HEE. YOUR MOUTH SAYS NO, BUT YOUR BODY SAYS YES. I CAN SEE YOU GREEDILY EYEING THIS GRAPH.
PAT PAT
IS THIS GUY THE REASON WHY DAD NEVER COMES HOME?
HEY! YOU'RE COMING HOME WITH US, RIGHT, TAKAMORI-KUN?!
I'M SORRY TO SAY THAT OHSHIBA-SENPAI IS A MAN DEDICATED TO HIS JOB, BOTH BODY AND SOUL.

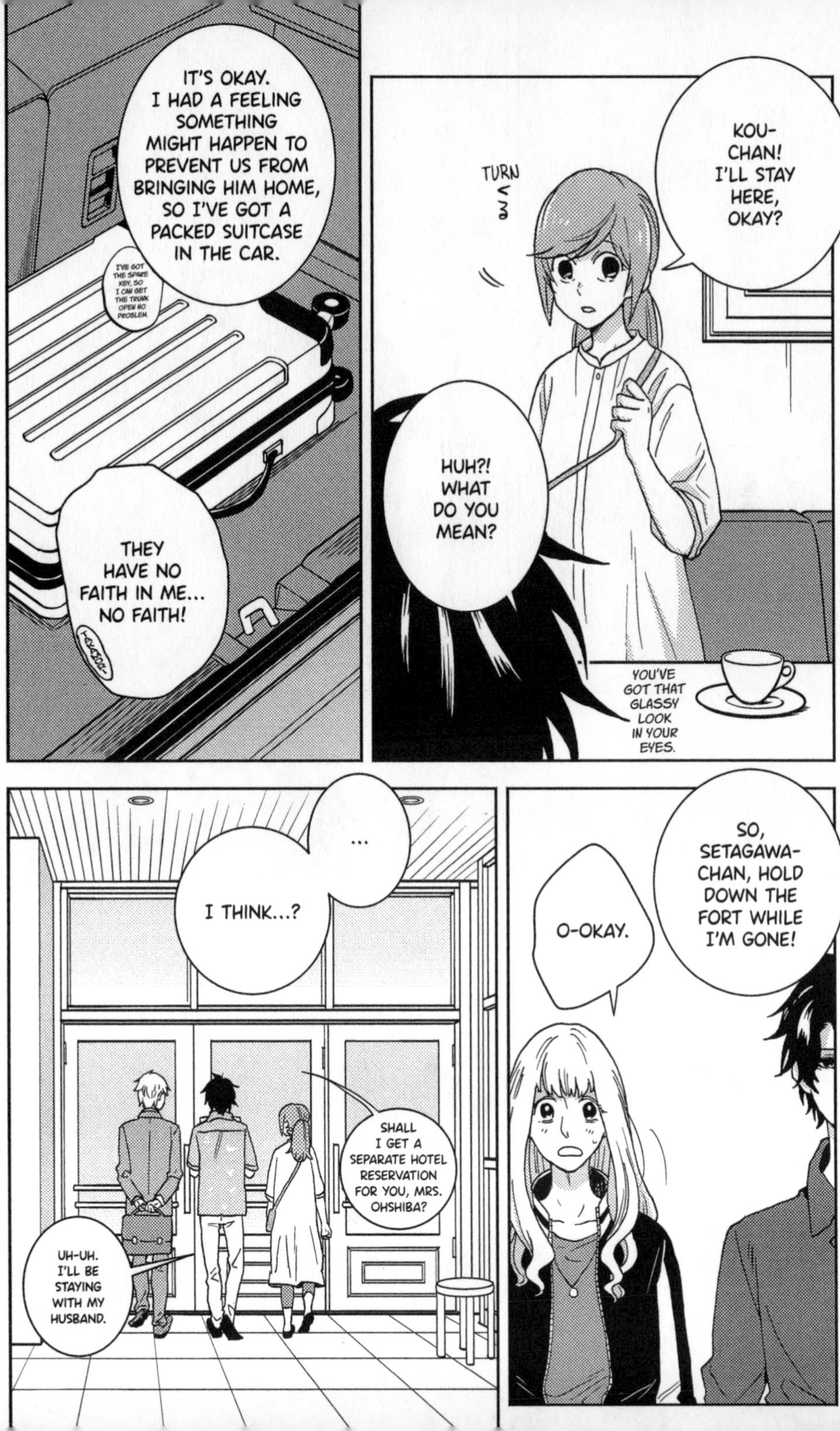
KOU-CHAN! I'LL STAY HERE, OKAY?
TURN
HUH?! WHAT DO YOU MEAN?
YOU'VE GOT THAT GLASSY LOOK IN YOUR EYES.
IT'S OKAY. I HAD A FEELING SOMETHING MIGHT HAPPEN TO PREVENT US FROM BRINGING HIM HOME, SO I'VE GOT A PACKED SUITCASE IN THE CAR.
I'VE GOT THE SPARE KEY, SO I CAN GET THE TRUNK OPEN NO PROBLEM.
THEY HAVE NO FAITH IN ME... NO FAITH!
SO, SETAGAWA-CHAN, HOLD DOWN THE FORT WHILE I'M GONE!
O-OKAY.
...
I THINK...?
SHALL I GET A SEPARATE HOTEL RESERVATION FOR YOU, MRS. OHSHIBA?
UH-UH. I'LL BE STAYING WITH MY HUSBAND.

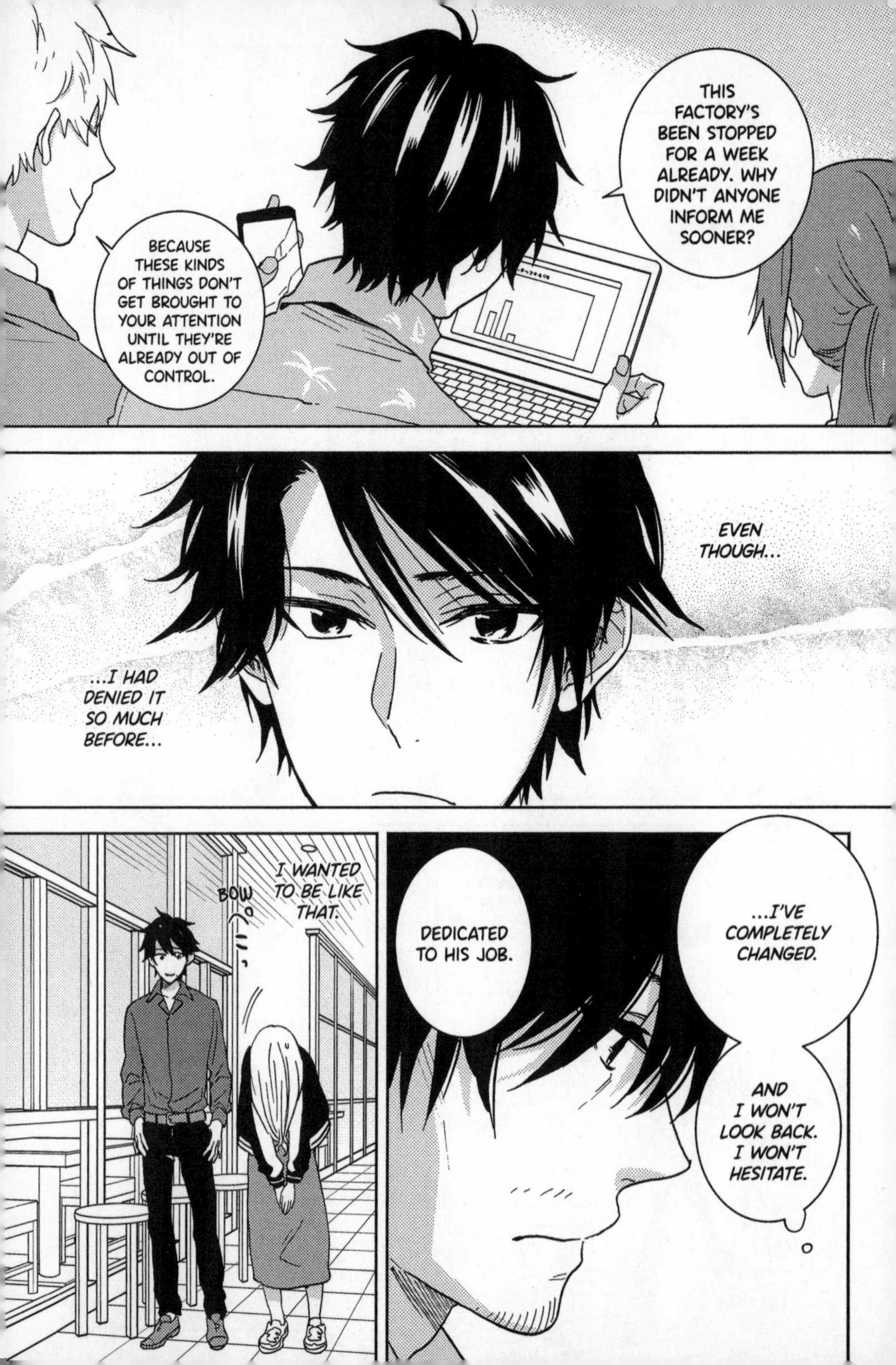
THIS FACTORY'S BEEN STOPPED FOR A WEEK ALREADY. WHY DIDN'T ANYONE INFORM ME SOONER?
BECAUSE THESE KINDS OF THINGS DON'T GET BROUGHT TO YOUR ATTENTION UNTIL THEY'RE ALREADY OUT OF CONTROL.
EVEN THOUGH...
...I HAD DENIED IT SO MUCH BEFORE...
...I'VE COMPLETELY CHANGED.
DEDICATED TO HIS JOB.
AND I WON'T LOOK BACK. I WON'T HESITATE.
I WANTED TO BE LIKE THAT.
BOW

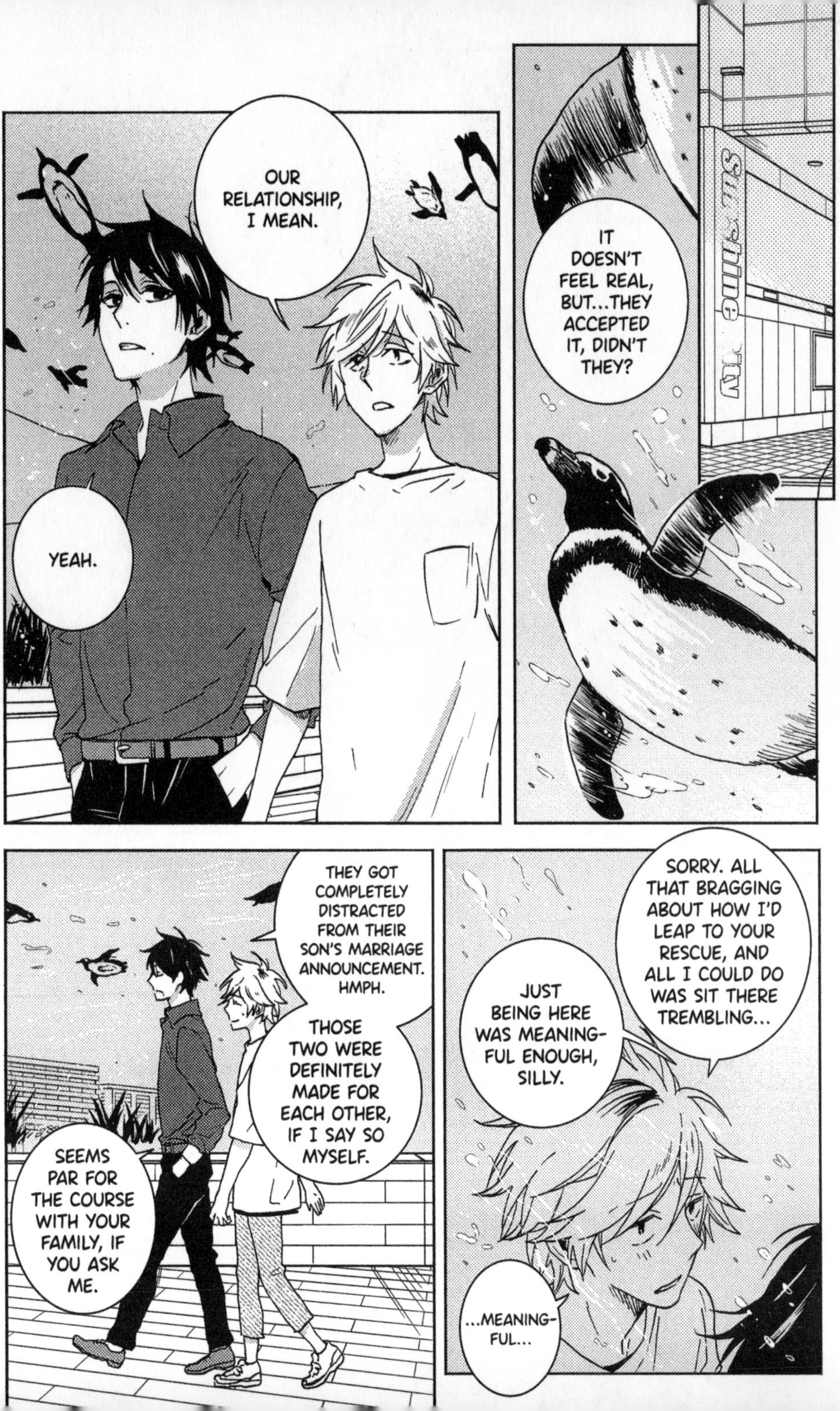
IT DOESN'T FEEL REAL, BUT...THEY ACCEPTED IT, DIDN'T THEY?
OUR RELATIONSHIP, I MEAN.
YEAH.
SORRY. ALL THAT BRAGGING ABOUT HOW I'D LEAP TO YOUR RESCUE, AND ALL I COULD DO WAS SIT THERE TREMBLING...
JUST BEING HERE WAS MEANING-FUL ENOUGH, SILLY.
...MEANING-FUL...
THEY GOT COMPLETELY DISTRACTED FROM THEIR SON'S MARRIAGE ANNOUNCEMENT. HMPH.
THOSE TWO WERE DEFINITELY MADE FOR EACH OTHER, IF I SAY SO MYSELF.
SEEMS PAR FOR THE COURSE WITH YOUR FAMILY, IF YOU ASK ME.

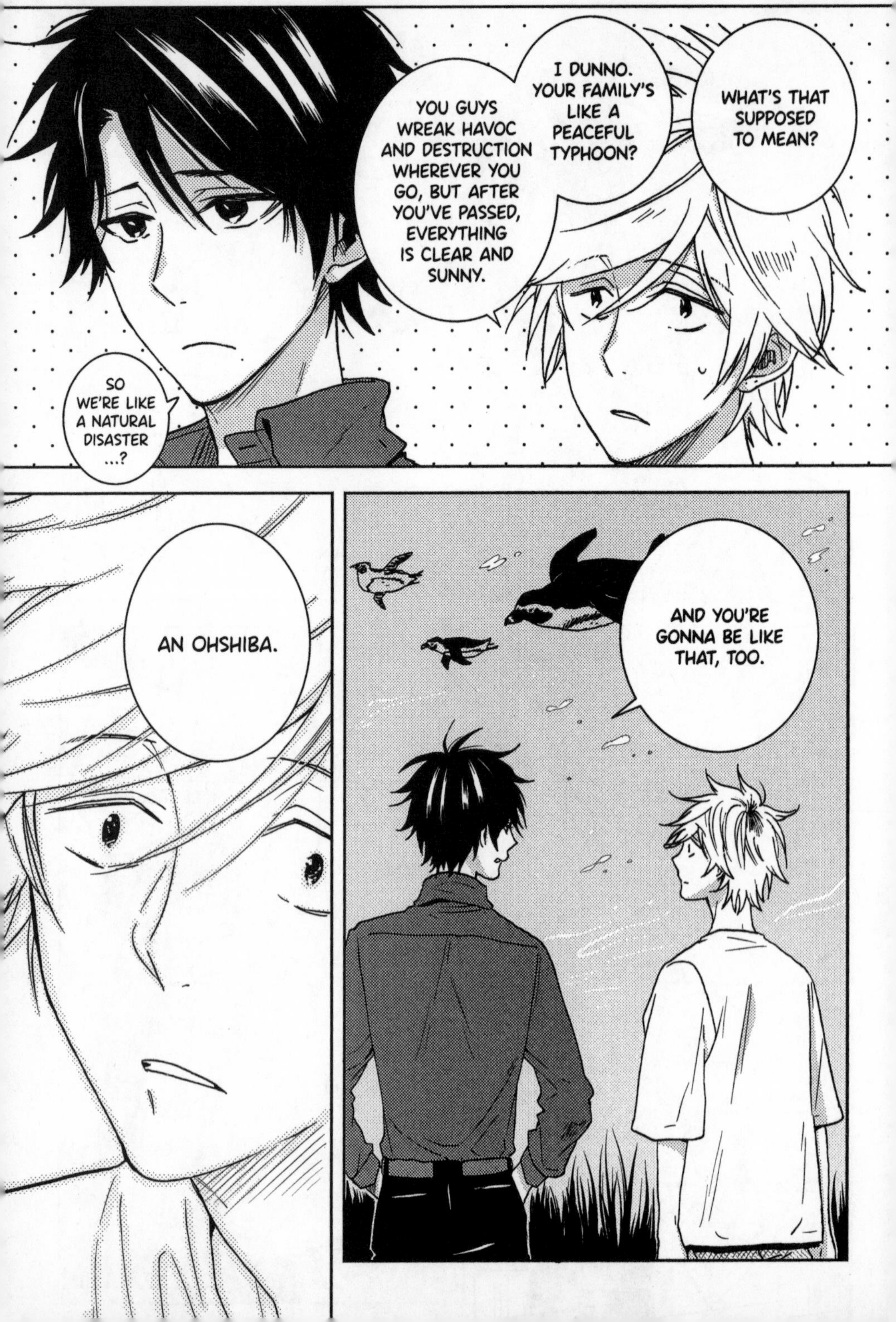
WHAT'S THAT SUPPOSED TO MEAN?
I DUNNO. YOUR FAMILY'S LIKE A PEACEFUL TYPHOON?
YOU GUYS WREAK HAVOC AND DESTRUCTION WHEREVER YOU GO, BUT AFTER YOU'VE PASSED, EVERYTHING IS CLEAR AND SUNNY.
SO WE'RE LIKE A NATURAL DISASTER ...?
AND YOU'RE GONNA BE LIKE THAT, TOO.
AN OHSHIBA.

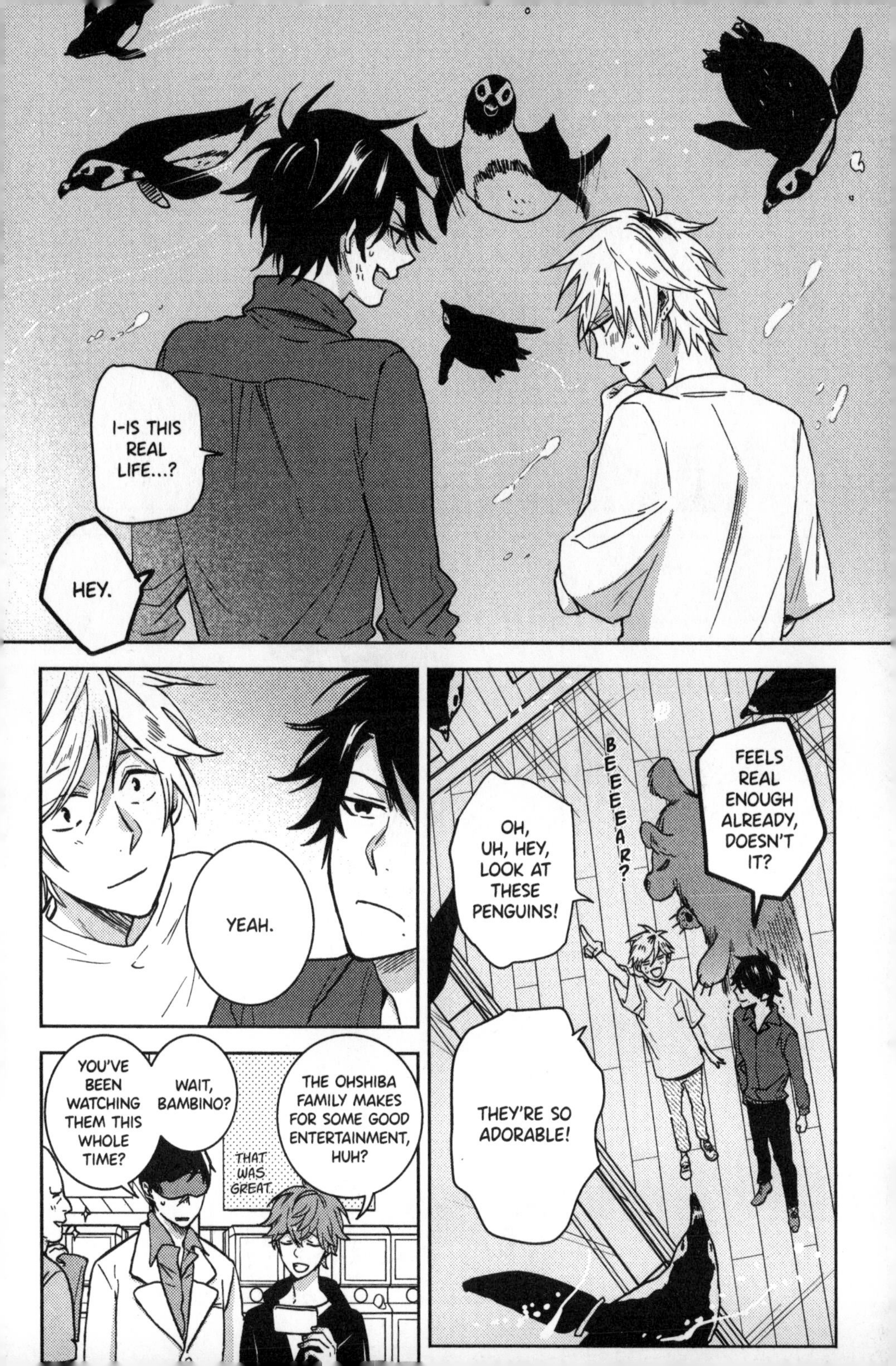
I-IS THIS REAL LIFE...?
HEY.
FEELS REAL ENOUGH ALREADY, DOESN'T IT?
BEEEEAR?
OH, UH, HEY, LOOK AT THESE PENGUINS!
THEY'RE SO ADORABLE!
YEAH.
THE OHSHIBA FAMILY MAKES FOR SOME GOOD ENTERTAINMENT, HUH?
THAT WAS GREAT.
WAIT, BAMBINO?
YOU'VE BEEN WATCHING THEM THIS WHOLE TIME?

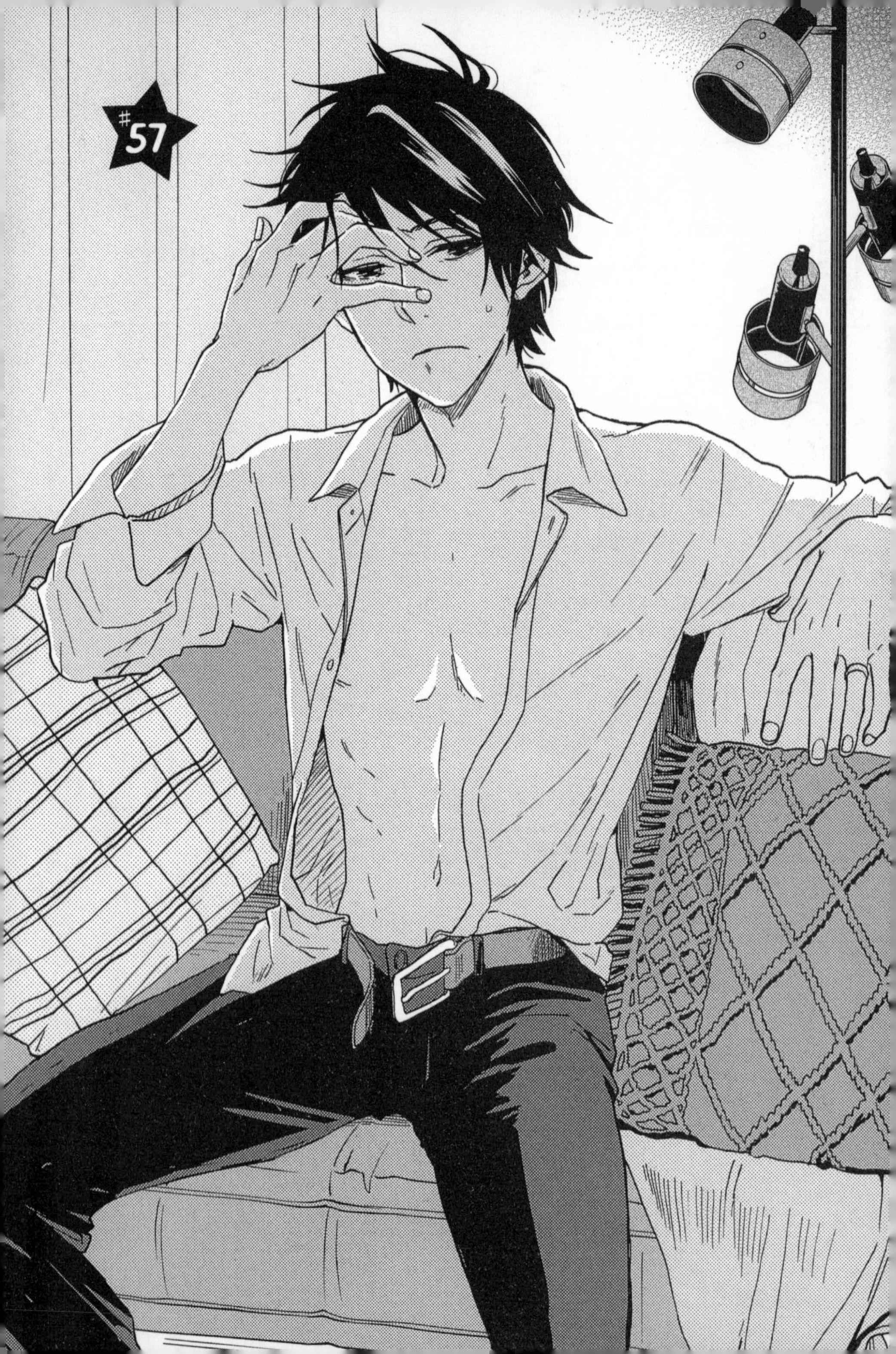
#57

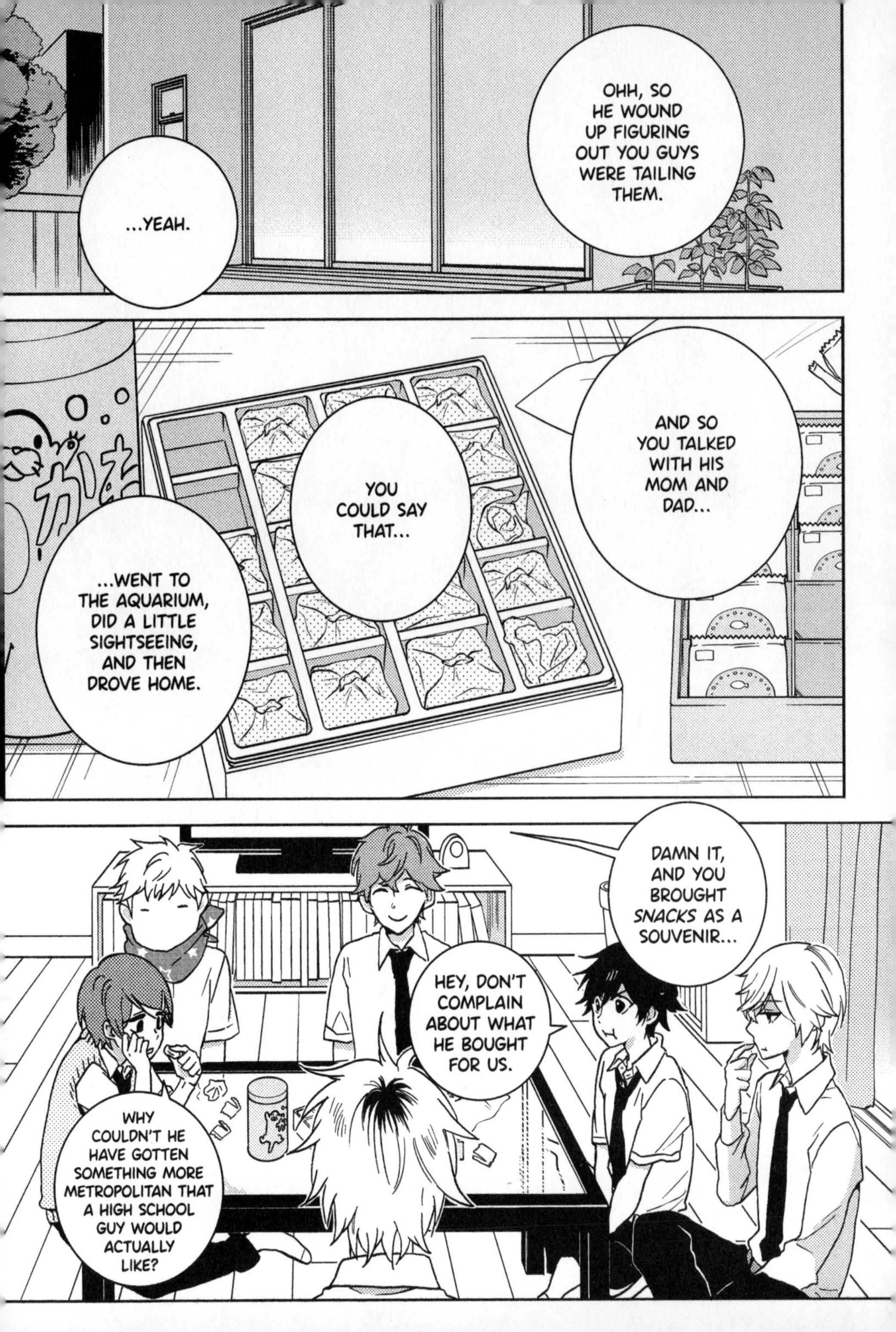
OHH, SO HE WOUND UP FIGURING OUT YOU GUYS WERE TAILING THEM.
...YEAH.
AND SO YOU TALKED WITH HIS MOM AND DAD...
YOU COULD SAY THAT...
...WENT TO THE AQUARIUM, DID A LITTLE SIGHTSEEING, AND THEN DROVE HOME.
DAMN IT, AND YOU BROUGHT *SNACKS* AS A SOUVENIR...
HEY, DON'T COMPLAIN ABOUT WHAT HE BOUGHT FOR US.
WHY COULDN'T HE HAVE GOTTEN SOMETHING MORE METROPOLITAN THAT A HIGH SCHOOL GUY WOULD ACTUALLY LIKE?

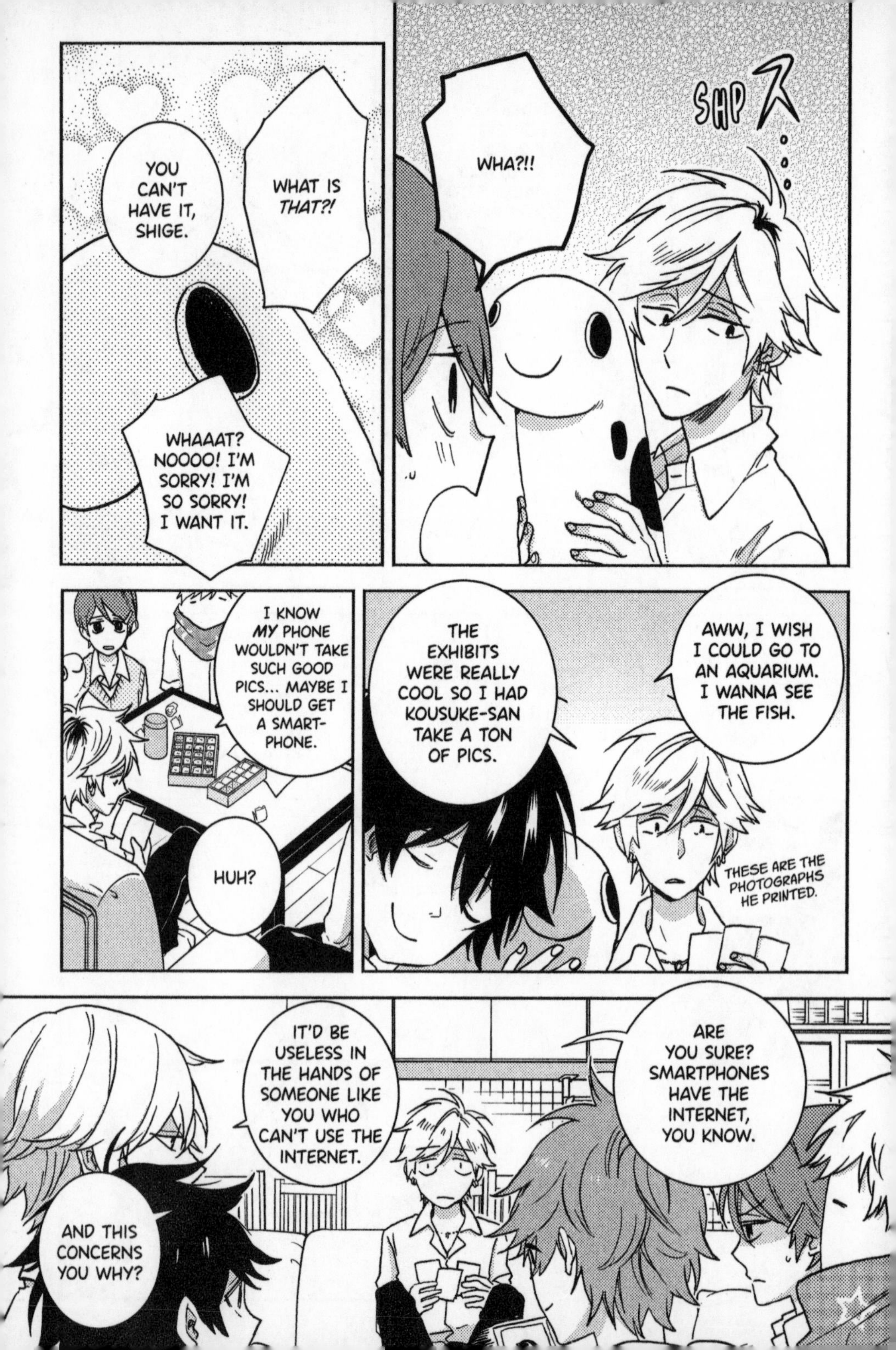
SHP ス
WHA?!!
WHAT IS THAT?!
YOU CAN'T HAVE IT, SHIGE.
WHAAAT? NOOOO! I'M SORRY! I'M SO SORRY! I WANT IT.
AWW, I WISH I COULD GO TO AN AQUARIUM. I WANNA SEE THE FISH.
THE EXHIBITS WERE REALLY COOL SO I HAD KOUSUKE-SAN TAKE A TON OF PICS.
THESE ARE THE PHOTOGRAPHS HE PRINTED.
I KNOW MY PHONE WOULDN'T TAKE SUCH GOOD PICS... MAYBE I SHOULD GET A SMART-PHONE.
HUH?
ARE YOU SURE? SMARTPHONES HAVE THE INTERNET, YOU KNOW.
IT'D BE USELESS IN THE HANDS OF SOMEONE LIKE YOU WHO CAN'T USE THE INTERNET.
AND THIS CONCERNS YOU WHY?

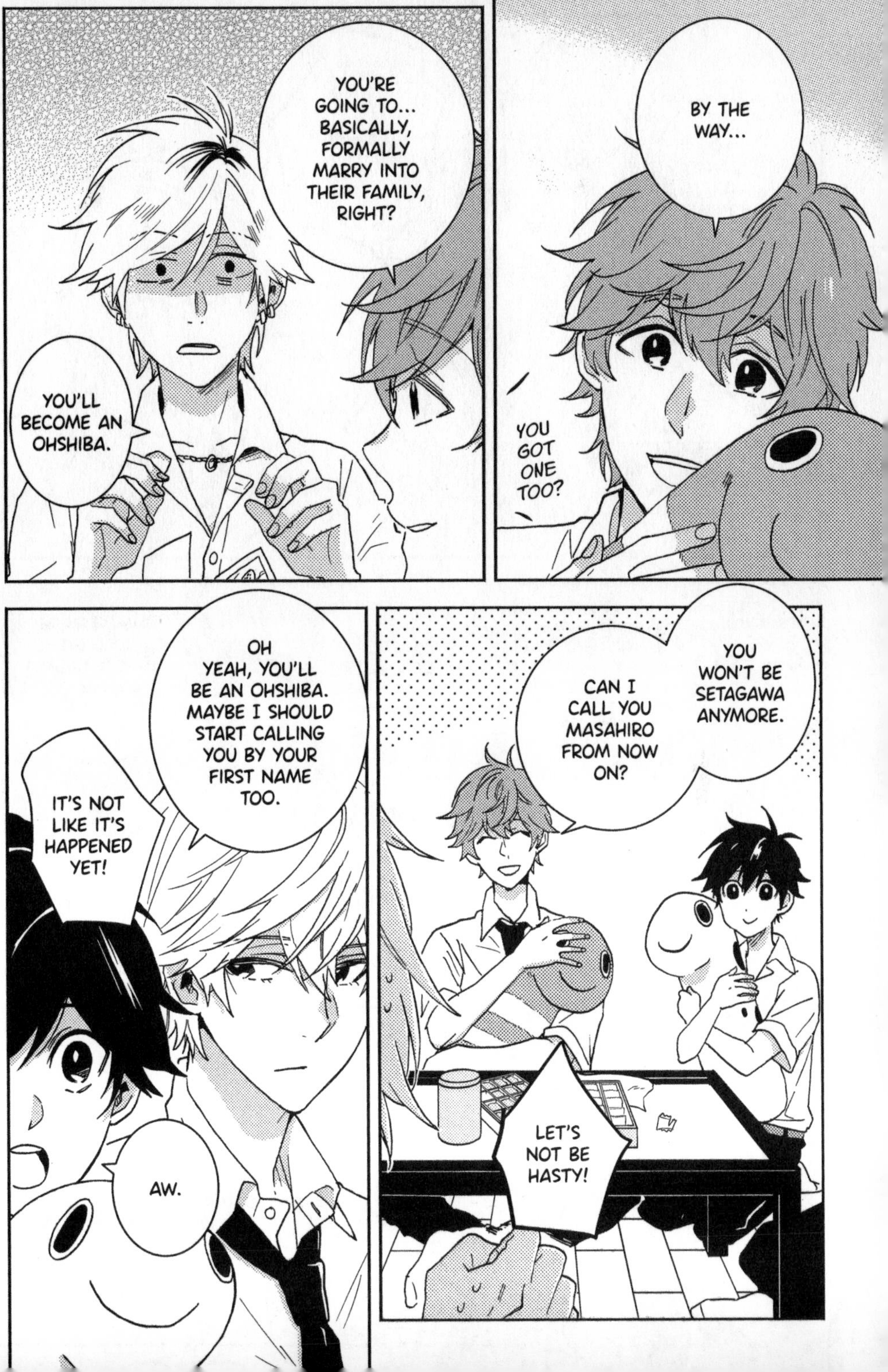
BY THE WAY...
YOU GOT ONE TOO?
YOU'RE GOING TO... BASICALLY, FORMALLY MARRY INTO THEIR FAMILY, RIGHT?
YOU'LL BECOME AN OHSHIBA.
YOU WON'T BE SETAGAWA ANYMORE.
CAN I CALL YOU MASAHIRO FROM NOW ON?
LET'S NOT BE HASTY!
OH YEAH, YOU'LL BE AN OHSHIBA. MAYBE I SHOULD START CALLING YOU BY YOUR FIRST NAME TOO.
IT'S NOT LIKE IT'S HAPPENED YET!
AW.

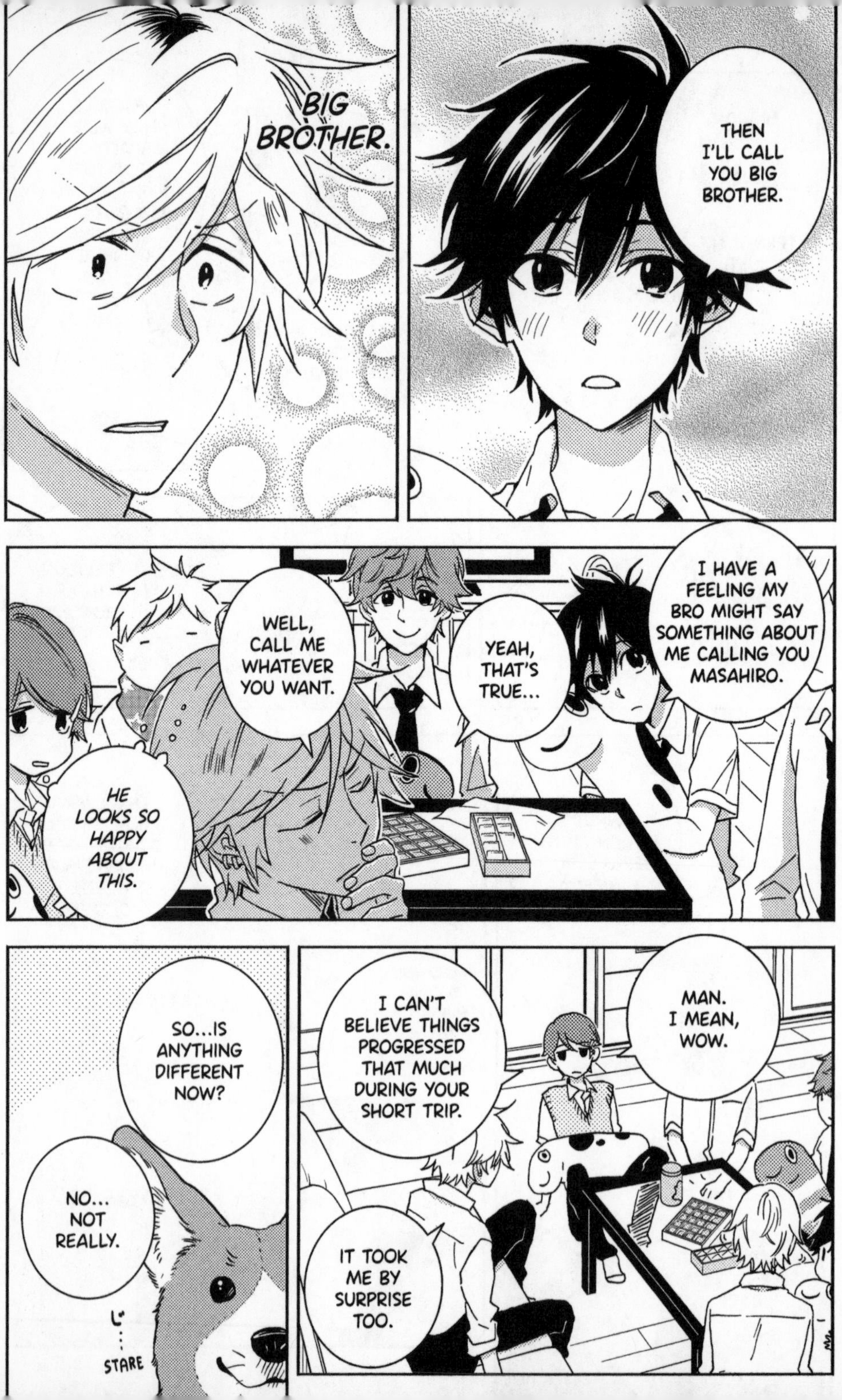
THEN I'LL CALL YOU BIG BROTHER.
BIG BROTHER.
I HAVE A FEELING MY BRO MIGHT SAY SOMETHING ABOUT ME CALLING YOU MASAHIRO.
YEAH, THAT'S TRUE...
WELL, CALL ME WHATEVER YOU WANT.
HE LOOKS SO HAPPY ABOUT THIS.
MAN. I MEAN, WOW.
I CAN'T BELIEVE THINGS PROGRESSED THAT MUCH DURING YOUR SHORT TRIP.
IT TOOK ME BY SURPRISE TOO.
SO...IS ANYTHING DIFFERENT NOW?
NO... NOT REALLY.
じ…
STARE

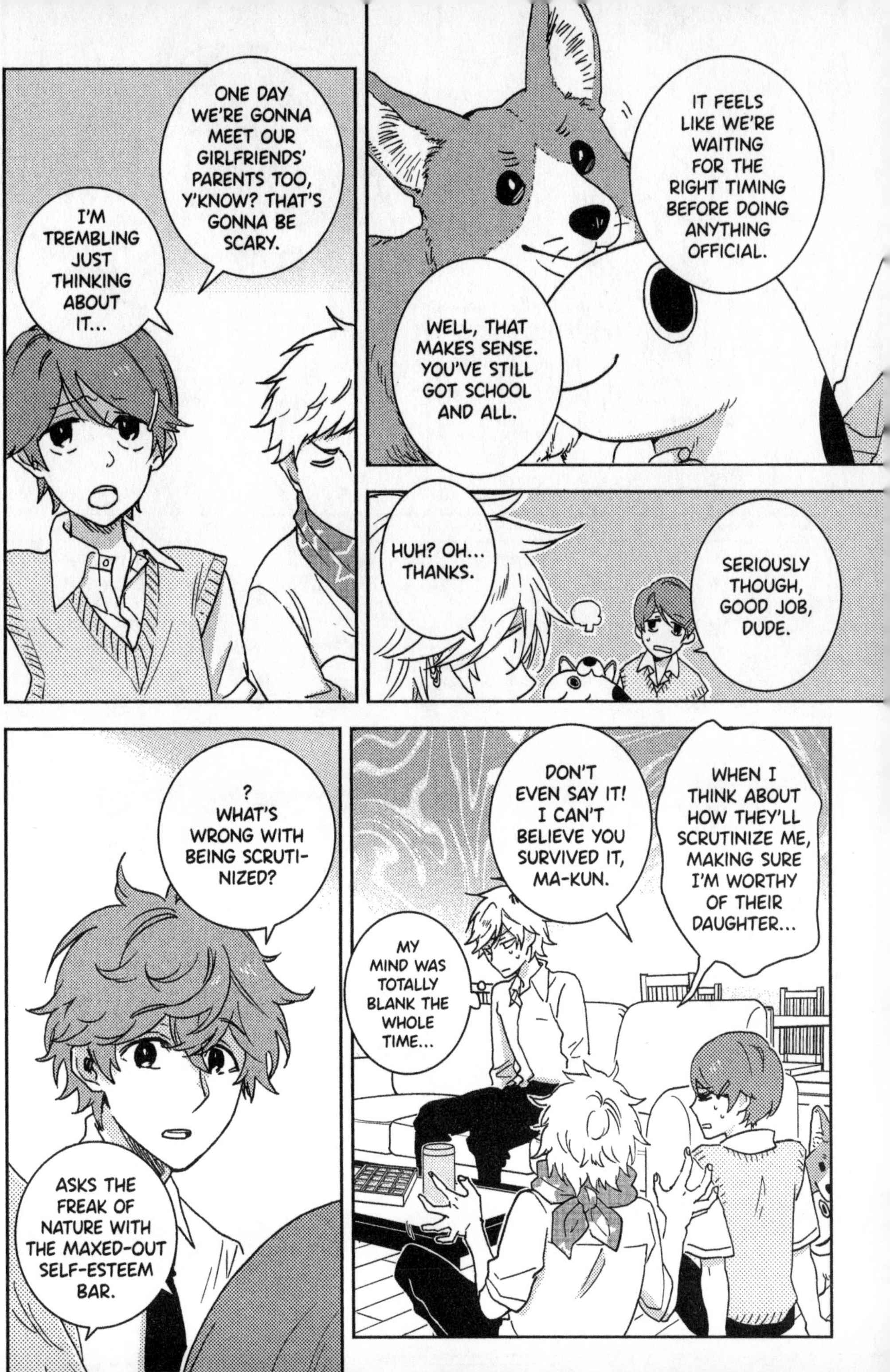
IT FEELS LIKE WE'RE WAITING FOR THE RIGHT TIMING BEFORE DOING ANYTHING OFFICIAL.
WELL, THAT MAKES SENSE. YOU'VE STILL GOT SCHOOL AND ALL.
SERIOUSLY THOUGH, GOOD JOB, DUDE.
HUH? OH... THANKS.
ONE DAY WE'RE GONNA MEET OUR GIRLFRIENDS' PARENTS TOO, Y'KNOW? THAT'S GONNA BE SCARY.
I'M TREMBLING JUST THINKING ABOUT IT...
WHEN I THINK ABOUT HOW THEY'LL SCRUTINIZE ME, MAKING SURE I'M WORTHY OF THEIR DAUGHTER...
DON'T EVEN SAY IT! I CAN'T BELIEVE YOU SURVIVED IT, MA-KUN.
MY MIND WAS TOTALLY BLANK THE WHOLE TIME...
? WHAT'S WRONG WITH BEING SCRUTI-NIZED?
ASKS THE FREAK OF NATURE WITH THE MAXED-OUT SELF-ESTEEM BAR.

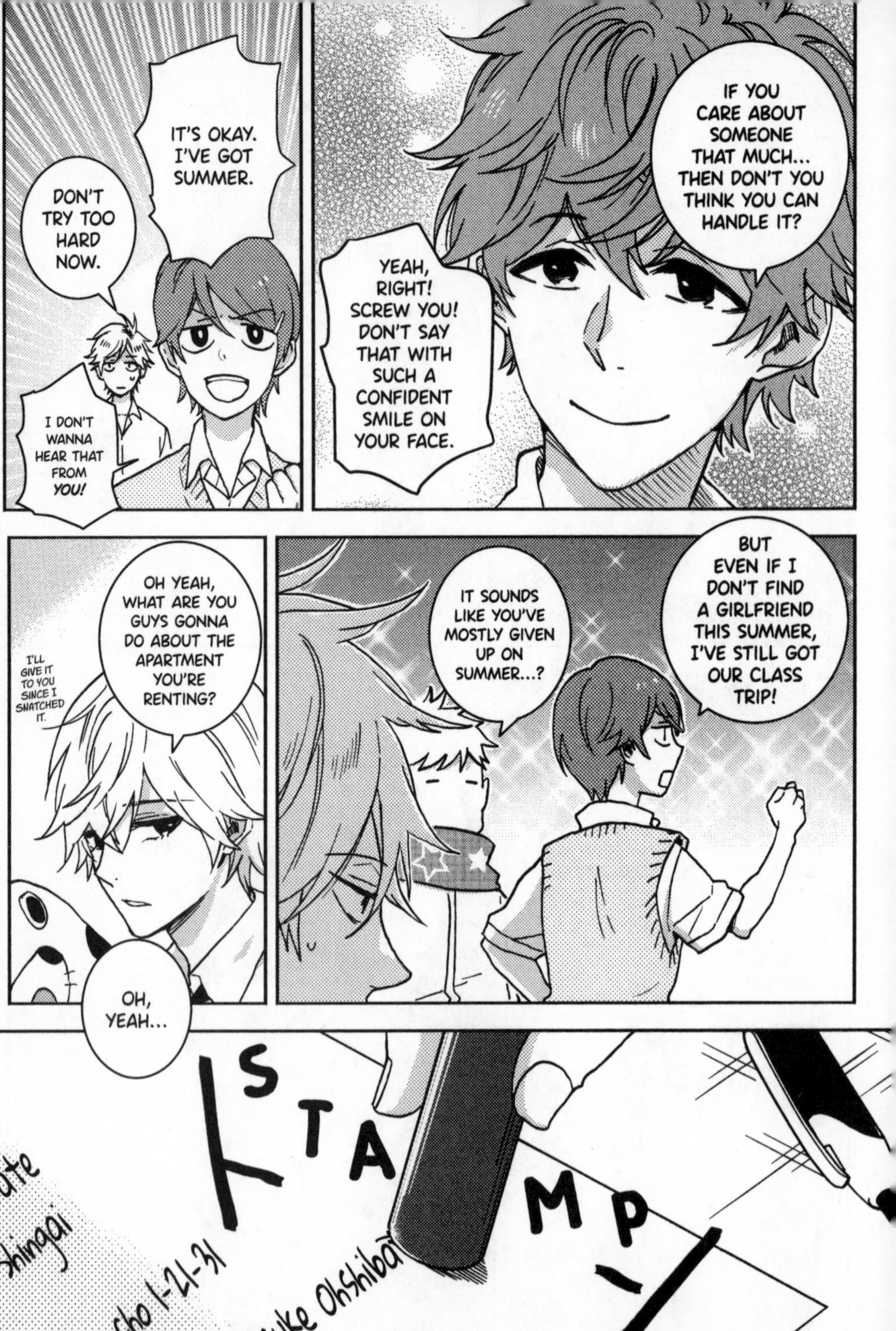

IF YOU CARE ABOUT SOMEONE THAT MUCH... THEN DON'T YOU THINK YOU CAN HANDLE IT?
YEAH, RIGHT! SCREW YOU! DON'T SAY THAT WITH SUCH A CONFIDENT SMILE ON YOUR FACE.
IT'S OKAY. I'VE GOT SUMMER.
DON'T TRY TOO HARD NOW.
I DON'T WANNA HEAR THAT FROM *YOU!*
BUT EVEN IF I DON'T FIND A GIRLFRIEND THIS SUMMER, I'VE STILL GOT OUR CLASS TRIP!
IT SOUNDS LIKE YOU'VE MOSTLY GIVEN UP ON SUMMER...?
OH YEAH, WHAT ARE YOU GUYS GONNA DO ABOUT THE APARTMENT YOU'RE RENTING?
I'LL GIVE IT TO YOU SINCE I SNATCHED IT.
OH, YEAH...
STAMP
cho 1-21-31
Kousuke Ohshiba

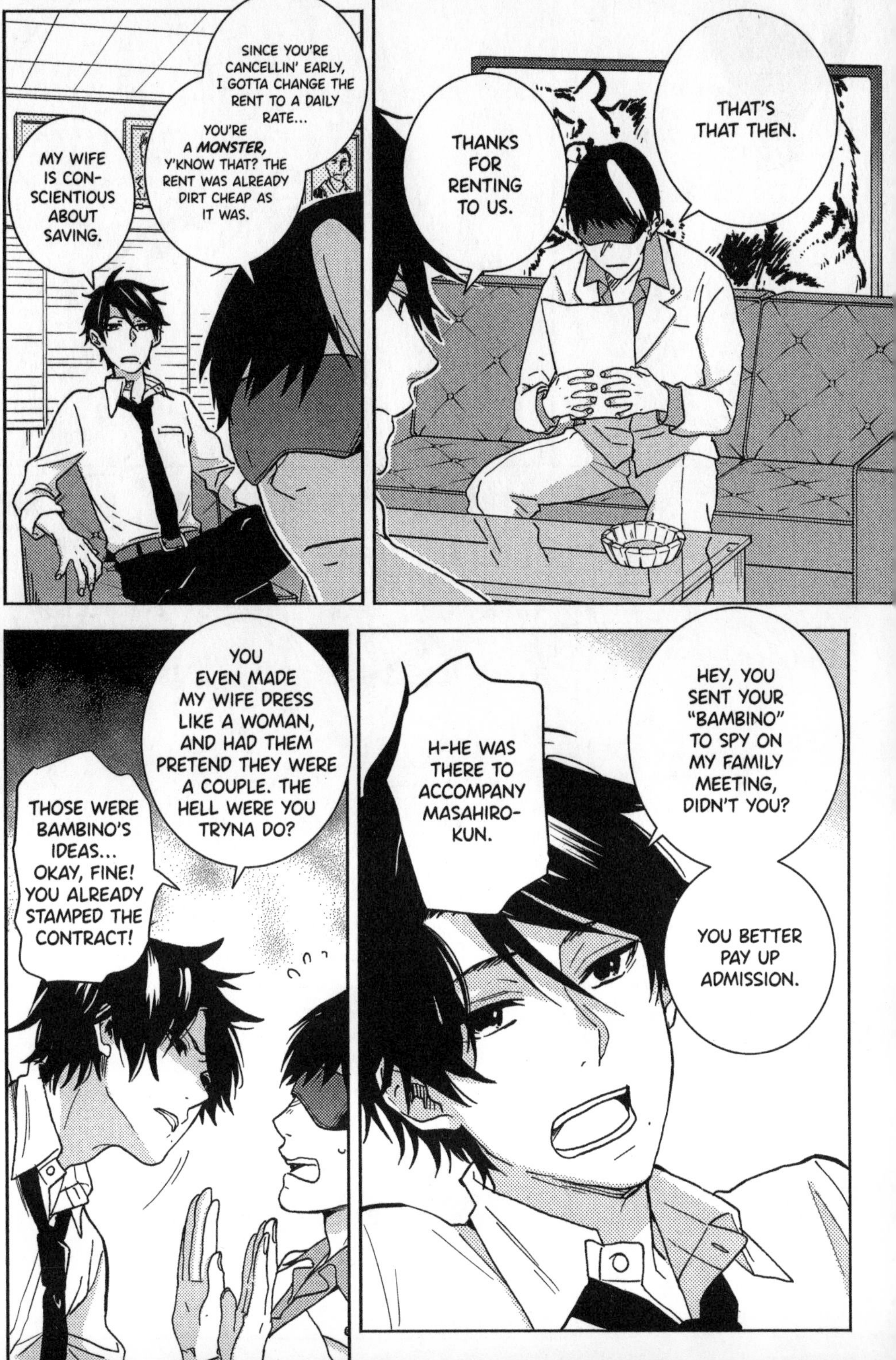
THAT'S THAT THEN.
THANKS FOR RENTING TO US.
SINCE YOU'RE CANCELLIN' EARLY, I GOTTA CHANGE THE RENT TO A DAILY RATE...
YOU'RE A **MONSTER,** Y'KNOW THAT? THE RENT WAS ALREADY DIRT CHEAP AS IT WAS.
MY WIFE IS CON-SCIENTIOUS ABOUT SAVING.
HEY, YOU SENT YOUR "BAMBINO" TO SPY ON MY FAMILY MEETING, DIDN'T YOU?
H-HE WAS THERE TO ACCOMPANY MASAHIRO-KUN.
YOU BETTER PAY UP ADMISSION.
YOU EVEN MADE MY WIFE DRESS LIKE A WOMAN, AND HAD THEM PRETEND THEY WERE A COUPLE. THE HELL WERE YOU TRYNA DO?
THOSE WERE BAMBINO'S IDEAS... OKAY, FINE! YOU ALREADY STAMPED THE CONTRACT!

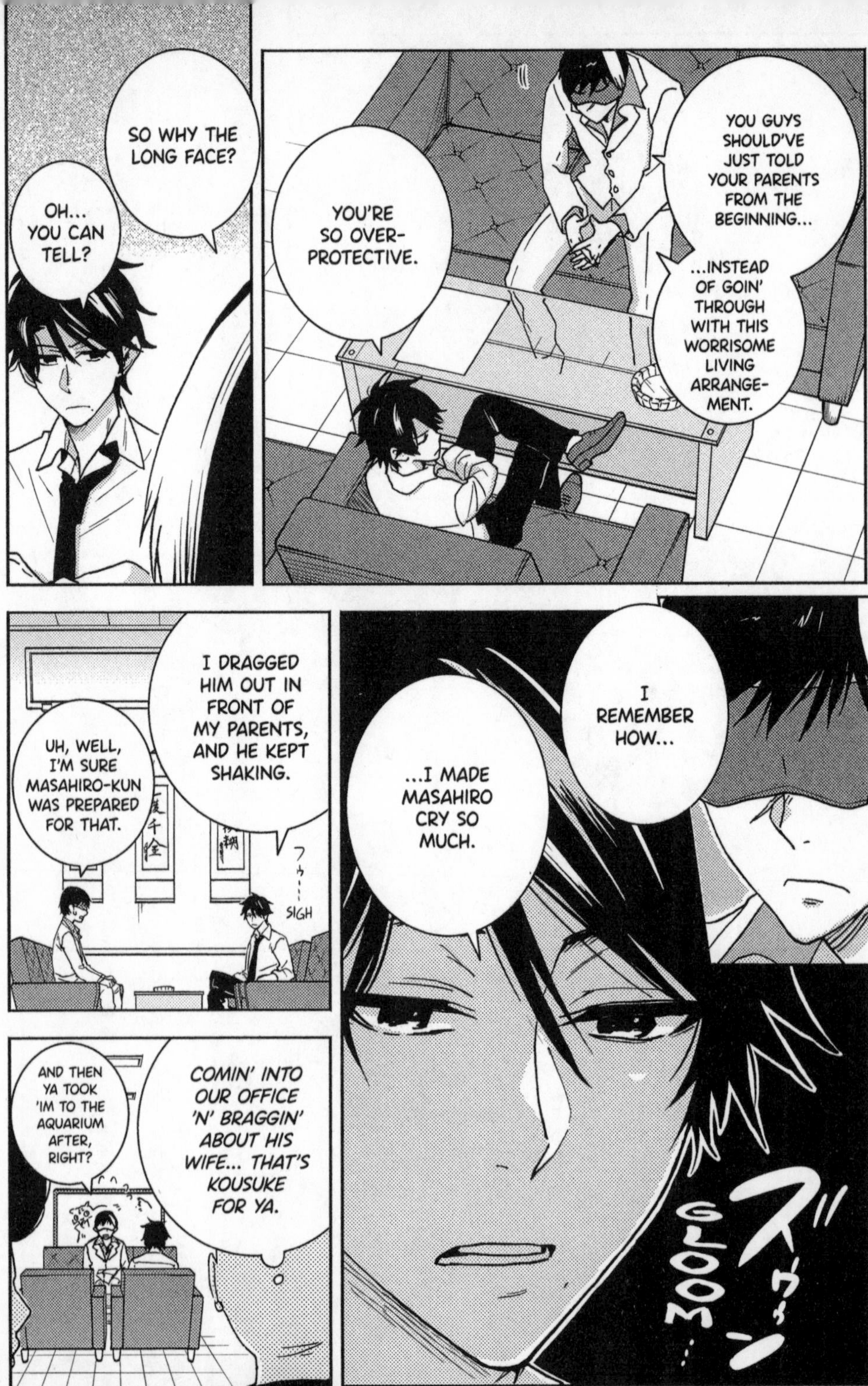
YOU GUYS SHOULD'VE JUST TOLD YOUR PARENTS FROM THE BEGINNING...
...INSTEAD OF GOIN' THROUGH WITH THIS WORRISOME LIVING ARRANGE-MENT.
YOU'RE SO OVER-PROTECTIVE.
SO WHY THE LONG FACE?
OH... YOU CAN TELL?
I REMEMBER HOW...
...I MADE MASAHIRO CRY SO MUCH.
GLOOM...
I DRAGGED HIM OUT IN FRONT OF MY PARENTS, AND HE KEPT SHAKING.
UH, WELL, I'M SURE MASAHIRO-KUN WAS PREPARED FOR THAT.
SIGH
COMIN' INTO OUR OFFICE 'N' BRAGGIN' ABOUT HIS WIFE... THAT'S KOUSUKE FOR YA.
AND THEN YA TOOK 'IM TO THE AQUARIUM AFTER, RIGHT?

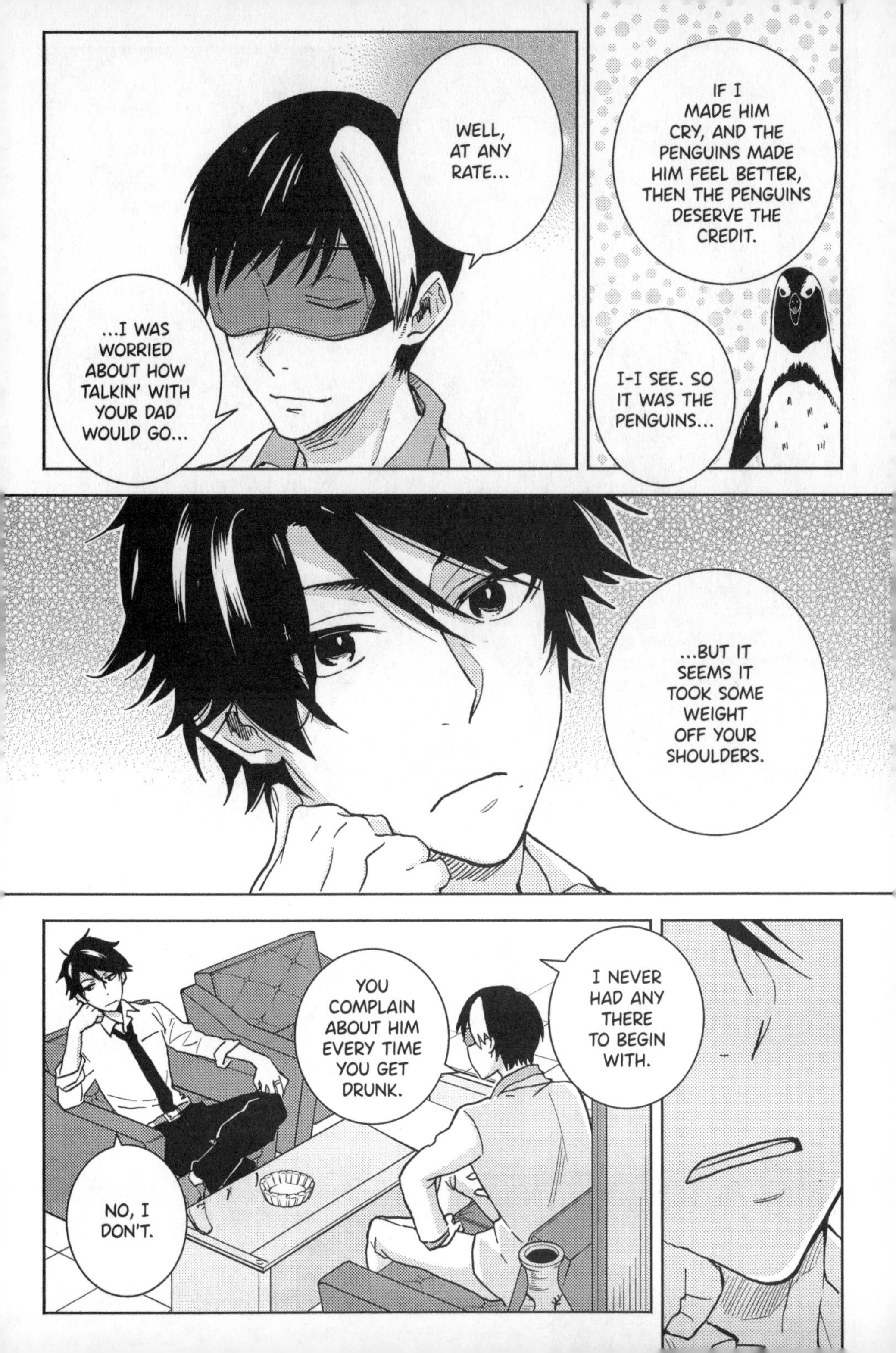
IF I MADE HIM CRY, AND THE PENGUINS MADE HIM FEEL BETTER, THEN THE PENGUINS DESERVE THE CREDIT.
I-I SEE. SO IT WAS THE PENGUINS...
WELL, AT ANY RATE...
...I WAS WORRIED ABOUT HOW TALKIN' WITH YOUR DAD WOULD GO...
...BUT IT SEEMS IT TOOK SOME WEIGHT OFF YOUR SHOULDERS.
I NEVER HAD ANY THERE TO BEGIN WITH.
YOU COMPLAIN ABOUT HIM EVERY TIME YOU GET DRUNK.
NO, I DON'T.

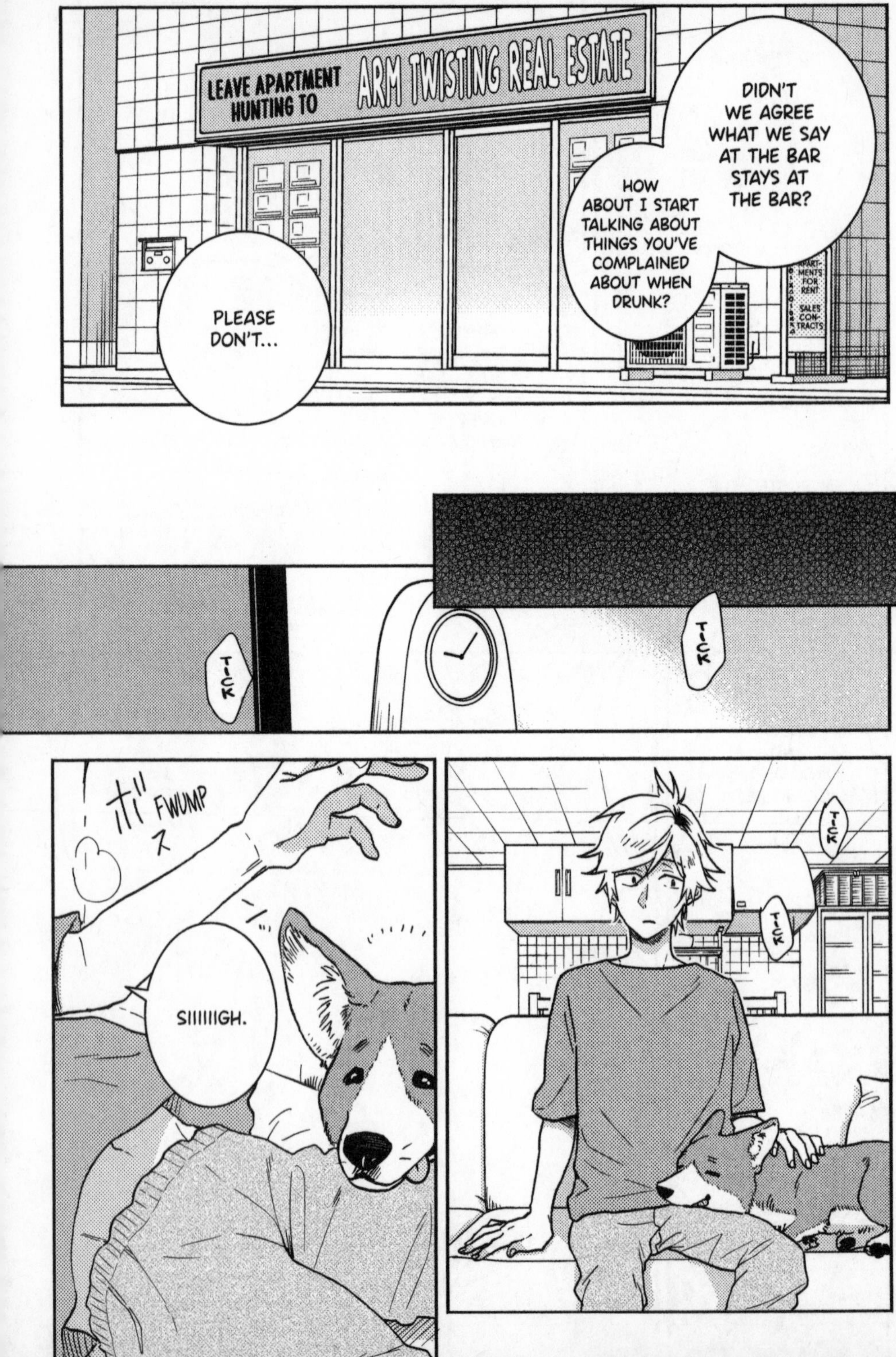
LEAVE APARTMENT HUNTING TO ARM TWISTING REAL ESTATE
DIDN'T WE AGREE WHAT WE SAY AT THE BAR STAYS AT THE BAR?
HOW ABOUT I START TALKING ABOUT THINGS YOU'VE COMPLAINED ABOUT WHEN DRUNK?
APARTMENTS FOR RENT
SALES CONTRACTS
PLEASE DON'T...
TICK
TICK
TICK
TICK
FWUMP
SIIIIIGH.

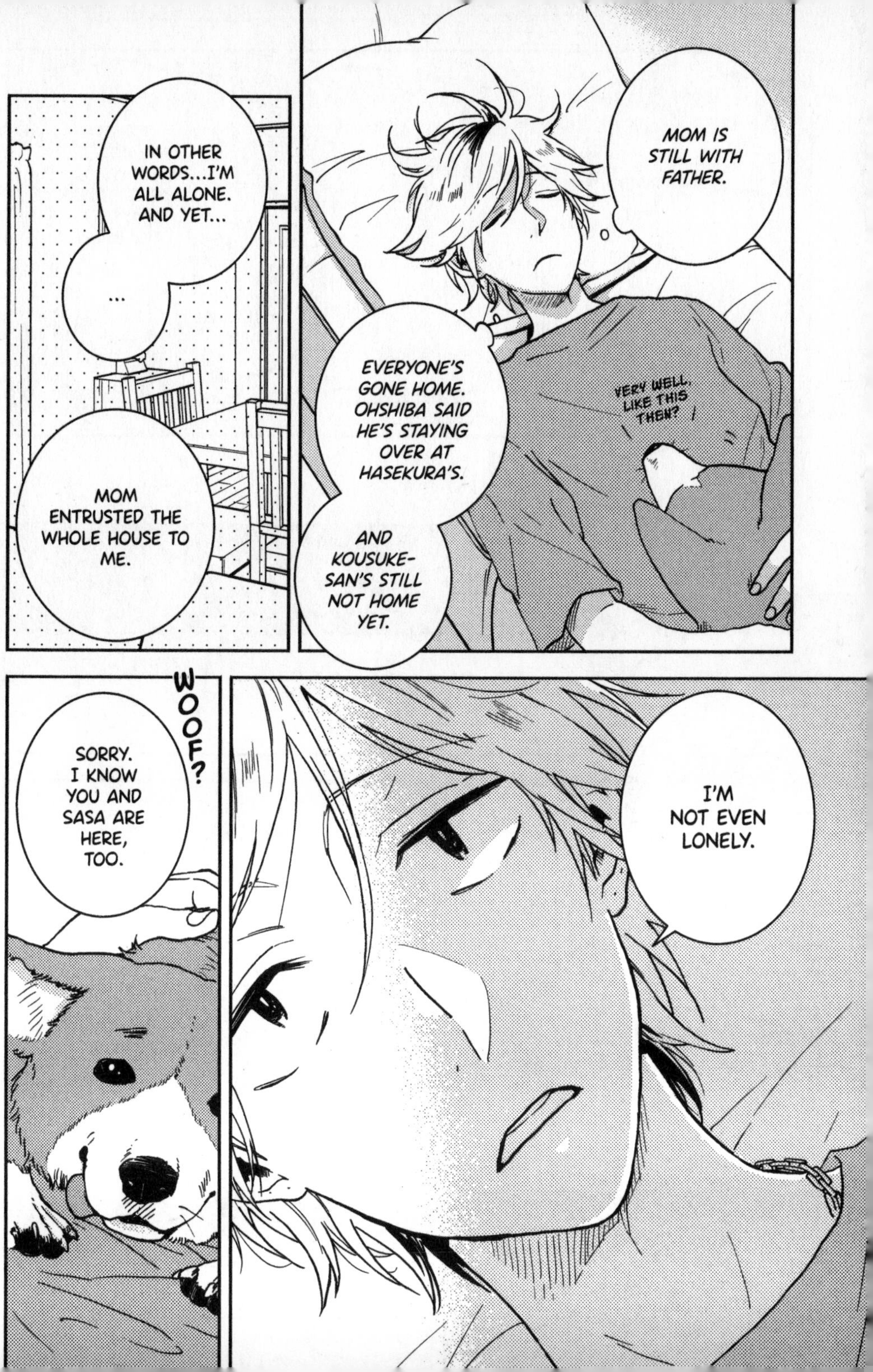
MOM IS STILL WITH FATHER.
VERY WELL, LIKE THIS THEN?
EVERYONE'S GONE HOME. OHSHIBA SAID HE'S STAYING OVER AT HASEKURA'S.
AND KOUSUKE-SAN'S STILL NOT HOME YET.
IN OTHER WORDS...I'M ALL ALONE. AND YET...
...
MOM ENTRUSTED THE WHOLE HOUSE TO ME.
I'M NOT EVEN LONELY.
WOOF?
SORRY. I KNOW YOU AND SASA ARE HERE, TOO.

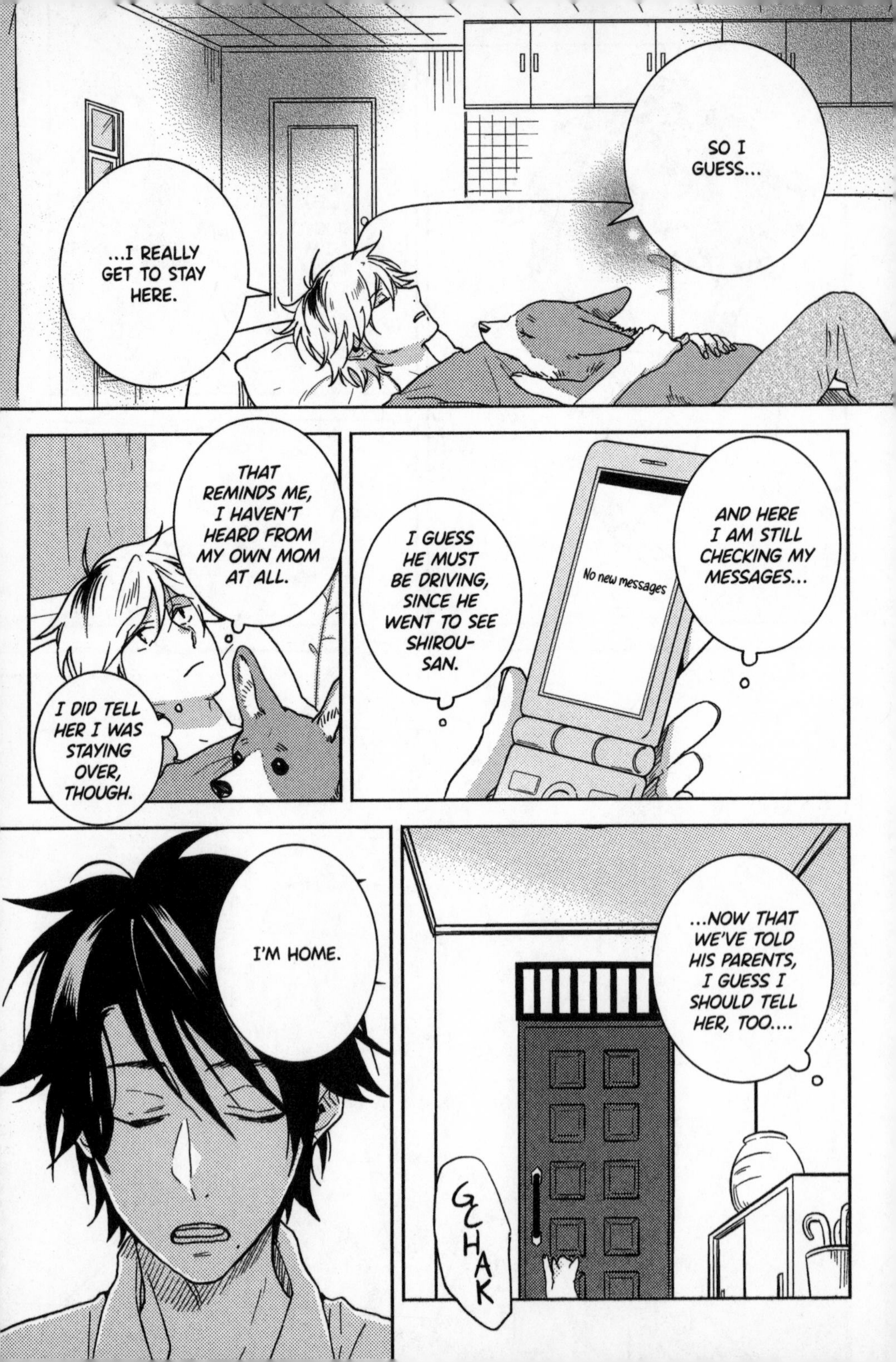
SO I GUESS...
...I REALLY GET TO STAY HERE.
AND HERE I AM STILL CHECKING MY MESSAGES...
No new messages
I GUESS HE MUST BE DRIVING, SINCE HE WENT TO SEE SHIROU-SAN.
THAT REMINDS ME, I HAVEN'T HEARD FROM MY OWN MOM AT ALL.
I DID TELL HER I WAS STAYING OVER, THOUGH.
...NOW THAT WE'VE TOLD HIS PARENTS, I GUESS I SHOULD TELL HER, TOO....
GCHAK
I'M HOME.

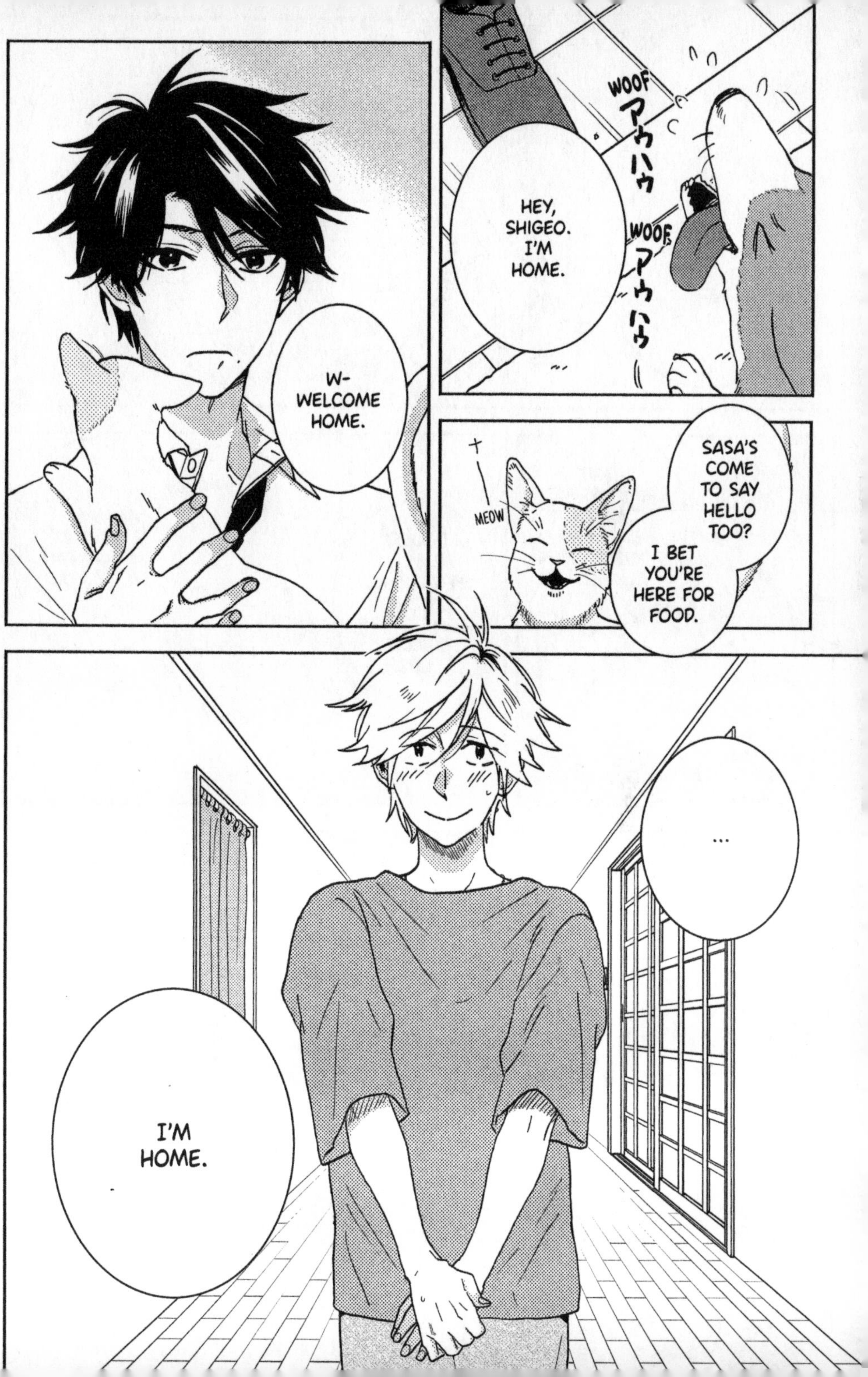
WOOF
アウハウ
WOOF
アウハウ
HEY, SHIGEO. I'M HOME.
MEOW
SASA'S COME TO SAY HELLO TOO?
I BET YOU'RE HERE FOR FOOD.
W- WELCOME HOME.
...
I'M HOME.

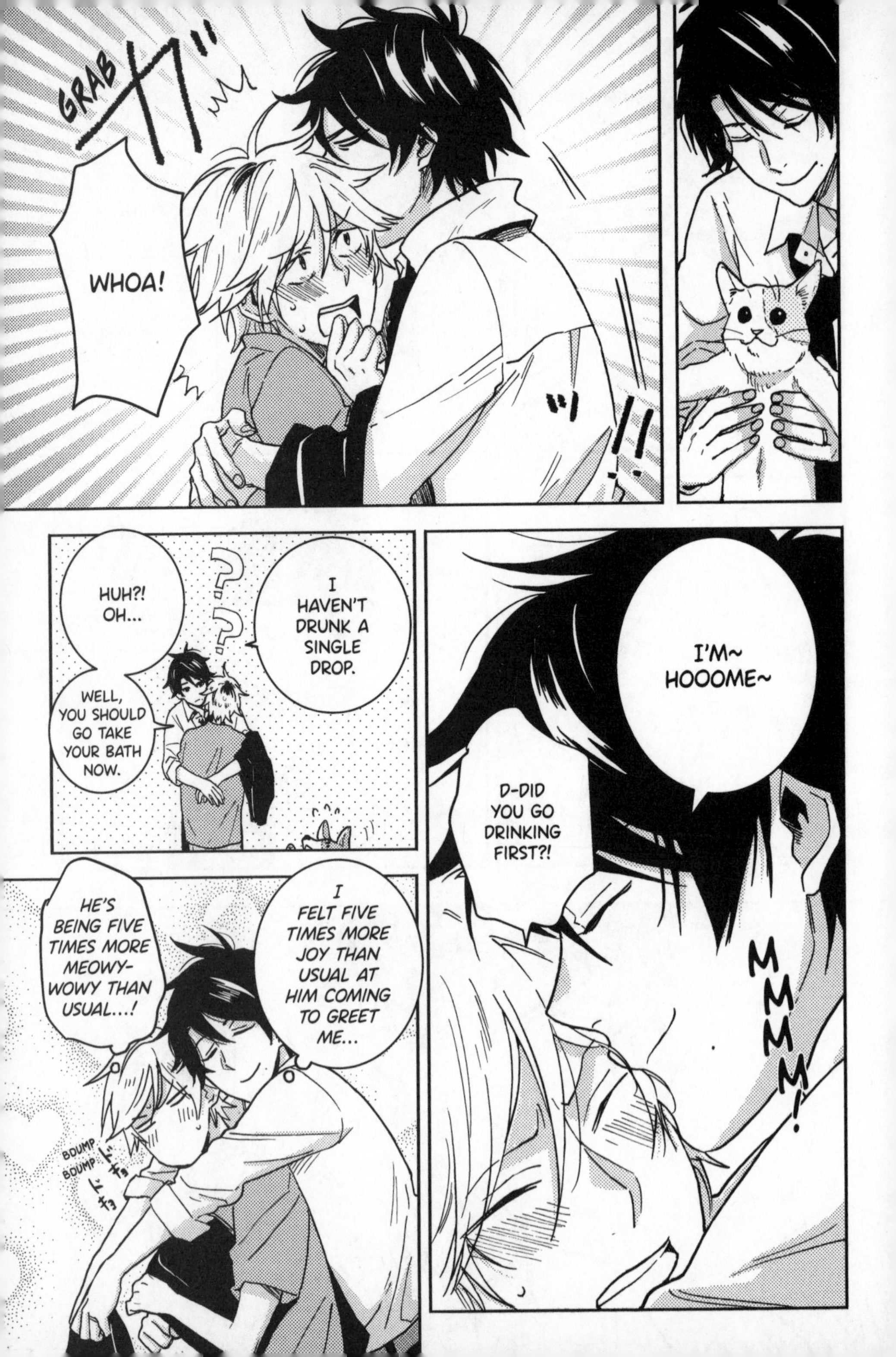
GRAB
WHOA!
I'M~ HOOOME~
D-DID YOU GO DRINKING FIRST?!
MMMM!
I HAVEN'T DRUNK A SINGLE DROP.
HUH?! OH...
WELL, YOU SHOULD GO TAKE YOUR BATH NOW.
I FELT FIVE TIMES MORE JOY THAN USUAL AT HIM COMING TO GREET ME...
HE'S BEING FIVE TIMES MORE MEOWY-WOWY THAN USUAL...!
BDUMP BDUMP

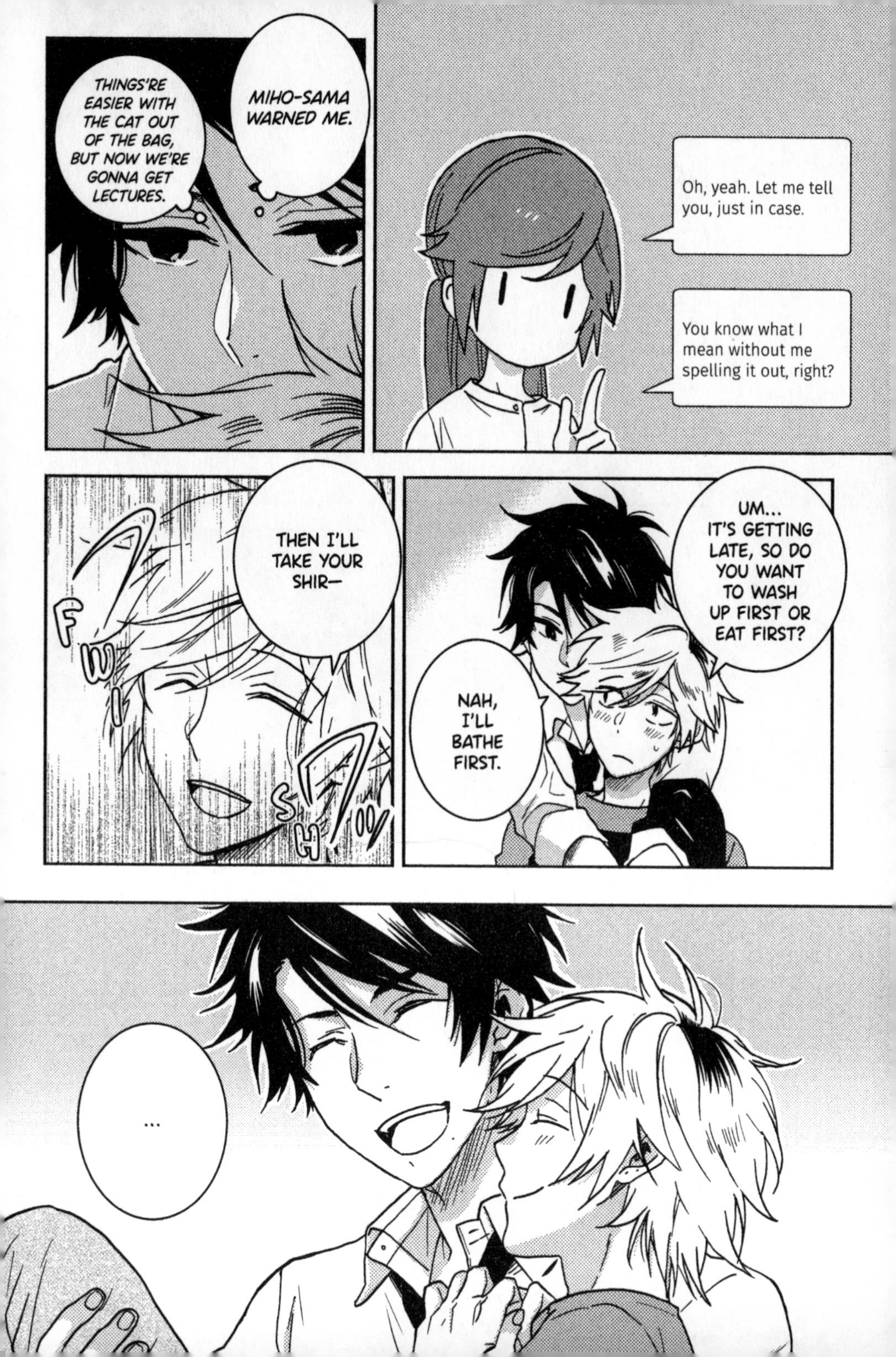
Oh, yeah. Let me tell you, just in case.
You know what I mean without me spelling it out, right?
MIHO-SAMA WARNED ME.
THINGS'RE EASIER WITH THE CAT OUT OF THE BAG, BUT NOW WE'RE GONNA GET LECTURES.
UM... IT'S GETTING LATE, SO DO YOU WANT TO WASH UP FIRST OR EAT FIRST?
NAH, I'LL BATHE FIRST.
THEN I'LL TAKE YOUR SHIR—
...

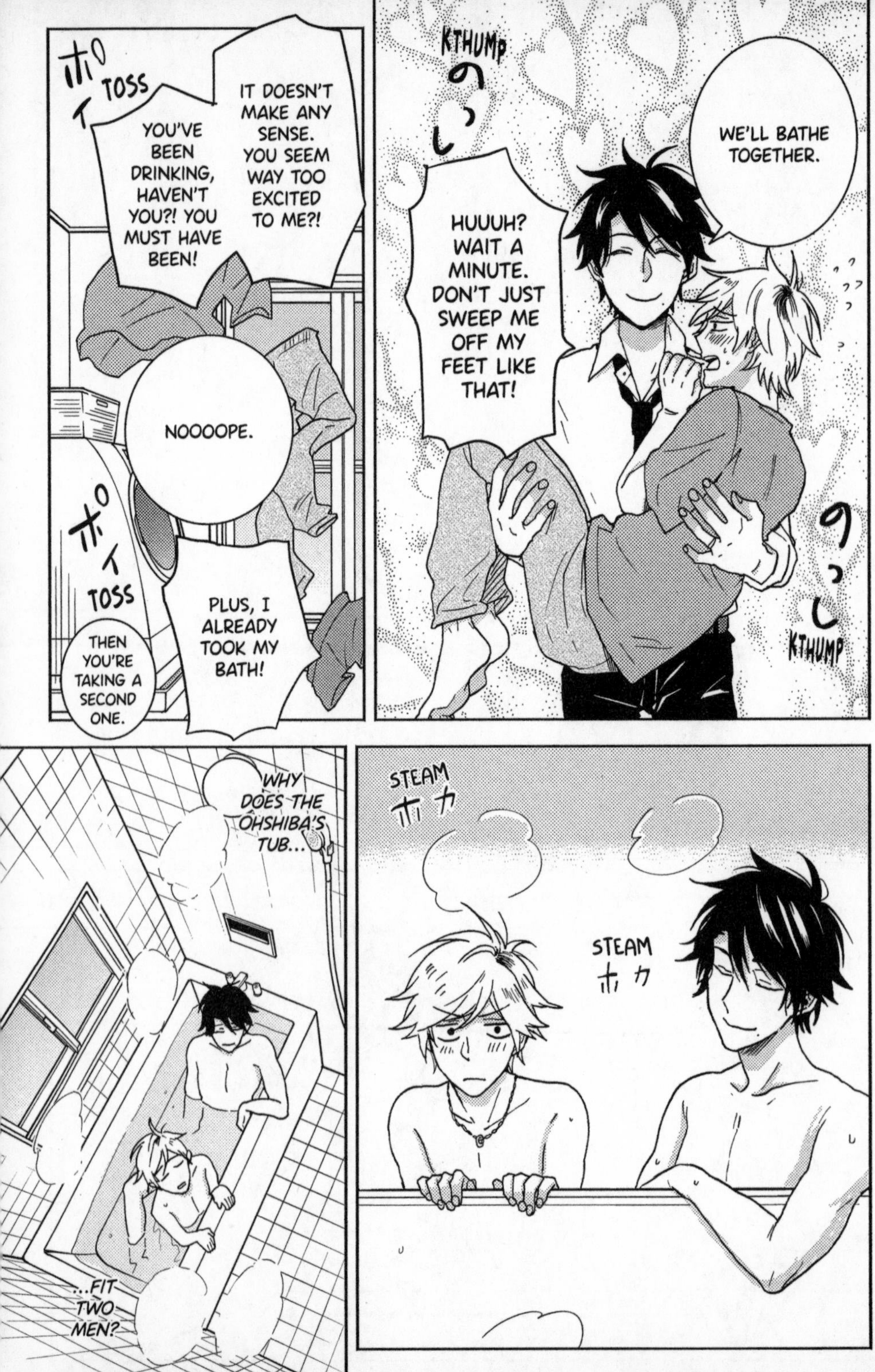
のっし
KTHUMP
WE'LL BATHE TOGETHER.
HUUUH? WAIT A MINUTE. DON'T JUST SWEEP ME OFF MY FEET LIKE THAT!
のっし
KTHUMP
ホイ
TOSS
IT DOESN'T MAKE ANY SENSE. YOU SEEM WAY TOO EXCITED TO ME?!
YOU'VE BEEN DRINKING, HAVEN'T YOU?! YOU MUST HAVE BEEN!
NOOOOPE.
ホイ
TOSS
PLUS, I ALREADY TOOK MY BATH!
THEN YOU'RE TAKING A SECOND ONE.
STEAM
ホカ
STEAM
ホカ
WHY DOES THE OHSHIBA'S TUB...
...FIT TWO MEN?

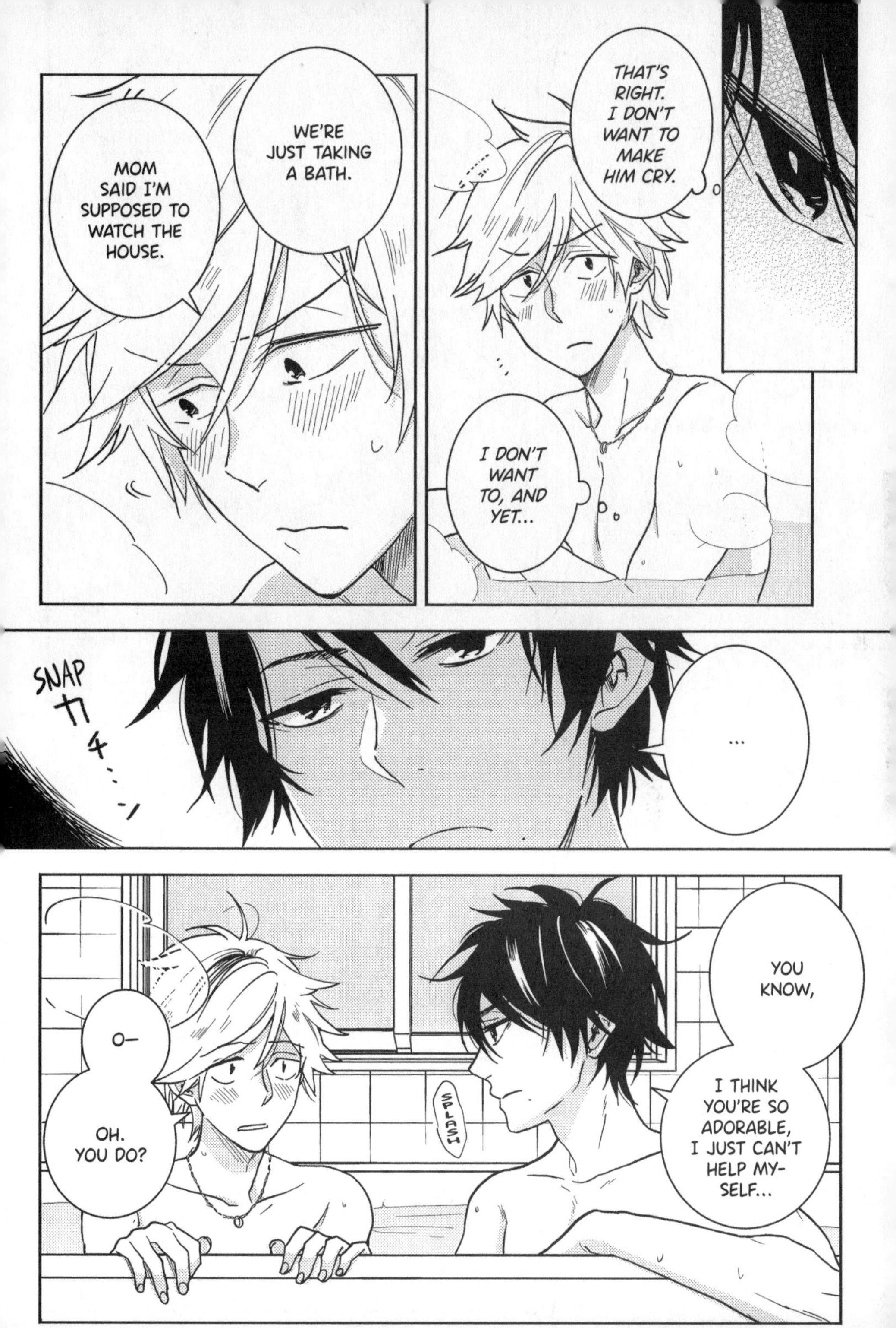
THAT'S RIGHT. I DON'T WANT TO MAKE HIM CRY.
I DON'T WANT TO, AND YET...
WE'RE JUST TAKING A BATH.
MOM SAID I'M SUPPOSED TO WATCH THE HOUSE.
...
SNAP
カチ…
YOU KNOW,
I THINK YOU'RE SO ADORABLE, I JUST CAN'T HELP MY-SELF...
SPLASH
O—
OH. YOU DO?

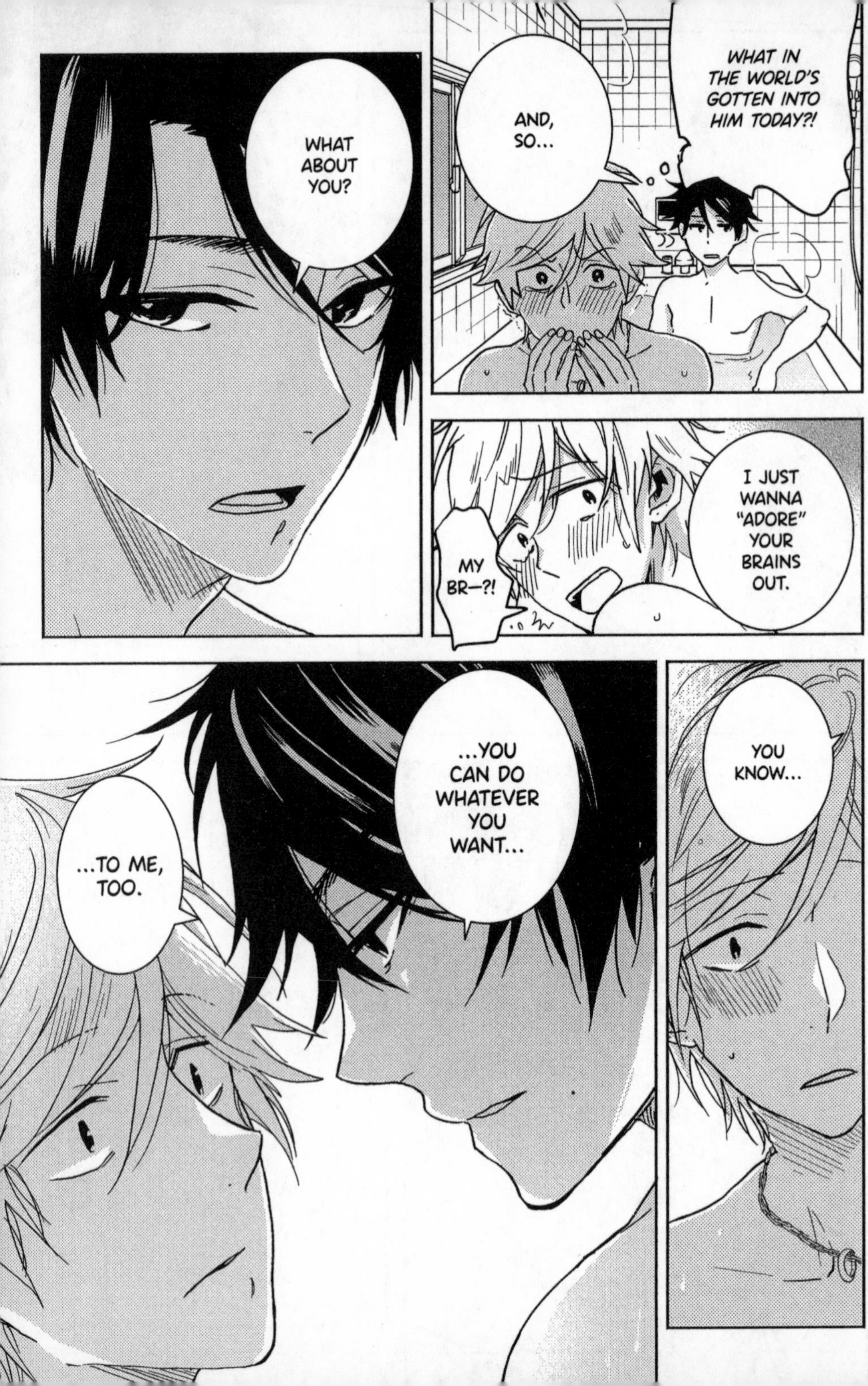
WHAT IN THE WORLD'S GOTTEN INTO HIM TODAY?!
AND, SO...
I JUST WANNA "ADORE" YOUR BRAINS OUT.
MY BR—?!
WHAT ABOUT YOU?
YOU KNOW...
...YOU CAN DO WHATEVER YOU WANT...
...TO ME, TOO.

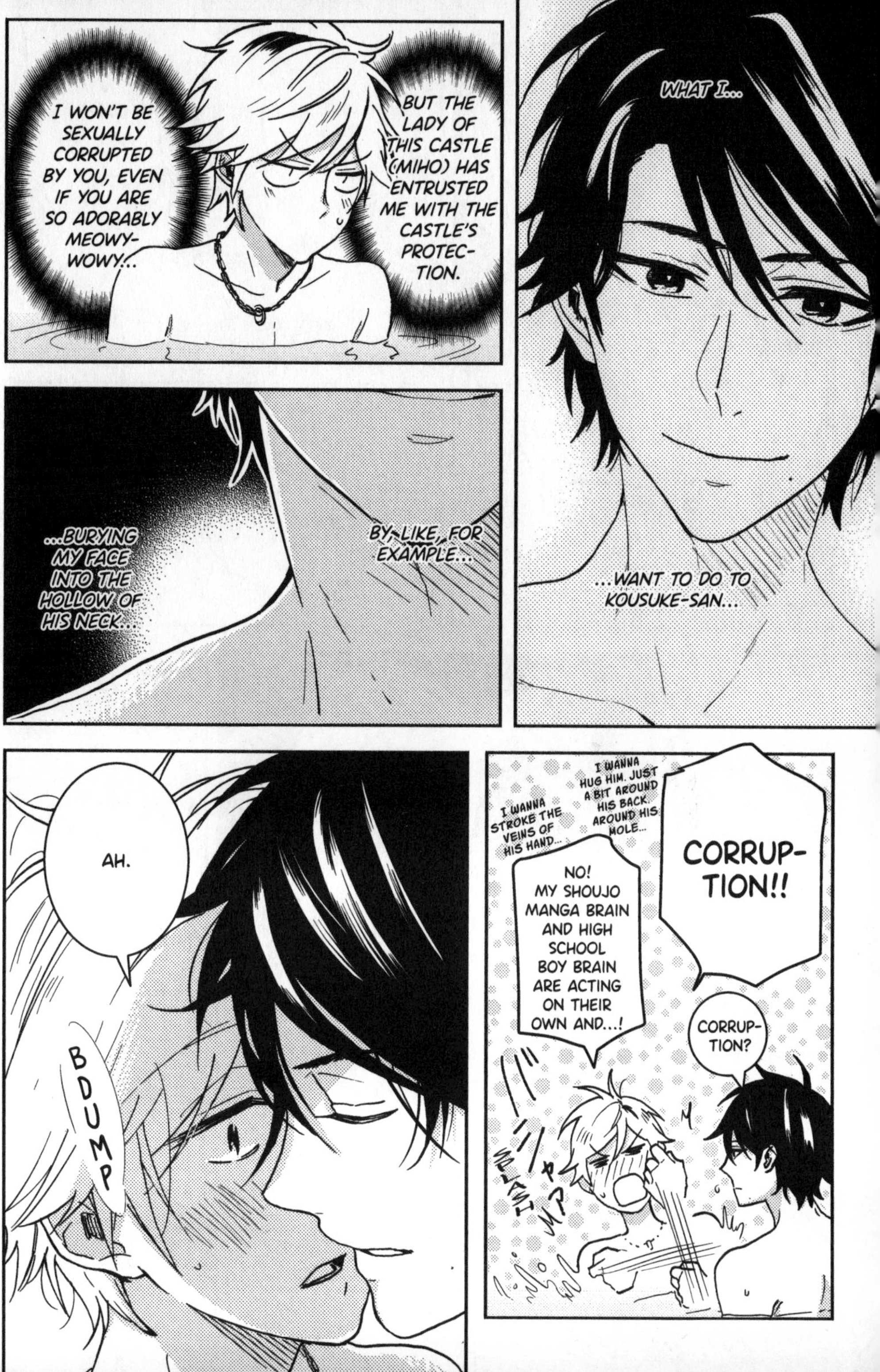
WHAT I...
...WANT TO DO TO KOUSUKE-SAN...
BUT THE LADY OF THIS CASTLE (MIHO) HAS ENTRUSTED ME WITH THE CASTLE'S PROTEC-TION.
I WON'T BE SEXUALLY CORRUPTED BY YOU, EVEN IF YOU ARE SO ADORABLY MEOWY-WOWY...
BY, LIKE, FOR EXAMPLE...
...BURYING MY FACE INTO THE HOLLOW OF HIS NECK...
CORRUP-TION!!
I WANNA HUG HIM. JUST A BIT AROUND HIS BACK. AROUND HIS MOLE...
I WANNA STROKE THE VEINS OF HIS HAND...
NO! MY SHOUJO MANGA BRAIN AND HIGH SCHOOL BOY BRAIN ARE ACTING ON THEIR OWN AND...!
CORRUP-TION?
SPLASH
AH.
BDUMP

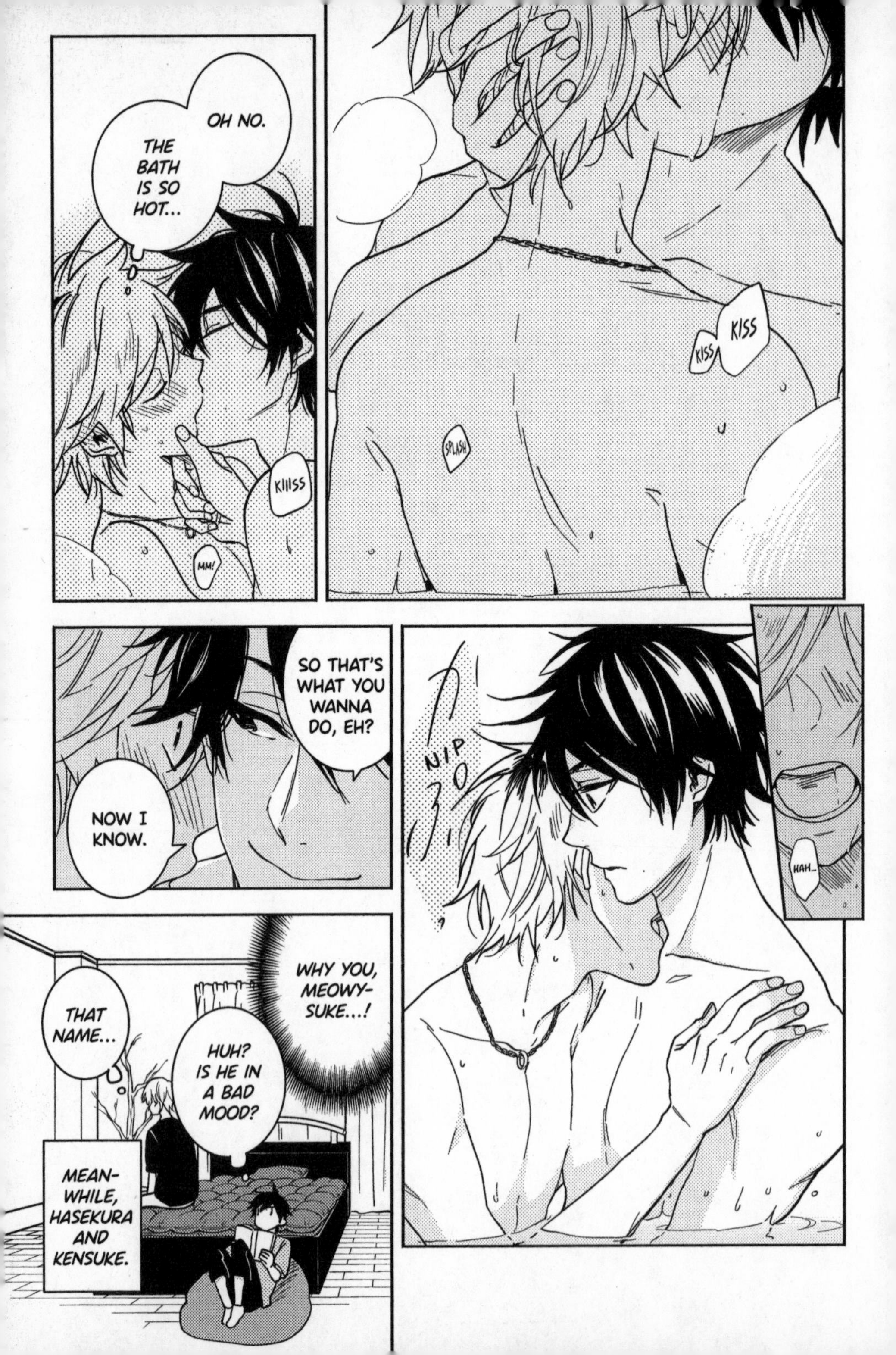
KISS
KISS
SPLASH
OH NO.
THE BATH IS SO HOT...
KIIISS
MM!
HAH...
NIP
SO THAT'S WHAT YOU WANNA DO, EH?
NOW I KNOW.
WHY YOU, MEOWY-SUKE...!
HUH? IS HE IN A BAD MOOD?
THAT NAME...
MEAN-WHILE, HASEKURA AND KENSUKE.

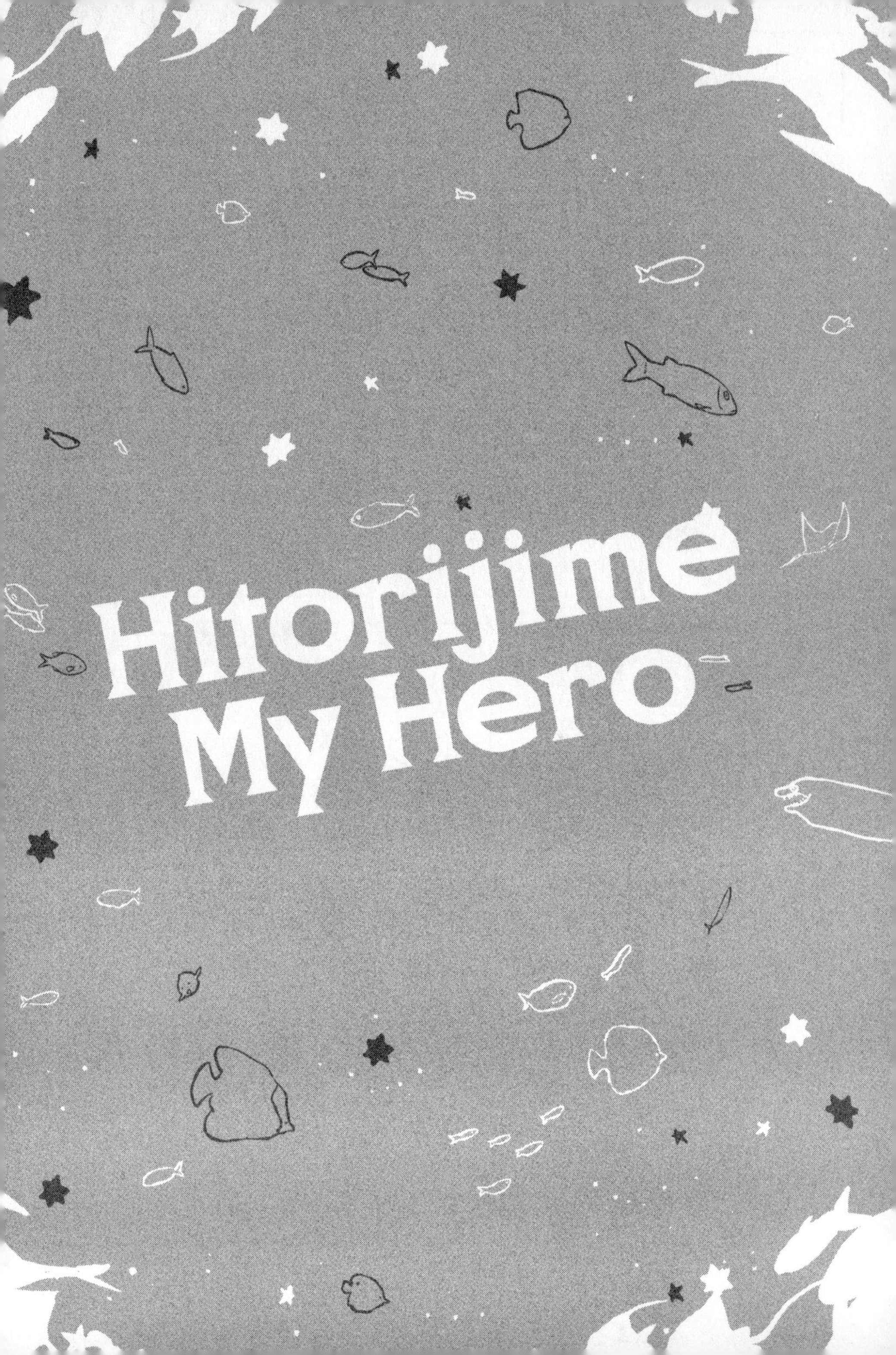
Hitorijime
My Hero

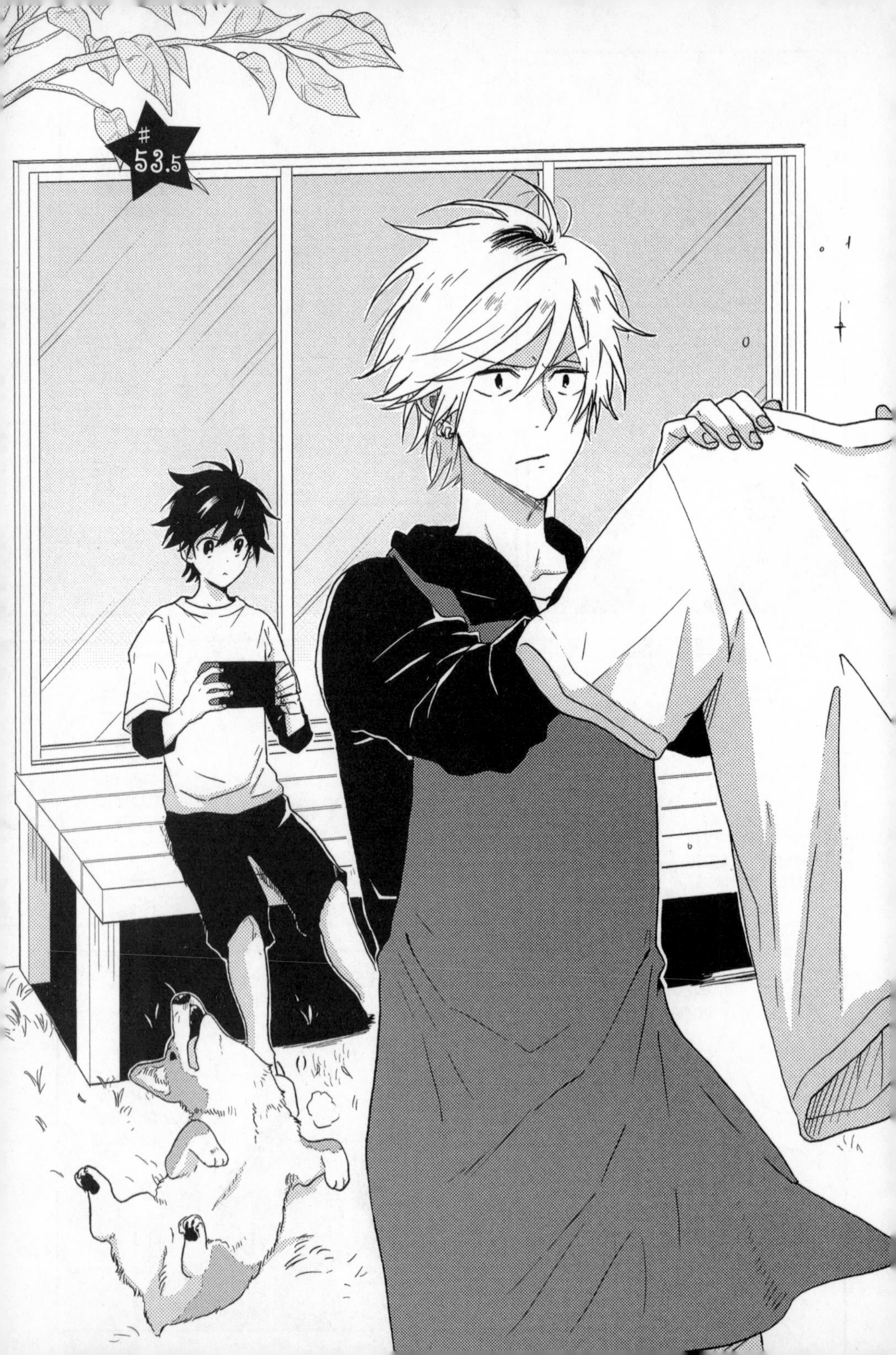
#
53.5

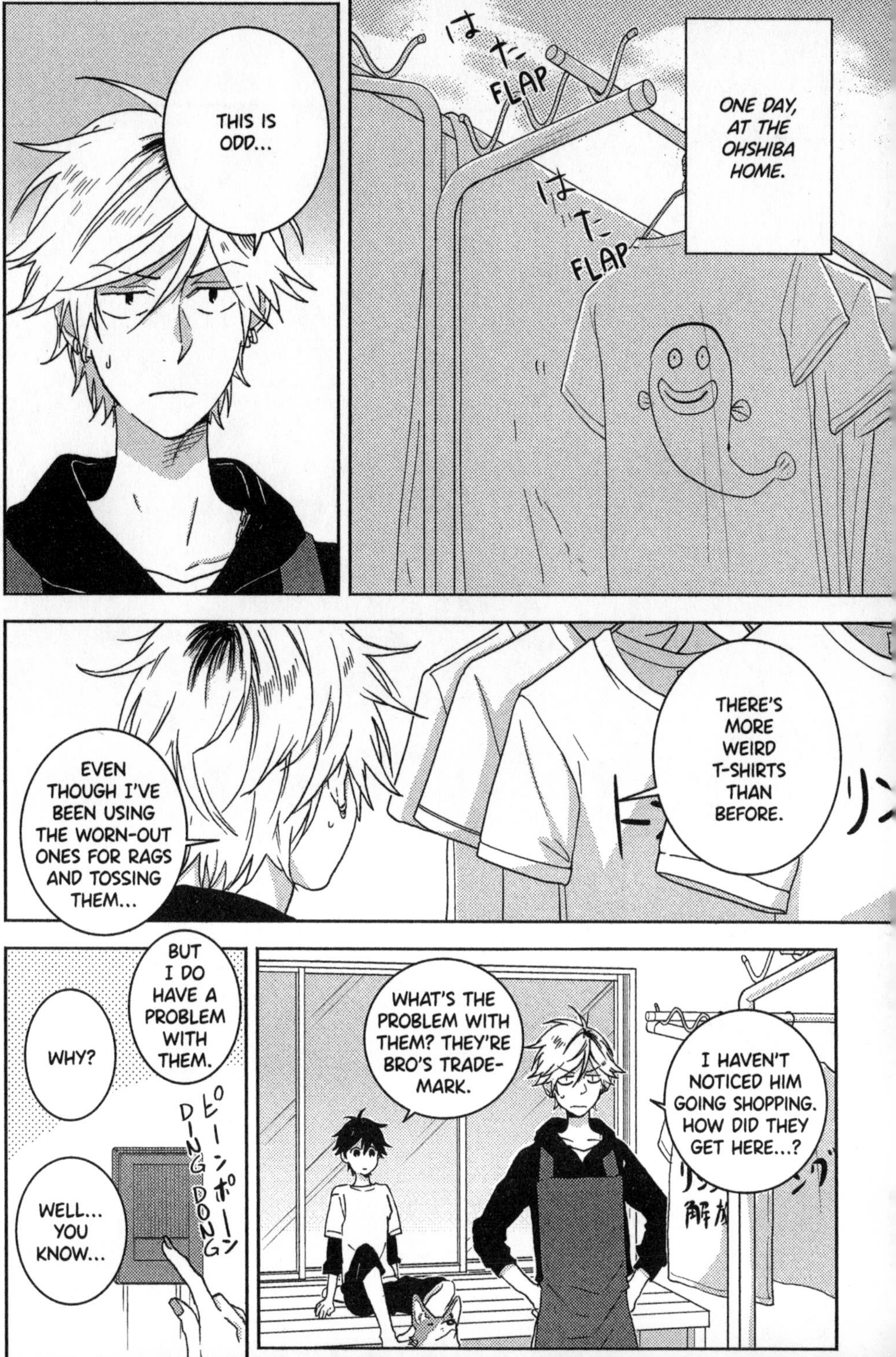

ONE DAY, AT THE OHSHIBA HOME.
はた
FLAP
はた
FLAP
THIS IS ODD...
THERE'S MORE WEIRD T-SHIRTS THAN BEFORE.
EVEN THOUGH I'VE BEEN USING THE WORN-OUT ONES FOR RAGS AND TOSSING THEM...
I HAVEN'T NOTICED HIM GOING SHOPPING. HOW DID THEY GET HERE...?
WHAT'S THE PROBLEM WITH THEM? THEY'RE BRO'S TRADE-MARK.
BUT I DO HAVE A PROBLEM WITH THEM.
WHY?
ピーンポーン
DING DONG
WELL... YOU KNOW...

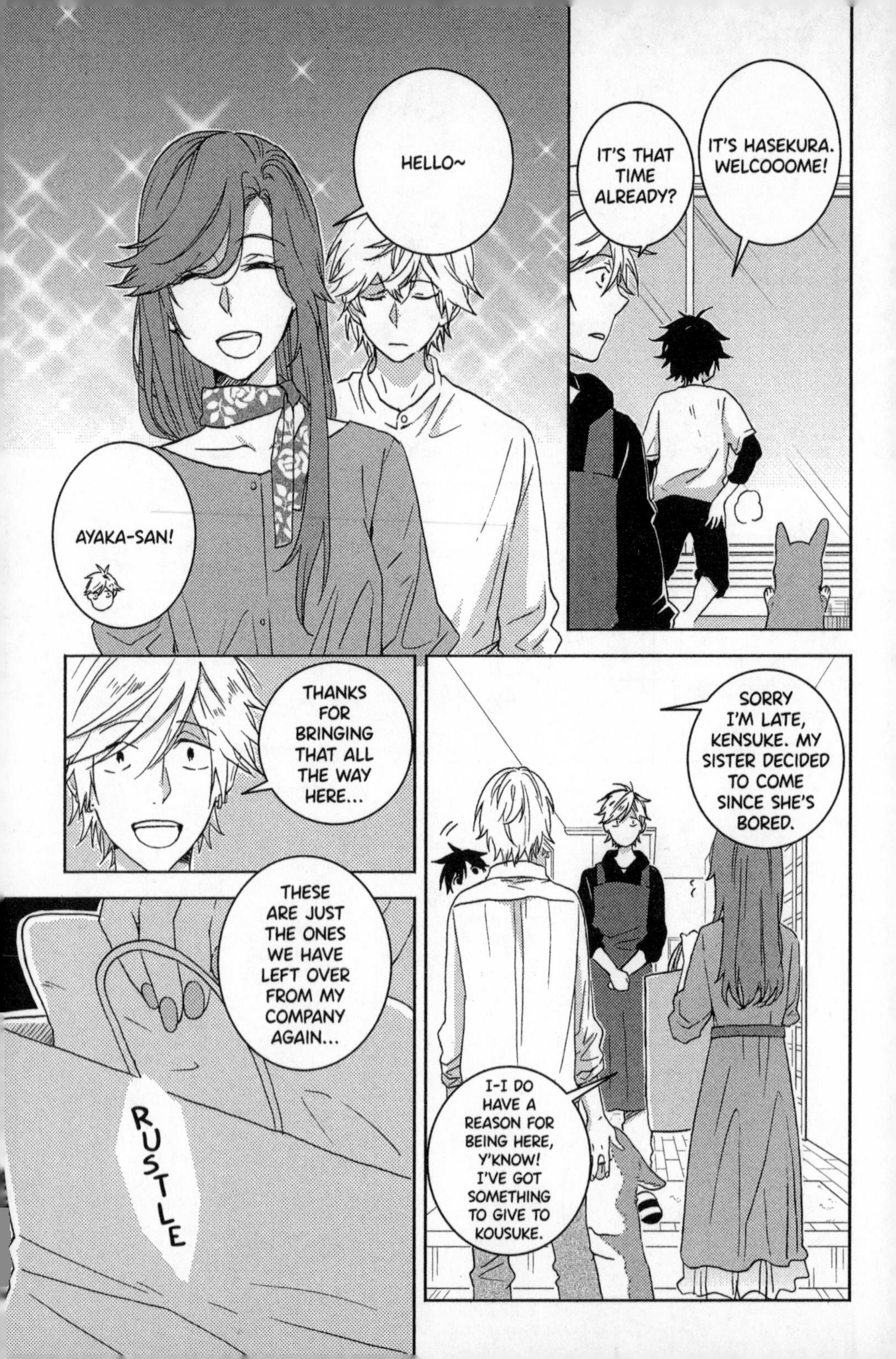
IT'S HASEKURA. WELCOOOME!
IT'S THAT TIME ALREADY?
HELLO~
AYAKA-SAN!
SORRY I'M LATE, KENSUKE. MY SISTER DECIDED TO COME SINCE SHE'S BORED.
I-I DO HAVE A REASON FOR BEING HERE, Y'KNOW! I'VE GOT SOMETHING TO GIVE TO KOUSUKE.
THANKS FOR BRINGING THAT ALL THE WAY HERE...
THESE ARE JUST THE ONES WE HAVE LEFT OVER FROM MY COMPANY AGAIN...
RUSTLE

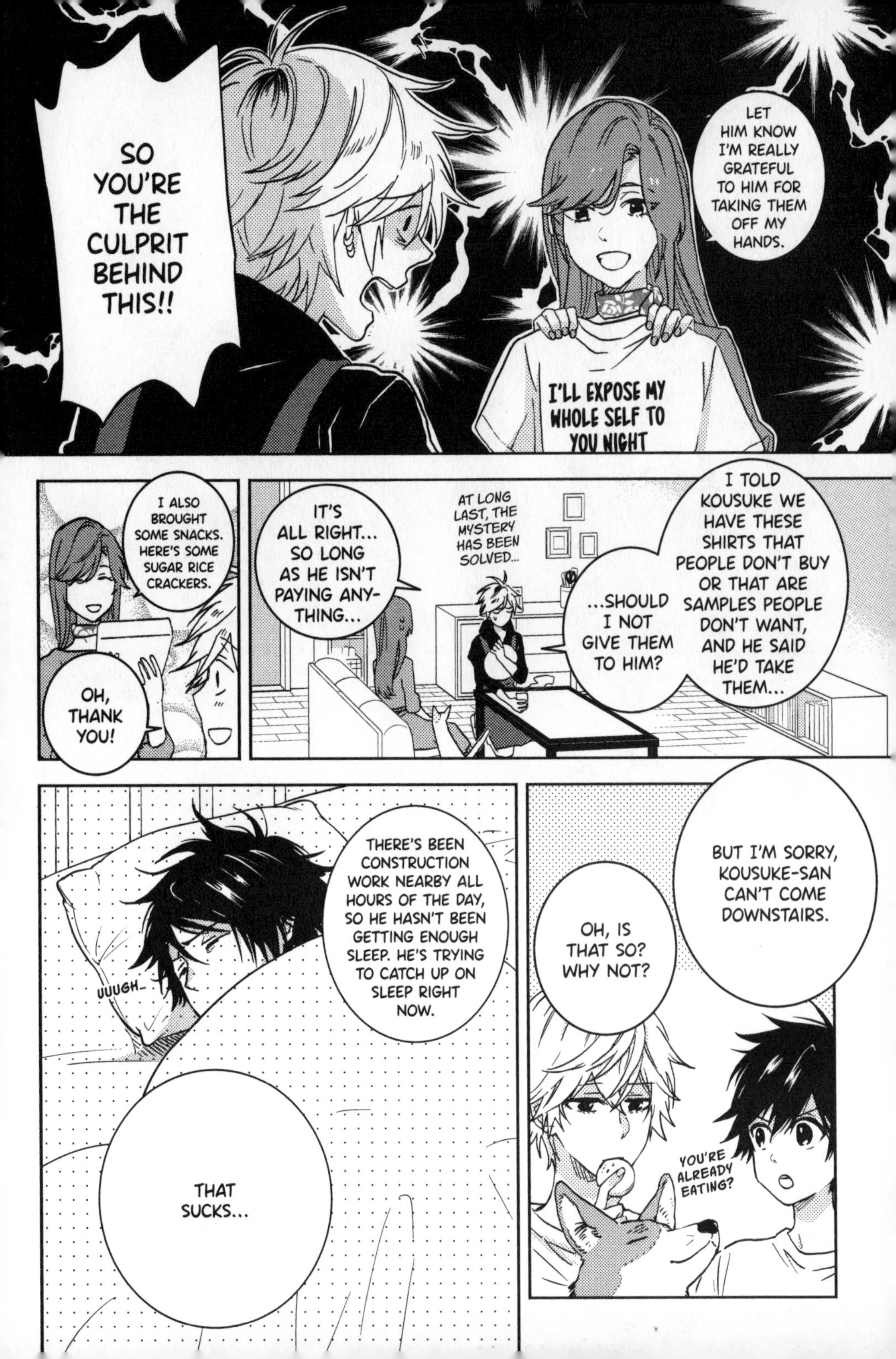
LET HIM KNOW I'M REALLY GRATEFUL TO HIM FOR TAKING THEM OFF MY HANDS.
SO YOU'RE THE CULPRIT BEHIND THIS!!
I'LL EXPOSE MY WHOLE SELF TO YOU NIGHT
I TOLD KOUSUKE WE HAVE THESE SHIRTS THAT PEOPLE DON'T BUY OR THAT ARE SAMPLES PEOPLE DON'T WANT, AND HE SAID HE'D TAKE THEM...
...SHOULD I NOT GIVE THEM TO HIM?
AT LONG LAST, THE MYSTERY HAS BEEN SOLVED...
IT'S ALL RIGHT... SO LONG AS HE ISN'T PAYING ANY-THING...
I ALSO BROUGHT SOME SNACKS. HERE'S SOME SUGAR RICE CRACKERS.
OH, THANK YOU!
BUT I'M SORRY, KOUSUKE-SAN CAN'T COME DOWNSTAIRS.
OH, IS THAT SO? WHY NOT?
YOU'RE ALREADY EATING?
THERE'S BEEN CONSTRUCTION WORK NEARBY ALL HOURS OF THE DAY, SO HE HASN'T BEEN GETTING ENOUGH SLEEP. HE'S TRYING TO CATCH UP ON SLEEP RIGHT NOW.
UUUGH...
THAT SUCKS...

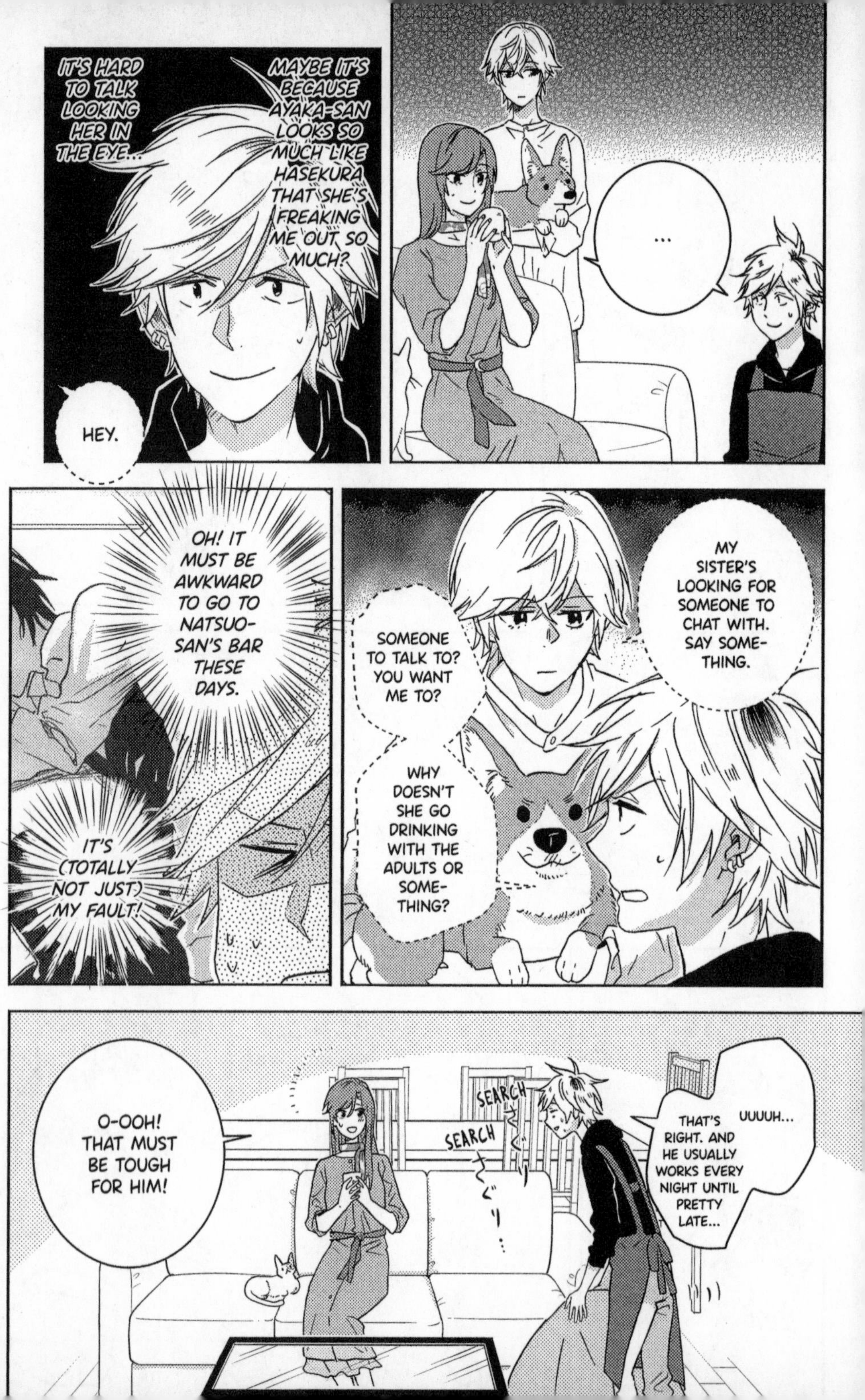
...
MAYBE IT'S BECAUSE AYAKA-SAN LOOKS SO MUCH LIKE HASEKURA THAT SHE'S FREAKING ME OUT SO MUCH?
IT'S HARD TO TALK LOOKING HER IN THE EYE...
HEY.
MY SISTER'S LOOKING FOR SOMEONE TO CHAT WITH. SAY SOME-THING.
SOMEONE TO TALK TO? YOU WANT ME TO?
WHY DOESN'T SHE GO DRINKING WITH THE ADULTS OR SOME-THING?
OH! IT MUST BE AWKWARD TO GO TO NATSUO-SAN'S BAR THESE DAYS.
IT'S (TOTALLY NOT JUST) MY FAULT!
UUUUH...
THAT'S RIGHT. AND HE USUALLY WORKS EVERY NIGHT UNTIL PRETTY LATE...
SEARCH
SEARCH
O-OOH! THAT MUST BE TOUGH FOR HIM!

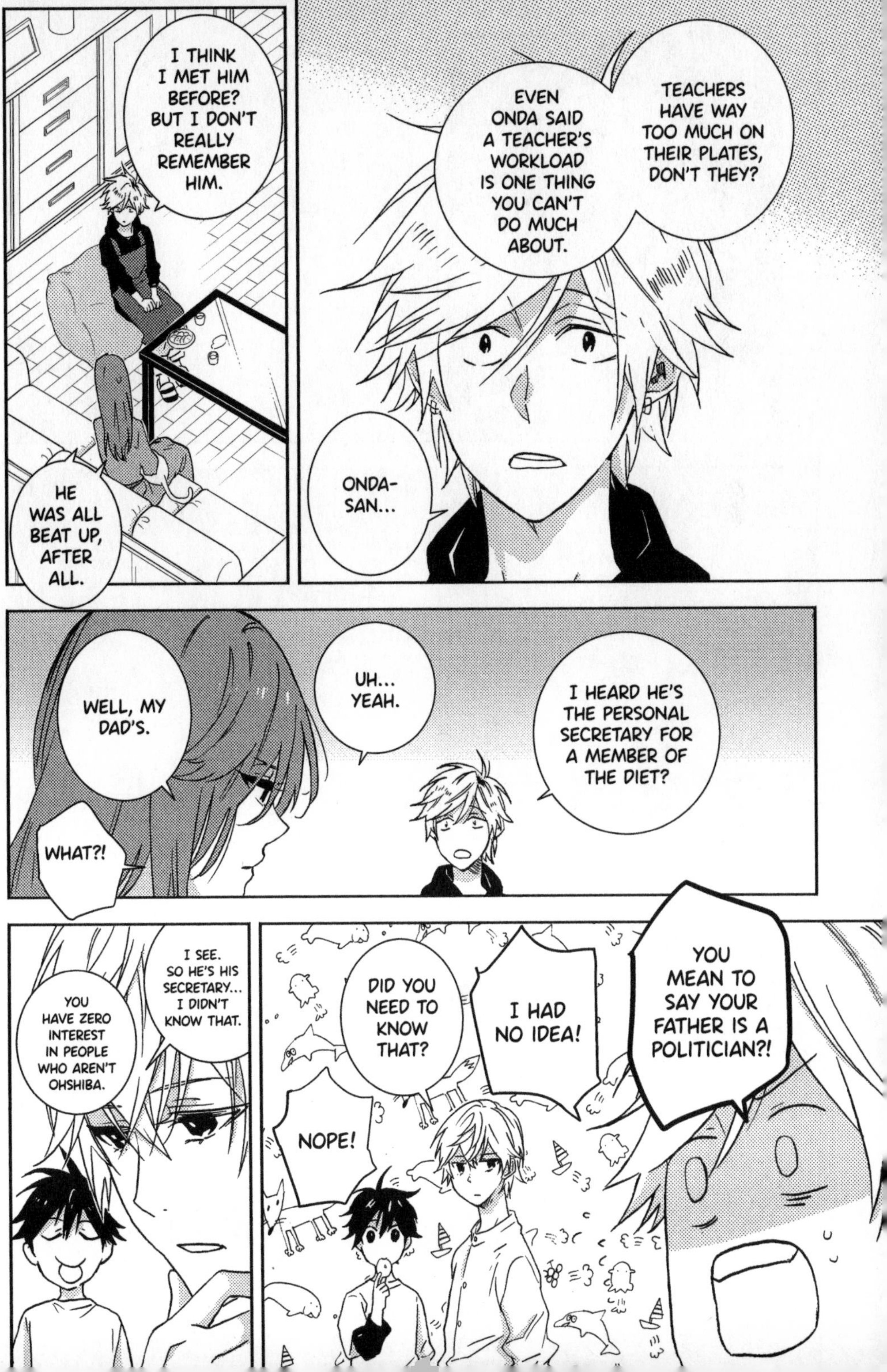
TEACHERS HAVE WAY TOO MUCH ON THEIR PLATES, DON'T THEY?
EVEN ONDA SAID A TEACHER'S WORKLOAD IS ONE THING YOU CAN'T DO MUCH ABOUT.
ONDA-SAN...
I THINK I MET HIM BEFORE? BUT I DON'T REALLY REMEMBER HIM.
HE WAS ALL BEAT UP, AFTER ALL.
I HEARD HE'S THE PERSONAL SECRETARY FOR A MEMBER OF THE DIET?
UH... YEAH.
WELL, MY DAD'S.
WHAT?!
YOU MEAN TO SAY YOUR FATHER IS A POLITICIAN?!
I HAD NO IDEA!
DID YOU NEED TO KNOW THAT?
NOPE!
I SEE. SO HE'S HIS SECRETARY... I DIDN'T KNOW THAT.
YOU HAVE ZERO INTEREST IN PEOPLE WHO AREN'T OHSHIBA.

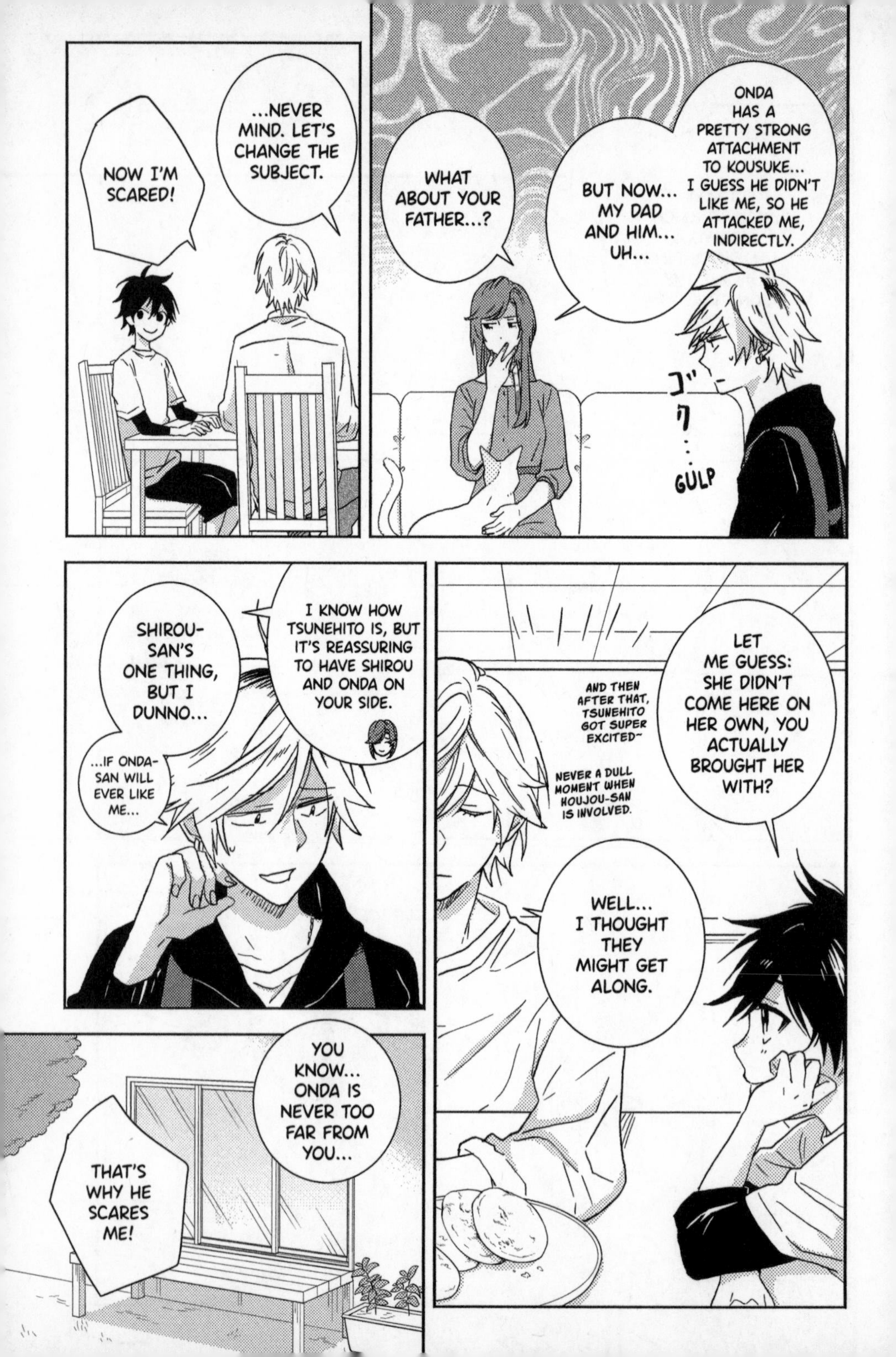
ONDA HAS A PRETTY STRONG ATTACHMENT TO KOUSUKE... I GUESS HE DIDN'T LIKE ME, SO HE ATTACKED ME, INDIRECTLY.
BUT NOW... MY DAD AND HIM... UH...
WHAT ABOUT YOUR FATHER...?
ゴク...
GULP
...NEVER MIND. LET'S CHANGE THE SUBJECT.
NOW I'M SCARED!
LET ME GUESS: SHE DIDN'T COME HERE ON HER OWN, YOU ACTUALLY BROUGHT HER WITH?
AND THEN AFTER THAT, TSUNEHITO GOT SUPER EXCITED~
NEVER A DULL MOMENT WHEN HOUJOU-SAN IS INVOLVED.
WELL... I THOUGHT THEY MIGHT GET ALONG.
I KNOW HOW TSUNEHITO IS, BUT IT'S REASSURING TO HAVE SHIROU AND ONDA ON YOUR SIDE.
SHIROU-SAN'S ONE THING, BUT I DUNNO...
...IF ONDA-SAN WILL EVER LIKE ME...
YOU KNOW... ONDA IS NEVER TOO FAR FROM YOU...
THAT'S WHY HE SCARES ME!

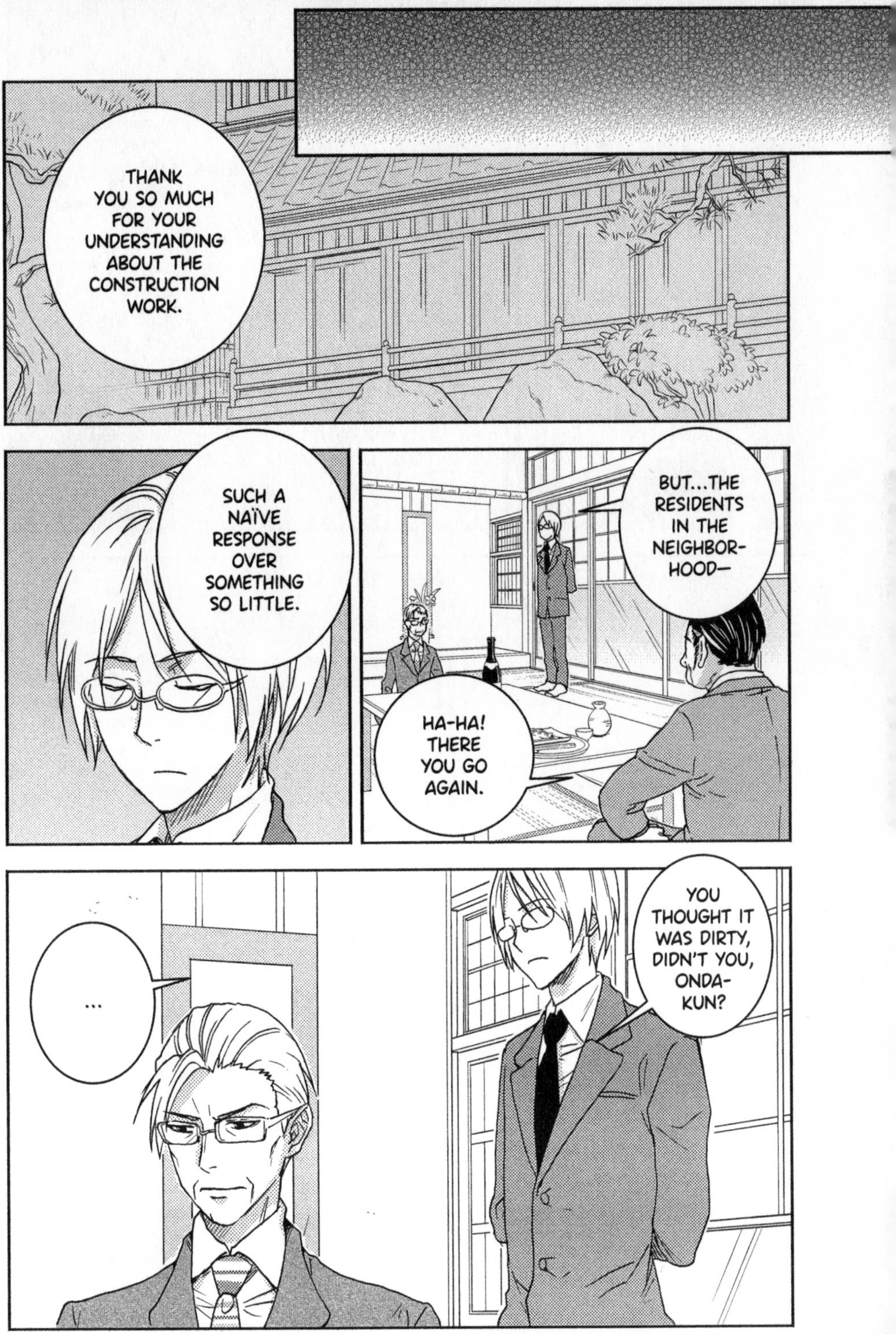
THANK YOU SO MUCH FOR YOUR UNDERSTANDING ABOUT THE CONSTRUCTION WORK.
BUT...THE RESIDENTS IN THE NEIGHBOR-HOOD—
HA-HA! THERE YOU GO AGAIN.
SUCH A NAÏVE RESPONSE OVER SOMETHING SO LITTLE.
YOU THOUGHT IT WAS DIRTY, DIDN'T YOU, ONDA-KUN?
...

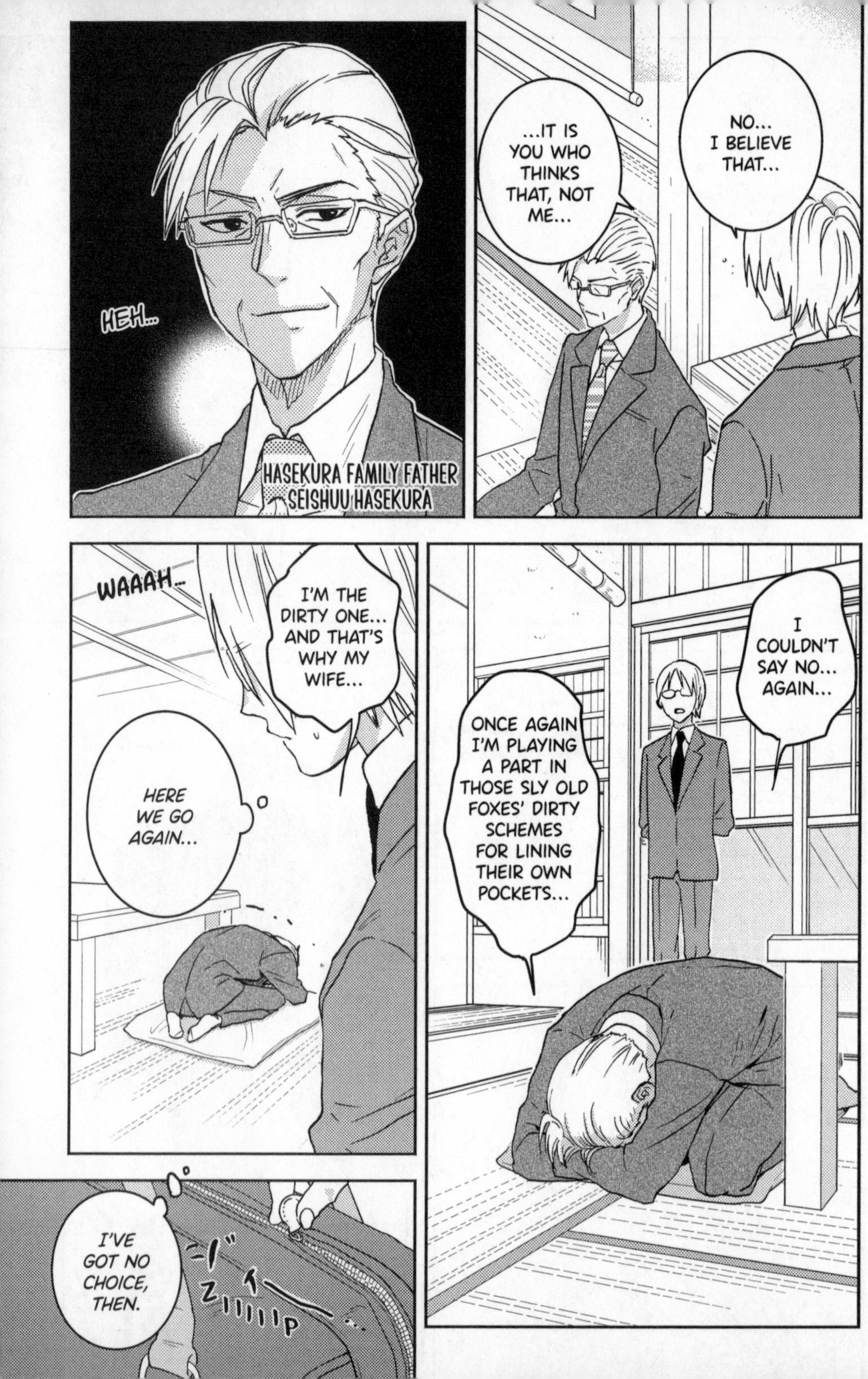
NO... I BELIEVE THAT...
...IT IS YOU WHO THINKS THAT, NOT ME...
HEH...
HASEKURA FAMILY FATHER SEISHUU HASEKURA
I COULDN'T SAY NO... AGAIN...
ONCE AGAIN I'M PLAYING A PART IN THOSE SLY OLD FOXES' DIRTY SCHEMES FOR LINING THEIR OWN POCKETS...
WAAAH...
I'M THE DIRTY ONE... AND THAT'S WHY MY WIFE...
HERE WE GO AGAIN...
I'VE GOT NO CHOICE, THEN.
ZIIIIIP

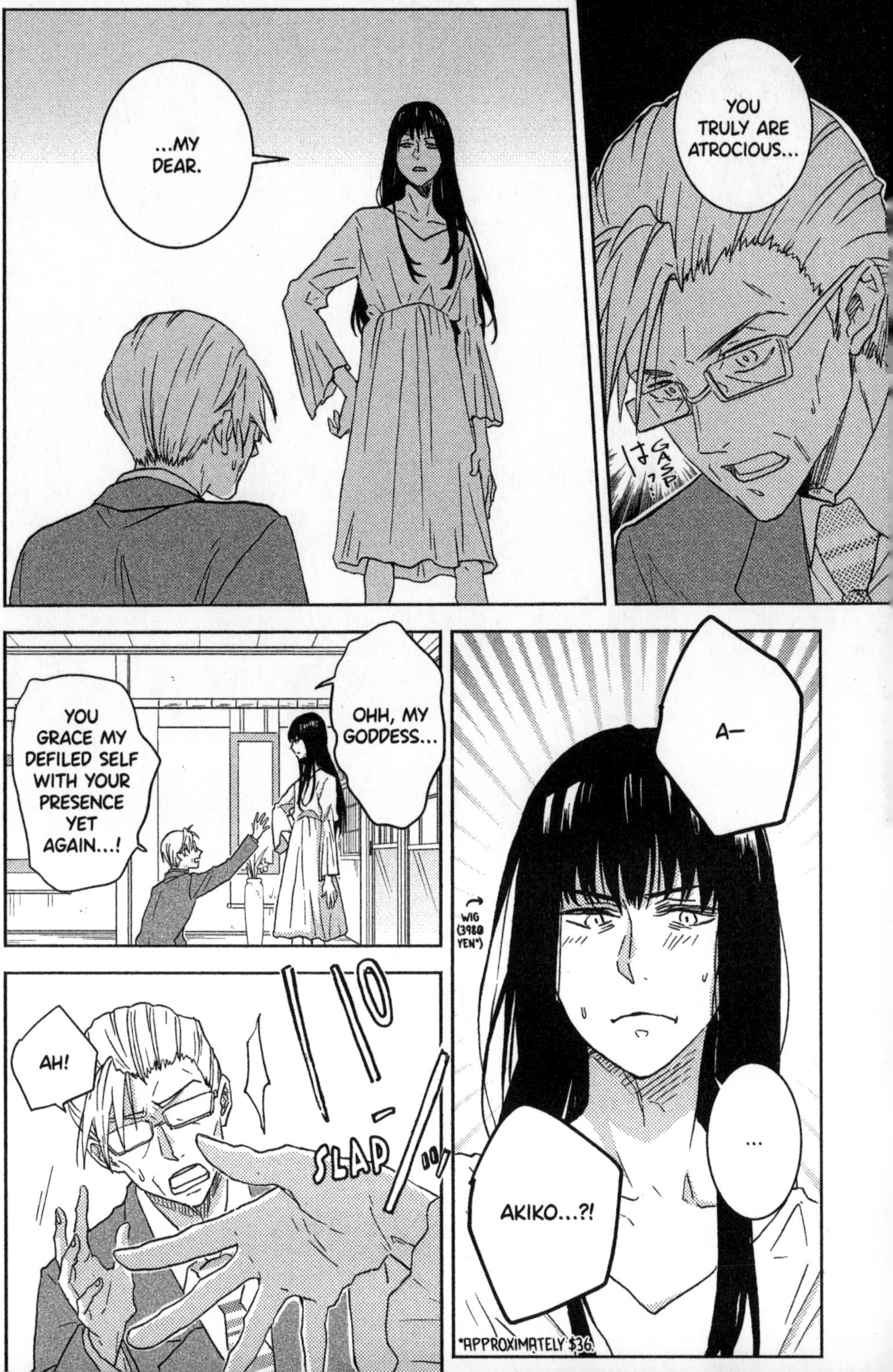
YOU TRULY ARE ATROCIOUS...
は GASP
...MY DEAR.
A—
WIG (3980 YEN*)
...
AKIKO...?!
*APPROXIMATELY $36.
OHH, MY GODDESS...
YOU GRACE MY DEFILED SELF WITH YOUR PRESENCE YET AGAIN...!
SLAP
AH!

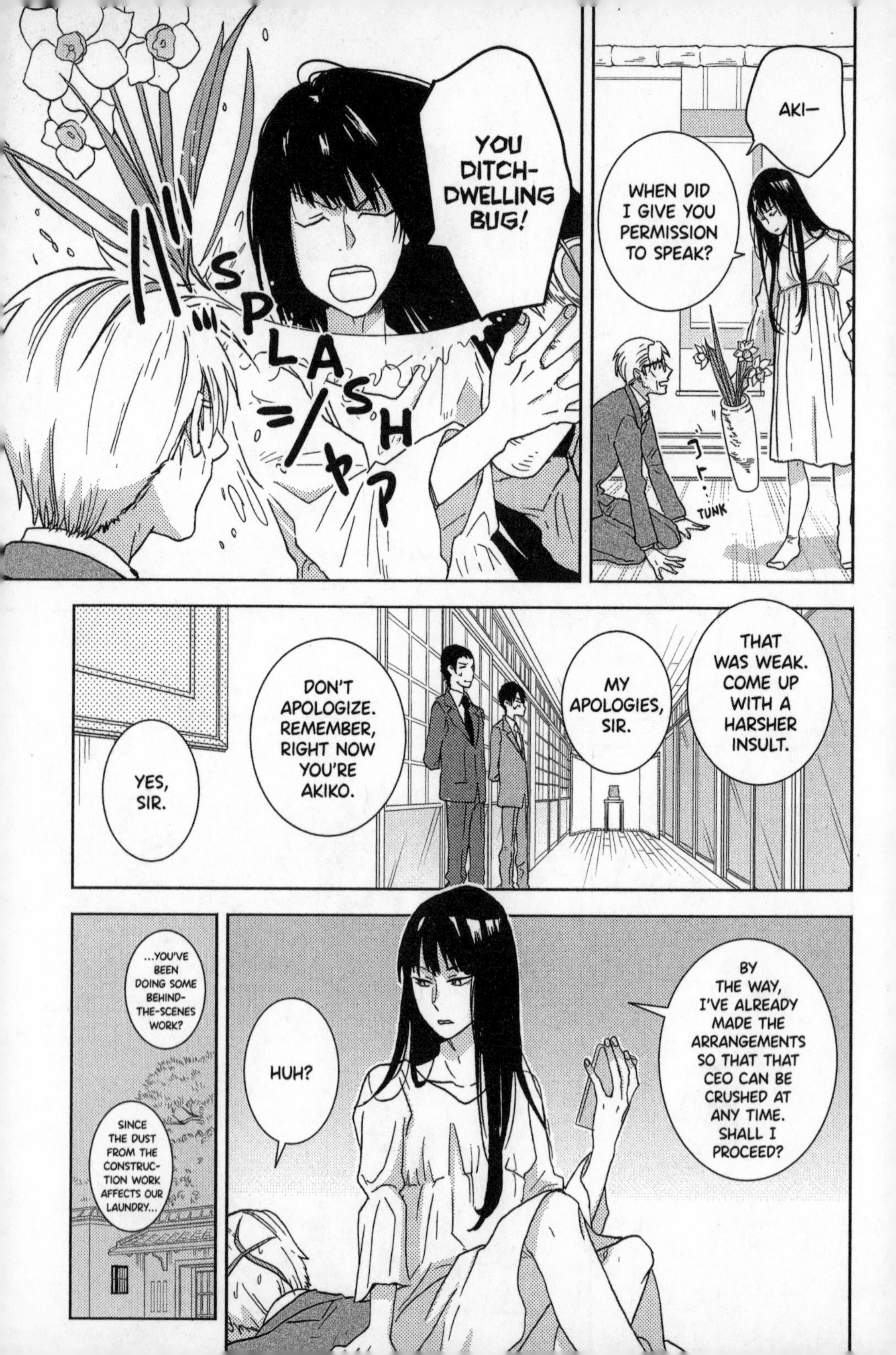
AKI—
WHEN DID I GIVE YOU PERMISSION TO SPEAK?
TUNK
YOU DITCH-DWELLING BUG!
SPLASH
THAT WAS WEAK. COME UP WITH A HARSHER INSULT.
MY APOLOGIES, SIR.
DON'T APOLOGIZE. REMEMBER, RIGHT NOW YOU'RE AKIKO.
YES, SIR.
BY THE WAY, I'VE ALREADY MADE THE ARRANGEMENTS SO THAT THAT CEO CAN BE CRUSHED AT ANY TIME. SHALL I PROCEED?
HUH?
...YOU'VE BEEN DOING SOME BEHIND-THE-SCENES WORK?
SINCE THE DUST FROM THE CONSTRUCTION WORK AFFECTS OUR LAUNDRY...

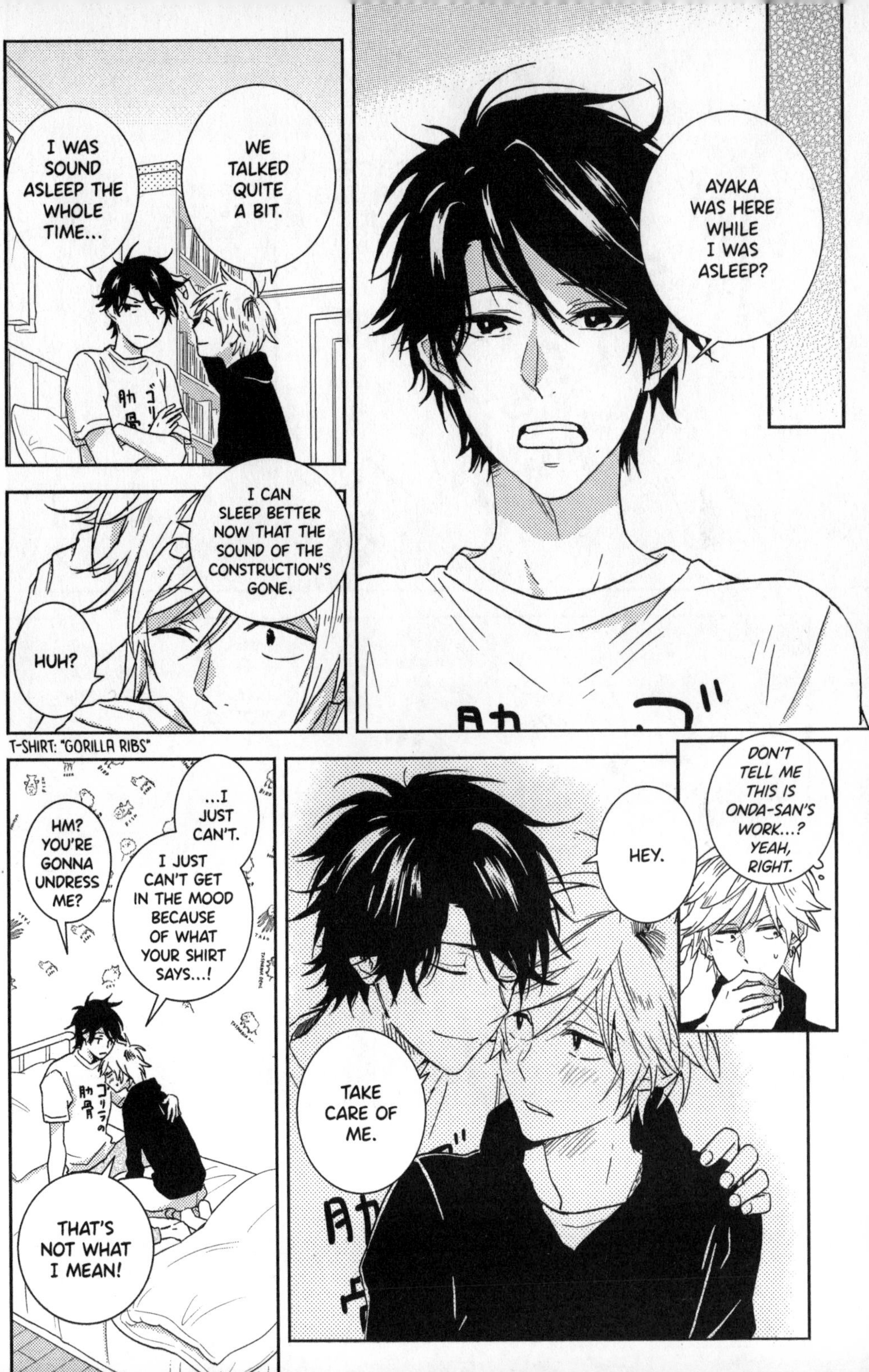
AYAKA WAS HERE WHILE I WAS ASLEEP?
WE TALKED QUITE A BIT.
I WAS SOUND ASLEEP THE WHOLE TIME...
I CAN SLEEP BETTER NOW THAT THE SOUND OF THE CONSTRUCTION'S GONE.
HUH?
T-SHIRT: "GORILLA RIBS"
DON'T TELL ME THIS IS ONDA-SAN'S WORK...? YEAH, RIGHT.
HEY.
TAKE CARE OF ME.
...I JUST CAN'T.
HM? YOU'RE GONNA UNDRESS ME?
I JUST CAN'T GET IN THE MOOD BECAUSE OF WHAT YOUR SHIRT SAYS...!
THAT'S NOT WHAT I MEAN!

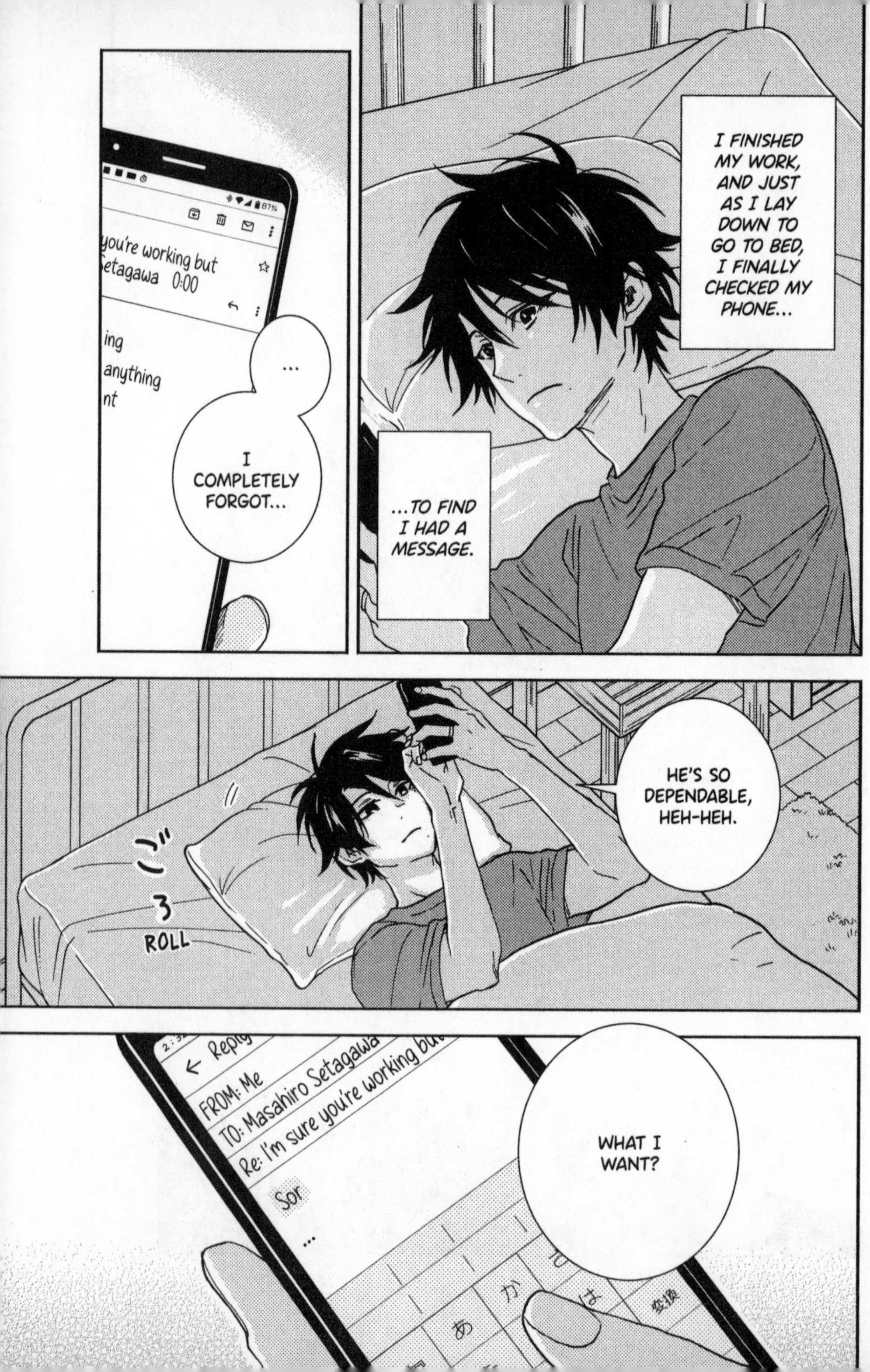
I FINISHED MY WORK, AND JUST AS I LAY DOWN TO GO TO BED, I FINALLY CHECKED MY PHONE...
...TO FIND I HAD A MESSAGE.
you're working but
Setagawa 0:00
ing
anything
nt
...
I COMPLETELY FORGOT...
ROLL
HE'S SO DEPENDABLE, HEH-HEH.
Reply
FROM: Me
TO: Masahiro Setagawa
Re: I'm sure you're working bu
Sor
...
WHAT I WANT?

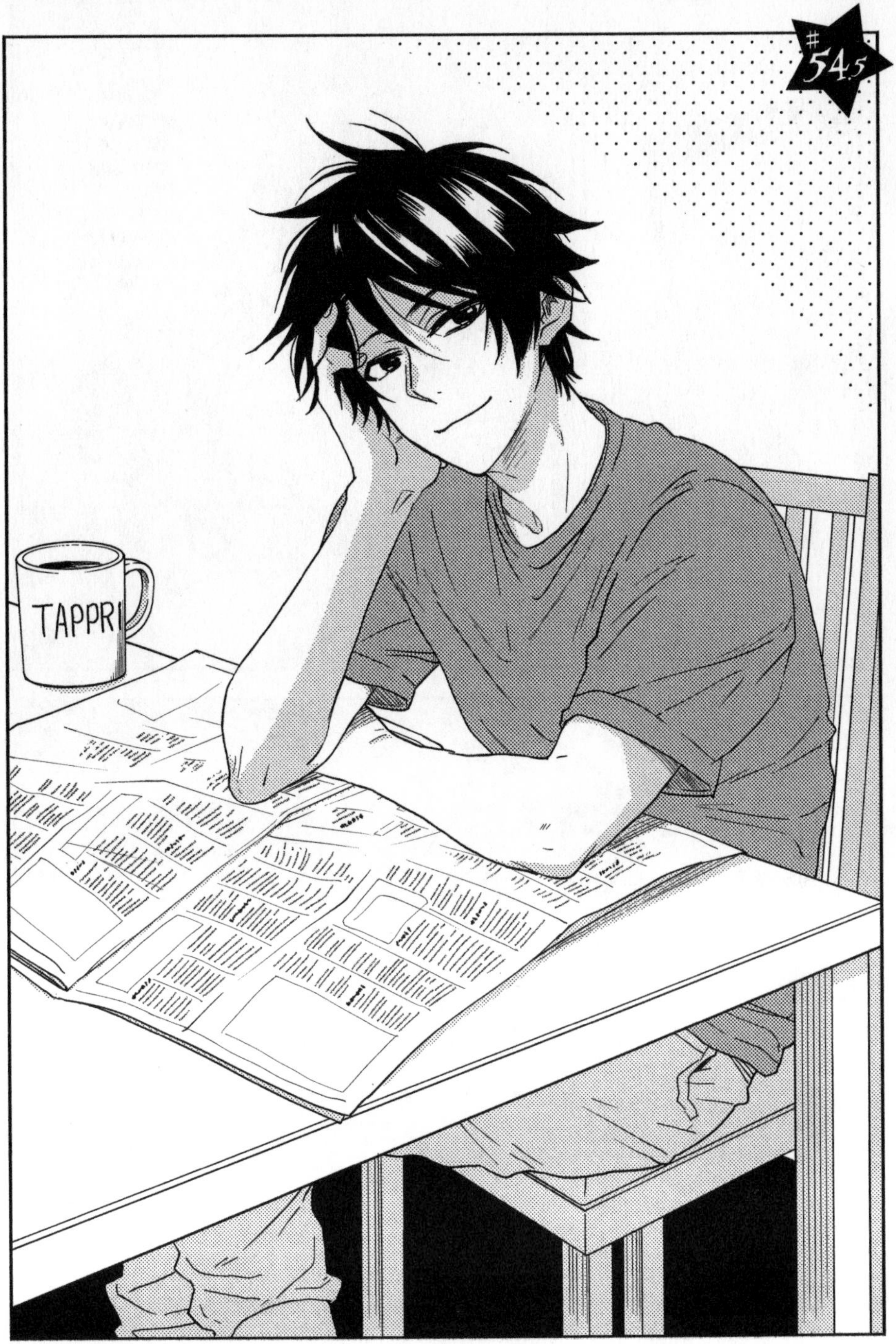
#54.5
TAPPRI

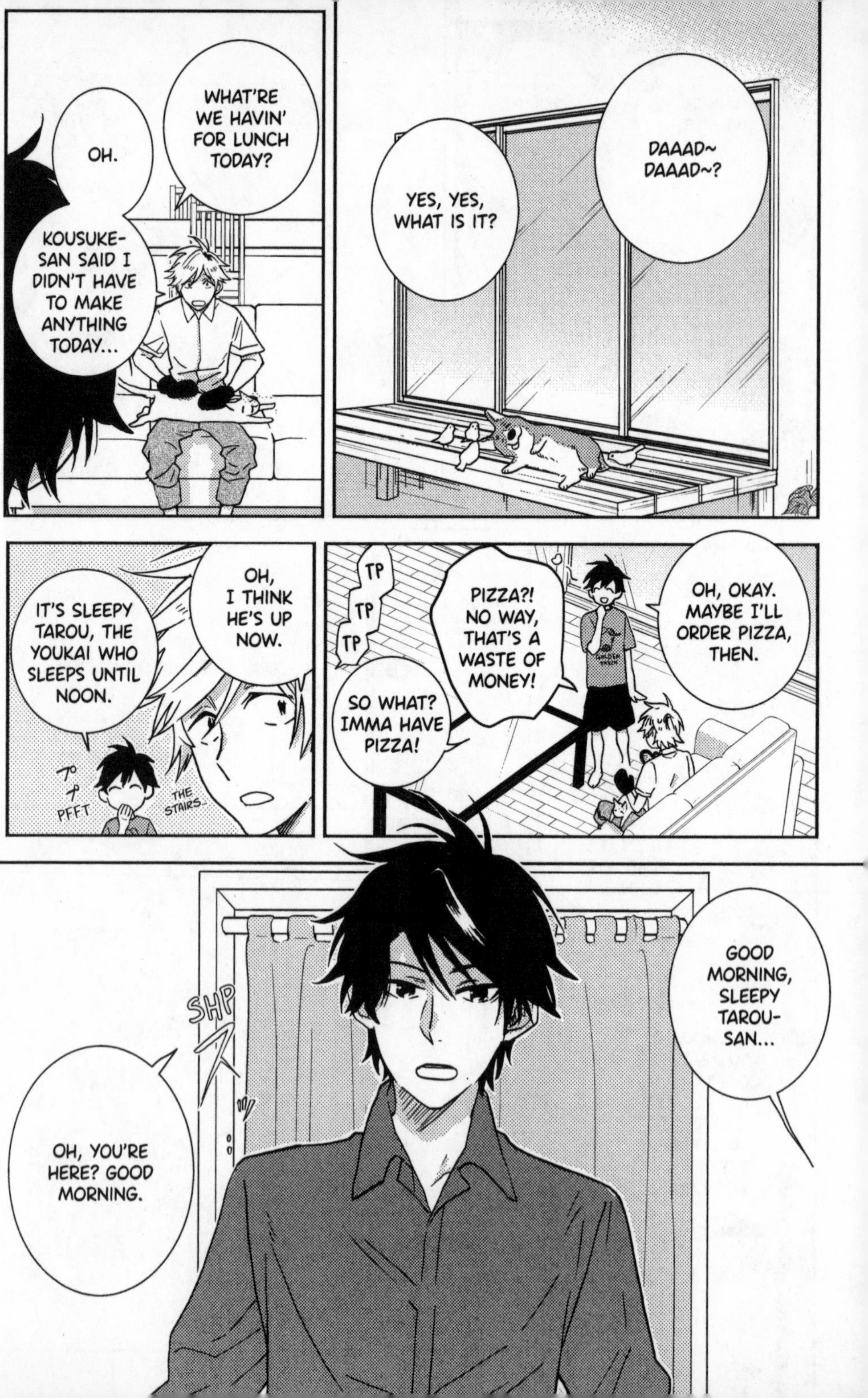
DAAAD~ DAAAD~?
YES, YES, WHAT IS IT?
WHAT'RE WE HAVIN' FOR LUNCH TODAY?
OH.
KOUSUKE-SAN SAID I DIDN'T HAVE TO MAKE ANYTHING TODAY...
OH, OKAY. MAYBE I'LL ORDER PIZZA, THEN.
PIZZA?! NO WAY, THAT'S A WASTE OF MONEY!
TP
TP
TP
SO WHAT? IMMA HAVE PIZZA!
OH, I THINK HE'S UP NOW.
IT'S SLEEPY TAROU, THE YOUKAI WHO SLEEPS UNTIL NOON.
THE STAIRS...
PFFT
GOOD MORNING, SLEEPY TAROU-SAN...
SHP
OH, YOU'RE HERE? GOOD MORNING.

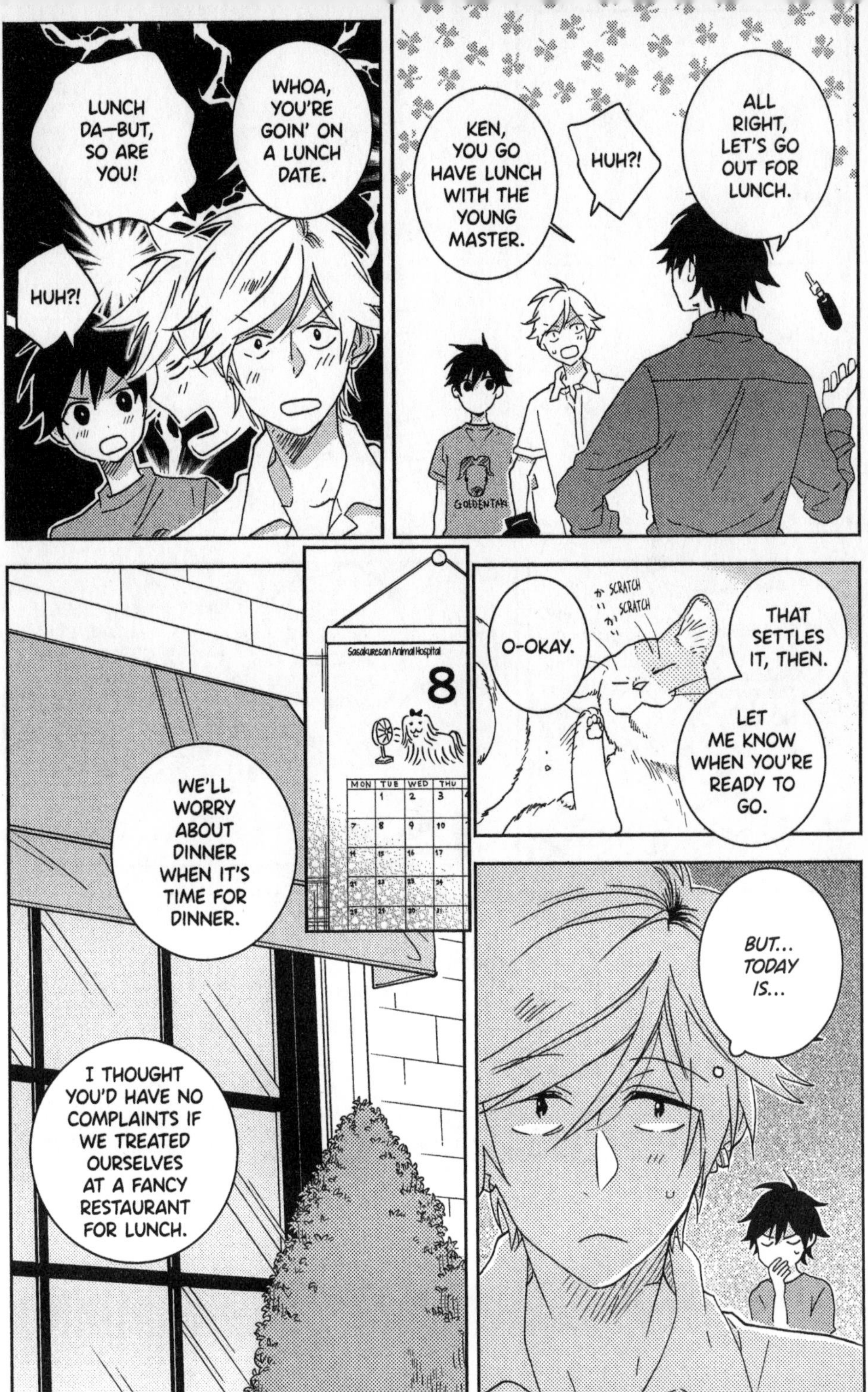
ALL RIGHT, LET'S GO OUT FOR LUNCH.
HUH?!
KEN, YOU GO HAVE LUNCH WITH THE YOUNG MASTER.
WHOA, YOU'RE GOIN' ON A LUNCH DATE.
LUNCH DA—BUT, SO ARE YOU!
HUH?!
THAT SETTLES IT, THEN.
LET ME KNOW WHEN YOU'RE READY TO GO.
かい SCRATCH
かい SCRATCH
O-OKAY.
BUT... TODAY IS...
Sasakuresan Animal Hospital
8
MON TUE WED THU
WE'LL WORRY ABOUT DINNER WHEN IT'S TIME FOR DINNER.
I THOUGHT YOU'D HAVE NO COMPLAINTS IF WE TREATED OURSELVES AT A FANCY RESTAURANT FOR LUNCH.

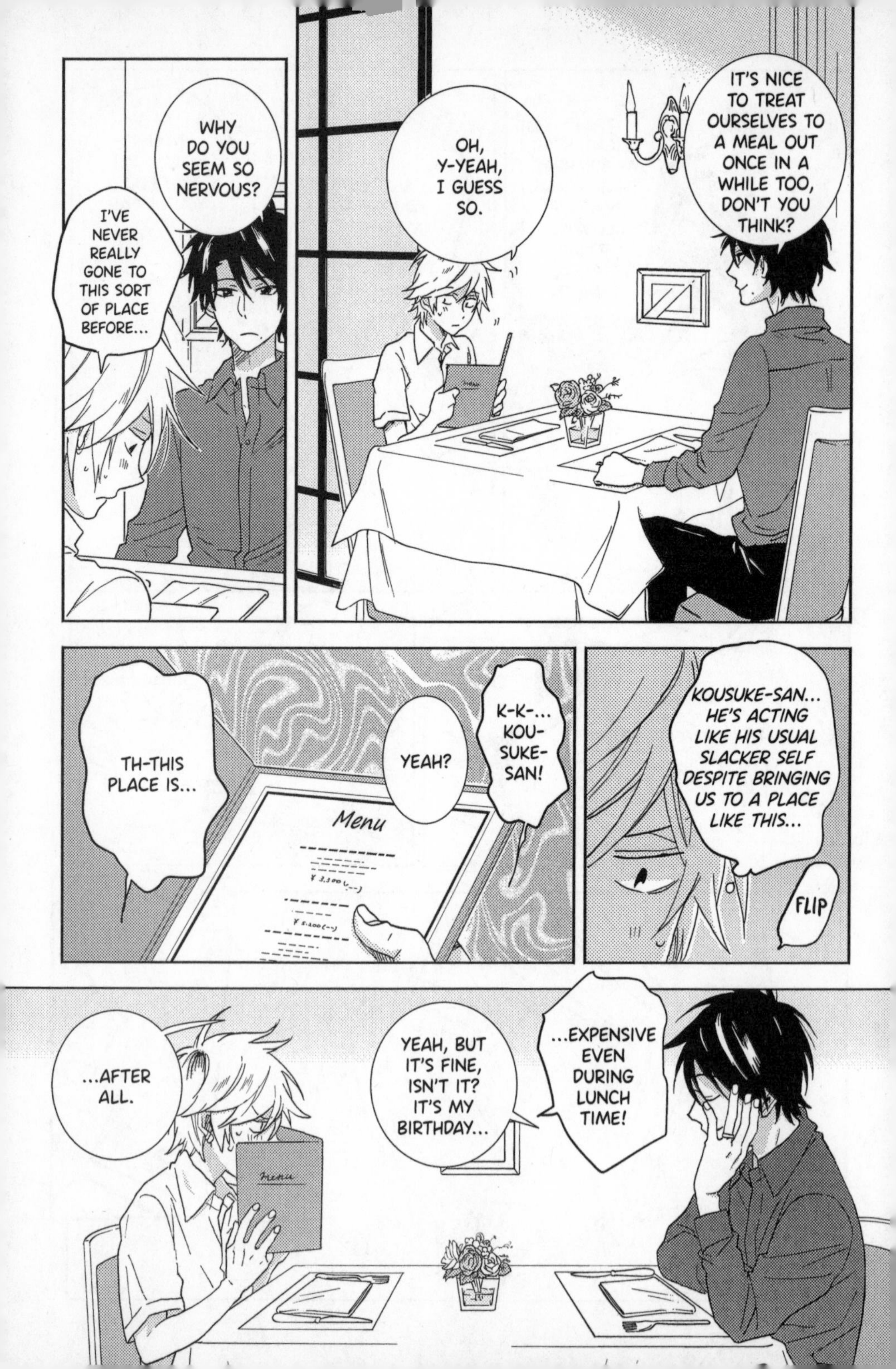
IT'S NICE TO TREAT OURSELVES TO A MEAL OUT ONCE IN A WHILE TOO, DON'T YOU THINK?
OH, Y-YEAH, I GUESS SO.
WHY DO YOU SEEM SO NERVOUS?
I'VE NEVER REALLY GONE TO THIS SORT OF PLACE BEFORE...
KOUSUKE-SAN... HE'S ACTING LIKE HIS USUAL SLACKER SELF DESPITE BRINGING US TO A PLACE LIKE THIS...
FLIP
K-K-... KOU-SUKE-SAN!
YEAH?
Menu
TH-THIS PLACE IS...
...EXPENSIVE EVEN DURING LUNCH TIME!
YEAH, BUT IT'S FINE, ISN'T IT? IT'S MY BIRTHDAY...
...AFTER ALL.

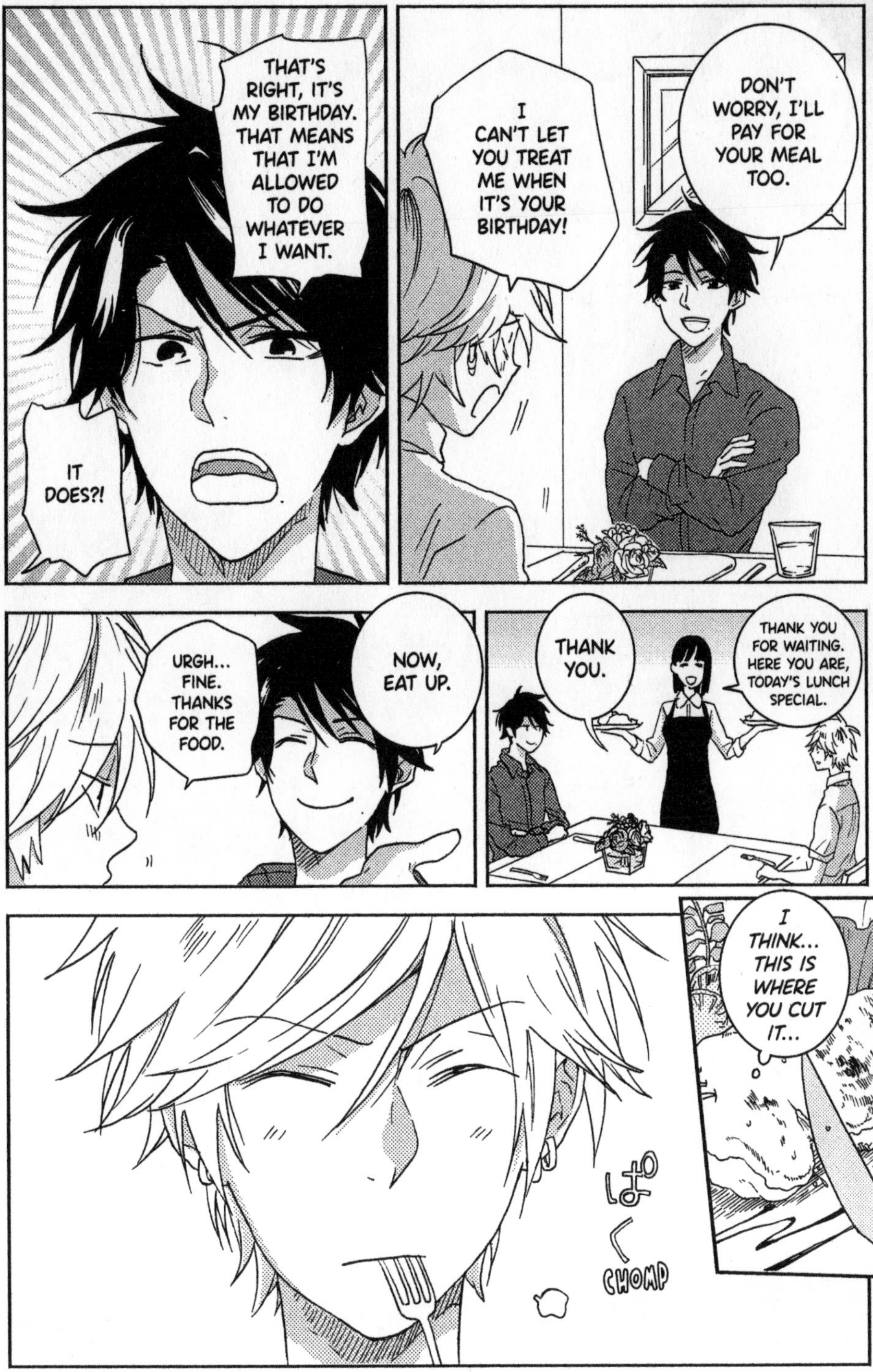
DON'T WORRY, I'LL PAY FOR YOUR MEAL TOO.
I CAN'T LET YOU TREAT ME WHEN IT'S YOUR BIRTHDAY!
THAT'S RIGHT, IT'S MY BIRTHDAY. THAT MEANS THAT I'M ALLOWED TO DO WHATEVER I WANT.
IT DOES?!
THANK YOU FOR WAITING. HERE YOU ARE, TODAY'S LUNCH SPECIAL.
THANK YOU.
NOW, EAT UP.
URGH... FINE. THANKS FOR THE FOOD.
I THINK... THIS IS WHERE YOU CUT IT...
ぱく
CHOMP

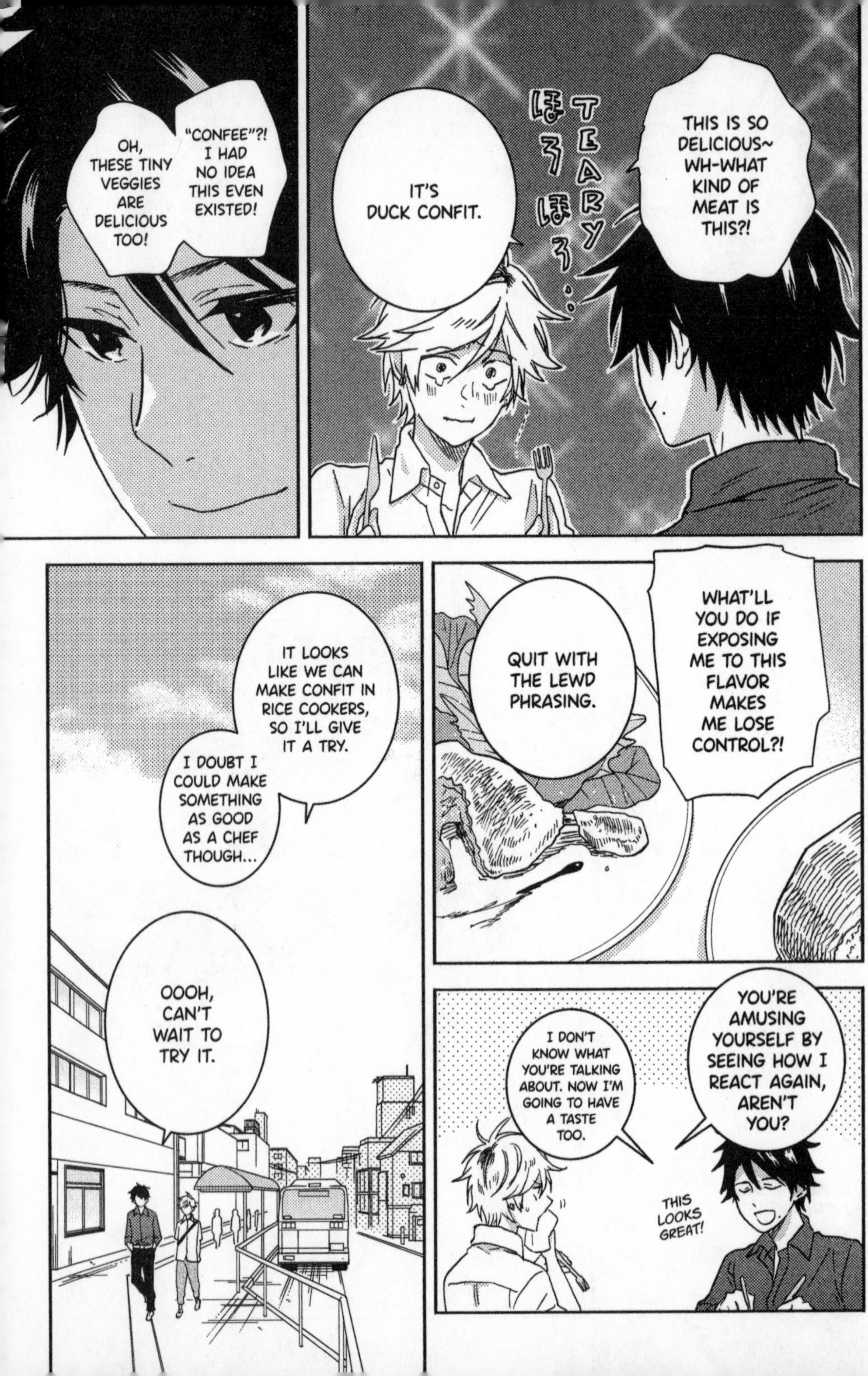
THIS IS SO DELICIOUS~ WH-WHAT KIND OF MEAT IS THIS?!
TEARY
ぽろぽろ
IT'S DUCK CONFIT.
"CONFEE"?! I HAD NO IDEA THIS EVEN EXISTED!
OH, THESE TINY VEGGIES ARE DELICIOUS TOO!
WHAT'LL YOU DO IF EXPOSING ME TO THIS FLAVOR MAKES ME LOSE CONTROL?!
QUIT WITH THE LEWD PHRASING.
YOU'RE AMUSING YOURSELF BY SEEING HOW I REACT AGAIN, AREN'T YOU?
I DON'T KNOW WHAT YOU'RE TALKING ABOUT. NOW I'M GOING TO HAVE A TASTE TOO.
THIS LOOKS GREAT!
IT LOOKS LIKE WE CAN MAKE CONFIT IN RICE COOKERS, SO I'LL GIVE IT A TRY.
I DOUBT I COULD MAKE SOMETHING AS GOOD AS A CHEF THOUGH...
OOOH, CAN'T WAIT TO TRY IT.

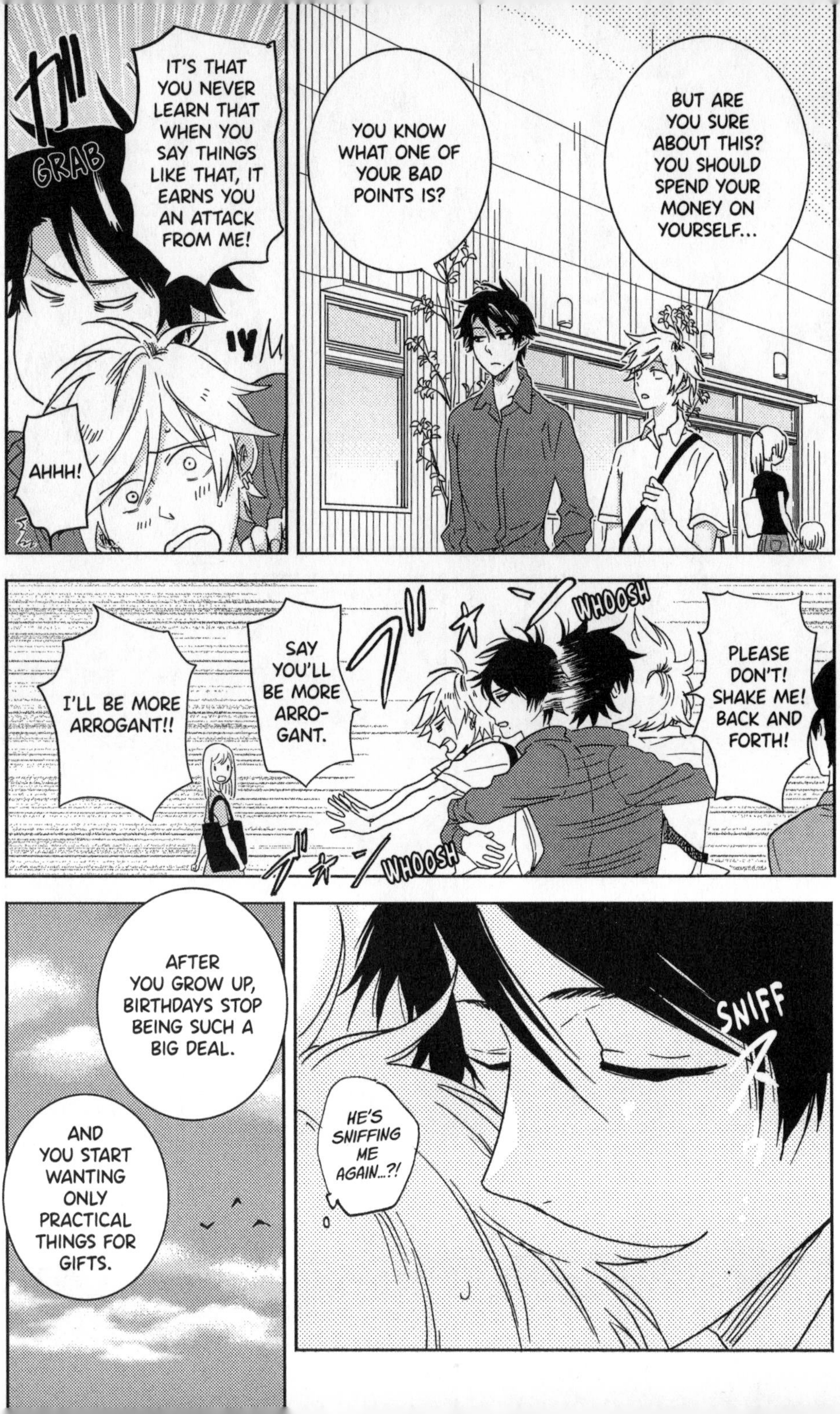
BUT ARE YOU SURE ABOUT THIS? YOU SHOULD SPEND YOUR MONEY ON YOURSELF...
YOU KNOW WHAT ONE OF YOUR BAD POINTS IS?
IT'S THAT YOU NEVER LEARN THAT WHEN YOU SAY THINGS LIKE THAT, IT EARNS YOU AN ATTACK FROM ME!
GRAB
AHHH!
WHOOSH
PLEASE DON'T! SHAKE ME! BACK AND FORTH!
SAY YOU'LL BE MORE ARRO-GANT.
I'LL BE MORE ARROGANT!!
WHOOSH
SNIFF
HE'S SNIFFING ME AGAIN...?!
AFTER YOU GROW UP, BIRTHDAYS STOP BEING SUCH A BIG DEAL.
AND YOU START WANTING ONLY PRACTICAL THINGS FOR GIFTS.

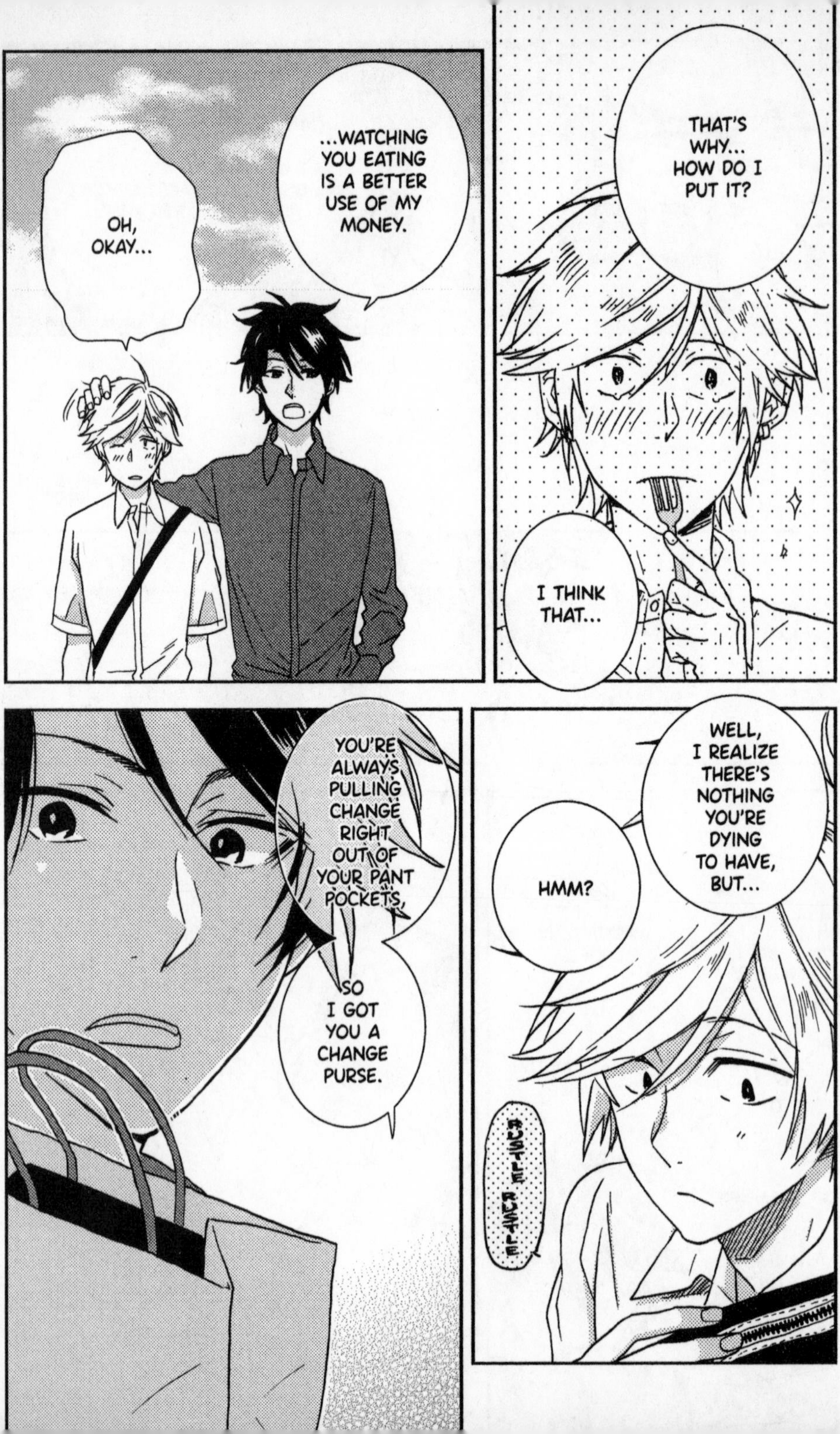
THAT'S WHY... HOW DO I PUT IT?
I THINK THAT...
...WATCHING YOU EATING IS A BETTER USE OF MY MONEY.
OH, OKAY...
WELL, I REALIZE THERE'S NOTHING YOU'RE DYING TO HAVE, BUT...
HMM?
RUSTLE RUSTLE
YOU'RE ALWAYS PULLING CHANGE RIGHT OUT OF YOUR PANT POCKETS,
SO I GOT YOU A CHANGE PURSE.

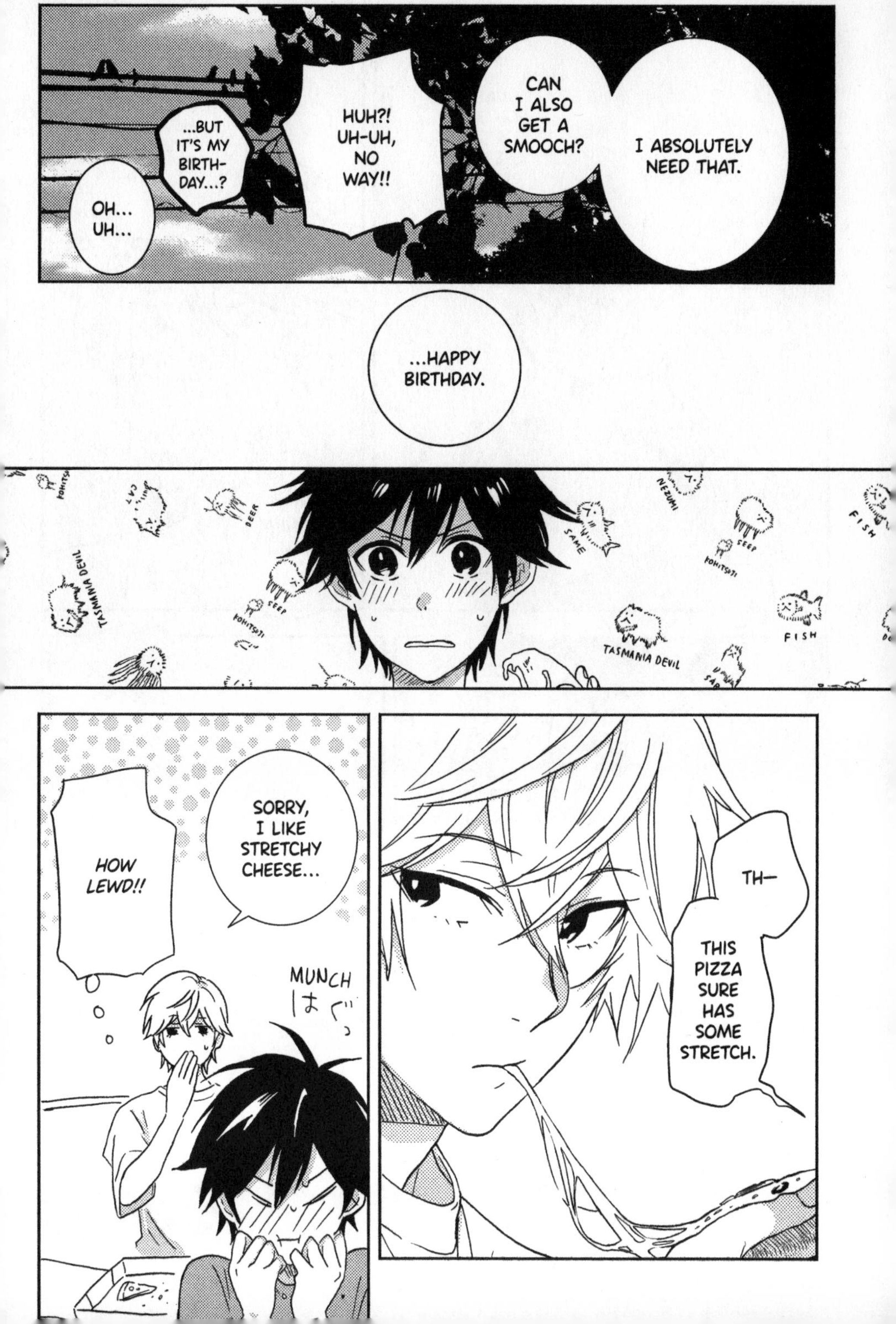
I ABSOLUTELY NEED THAT.
CAN I ALSO GET A SMOOCH?
HUH?! UH-UH, NO WAY!!
...BUT IT'S MY BIRTHDAY...?
OH... UH...
...HAPPY BIRTHDAY.
FISH
SEEP
KOHITSUJI
FISH
TASMANIA DEVIL
NEZUMI
SAME
DEER
CAT
KOHITSUJI
TASMANIA DEVIL
SEEP
KOHITSUJI
TH—
THIS PIZZA SURE HAS SOME STRETCH.
SORRY, I LIKE STRETCHY CHEESE...
HOW LEWD!!
MUNCH はぐっ

SHAMELESSLY
STRETCHED OUT...

COMMENT FROM
THE PIZZA

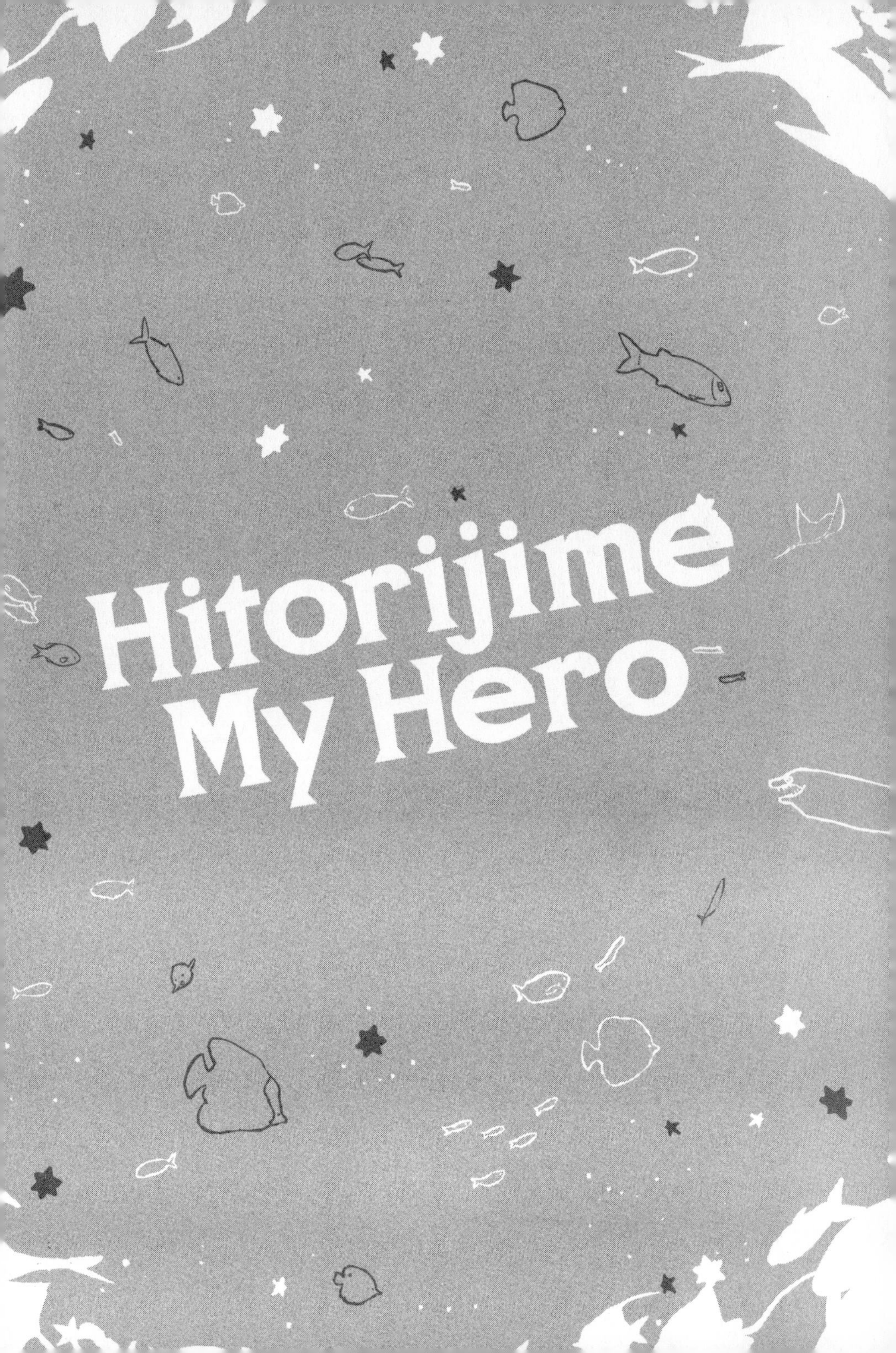
Hitorijime
My Hero

★ INTOXICATION AND DISORDER ★

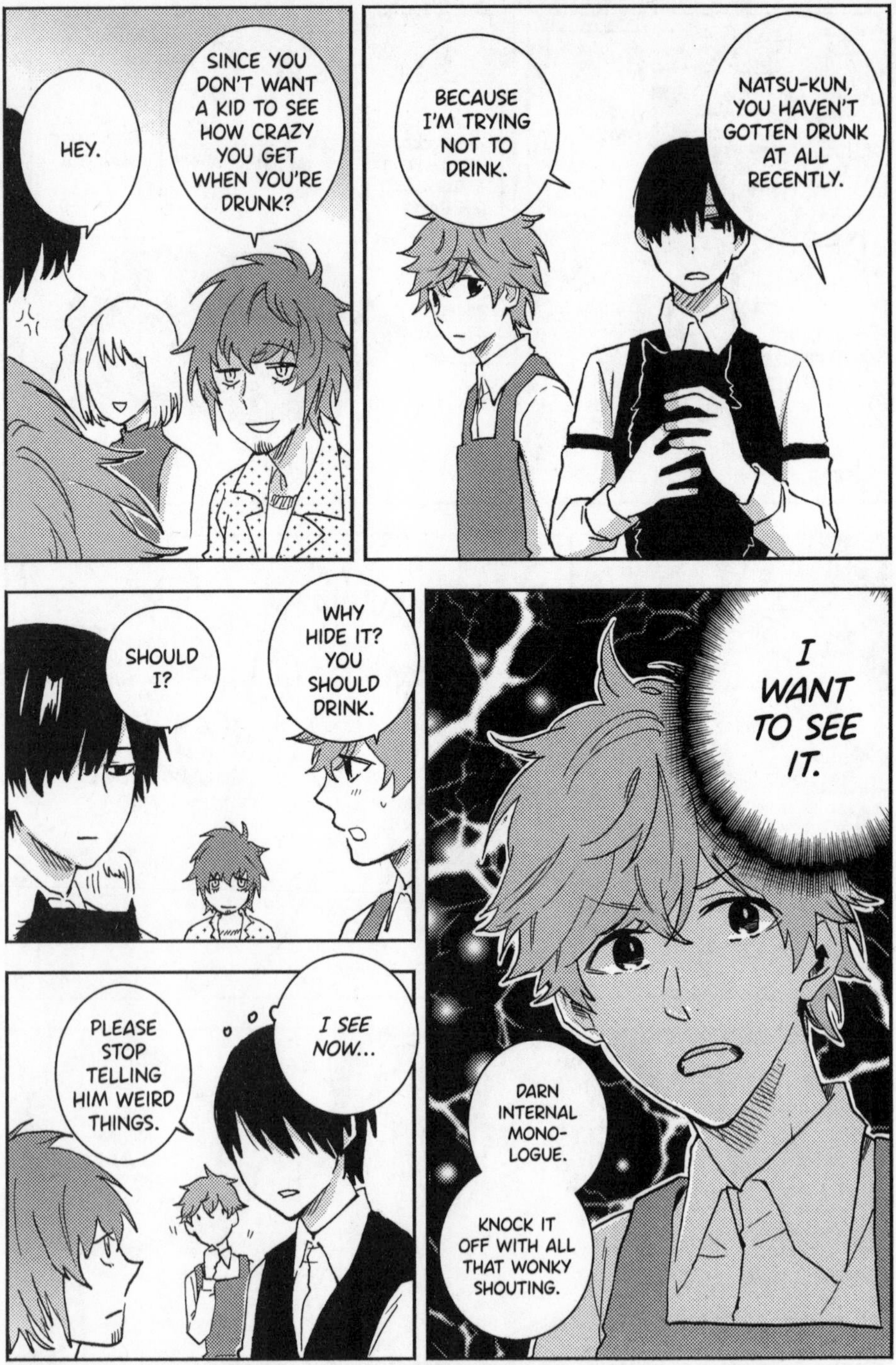

NATSU-KUN, YOU HAVEN'T GOTTEN DRUNK AT ALL RECENTLY.
BECAUSE I'M TRYING NOT TO DRINK.
SINCE YOU DON'T WANT A KID TO SEE HOW CRAZY YOU GET WHEN YOU'RE DRUNK?
HEY.
I WANT TO SEE IT.
DARN INTERNAL MONO-LOGUE.
KNOCK IT OFF WITH ALL THAT WONKY SHOUTING.
WHY HIDE IT? YOU SHOULD DRINK.
SHOULD I?
I SEE NOW...
PLEASE STOP TELLING HIM WEIRD THINGS.

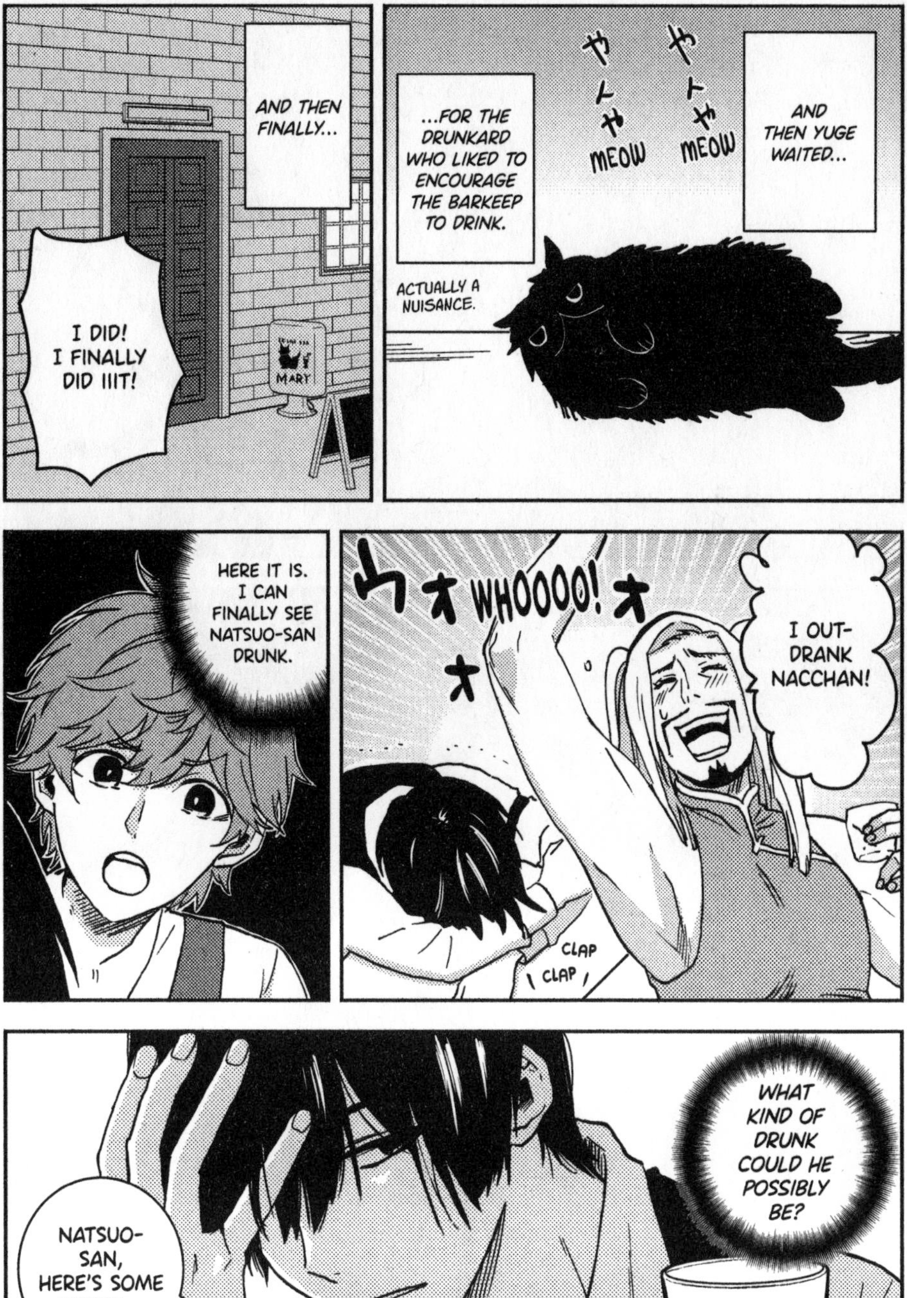
AND THEN YUGE WAITED...
MEOW
MEOW
...FOR THE DRUNKARD WHO LIKED TO ENCOURAGE THE BARKEEP TO DRINK.
ACTUALLY A NUISANCE.
AND THEN FINALLY...
I DID! I FINALLY DID IIIT!
WHOOOO!
I OUT-DRANK NACCHAN!
CLAP
CLAP
HERE IT IS. I CAN FINALLY SEE NATSUO-SAN DRUNK.
WHAT KIND OF DRUNK COULD HE POSSIBLY BE?
NATSUO-SAN, HERE'S SOME WATER...

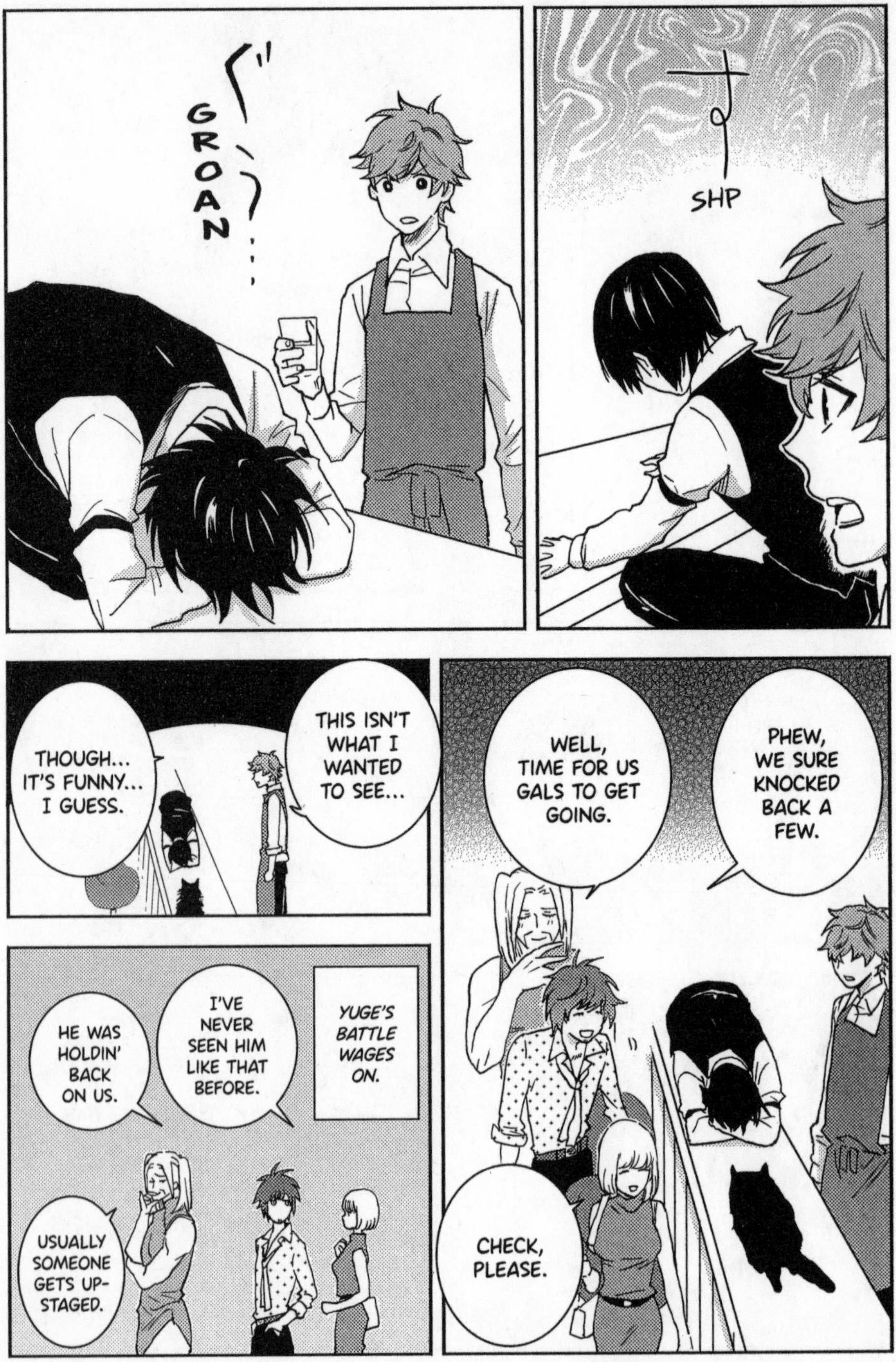
SHP
GROAN...
PHEW, WE SURE KNOCKED BACK A FEW.
WELL, TIME FOR US GALS TO GET GOING.
CHECK, PLEASE.
THIS ISN'T WHAT I WANTED TO SEE...
THOUGH... IT'S FUNNY... I GUESS.
YUGE'S BATTLE WAGES ON.
I'VE NEVER SEEN HIM LIKE THAT BEFORE.
HE WAS HOLDIN' BACK ON US.
USUALLY SOMEONE GETS UP-STAGED.

★ AN UNEXPECTED REALIZATION ★

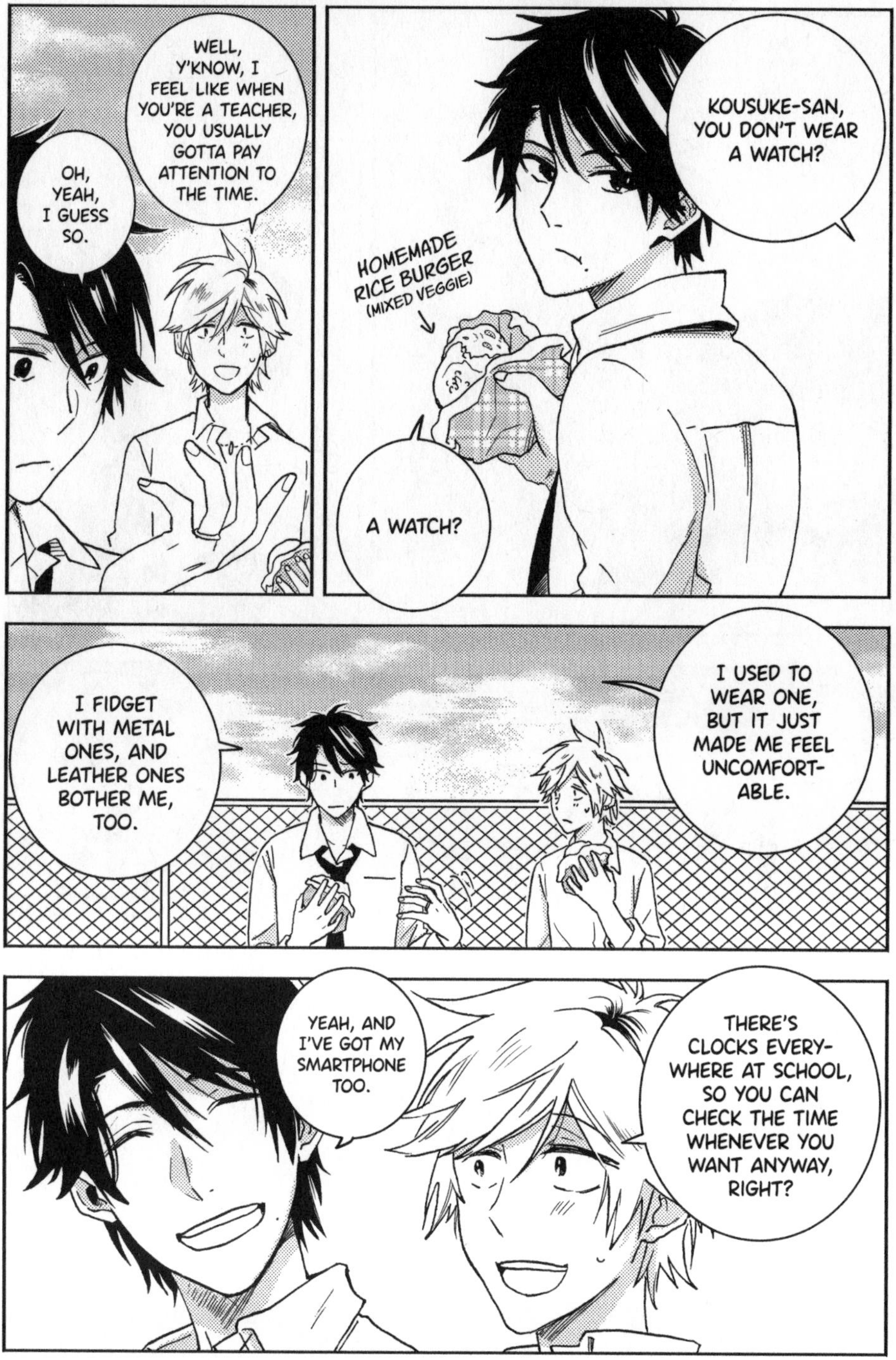
KOUSUKE-SAN, YOU DON'T WEAR A WATCH?
HOMEMADE RICE BURGER (MIXED VEGGIE)
A WATCH?
WELL, Y'KNOW, I FEEL LIKE WHEN YOU'RE A TEACHER, YOU USUALLY GOTTA PAY ATTENTION TO THE TIME.
OH, YEAH, I GUESS SO.
I USED TO WEAR ONE, BUT IT JUST MADE ME FEEL UNCOMFORT-ABLE.
I FIDGET WITH METAL ONES, AND LEATHER ONES BOTHER ME, TOO.
THERE'S CLOCKS EVERY-WHERE AT SCHOOL, SO YOU CAN CHECK THE TIME WHENEVER YOU WANT ANYWAY, RIGHT?
YEAH, AND I'VE GOT MY SMARTPHONE TOO.

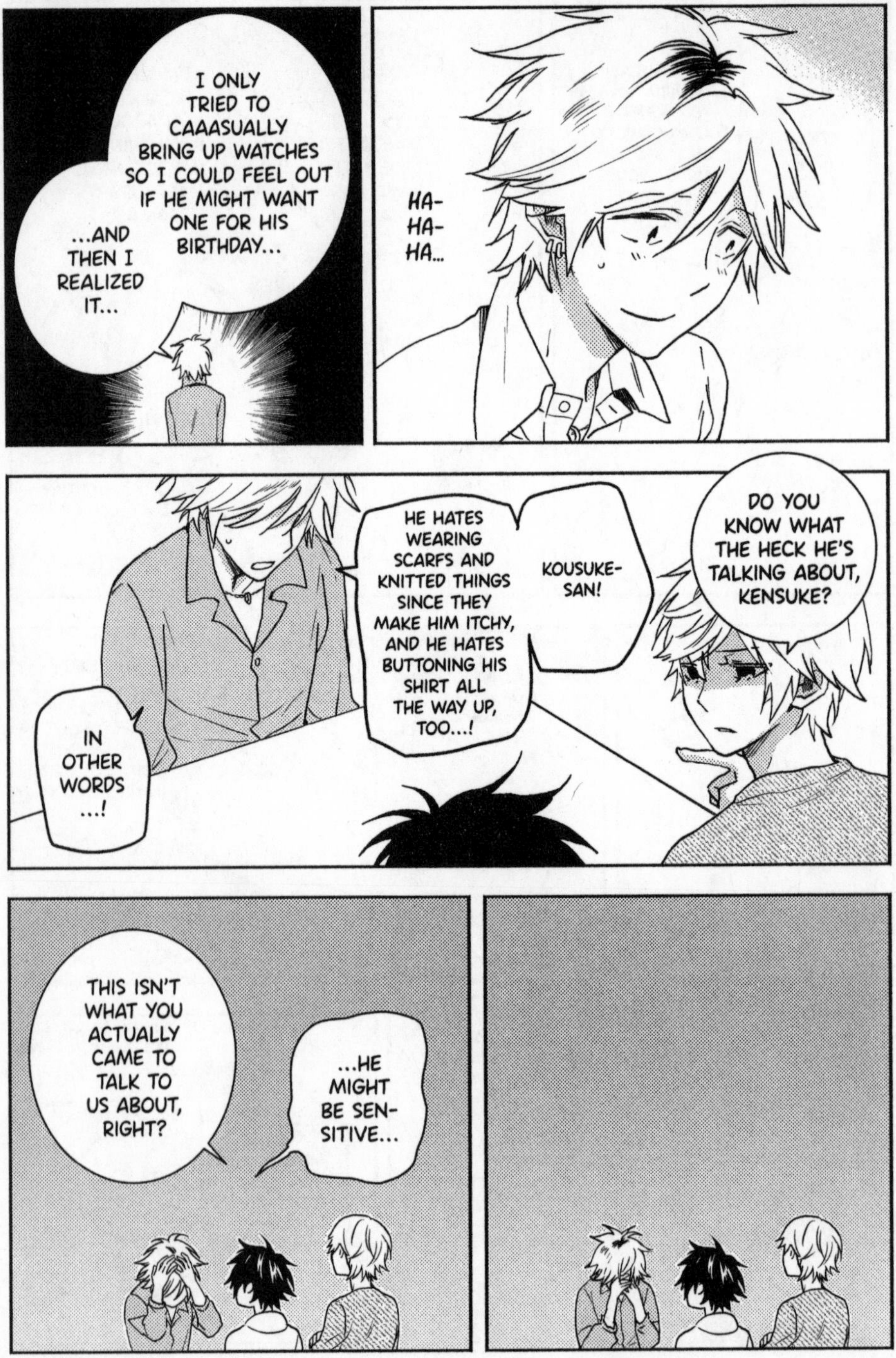
HA-HA-HA...
I ONLY TRIED TO CAAASUALLY BRING UP WATCHES SO I COULD FEEL OUT IF HE MIGHT WANT ONE FOR HIS BIRTHDAY...
...AND THEN I REALIZED IT...
DO YOU KNOW WHAT THE HECK HE'S TALKING ABOUT, KENSUKE?
KOUSUKE-SAN!
HE HATES WEARING SCARFS AND KNITTED THINGS SINCE THEY MAKE HIM ITCHY, AND HE HATES BUTTONING HIS SHIRT ALL THE WAY UP, TOO...!
IN OTHER WORDS ...!
...HE MIGHT BE SEN-SITIVE...
THIS ISN'T WHAT YOU ACTUALLY CAME TO TALK TO US ABOUT, RIGHT?

★ DAD'S LESSON ★

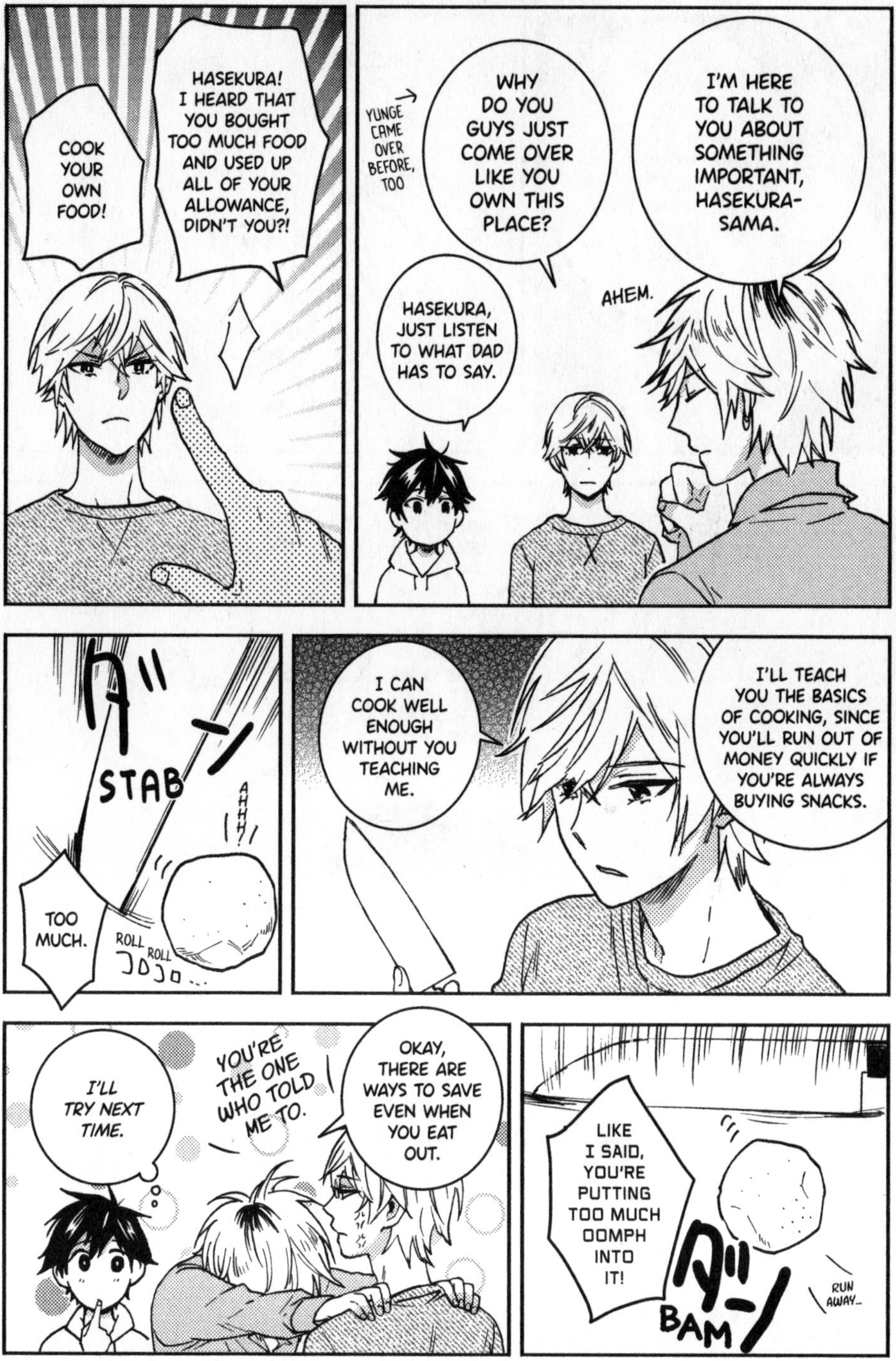
I'M HERE TO TALK TO YOU ABOUT SOMETHING IMPORTANT, HASEKURA-SAMA.
AHEM.
WHY DO YOU GUYS JUST COME OVER LIKE YOU OWN THIS PLACE?
YUNGE CAME OVER BEFORE, TOO
HASEKURA, JUST LISTEN TO WHAT DAD HAS TO SAY.
HASEKURA! I HEARD THAT YOU BOUGHT TOO MUCH FOOD AND USED UP ALL OF YOUR ALLOWANCE, DIDN'T YOU?!
COOK YOUR OWN FOOD!
I'LL TEACH YOU THE BASICS OF COOKING, SINCE YOU'LL RUN OUT OF MONEY QUICKLY IF YOU'RE ALWAYS BUYING SNACKS.
I CAN COOK WELL ENOUGH WITHOUT YOU TEACHING ME.
STAB
AHH?!
TOO MUCH.
ROLL ROLL
LIKE I SAID, YOU'RE PUTTING TOO MUCH OOMPH INTO IT!
BAM
RUN AWAY...
OKAY, THERE ARE WAYS TO SAVE EVEN WHEN YOU EAT OUT.
YOU'RE THE ONE WHO TOLD ME TO.
I'LL TRY NEXT TIME.

FIRST RUN

Hitorijime My Hero #52 gateau magazine April 2020 issue

Hitorijime My Hero #53 gateau magazine May 2020 issue

Hitorijime My Hero #54 gateau magazine July 2020 issue

Hitorijime My Hero #55 gateau magazine October 2020 issue

Hitorijime My Hero #56 gateau magazine November 2020 issue

Hitorijime My Hero #57 gateau magazine December 2020 issue

Hitorijime My Hero #53.5 gateau magazine June 2020 issue

Hitorijime My Hero #54.5 gateau magazine September 2020 issue

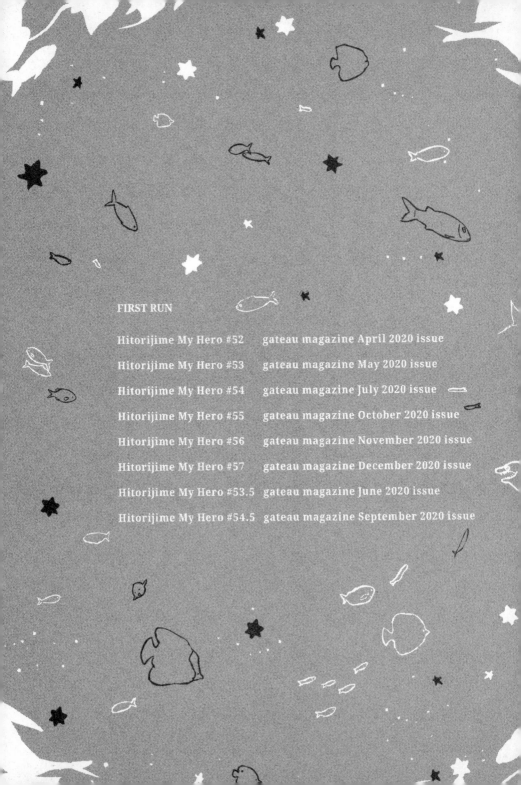

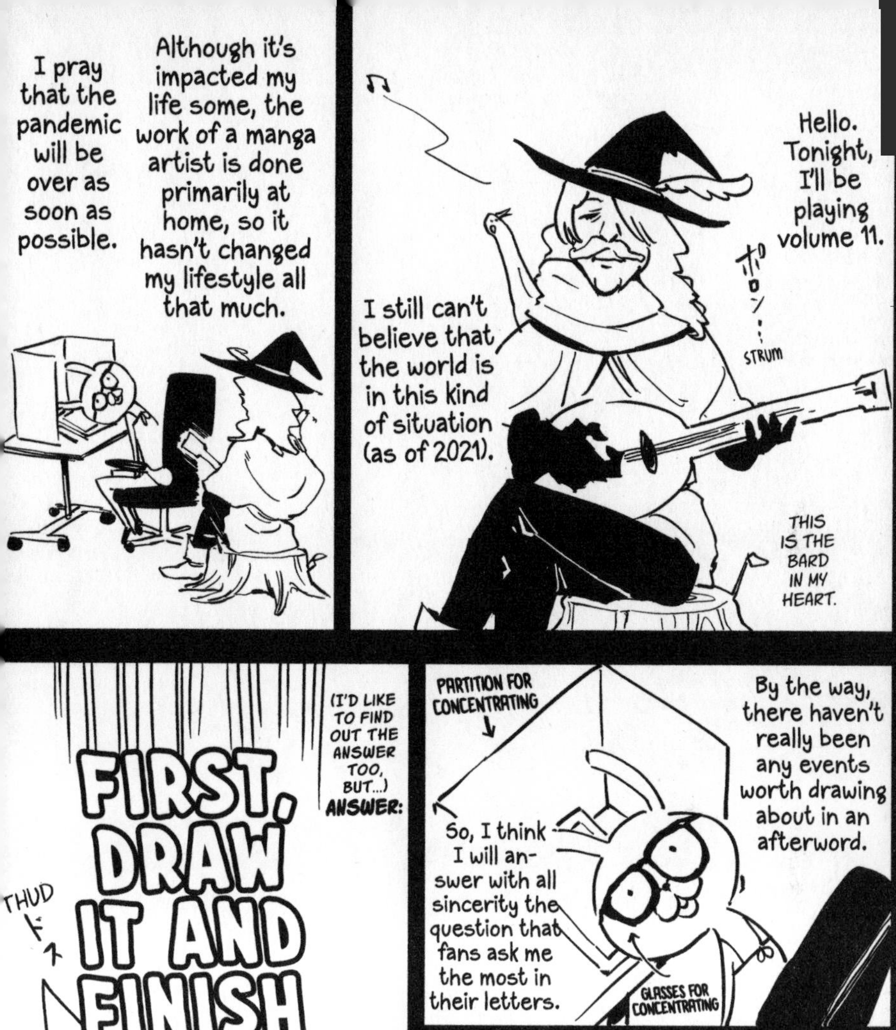
Hello. Tonight, I'll be playing volume 11.
ポロン…
STRUM
I still can't believe that the world is in this kind of situation (as of 2021).
THIS IS THE BARD IN MY HEART.
Although it's impacted my life some, the work of a manga artist is done primarily at home, so it hasn't changed my lifestyle all that much.
I pray that the pandemic will be over as soon as possible.
By the way, there haven't really been any events worth drawing about in an afterword.
PARTITION FOR CONCENTRATING
So, I think I will an-swer with all sincerity the question that fans ask me the most in their letters.
GLASSES FOR CONCENTRATING
The ques-tion is...
..."How do I get better at"...
"drawing manga (pictures)?"
(I'D LIKE TO FIND OUT THE ANSWER TOO, BUT...)
ANSWER:
FIRST, DRAW IT AND FINISH IT.
ドス
THUD

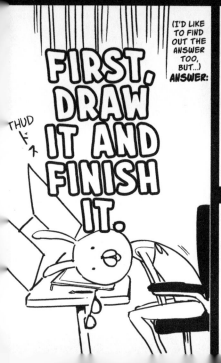

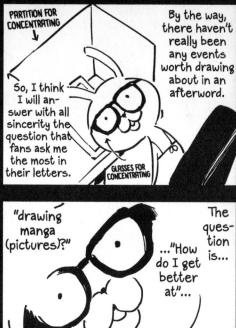

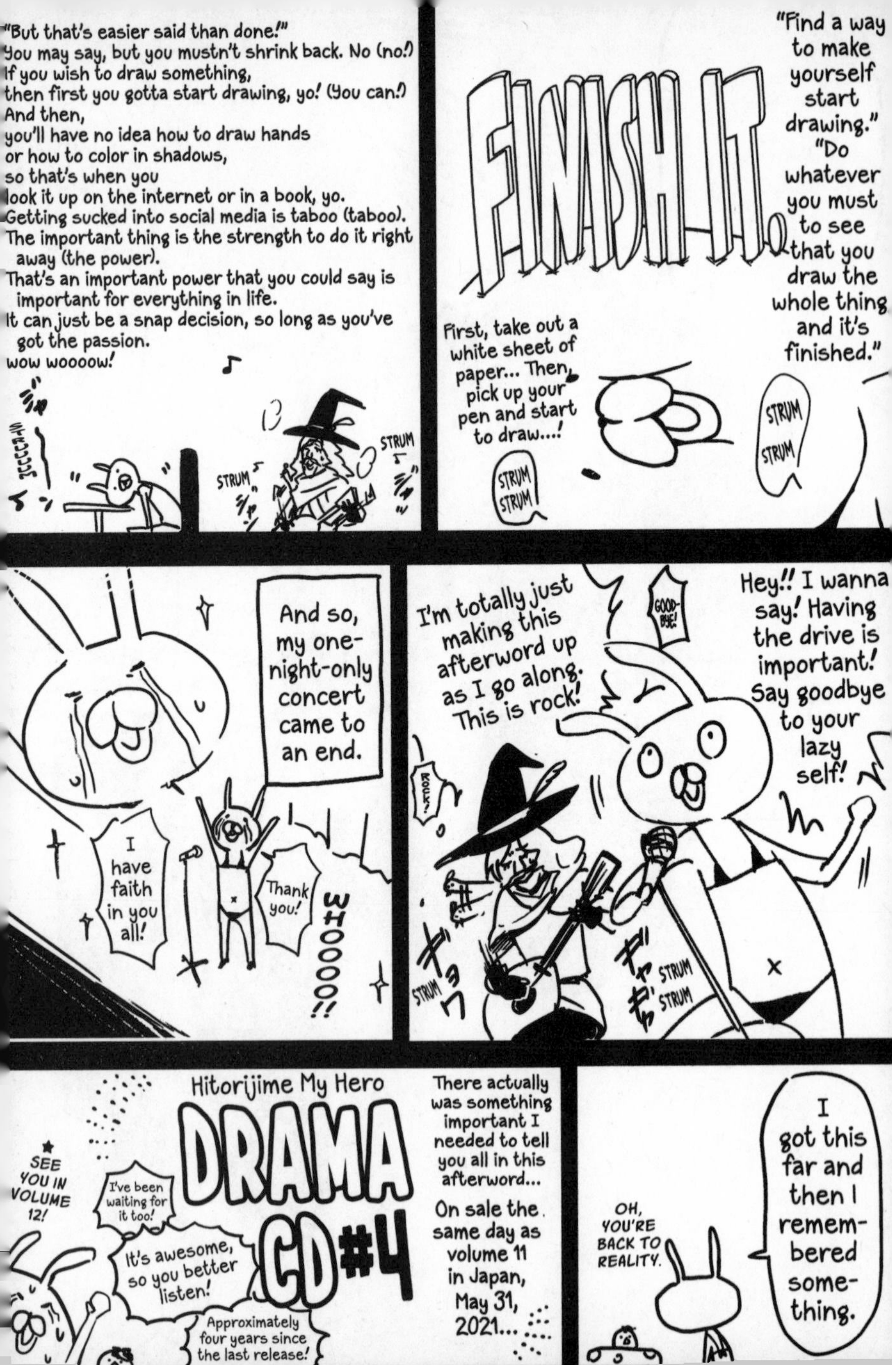

"Find a way to make yourself start drawing." "Do whatever you must to see that you draw the whole thing and it's finished."
FINISH IT.
First, take out a white sheet of paper... Then, pick up your pen and start to draw...!
STRUM STRUM
STRUM STRUM
"But that's easier said than done!"
You may say, but you mustn't shrink back. No (no!)
If you wish to draw something,
then first you gotta start drawing, yo! (You can!)
And then,
you'll have no idea how to draw hands
or how to color in shadows,
so that's when you
look it up on the internet or in a book, yo.
Getting sucked into social media is taboo (taboo).
The important thing is the strength to do it right away (the power).
That's an important power that you could say is important for everything in life.
It can just be a snap decision, so long as you've got the passion.
wow woooow!
STRUM
STRUM
Hey!! I wanna say! Having the drive is important! Say goodbye to your lazy self!
GOOD-BYE!
I'm totally just making this afterword up as I go along. This is rock!
ROCK!
STRUM
STRUM STRUM
And so, my one-night-only concert came to an end.
I have faith in you all!
Thank you!
WHOOOOO!!
I got this far and then I remembered something.
OH, YOU'RE BACK TO REALITY.
There actually was something important I needed to tell you all in this afterword...
On sale the same day as volume 11 in Japan, May 31, 2021...
Hitorijime My Hero
DRAMA CD #4
I've been waiting for it too!
It's awesome, so you better listen!
Approximately four years since the last release!
SEE YOU IN VOLUME 12!

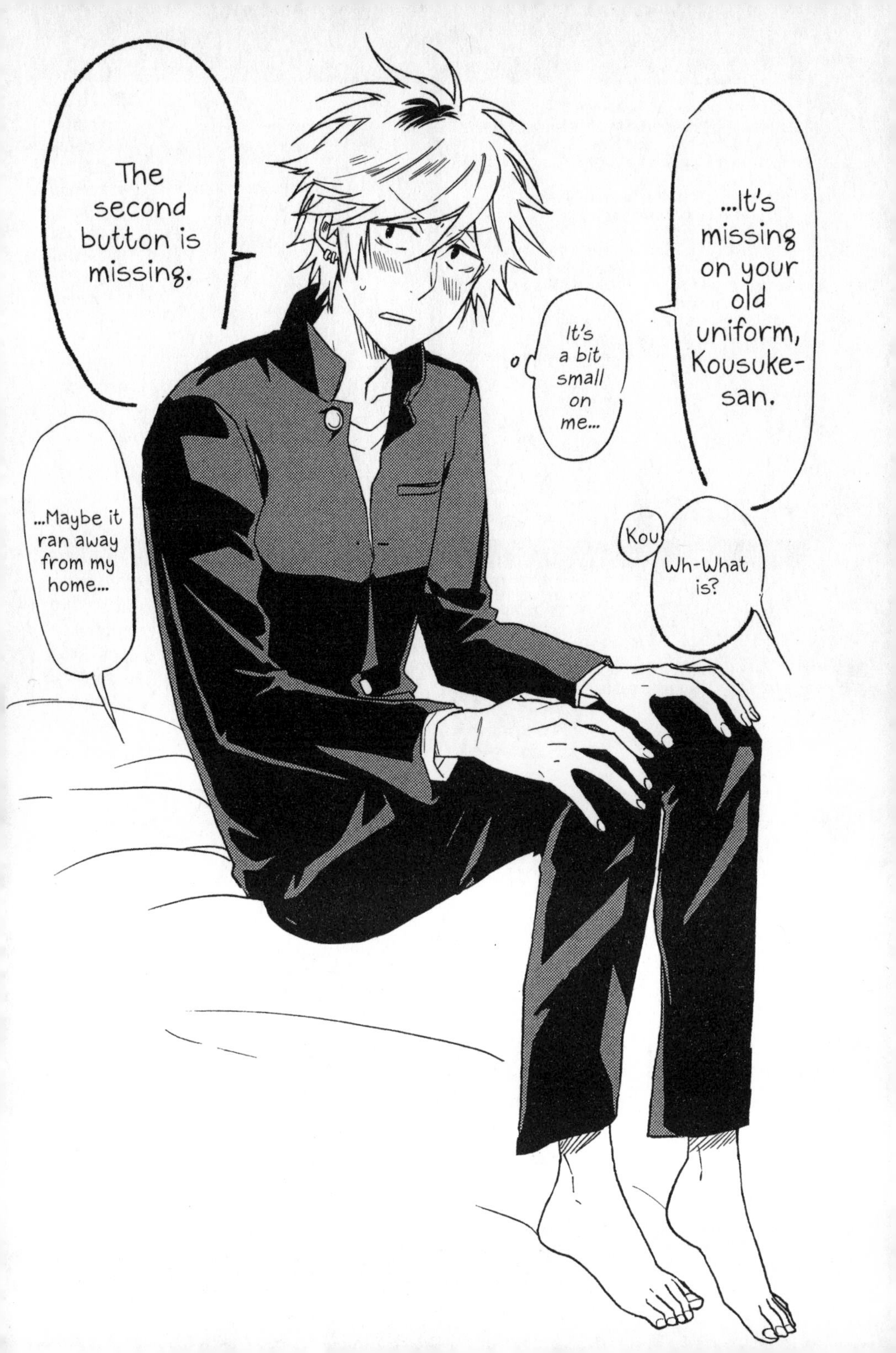
...It's missing on your old uniform, Kousuke-san.
It's a bit small on me...
The second button is missing.
Kou
Wh-What is?
...Maybe it ran away from my home...

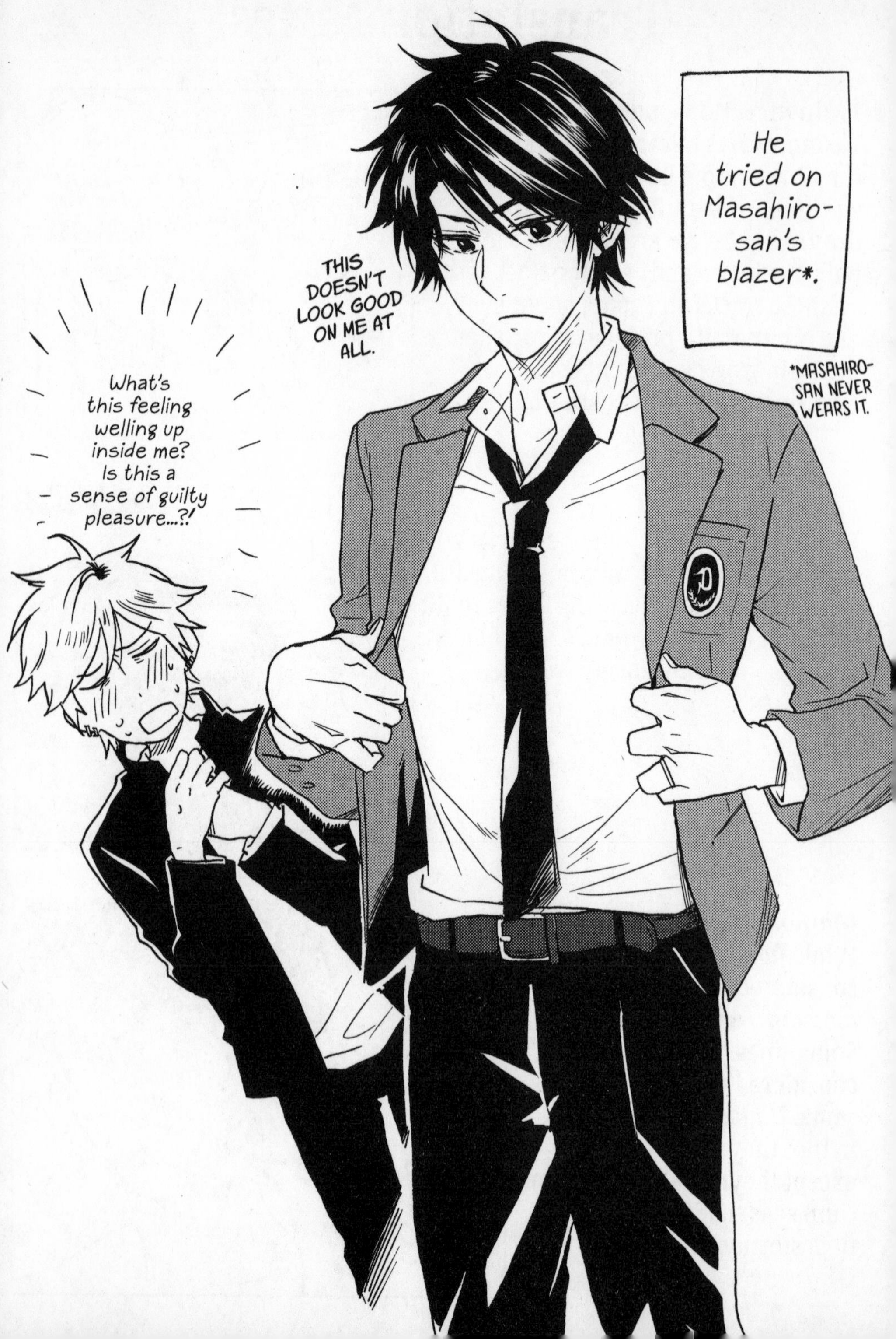
He tried on Masahiro-san's blazer*.
*MASAHIRO-SAN NEVER WEARS IT.
THIS DOESN'T LOOK GOOD ON ME AT ALL.
What's this feeling welling up inside me? Is this a sense of guilty pleasure...?!

Translation Notes

Train directions, page 5
Takamori was talking about riding on the JR Yamanote line, which is a train track that's essentially a loop around the greater Tokyo area. Trains run both clockwise and counter-clockwise on these tracks and come about every five minutes. It's pretty easy to get on the train going in the opposite direction if you're not careful.

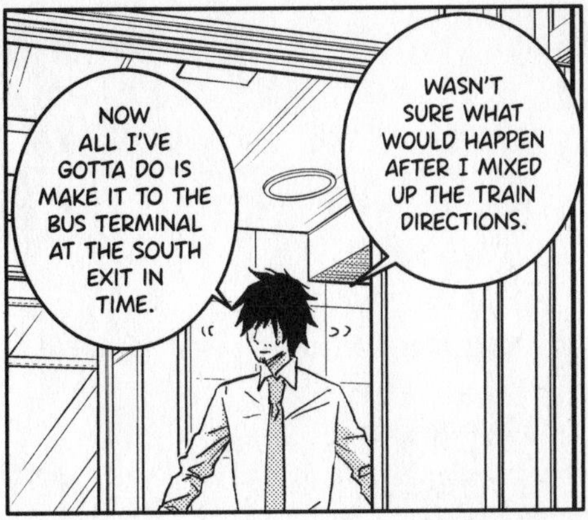
WASN'T SURE WHAT WOULD HAPPEN AFTER I MIXED UP THE TRAIN DIRECTIONS.
NOW ALL I'VE GOTTA DO IS MAKE IT TO THE BUS TERMINAL AT THE SOUTH EXIT IN TIME.

***Funayurei*, page 36**
Funayurei are believed to be spirits who died at sea who have become vengeful ghosts that sink ships using ladles to fill the boats and make them sink. They are said to come with stormy weather.

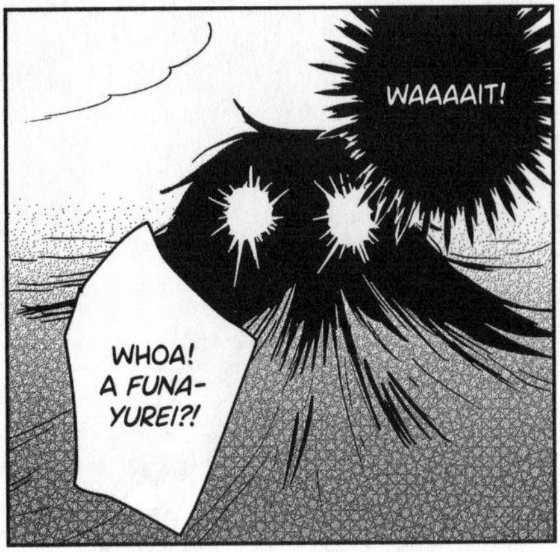
WAAAAIT!
WHOA! A FUNA-YUREI?!

***Umibouzu*, page 38**
While *funayurei* are considered spirits, *umibouzu* are *youkai.* Sometimes they're considered to be one and the same. *Umibouzu* are similar in that they also sink ships, except they usually appear on calm seas that then suddenly turn stormy.

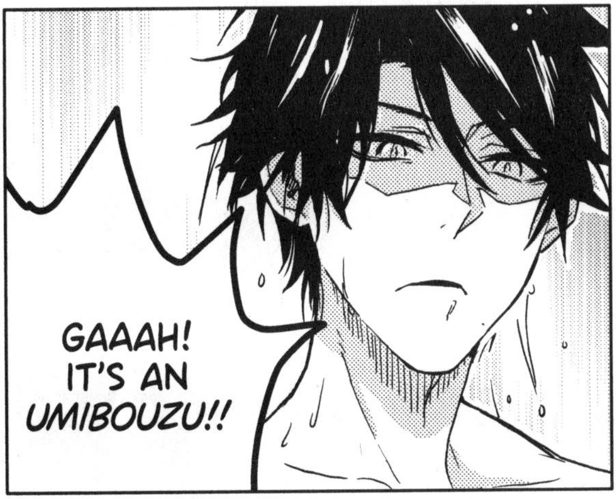
GAAAH! IT'S AN UMIBOUZU!!

ETC only, page 41
ETC is the name of the automatic toll payment system used in Japan.

TOKYO
TOLLBOOTH
700 YEN IS YOUR CHANGE.
ETC ONLY

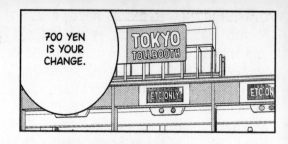

Mako, page 59
"Ko" is a common character used in the names of women in Japan. Yuge is using the "Ma" from Masahiro's name and adding "ko" to give him a more feminine-sounding name while he's in disguise.

BUT THAT'S GOTTA BE SOME KIND OF ACTRESS OR MODEL!
LISTEN TO ME AND STOP FLESHING OUT MY CHARACTER.
MAKO, YOU'RE A TALL HARAJUKU GIRL. YOU LOVE CORIANDER AND...
HE'S CALLING ME...

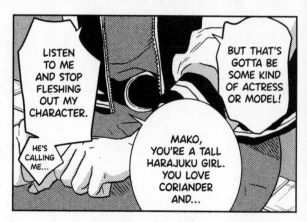

Animate, page 87
Animate is the name of a famous store chain that sells anime, manga, light novels, related CDs, visual novels, and all other kinds of merchandise related to those industries.

TP
TP
TP

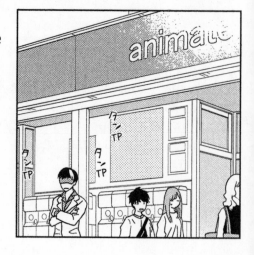

Urashima's jeweled box, page 96
"Urashima's jeweled box" refers to the tale of Urashima Tarou, a fisherman who was invited to the Dragon Palace under the sea by Princess Otohime after saving a turtle. He spent a few days there, and upon leaving was given a jeweled box he was told never to open. When he returned to the surface, he discovered at least a hundred years had passed and everyone he knew was gone. In his grief, he forgot the warning and opened the box, which instantly turned him into an old man.

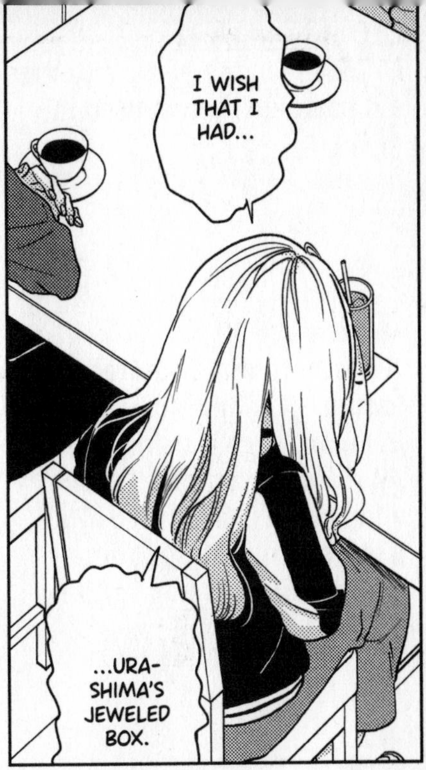
I WISH THAT I HAD...
...URASHIMA'S JEWELED BOX.

Pizza is a waste of money, page 143
Pizza in Japan is much more expensive than in the United States. A single large sized pizza can easily cost $25-$40 depending on the toppings and the crust. Basic plain cheese is usually not so expensive, though.

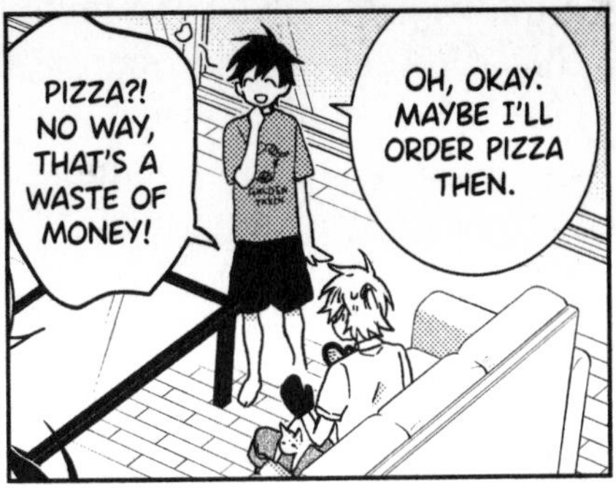
OH, OKAY. MAYBE I'LL ORDER PIZZA THEN.
PIZZA?! NO WAY, THAT'S A WASTE OF MONEY!

Young characters and steampunk setting, like *Howl's Moving Castle* and *Battle Angel Alita*

Beyond the Clouds © 2018 Nicke / Ki-oon

A boy with a talent for machines and a mysterious girl whose wings he's fixed will take you beyond the clouds! In the tradition of the high-flying, resonant adventure stories of Studio Ghibli comes a gorgeous tale about the longing of young hearts for adventure and friendship!

One of CLAMP's biggest hits returns in this definitive, premium, hardcover 20th anniversary collector's edition!

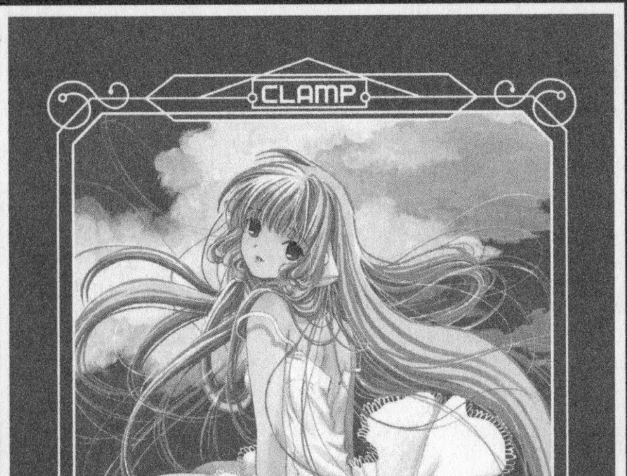
CLAMP
1 Chobits
20TH ANNIVERSARY EDITION

"A wonderfully entertaining story that would be a great installment in anybody's manga collection."
— Anime News Network

"CLAMP is an all-female manga-creating team whose feminine touch shows in this entertaining, sci-fi soap opera."
— Publishers Weekly

Poor college student Hideki is down on his luck. All he wants is a good job, a girlfriend, and his very own "persocom"—the latest and greatest in humanoid computer technology. Hideki's luck changes one night when he finds Chi—a persocom thrown out in a pile of trash. But Hideki soon discovers that there's much more to his cute new persocom than meets the eye.

KC KODANSHA COMICS

Knight of the Ice ©Yayoi Ogawa/Kodansha Ltd.

SKATING THRILLS AND ICY CHILLS WITH THIS NEW TINGLY ROMANCE SERIES!

A rom-com on ice, perfect for fans of *Princess Jellyfish* and *Wotakoi*. Kokoro is the talk of the figure-skating world, winning trophies and hearts. But little do they know... he's actually a huge nerd! From the beloved creator of *You're My Pet* (*Tramps Like Us*).

Chitose is a serious young woman, working for the health magazine *SASSO*. Or at least, she would be, if she wasn't constantly getting distracted by her childhood friend, international figure skating star Kokoro Kijinami! In the public eye and on the ice, Kokoro is a gallant, flawless knight, but behind his glittery costumes and breathtaking spins lies a secret: He's actually a hopelessly romantic otaku, who can only land his quad jumps when Chitose is on hand to recite a spell from his favorite magical girl anime!

A SMART, NEW ROMANTIC COMEDY FOR FANS OF *SHORTCAKE CAKE* AND *TERRACE HOUSE!*

A romance manga starring high school girl Meeko, who learns to live on her own in a boarding house whose living room is home to the odd (but handsome) Matsunaga-san. She begins to adjust to her new life away from her parents, but Meeko soon learns that no matter how far away from home she is, she's still a young girl at heart — especially when she finds herself falling for Matsunaga-san.

PERFECT WORLD

Rie Aruga

A TOUCHING NEW SERIES ABOUT LOVE AND COPING WITH DISABILITY

An office party reunites Tsugumi with her high school crush Itsuki. He's realized his dream of becoming an architect, but along the way, he experienced a spinal injury that put him in a wheelchair. Now Tsugumi's rekindled feelings will butt up against prejudices she never considered — and Itsuki will have to decide if he's ready to let someone into his heart...

"Depicts with great delicacy and courage the difficulties some with disabilities experience getting involved in romantic relationships... Rie Aruga refuses to romanticize, pushing her heroine to face the reality of disability. She invites her readers to the same tasks of empathy, knowledge and recognition."
—Slate.fr

"An important entry [in manga romance]... The emotional core of both plot and characters indicates thoughtfulness... [Aruga's] research is readily apparent in the text and artwork, making this feel like a real story."
—Anime News Network

KC KODANSHA COMICS

The boys are back, in 400-page hardcovers that are as pretty and badass as they are!

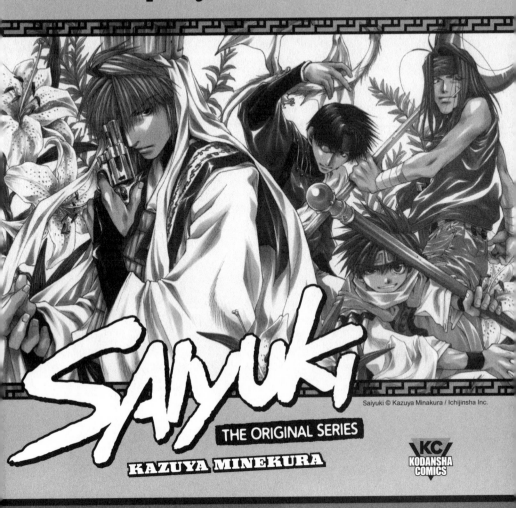

Saiyuki © Kazuya Minakura / Ichijinsha Inc.

SAIYUKI
THE ORIGINAL SERIES
KAZUYA MINEKURA

"AN EDGY COMIC LOOK AT AN ANCIENT CHINESE TALE." —YALSA

Genjo Sanzo is a Buddhist priest in the city of Togenkyo, which is being ravaged by yokai spirits that have fallen out of balance with the natural order. His superiors send him on a journey far to the west to discover why this is happening and how to stop it. His companions are three yokai with human souls. But this is no day trip — the four will encounter many discoveries and horrors on the way.

FEATURES NEW TRANSLATION, COLOR PAGES, AND BEAUTIFUL WRAPAROUND COVER ART!

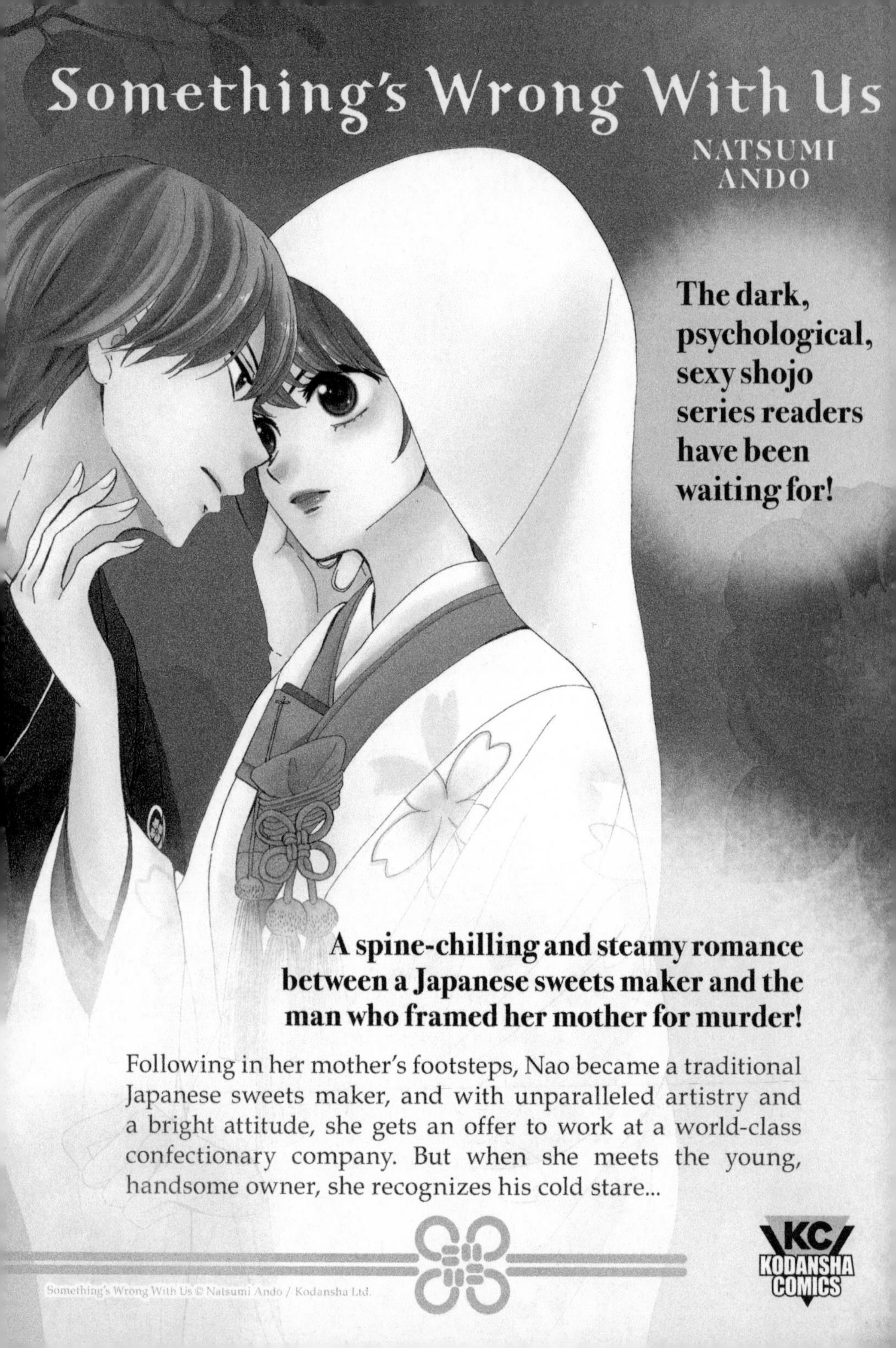

Something's Wrong With Us

NATSUMI ANDO

The dark, psychological, sexy shojo series readers have been waiting for!

A spine-chilling and steamy romance between a Japanese sweets maker and the man who framed her mother for murder!

Following in her mother's footsteps, Nao became a traditional Japanese sweets maker, and with unparalleled artistry and a bright attitude, she gets an offer to work at a world-class confectionary company. But when she meets the young, handsome owner, she recognizes his cold stare...

The adorable new odd-couple cat comedy manga from the creator of the beloved *Chi's Sweet Home*, in full color!

Praise for Chi's Sweet Home

"Nearly impossible to turn away... a true all-ages title that anyone, young or old, cat lover or not, will enjoy. The stories will bring a smile to your face and warm your heart."

~School Library Journal

Sue & Tai-chan

Konami Kanata

Sue is an aging housecat who's looking forward to living out her life in peace... but her plans change when the mischievous black tomcat Tai-chan enters the picture! Hey! Sue never signed up to be a catsitter! *Sue & Tai-chan* is the latest from the reigning meow-narch of cute kitty comics, Konami Kanata.

KC KODANSHA COMICS

THE SWEET SCENT OF LOVE IS IN THE AIR! FOR FANS OF OFFBEAT ROMANCES LIKE *WOTAKOI*

VOL. 1

KINTETSU YAMADA

Sweat and Soap © Kintetsu Yamada / Kodansha Ltd.

In an office romance, there's a fine line between sexy and awkward... and that line is where Asako — a woman who sweats copiously — meets Koutarou — a perfume developer who can't get enough of Asako's, er, scent. Don't miss a romcom manga like no other!

KC KODANSHA COMICS

CUTE ANIMALS AND LIFE LESSONS, PERFECT FOR ASPIRING PET VETS OF ALL AGES!

YUZU THE PET VET

1

BY
MINGO ITO

In collaboration with
NIPPON COLUMBIA CO., LTD.

Yuzu the Pet Vet © Mingo Ito / NIPPON COLUMBIA CO., LTD./ Kodansha Ltd

For an 11-year-old, Yuzu has a lot on her plate. When her mom gets sick and has to be hospitalized, Yuzu goes to live with her uncle who runs the local veterinary clinic. Yuzu's always been scared of animals, but she tries to help out. Through all the tough moments in her life, Yuzu realizes that she can help make things all right with a little help from her animal pals, peers, and kind grown-ups.

Every new patient is a furry friend in the making!

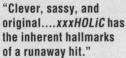

A Kodansha Comics Trade Paperback Original
Hitorijime My Hero 11 copyright © 2021 Memeco Arii
English translation copyright © 2021 Memeco Arii

Published in the United States by Kodansha Comics, an imprint of Kodansha USA Publishing, LLC, New York.

Publication rights for this English edition arranged through Kodansha Ltd., Tokyo.

First published in Japan in 2021 by Ichijinsha Inc., Tokyo.

ISBN 978-1-64651-217-1

Printed in the United States of America.

www.kodansha.us

9 8 7 6 5 4 3 2
Translation: Julie Goniwich
Lettering: Michael Martin
Editing: Greg Moore
Kodansha Comics edition cover design by Phil Balsman

Publisher: Kiichiro Sugawara

Director of publishing services: Ben Applegate
Associate director of operations: Stephen Pakula
Publishing services managing editorial: Madison Salters, Alanna Ruse
Production managers: Emi Lotto, Angela Zurlo